THE LATE SIGM

MW00827301

Freud is best remembered for two applied works on society, *The Future of an Illusion* and *Civilization and Its Discontents*. Yet the works of the final period are routinely denigrated as merely supplemental to the earlier, more fundamental "discoveries" of the unconscious and dream interpretation. In fact, the "cultural Freud" is sometimes considered an embarrassment to psychoanalysis.

Dufresne argues that the late Freud, as brilliant as ever, was actually revealing the true meaning of his life's work. And so while *Future, Civilization*, and his final work *Moses and Monotheism* may be embarrassing to some, they validate beliefs that Freud always held – including the psychobiology that provides the missing link between the individual psychology of the early period and the psychoanalysis of culture of the final period. The result is a lively, balanced, and scholarly defense of the late Freud that doubles as a major reassessment of psychoanalysis of interest to all readers of Freud.

TODD DUFRESNE is Professor of Philosophy at Lakehead University. He is the author or editor of *Returns of the "French Freud"* (1997), *Tales from the Freudian Crypt* (2000), *Killing Freud* (2003), *Against Freud* (2007), Freud's *Beyond the Pleasure Principle* (2011), *The Future of an Illusion* (2012), *Civilization and Its Discontents* (2016), and others.

THE LATE SIGMUND FREUD

Or, The Last Word on Psychoanalysis, Society,
and All the Riddles of Life

TODD DUFRESNE

Lakehead University, Ontario

CAMBRIDGE
UNIVERSITY PRESS

CAMBRIDGE
UNIVERSITY PRESS

University Printing House, Cambridge CB2 8BS, United Kingdom

One Liberty Plaza, 20th Floor, New York, NY 10006, USA

477 Williamstown Road, Port Melbourne, VIC 3207, Australia

4843/24, 2nd Floor, Ansari Road, Daryaganj, Delhi – 110002, India

79 Anson Road, #06–04/06, Singapore 079906

Cambridge University Press is part of the University of Cambridge.

It furthers the University's mission by disseminating knowledge in the pursuit of education, learning, and research at the highest international levels of excellence.

www.cambridge.org
Information on this title: www.cambridge.org/9781107178724
DOI: 10.1017/9781316827321

First published 2017

Printed in the United States of America by Sheridan Books, Inc.

A catalogue record for this publication is available from the British Library.

ISBN 978-1-107-17872-4 Hardback
ISBN 978-1-316-63102-7 Paperback

Humans knew they had spirit,
I had to show them that they also have drive.

(Freud & Binswanger, 2003, p. 238)

Contents

Preface

There is so much to say about the final phase of Sigmund Freud's life and work that it is difficult to know where to start and what to include. Probably the best place to start is *Beyond the Pleasure Principle* of 1920, a slight yet difficult book that revolutionized the meaning of psycho-analysis and made the cultural works possible. We will have many oppor-tunities to plumb the changes wrought by this book, since my main focus is everything that comes after it, everything that overlaps with the most popular and accessible works of Freud, namely those works of the late period often referred to as the "cultural Freud." These are the works that general readers and students favor, precisely because in them Freud tackles the biggest questions of life and society. Nothing in Freud seems so accessible and relevant to our lives even today.

Freud's expansive outlook is eccentric territory for someone formally trained in medicine and neurology – territory more typically suited to sociologists, anthropologists, political scientists, historians, psychologists, and, perhaps most especially, philosophers. Yet Freud was hardly typical. His combination of intelligence, curiosity, creativity, and ambition has been nearly unequalled in the history of Western thought. Today we can barely recognize let alone comprehend this kind of person: a product of *Mitteleuropa*, classically educated and functional in six languages, includ-ing Greek and Latin; disciplined in work, both as a therapist during the day and as a prodigious writer of essays, books, and letters in the evening; comfortable in disparate fields, from science to literature; intellectually gifted far beyond the average; and the beneficiary of cultural norms that ensured his freedom from the prosaic aspects of everyday life, including activities such as childcare, cooking, and cleaning. In this lattermost respect Freud was one of the last great bourgeois patriarchs. As such he owes a considerable debt to his wife Martha, his live-in sister-in-law (and likely lover) Minna, his daughter Anna, and their long-serving house-keeper, Paula Fichtl. A similar debt extends to pliable friends and followers, mostly but not exclusively men, who performed important tasks for him, including roles as secretaries of the Vienna Psychoanalytic Society, organizers of international meetings, journal editors, sounding boards, and defenders of "the cause."

The big questions of life and society are posed most insistently in two famous works of the late period, *The Future of an Illusion* (1927) and *Civilization and Its Discontents* (1930), and in one embarrassing work at the very end of Freud's life, *Moses and Monotheism* (1939). At the center of these works is the role of illusion and even delusion in civilization, and with it the meaning of objectivity, reality, and science; and, beneath all of that, the connection between the everyday present and the repressed, unconscious past. Like the best kind of philosopher, Freud asks simple but fundamental questions. Who are we? Why do we believe what we believe? From where do we get the answers to all the big questions of existence? Or more negatively: Why have we failed to achieve the dreams of reason and freedom? Why are we so unhappy in advanced Western society? Why so guilty? Why so neurotic?

It is remarkable that a man living among us only a few generations ago could devise such an original, intricate, and comprehensive system of thought, one that contrasts so emphatically with much that came before it. Of course psychoanalysis did not come into existence from scratch, ex nihilo. Freud lifted from the poets, like Sophocles, Shakespeare, Heine, and Goethe; pilfered from the philosophers, like Hartmann, Schopenhauer, and Nietzsche; and was schooled in the practices of hypnosis, hysteria, and psychotherapy by Charcot, Bernheim, Breuer, and many others. Yet Freud's Olympian achievement cannot be denied. For here was someone who entirely reconceived what it means to be a human individual, and on that basis did the same with human society – our mass psychology. What does it mean to be a mass individual, a social subject, and a product of deep history?

In a lecture of 1933 Freud denied that psychoanalysis had become a *Weltanschauung*, a worldview. But psychoanalysis was indeed a worldview, and long before the end of Freud's life. Why did Freud deny it? The answer is simple: Freud feared that the science of psychoanalysis might be confused for those worldviews called religion, magic, mysticism, and the occult. If psychoanalysis was real, objective, scientific, then it wasn't just another perspective among all the others. Not incidentally, those others include the psychological approaches named after the early dissidents of psychoanalysis: Adlerian, Jungian, Rankian, and Reichean psychologies. Part of the story of the cultural Freud is an engagement, not always explicit, with these alternative worldviews; an engagement and, it must be admitted, a willful demolition of their challenge to the singular truth of Freudian psychoanalysis.

* * *

In 1923 Freud fell seriously ill with cancer of the jaw. His doctors gave him five years to live – a prognosis likely to sharpen the mind, even the mind of someone revered as a genius. So the man who always thought he was dying, who for years found portents of his death in superstitions about numbers, finally received a death sentence. Freud would later write: "it seemed as though my life would soon be brought to an end by the recurrence of malignant disease; but surgical skill saved me in 1923 and I was able to continue my life and my work, though no longer in freedom from pain" (*SE*, 1935/1991, p. 71). The miracle is that Freud lived for another sixteen years beyond the initial diagnosis, enough time to experience the torture of thirty-one operations on his jaw and upper palate, the latter of which was removed and fitted with a prosthesis that made speaking difficult. Old and sick, Freud frequently complained that he was finished and had nothing left to say. Each new work was purported to be his last. And while it's true that Freud's prodigious output fell after 1923, he never stopped writing, editing, and publishing new works. That's saying too little. Freud continued to publish the two works for which he is most famous today, namely, *The Future of an Illusion* (1927) and *Civilization and Its Discontents* (1930).

Paradoxically, in old age Freud's thinking became both more risky *and* more dogmatic. On the one hand, he revolutionized psychoanalysis with the sometimes wild, often unsubstantiated speculations of *Beyond the Pleasure Principle*. His most famous claim: human existence is governed by the life and death drives, by a warring dualism. "According to our hypothesis," Freud says, "human instincts are of only two kinds: those which seek to preserve and unite – which we call 'erotic', exactly in the sense in which Plato uses the word 'Eros' in his *Symposium* . . . – and those which seek to destroy and kill and which we group together as the aggressive or destructive instinct" (*SE*, 1933b/1991, p. 209). Such was the crux of what must be called, in the context of psychoanalysis, an entirely new theory of human nature.

On the other hand, Freud's speculations had a way of becoming shibboleths; and indeed the late Freud was still dictating, or trying to dictate, the law to his followers. Consider his lifelong belief in the Lamarckian inheritance of acquired characteristics, which disregards the rediscovery of

Mendelian genetics in 1900. "I can say," Freud tells a student, "that the older I get the more sure I grow of everything" (Wortis, 1954, p. 92). The cultural works are the uneven result of this mix of curiosity and certainty, intellectual freedom and dogmatism.

Freud was sixty-four years old when he published *Beyond the Pleasure Principle*. By then psychoanalysis was established with journals, followers, and training institutes all over the world – thanks primarily to Freud's impressive output of essays and books, his personal fame, the dogged efforts of his closest followers, and the widespread use of psychoanalysis as a treatment of war neuroses during the First World War. The truth is that few psychoanalysts were pleased that Freud, in 1920, had single-handedly altered the theoretical foundation of the practice they all shared – the theory of sexual fantasy. Not without justification, many viewed the new dualism of life and death drives as a threat to establishment psycho-analysis. Certainly it was too much for most medically trained followers, who often ignored the shift as inconsequential to therapeutic practice. At the time few understood that the new theories of *Beyond* were actually the untimely return of Freud's oldest ideas, if not the frank admission that these theories had, in any case, always been operating just below the surface of everything. Even fewer understood how all the late works, including the explorations of "ego psychology," were also invested in the late dualism. There really was no escape, at least beyond a fundamental misunderstanding of what Freudianism actually means.

After the publication of *Beyond* analysts tended to pursue one of two strategies: stick with the "early" Freud of sexuality or accommodate in some way the "late" Freud of the death drive. I submit that this is a false, if not incoherent, choice; the early, middle, and late phases of Freud's work are not so easily partitioned. Despite authentic shifts in Freud's thinking, there is a very high degree of coherence and continuity. Consequently, I recommend a different and simple way forward: to follow Freud's speculations, no matter how bizarre or embarrassing, as faithfully as possible as he derives the big answers to what he calls "all the riddles of life." For, as we will see, no one was as radical as Freud himself. Or as interesting. It behooves us to try to keep up with him.

* * *

Among intellectuals there is a tendency to rank theory above history and history above biography, in extremis, to rank abstraction over gossip. Consequently, one finds entire books, written by thoroughly decent authors, devoted to some theory with hardly a word about the people and events, the sometimes undignified context, that made that theory possible. That is not my approach. Freud often had intellectually valid reasons for pursuing some idea, and it falls upon us to comprehend the logical coherence of his thinking as a whole. But Freud's intellectual pursuits were rarely untainted by everyday concerns about priority, competition, rivalry, insecurity, defensiveness, anger, friendship, and so on. In fact, I am more convinced than ever that the key to understanding Freud and psychoanalysis lies at the intersection of theory, history, and biography. In a way this shouldn't be surprising. Psychoanalysis is precisely the theory of one man's autobiography writ large and applied universally to all human beings. That this project, stripped bare as such, is audacious is an understatement. It is nothing short of *fantastic*. Yet, for all of that, Freud's own insistence on an embodied theory of consciousness is more often honored in the breach than in the observance. It is rare to find scholars willing, suited, or even trained to cross the boundaries between abstraction and gossip – to follow Freud where he takes us. As a result it is not just casual readers who are left baffled by Freud's theories; it is professional readers as well, with surprisingly few exceptions.

My goal is to do justice to Freud's own fantastical self-conception about psychoanalysis without, for all that, forgoing the obligation to access and contemplate all the key primary and secondary texts that have, over the last eighty years or so since his death, utterly transformed and enhanced our understanding of Freud's accomplishment. Given the immensity of the literature on psychoanalysis, the challenge is considerable and often overwhelming. In this respect it is not really a question of new sources or fresh archival discoveries. We already have loads of information about Freud. It is rather a question of synthesis and meta-analysis, of *thinking*, a kind of exercise denigrated in a world banally dedicated to measuring and accumulating. But let's recall that Freud himself was a *thinker*, not a data collector; despite Freud's self-serving rhetoric of clinical observation and empiricism, the advancement of ideas was always a matter of creative sifting and rearrangement – of what Freud, in *Beyond the Pleasure Principle*, calls "speculation." My approach, therefore, has been to treat Freud as a legitimate speculator, thinker, in a word, as a *philosopher* with something fundamental to say about everyday existence.

Freud was well aware that his work often had the ring, not just of speculation but of fiction, an awareness fueled by his considerable gifts as a writer, his appreciation for the detective novels of Arthur Conan Doyle, and his love of classical literature more generally. In this respect it is appropriate that Freud failed to win the Nobel Prize, which he coveted, and instead won the Goethe Prize for literature. For it's not only his clinical case studies that read like detective stories. The theoretical innovations themselves are just as intricately devised, caught up in a web of connections across many works, across different time periods, and brought to life within a nexus of complex human relationships. Over and over again the genesis of some theoretical innovation is revealed to be highly personal, the result of Freud's engagement with disgruntled former colleagues, intimate friends and supporters, and highly regarded outsiders. For lay readers the silver lining is fairly obvious: the most obtuse theories are almost always part of a far more accessible, more human story. More to the point, the human stories are at the core of what psychoanalysis meant for Freud and his earliest followers. It also reveals why these stories, heroic or otherwise, are still capable of attracting new readers to the theories of psychoanalysis. As a result I have in *The Late Sigmund Freud* tried to ground the theory in the story whenever that is possible and sensible.

The more Freud published, the better known he became, the more he won over adherents, and the more significant became his engagement with a range of important contemporaries. Naturally this is most true of the last phase of Freud's work, when his fame drew other celebrated men and women into his orbit, or gave him an excuse to reach out to such men and women himself. Freud's response to these people was very different in tone from his daily responses to followers. As convention dictates he was more indulgent, generous, kind – in short, more friendly. By contrast Freud could be intolerant and demanding of his closest friends and followers, whom he expected to toe the party line.

Rarely do we think seriously about psychoanalysis as a vehicle for personal and professional exchanges between friends, colleagues, and cor-respondents. Yet debate about psychoanalysis was Freud's window onto the world, not just the subject of exchange but the means and style as well. Freud sought out and maintained friendships with a community of people, the better to test the warp and woof of his intellectual beliefs. Significant followers discussed in *The Late Sigmund Freud* include Sándor Ferenczi, Wilhelm Reich, Theodor Reik, Oskar Pfister, Arnold Zweig, James Strachey, Ernest Jones, Hilda Doolittle (H.D.), Herbert Silberer, Wilhelm Stekel, and Carl Jung. Any examination of the cultural works must contend with their influence on the direction of Freud's thought. Of course we already know what Freud thought of his followers. Those beliefs are recorded in *Totem and Taboo*, where Freud argues that everyday civility is window dressing for an ancient hatred. Civilization, including the society of psychoanalysts, is founded upon the murder of the primal father and subsequent establishment of a community of guilt-ridden brothers. Such was, in a nut shell, the psychoanalytic "horde."

Freud's formula is beautifully rendered in *The Minutes of the Vienna Psychoanalytic Society*, where on 11 December 1912 Freud states that "law is what the father does; religion is what the son has" (Nunberg & Federn, 1975, Vol. 4, p. 136). Ever since *Totem and Taboo* everyone understands how, for Freud, the band of brothers called psychoanalysts were subject to the Oedipus complex, the need to kill father Freud to win the mother. The most ambitious among them wanted "Lady Psychoanalysis" for themselves. The same cannot be said of Freud's famous friends outside of psychoanalysis. From the perspective of psychoanalysis, they were agnostics or worse. These great men in Freud's life were also, almost without exception, celebrated advocates of peace, love, and community. Their names, sometimes forgotten today, were during Freud's lifetime close to legendary: Romain Rolland, Stefan Zweig, Havelock Ellis, and Albert Einstein. Their friendships with Freud were the site of passionately contested worldviews, the loving peaceniks versus the lone pessimist, the fantasists versus the realist. None of this is incidental, as the contest of worldviews is an essential theme that dominates the works and thought of the late Freud: the battle over what counts as "reality," over what is illusory, and what is objective knowledge of the external world. That this battle over "science" extends, inevitably, to an assessment of the reality of psychoanalysis itself goes without saying. For if anything the objectivity and uncertain future of psychoanalysis is the *primary impulse* behind almost everything Freud wrote in the late phase. As always, psychoanalytic theorizing is always most applicable to, and most true about, psychoanalysis. In this sense, the *theory* of psychoanalysis was in a sense already the first "applied" psychoanalysis, the "object" wherein the application found its most literal and (to close the circle) most correct confirmation.

* * *

As in *Tales from the Freudian Crypt* (Dufresne, 2000), *The Late Sigmund Freud* is an attempt to better understand the influence of the death drive theory of 1920. But whereas the former work focused on the myriad responses to *Beyond the Pleasure Principle*, the current work focuses on its impact on Freud's own work. It is offered as a work of scholarship, replete with citations, recourse to original German terms, and acknowledgment of secondary sources and contemporary debates. In short, there is much wrestling with Freud's meaning in the context of Freud Studies. Yet, for all that, this book has been designed for a wide audience of general readers interested in a range of themes. These themes include the following: Freud's life and work; religion, including the origins of monotheism; culture and society, most especially the origins and conditions of love and hate; war, human nature, and the future of culture and civility; the possibilities of happiness given the complications of guilt and conscience; group feeling, friendship, homosexuality, and community; the role that Jewishness and anti-Semitism play in Freud's late work; Freud's relationships with key followers and with celebrated correspondents; and, finally, the glory of a life of the mind lived at the highest level, even when the arguments are frankly absurd. It is my basic contention that the story of Freud's engagement with the problems of *Kultur* is not only the most fascinating part of Freud's legacy, but also the most misunderstood.

Of course the stakes are very high. Let me put it as plainly as possible: the apparent accessibility of the cultural Freud, the Freud we all read as college and even as high school students, is an illusion based on oversimplified assumptions, decades of misreadings, and all around complacency. *The Late Sigmund Freud* seeks to restore the coherence of Freud's late speculations and, in the process, renew our understanding of Freudian psychoanalysis as a whole. To this end, I argue that the cultural works, often derided as superfluous to Freud's supposed discovery of the unconscious, are in fact the revelation of everything Freud held dear to the theory and practice of psychoanalysis. Far from expendable, therefore, the late works are the crowning achievement of Freud's life as a thinker, as a philosopher doing sociology, for better and for worse.

This bears repeating. The unusual and even bizarre claims found in Freud's final thoughts about culture – all of them written under the influence of his earliest speculations about biology and history – are actually the perfectly coherent, logical consequence of all the other seemingly non-embarrassing features that scholars usually accept without question (e.g., the unconscious, dream interpretation, symbolism, transference, repression, psychic determinism, and repetition compulsion). This is why I am not embarrassed so much as fascinated by the late Freud. I am certainly not trying to "save Freud from himself," or correct his mistakes. I am rather trying to demonstrate why the dumbfounding conclusions of the late Freud are, most especially from Freud's perspective, fully justified and coherent; that the cultural Freud merely draws the logical but radical conclusions of his basic theory; that this basic theory is heavily invested in the discourses of psycho-Lamarckianism and recapitulation; and that Freud is, in his final works, bluntly instructing his readers about the "true" meaning of his life's work in precisely these terms. So no,

Freud never lost the thread of psychoanalysis in these embarrassing works; it is his readers, followers and detractors alike, who have lost the thread. In this respect the condescending and truly ahistorical project of "correcting Freud's mistakes" has blinded us to what Freud actually says and does in the late period. Simply put, the old Freud had his reasons; was saying much more about psychoanalysis that can be told in the mirror of his own unanalyzed unconscious; and, brilliant as ever, was hardly the victim of a bumbling, deficient, geriatric "late style." Such dubious claims about the late Freud are, in fact, among the last great myths still in wide circulation about Freud and psychoanalysis. *The Late Sigmund Freud* demonstrates, I hope decisively, that the old Freud capably and expertly navigated the meaning of *his own work*. Consequently, he has never needed others to do it for him after his death, let alone do it "better." The irony is that after decades of obfuscating "help," Freud is in desperate need of a sympathetic critic to clear the decks and reveal the radicality of his fundamental positions about culture. That, in any case, has been my goal.

* * *

Recourse to biography can result in a naive reductionism. Sometimes scholars reduce Freud's most unusual and embarrassing theoretical claims to an event in his life, or even to a piece of his unanalyzed unconscious – neatly avoiding the arguments by treating them as symptoms. This game also works the other way around: sometimes scholars reduce their own lived experiences and inner lives to Freud's theories. Take three interrelated examples. The respected historian of Jewish culture Yosef Yerushalmi, otherwise careful to avoid "subjectivism" in a 1991 book on Freud's *Moses*, nonetheless adds an open letter to Freud: "Dear and most highly esteemed Professor Freud" (1991, p. 81). The father of deconstruction Jacques Derrida, in what is essentially a long review of Yerushalmi's book, thereupon adds his own autobiographical morsels to the mix: "By chance, I wrote these last words on the edge of Vesuvius, right near Pompeii, less than eight days ago" (1996, p. 97). Following them, the philosopher Richard J. Bernstein (1998) includes yet another open letter in his own Moses book, this one to Yerushalmi but running alongside Derrida: "At this point I would like to bring Derrida into our conversation" (p. 95). By this process, the three men have written themselves into a delirious history of Freudism, one on top of the other, not simply as commentators but as participants – finally, as brothers.

Such inclinations are understandable as artistic experiment, as beautiful gestures of fellowship, or even, if you prefer, as spirited intercourse across time and space. But I have avoided it. _The Late Sigmund Freud_ is primarily about the final phase of Freud's work, the late or cultural Freud. But it is also about "the late Sigmund Freud," i.e., about the Freud we continue to read even after belief in his basic findings has faded – at least for most people outside of institutional psychoanalysis. Certain scholars, often analysts, speak rather dramatically about "Freud bashing" and the "death of psychoanalysis," features I mock in a book of essays called _Killing Freud_. But then as now I prefer to speak about "critical Freud studies," that is, a moment in time when we can finally debate Freud without belief, without love or hate, and without the need to engage in psychoanalysis as active participants. In these respects I am simply not interested in adding my autobiographical tidbits to the literature. For one thing, love letters to Freud are boring. For another, they are presumptuous. Instead I take my cue from my young students who routinely read Freud the same way they read Plato or Rousseau – as a worthy and remarkable figure of history. So when Freud, for example, speaks of the illusion of religion, these secular readers _automatically_ wonder about the illusion of psychoanalysis. This is a Freud given to examination without the prerequisite of belief or conversion. As such it is nonpartisan, curious, amused, perplexed, secular, interested. One could almost say _disinterested_ – and why not? That one is fated to fall short of a now unfashionable value says very little about the value itself. That the project is potentially open to subsequent deconstruction says very little about the merit of constructing arguments, of risking one's thought. The likely charge, moreover, that this approach is a subtle restitution of positivism is, I think, utter nonsense. The point is not to reveal the "truth of Freud," but to reveal what it was that Freud believed and thought, to wit, _Freud's truth_; to accept his own rhetoric and see where it leads. That's it. Positivism has nothing to do with careful reading and a sensitivity to context.

I have spent a long time thinking and writing about Freud and psychoanalysis. And I have learned a lot during the writing of this book; the field is amazingly rich, in part, because Freud's work is amazingly rich. But this is it; I'm done. Aside from minor contributions, _The Late Sigmund Freud_ is my last word on Freud. Knowing this to be the case, I have taken special care to be as balanced and non-polemical as possible, so that every reader, not just critics, can enjoy what follows. That said, "critical Freud studies" is just that – critical. So I pull my punches and register my sincere respect but always underline difficulties when it is warranted. The result is the best work I could muster. Whether I sometimes say too little, too much, or the wrong thing I leave to readers to decide.

The book is divided into three main chapters plus the opening and closing discussions. There really is continuity from beginning to end, since I've followed Freud's career more or less chronologically from the Introduction through to the end of Chapter 3. The Introduction discusses *Beyond the Pleasure Principle*; the first chapter, *The Future of an Illusion*; the second, *Civilization and Its Discontents*; and the third, *Moses and Monotheism*. Within those three chapters I take numerous detours when the material requires it; for the core discussions of death, religion, civilization, and prehistory, respectively, also touch, for example, on related discussions of philosophy, Marxism, mysticism, guilt, homosexuality, anti-Semitism, and the occult. Note, however, that in the Conclusion I return to the period of time that *precedes* the founding of the "cultural Freud" – roughly 1900–19. Why begin with the cultural works and only later consider these early foundations? First of all, because the cultural works are the most accessible and well-read works of Freud, are often read as stand-alone works, and are as good a place to start as any. Second, because the most immediate foundation for the cultural works is *Beyond the Pleasure Principle*, which is duly discussed in the Introduction. Third, because Freud's final cultural work, *Moses and Monotheism*, is ultimately an elaborate response to Freud's greatest and most dangerous follower, Carl Jung. And since Jung left psychoanalysis in 1913–14 – many years before the "late Freud" proper begins – it makes sense, finally, to reconsider this formative earlier period.

And so, my Conclusion follows Freud back to the period before *Beyond the Pleasure Principle* was written to reveal continuities not always apparent to casual readers of the cultural Freud. In other words, I end the book with the "middle period" of Freud's thinking because it is a hinge between the origins of psychoanalysis proper and its final shape as a wild theory of culture; and, in truth, I return to Freud's "early period" in the chapters before that. So ultimately my examination of the late Freud touches on everything associated with Freudian psychoanalysis. In these respects let me emphasize again the ultimate argument of *The Late Sigmund Freud*: namely, that the seemingly miscellaneous or even disposable cultural works are in fact the essential message, albeit a radical message, of psychoanalysis as a whole.

Finally, in a Coda I attempt to characterize the totality of Freud's project to understand culture by turning to two short works, quirky in many ways, published consecutively in the early 1930s. In one Freud speculates about the origin of fire, and in the other he debates the possibilities of peace with Albert Einstein. I essentially argue that the two works contain in miniature all the major features of the late Freud, even pointing toward what will become his final major word on psychoanalysis, *Moses and Monotheism*. It is my last chance to argue my case, and close the book by applying everything I have discovered.

So there is a logic to the presentation. Nonetheless, readers are invited to approach things differently than presented. Some might skip over chapters dealing with key cultural works they don't favor; or, they could begin with the Conclusion and Coda and only then continue with the Introduction or Chapter 1; or, if they are already versed in the theories of *Beyond*, they could skip the Introduction. In short, readers should feel free to make the book their own by finding their own way through it as it strikes their interests and inclinations.

Acknowledgments

I have many people and organizations to thank for supporting me during the period I wrote *The Late Sigmund Freud*. Parts of this book were written with the support of the Social Sciences and Humanities Research Council of Canada, which has been good to me since 1997. And parts were assisted by my two-year stint (2008–10) as Lakehead University Research Chair in Social and Cultural Theory. But the project really took flight in 2010–11 during a sabbatical at the Institute for the History and Philosophy of Science and Technology at the University of Toronto, where I was a visiting professor. Special thanks for the collegiality of Denis Walsh and, from the Department of Philosophy, Mark Kingwell. A sincere thanks to my partner, Clara Sacchetti, who has endured talk about Freud more than is decent and reasonable, and to Chloe for the same.

This is also the place to register my gratitude for the work of James Strachey. Every English reader owes a debt to Strachey, whose monumental work of translation has formed the ground against which every English reader thinks about Freud. Yet everyone knows about his limitations: Strachey's Freud is Victorian in style, needlessly scientistic, wordy, and unfunny in a way that violates Freud's own approach. Fortunately, the expiration of old copyright restrictions means that we are now living in a golden age of new translations of Freud's work. I have freely consulted old and new translations, and have always returned to the original German when citing Freud's work – without, I hope, making a fetish of the exercise. In this respect I have had one great advantage. The translator Gregory Richter and I published three editions of Freud's work at Broadview Books, and so I have consulted his translations and have abused his good-will whenever I have had a question. This has ensured that my bumbling through the German and French has often been helped along by the good sense and generosity of a gifted scholar. Aris Carastathis also helped me out with a passage from Greek. Of course any remaining blunders of translation are mine alone. I sent the manuscript to three friends willing to share their reactions: Greg Richter, Fuhito Endo, and Miranda Niittynen. Many thanks (and apologies). I am also grateful to three anonymous reviewers at CUP who reviewed the manuscript, made constructive comments, corrected some blunders, and helped me improve the work. Emma Woodley did an expert job in helping me convert my references to proper Cambridge style. And my friend, the artist Mark Nisenholt, kindly tweaked and improved Freud's own doodle of a fish in water, which appears on the book cover. I would also like to acknowledge the support and good sense of my editor at Cambridge, Janka Romero, and the patience of my content manager, Adam Hooper.

A handful of Freud scholars have influenced the direction and substance of my work in psychoanalysis over the years, two of whom deserve to be singled out: Mikkel Borch-Jacobsen, easily the best philosopher of Freud and psychoanalysis; and Frank Sulloway, easily the best thinker of the theoretical foundation of Freud's work. I owe you both for your models of scholarship and for your support in the past.

This book project began in earnest with steps taken as editor of three volumes on the late Freud for Broadview Books. Some small parts of my discussion of *Beyond the Pleasure Principle* and *Civilization and Its Discontents* echo remarks I make in the editor introductions I wrote for the editions of 2011 and 2016, while significant parts of my discussion of Freud's *Future of an Illusion* (in Chapter 1) appear as my introduction to *The Future of an Illusion* published at Broadview in 2012. I would like to thank Leslie Dema, my Broadview editor, for permitting their appearance here. Cheers.

This book is dedicated to life, love, happiness, and the future; it is dedicated, in short, to my daughter Chloe.

Introduction
Death and the Cultural Turn in Psychoanalysis

There is a moment, dear to readers in the humanities, when Freud explicitly acknowledges a shift in his work away from clinical concerns. It occurs in a "Postscript" of 1935 appended to his *Selbstdarstellung*, his "self-presentation" better known as "An Autobiographical Study" (*SE*, 1935/1991). In it Freud reflects on his work of the 1920s, and admits, ironically or otherwise, that he has "regressed" to his earliest interests in "cultural problems" (*SE*, 1935/1991, p. 72). So while he had already ventured, for example, to offer analyses of jokes in 1905, obsession and rituals in religion in 1907, Leonardo da Vinci's repressed homosexuality in 1910, Michelangelo's Moses statue in 1913, and "the origins of religion and morality" in *Totem and Taboo* in 1913, the late cultural works push more decisively into this territory. "I perceived ever more clearly," Freud writes,

> that the events of history, the interactions between human nature, cultural developments and the precipitates of primaeval experiences (the most prominent example of which is religion) are no more than a reflection of the dynamic conflicts between the ego, the id and the super ego, which psychoanalysis studies in the individual – are the very same processes repeated upon a wider stage. (SE, 1935/1991, p. 72)

In short, Freud had discovered the link between individual psychology and the history of society, and so rediscovered his youthful interest in *Kultur* – a German word meaning culture, society, and civilization.

The work that generates this apparent shift in perspective is a strangely elliptical, highly speculative, fifty-six-page book called *Beyond the Pleasure Principle*. It is the culmination of the theoretical work of the middle phase and the foundation for all of Freud's late cultural works – including the best-known work of his career, *Civilization and Its Discontents*. In a 1926 interview Freud declares that "Death is the mate of Love. Together they rule the world. This is the message of my book, 'Beyond the Pleasure Principle'" (Viereck, 1930, p. 32). Or as he had already put it in a letter of May 14, 1922, to the Viennese playwright and novelist Arthur Schnitzler, *Beyond the Pleasure Principle* attempts "to reveal Eros and the death instinct as the motivating powers whose interplay dominates all the riddles of life" (Freud, 1960b, p. 339). "All the riddles of life": Freud could not have been more bullish about the reach of his new work.

Like Freud but six years younger, Schnitzler was trained as a physician at the University of Vienna, worked at the General Hospital, and became a neuropathologist (Ellenberger, 1970, p. 471). Unlike Freud, Schnitzler was also a famous artist known as a key member of the *Jung Wien* group of artists, which included other writers such as Stefan Zweig and Hermann Bahr (Freud, 1992, p. 65). To Schnitzler on the occasion of his birthday, Freud confessed in 1922 that he feared him as a *Doppelgängerscheu*, a double whose interests overlapped with his own – so much so that Freud avoided meeting him (Jones, 1957, p. 443). "Whenever I get deeply absorbed in your beautiful creations," Freud writes, "I invariably seem to find beneath their poetical surface the very propositions, interests, and conclusions which I know to be my own" (Freud, 1960b, p. 339). The two secular Jews shared a history in neurology, hypnosis, and psychopathology, a fascination with dreams and human sexuality, an inclination toward determinism (at least early on, for Schnitzler), and a commitment to "the polarity of love and death." This letter was in fact the second time Freud reached out to praise Schnitzler, the first time being on May 8, 1906. Referring to the Dora case, Freud speaks of "the far-reaching conformity existing between your opinions and mine on many psychological and erotic problems"; his own "astonishment" and "envy" that Schnitzler's work expresses a "secret knowledge which I had acquired by painstaking investigation"; and also satisfaction that Schnitzler himself has "derived inspiration" from Freud (Freud, 1960b, p. 251). Freud experienced these overlaps as "uncanny." As implied in 1906, Freud trots out a claim that he often made about artists, namely that "you know through intuition – or rather from detailed self-observation – everything that I have discovered by laborious work on other people" (p. 340; cf., Viereck, 1930, p. 38). Here as elsewhere Freud is careful to contrast artistic intuition, self-observation, and fiction with scientific observation of everyday life and reality. As we will see, it would come to inform his general attitude in his late works.

Freud would have known quite a bit about Schnitzler, and not just because of their shared cultural and ethnic background in Vienna; or because they lived a few blocks away from each other; or because Schnitzler had in 1888 defended Freud during the cocaine scandal (Marcuse, 1973, p. 405); or because Schnitzler had become famous; or because the members of the

Vienna Psychoanalytic Society sometimes discussed his work, once as the main event (see Nunberg & Federn, 1975, Vol. 3, pp. 172–5); or even because Freud played tarock with Julian Schnitzler, the well-regarded surgeon and Arthur's younger brother (Jones, 1957, p. 84; Freud, 1992, p. 44). Freud could not fail to know about Schnitzler because they shared friends in common, including the analysts Lou Andreas-Salomé, Fritz Wittels, and Theodor Reik (Jones, 1955, p. 176). Reik's first book, *Arthur Schnitzler as Psychologist* (1913), was even dedicated to Freud – thereby closing the circle. Freud read Schnitzler's plays and novels, already in 1898 saying of *Paracelsus* that "I was astonished to see what such a writer knows about these things" (Jones, 1953, p. 346); the play features hypnosis and hysteria, which it exposes as being caught up with "fabrication and role acting" (Ellenberger, 1970, p. 472). As for Schnitzler, he read (at least) Freud's early translations of Charcot and Bernheim, *The Interpretation of Dreams*, and *The Ego and the Id* (Wisely, 2004, pp. 128, 131, 137).

Freud and Schnitzler did finally meet – by happenstance – while vacationing in Berchtesgaden, a small town in the Bavarian Alps, in August of 1922. There Schnitzler reluctantly discussed with Freud his recent divorce, but experienced no epiphanies (Wisely, 2004, p. 137). In an interview with George Viereck, Schnitzler admitted that his medical training helped him understand psychology – and also Freudianism:

> My medical training helps me to understand the problem of human conduct. I anticipated the Freudian theory of the dream in my plays ... In some respects I am the double of Professor Freud. Freud himself once called me his psychic twin. I tread in literature the same path which Freud explores with amazing audacity in science ... In hailing him as such I am not bound to accept every vagary of his pupils. Somewhere, in the depths, Freud is right. But one must not take him too literally, nor is it safe to generalize from his conclusions. (Viereck, 1930, pp. 333–4)

The truth is that Schnitzler was wary of psychoanalysis. To one correspondent he privately complained that "I have scruples about the one-sidedness of the psychoanalytical method practiced by [Freud] and other students" (Berlin & Levy, 1978, p. 112); it was a complaint echoed by Romain Rolland and Carl Jung. It wasn't just that Freud had "historical truth," a concept I discuss in Chapter 3, while Schnitzler had something he called "fictional truth."[1] It was that Schnitzler was less pessimistic than Freud and far more interested in moral responsibility. Despite their many similarities, then, it

---

[1] "I realized," Schnitzler says, "that there was such a thing as 'fictional truth'" (Kupper & Rollman-Branch, 1973, p. 425).

is important to note that the two men came to quite different conclusions about very similar terrain (Ellenberger, 1970, pp. 473–4).[2]

As for Freud's reference, in his letter, to "all the riddles of life," it is textually rich and not entirely innocent. In his characteristic way Freud was both complimenting Schnitzler and undermining his originality – pointing the way back to an earlier literary precursor, the Russian novelist Leo Tolstoy. The riddles phrase first appears late in "The Death of Ivan Ilych" (1934/1886), where the dying Ivan, a lawyer, grapples with the meaning of life. Here is the passage in full:

> "Maybe I did not live as I ought to have done," it suddenly occurred to him. "But how could that be, when I did everything properly?" he replied, and immediately dismissed from his mind this, the sole solution to all the riddles of life and death, as something quite impossible. "Then what do you want now? To live? Live as you have lived in the law courts when the usher proclaimed 'The judge is coming!' 'The judge is coming, the judge!'" he repeated to himself. "Here he is, the judge. But I am not guilty!" he exclaimed angrily. "What is it for?" And he ceased crying, but turning his face to the wall continued to ponder on the same question: Why, and for what purpose, is there all this horror? But however much he pondered he found no answer. And whenever the thought occurred to him, as it often did, that it all resulted from his not having lived as he ought to have done, he at once recalled the correctness of his whole life and dismissed so strange an idea. (pp. 64–5)

The nineteenth century is full of examples of what Germans called *Weltschmertz*, an attitude of world-weariness most explored by artists and their wealthy patrons. Like many people, Ivan Ilych wondered if he had wasted his life on appearances and conventions. But Freud never made Ivan's mistake: with *Beyond the Pleasure Principle* he had finally faced up to "all the riddles of life and death," territory always suited to artists like Tolstoy and Schnitzler but finally known to scientists like Freud. More to the point, with his late dualism of the life and death drives Freud had validated his own life as well lived. If so, then his compliment to Schnitzler doubled as a compliment to himself.

With *Beyond the Pleasure Principle* Freud was advancing the darkest possible claim about human nature: that we possess a demoniacal impulse that undermines life, love, and sociality; and, just as disturbingly and

---

[2] In his *Diary* entry of October 21, 1931, Freud recorded Schnitzler's death: "+ Arthur Schnitzler . . . " Freud's last letter to Schnitzler was a note of thanks for Schnitzler's birthday greeting (Freud's birthday was May 6) earlier that year, and an occasion to send a similar greeting to Schnitzler (Freud, 1992, p. 110).

indeed paradoxically, that this impulse is a significant part of biological evolution, human progress, and the claims of civilization. The linchpin of these dark presentiments is the theory of the death drive, *Todestrieb* – according to which life or Eros is compromised in advance by an over-whelming drive for quietude, constancy, nonexistence – and its correlate, *Aggressionstrieb*, the aggressive drive. The death drive aims to kill the individual from the inside (masochism), while the aggressive drive turns this aggression outward to kill others (sadism). Freud speculates that perhaps this death drive (and its correlate) is "beyond the pleasure principle."

It is poorly appreciated that Freud by the phrase "beyond the pleasure principle" means a "beyond of science" or, more exactly, a beyond of the science of the pleasure principle. Freud asks whether it is possible that affect, for example a traumatic experience, can ever escape the domain of sexuality and the pleasure principle. In this sense the new theory Freud comes up with is not properly "the theory of psychoanalysis" at all, as is often assumed, but rather a new field called "metapsychology." What is beyond the pleasure principle is beyond psychoanalysis, namely metapsy-chology or, better put, meta-psychoanalysis.[3]

1   Thought beyond All Demonstration: Or, How to be "Meta"

What psychoanalysts have understood better than anyone, and to their credit, is that Freud in *Beyond* threatens the very foundations of what it means to practice psychoanalysis; that the new "meta" perspective under-cuts the prosaic psychoanalysis of everyday life. To Freud's credit he ignores this danger. Psychoanalysis was his creation, and unlike his followers he was free to imperil its practice with a high-stakes metapsy-chology only loosely tied to empirical verification and clinical utility. For this reason *Beyond* is often considered to be Freud's most difficult, most philosophical, and consequently most disposable work. Yet even if *Beyond* qualifies as a "masterpiece" of "transcendental" thinking along Kantian lines, as the French philosopher Gilles Deleuze (1991, p. 111) contends, it is not because it breaks decisively and irrevocably from scientific discourse.

---

[3] Freud's metapsychology exhibits three basic approaches to the psyche: the "topographical" or "dynamic" approach, which contrasts conscious and unconscious elements; the "economic" approach, which studies the "energy" of the psyche as represented by the life and death drives; and the "structural" approach, which describes the psyche as id, ego, and superego. After 1923, the "late Freud" employs all three approaches, although the "economic" examination of drives is dominant and is at the heart of what Freud means when he speaks of "metapsychology."

On the contrary, *Beyond* represents a remarkable return of some of Freud's oldest "pre-psychoanalytic" preoccupations with nineteenth-century science. In fact, many of the central ideas of *Beyond* are the uncanny repetition of ideas first floated, during his cocaine phase, in the *Project for a Scientific Psychology* of 1895 – an ambitious and at times grandiose attempt to bridge the distance between psyche and neurology or, more broadly, between psychology and biology. That Freud abandoned the *Project* hardly means that he abandoned his speculations; it just means he couldn't make it work.

Beyond and the *Project* coincide with four notable features: the so-called economic perspective, according to which quantities of energy flow through the psyche; the pleasure principle, *das Lustprinzip*, which according to psychoanalysis dominates psychic life; the importance of repetition; and the theory of constancy, influenced by well-known ideas about energy conservation, entropy, and thermodynamics as first applied to psychology by Gustav Fechner (see Ellenberger, 1970, p. 218). As the English psychoanalyst and Freud translator James Strachey rightly says, "The 'Project,' or rather its invisible ghost, haunts the whole series of Freud's theoretical writings to the very end" (*SE*, 1895a/1991, p. 290).

In 1979 the historian of science Frank Sulloway was the first scholar to systematically demonstrate, and decisively so, Strachey's claim – namely, that Freud's early commitments to nineteenth-century theories of biology, the "metabiology," inform nearly all theory innovation in the history of psychoanalysis. The book was and remains a revelation. But Freud's biologism was already well-documented in the literature, not just by Strachey but in Ernest Jones's official biography of Freud (see Jones, 1957, pp. 310–13) and again in Philip Rieff's (and Susan Sontag's) great book, *Freud: The Mind of the Moralist* (1961, pp. 219–20). Yet these insights have also been ignored by nearly everyone.

A key feature of the metabiology is Freud's unwavering belief in Jean-Baptiste Lamarck's theory that evolution is fueled by the inheritance of acquired characteristics, a claim that perfectly complements the theory of recapitulation championed by Ernst Haeckel. According to Haeckel's once-popular view, individuals in the present ontogenetically repeat the (phylogenetic) history of the species. As Freud states in a letter of July 1915 to his close friend and collaborator Sándor Ferenczi, "What are now neuroses were once phases of the human condition" (1915/1987, p. 10). Or as he states very plainly in chapter five of *Beyond*, and just before his famous speculation about a conservative (entropic) drive, "ultimately it must be the developmental history of our earth and its relation to the sun that has left its mark on the evolution of the species" (Freud, 1920/2011, p. 77; *SE*, 1920a/1991, p. 38).

What is amazing is how scores of otherwise sophisticated readers have ignored such passages. Yet Freud and Ferenczi contemplated writing a joint work on "Lamarck and Psychoanalysis" in the years immediately preceding the writing of *Beyond*. In a letter of November 11, 1917, Freud explains the project to Karl Abraham, who had already published his own Lamarckian speculations in 1910:

> Have I really not told you about the Lamarck idea? It arose between Ferenczi and me, but neither of us has the time or spirit to tackle it at present. The idea is to put Lamarck entirely on our grounds and to show that his "need," which creates and transforms organs, is nothing but the power of the *Unc.* [unconscious] ideas over one's own body, of which we see remnants in hysteria, in short the "omnipotence of thoughts." This would actually supply a Ψα [psychoanalytic] explanation of expediency; it would put the coping stone on Ψα [psychoanalysis]. Two big principles of change (of progress) would emerge; the change through adaptation of one's body and the subsequent change through transformation of the external world (autoplastic and heteroplastic), etc. (Freud & Abraham, 2002, pp. 361–2)

Lamarckian inheritance would complete psychoanalysis, and would put the final "coping stone" in place. It is true that the proposed project was never completed as planned. But it was indeed tackled in their own individual works: Freud in *Beyond the Pleasure Principle* and Ferenczi in *Thalassa: A Theory of Genitality* (1924/1968). Not surprisingly, both works reflect the other. It is also true that other analysts contributed importantly to these phylogenetic speculations. In "The Cultural Significance of Psychoanalysis" of 1920, the dutiful Karl Abraham continued to make a case that "modern biology" demonstrates the truth of recapitulation. "Modern biology," writes the Berliner, "has shown how the organic development of the individual recapitulates in abbreviated form that of the species. Psychoanalysis has extended this biogenetic law [of recapitulation] first postulated by Haeckel to the psychic realm" (1955b, p. 134). Such commitments are, therefore, very clear to anyone willing to look.

It was with the old metabiology in mind that Freud thought that psychoanalysis, on the analogue of archaeology, could penetrate history to its collective, prehistorical roots – as in the fantasies of *Totem and Taboo* (1913b/1991) and *Moses and Monotheism* (1939/1991) – and reveal what Romantic philosophers called *Urphänomene*. For example, one could literally correlate what Freud calls "the hard school of the Ice Age" (1915/1987, pp. 13–14) with the period of "cold indifference" that characterizes adolescent attitudes today about members of the opposite sex (see Ferenczi, 1913/1956, pp. 201–2; Freud, 1915/1987, p. 10). The idea is repeated again in *Thalassa*, but was first proposed by Ferenczi in his essay of 1913, "Stages in the Development of the Sense of Reality." As we will see in the Conclusion, these ideas were characteristic speculations of the "middle" period of Freud's working life and are of the utmost importance for understanding the cultural Freud.

Yet if key members of Freud's inner circle were committed to understanding the prehistorical origins of psychology, most psychoanalysts were not enthused. In private letters Ernest Jones, for instance, urged Freud to excise his Lamarckian views (see Jones, 1957, p. 313). What this means is that the metabiology was already an embarrassment in Freud's own life, at least among his scientifically literate followers. Consequently the charge of "Whig" history is wrongheaded; critics today are not imputing a different set of scientific standards to the ones that informed Freud's own contemporaries. Freud very knowingly and stubbornly held steadfast to the old metabiology, which, as we will see, was hardly disposable. In his last major work, *Moses and Monotheism* (1939), Freud candidly admits, "My position, no doubt, is made more difficult by the present attitude of biological science, which refuses to hear of the inheritance of acquired characteristics by succeeding generations. I must, however, in all modesty confess that nevertheless I cannot do without this factor in biological evolution" (*SE*, 1939/1991, p. 100). Freud rarely backed down from his own hard-won views – the contrary "attitude" of biological science be damned.

If psychoanalysts have had trouble accepting that Freud in 1920 explicitly reinvested psychoanalytic theory in the failed, outdated, pre-psychoanalytic, biologistic, and mechanistic ideas of the *Project*, it has been no less troubling for scholars. On the one hand, humanities scholars have tended to be intrigued by the death drive theory. On the other, they are rarely interested in following Freud's own biologism. Even post-structuralists, who cut their teeth on close textual analysis, share an almost willful disregard for Freud's unwavering biologism. For some the death drive theory has thus become just another metaphor for human aggressivity and war – a conclusion, built on a stunning degree of ahistoricism, that is nearly as troubling as the motivated whitewashing that characterizes so much of the work published by psychoanalysts.

Scholars, however, are at least professionally inclined to tolerate and even enjoy the problems of interpretation that attend to a work like *Beyond*. In this sense they share with the Freud of *Beyond* a boundless curiosity about ultimate questions, and are far more indulgent of uncertain theoretical speculations than are therapists. And this is true even if, in the end, they too seek to tweak or otherwise repair Freud's thought (see Lear, 2000, p. 153). Philosophers and literary critics, for example, grant Freud the utility of a thought experiment and agree to follow an interesting train of thought on the grounds that Freud himself gives, namely, as "an *advocatus diaboli* who does not, for all that, sign a pact with the devil" (Freud, 1920/2011, p. 95; *SE*, 1920a/1991, p. 59). What these scholars also share with the late Freud, no doubt ironically, is an ambiguous relationship to therapy and treatment. Typically scholars do not seek to cure the soul but to understand something about it; or, even more often, to engage the discourses of the soul without doctrinal commitments one way or another. The efficacy of psychoanalytic therapy is therefore often ignored by scholars, swept under the rug along with the ethics of psychoanalytic practice.

Therapists, by contrast, ignore the nuts-and-bolts issue of efficacy at their own peril. When Freud announced the death drive theory, his colleagues had good reason to worry: the new, highly abstract theory undermined the fairly well-established theory of sexuality. Worse, the death drive theory countenanced a disturbing form of therapeutic nihilism. For if life really is set asunder by the forces of death, and these forces are the genetic inheritance of our phylogenetic past, then there is, in the final analysis, very little any therapy can do to assuage the roots of human suffering. We really are dealing with what Jonathan Lear calls a "metaphysical principle" with "teleological" and "cosmic" dimensions (2000, pp. 137–41). More simply put, nature trumps nurture – a troubling conclusion for anyone seeking to ameliorate human suffering. In Norman O. Brown's words, Freud's late dualism is therefore quite simply a form of "suicidal therapeutic pessimism" (1959, p. 81).

Beyond the Pleasure Principle couldn't be any darker. It is not just that one is left with the choice of dying in one's own way. Or even, as Freud clarifies in 1930, that one is left with a tragic, radically antisocial choice: destroy others or destroy one's self, sadism or masochism. It is also, as Freud concludes in "Analysis Terminable and Interminable" of 1937, that the practice of psychoanalysis is thereby rendered interminable. For if life is given over to endless struggle with the demons of one's own phylogenetic past, and with the pasts of other people similarly stricken, then our "discontent" with civilization is inevitable. Short of death, there is no cure for existence. As a result Freud evinced none of the *furor therapeuticus* that distinguished well-intending but overzealous physicians. Far from it. As Ferenczi reports, Freud in 1932 confessed that "neurotics are a rabble, good only to support us financially and to allow us to learn from their cases: psychoanalysis as a therapy may be worthless" (1932/1995, pp. 185–6).

Even though Ferenczi was an eager partner in Freud's biological speculations, he finally recoiled from the dark, tragically overdetermined ends of the new metapsychology. Ferenczi cared deeply for his patients, ultimately believing that therapy must trump metapsychology and, along with it, the vaunted principle of analyst neutrality. Consequently Ferenczi developed a new "active technique" based on his conviction that neurotic patients suffer from lack of love. The goal of therapy was, therefore, to compensate for this lack. In a letter of December 13, 1931, Freud characterized Ferenczi's technique this way: "I see that the difference between us comes to a head in the smallest thing, a detail in technique, which certainly deserves to be discussed. You have made no secret of the fact that you kiss your patients and let them kiss you; I had also heard the same thing from my patients [via Clara Thompson]" (Freud & Ferenczi, 2000, p. 422). Freud then points out that a kiss always includes an erotic component, and urges Ferenczi to keep his active technique private. Then he describes a classic slippery slope:

> Now, picture to yourself what will be the consequence of making your technique public? There is no revolutionary who is not knocked out of the field by a still more radical one. So-and-so many independent thinkers in technique will say to themselves: Why stop at a kiss? Certainly, one will achieve still more if one adds "pawing," which, after all, doesn't make any babies. And then bolder ones will come along who will take the further step of peeping and showing, and soon we will have accepted into the technique of psychoanalysis the whole repertoire of demiviergerie and petting parties [in English], with the result being a great increase of interest in analysis on the part of analysts and those who are being analyzed. The new ally will, however, easily lay too much claim to this interest for himself, the younger of our colleagues will be hard put, in the relational connections they have made, to stop at the point where they had originally intended, and Grandfather [in English] Ferenczi, looking at the busy scenery that he has created, will possibly say to himself: Perhaps I should have stopped in my technique of maternal tenderness *before* the kiss. (p. 422)

Or as Freud put it rather more succinctly to Sandor Rado, "we cannot make a whorehouse out of the psychoanalytic situation" (in Roazen & Swerdloff, 1995, p. 108). Obviously Freud thought that Ferenczi's new technique was a potential public relations nightmare for psychoanalysis – the kind of thing he had grown to expect from Jung years before, but not from dependable Ferenczi. As a result Freud was forced to make his case, as he says, "unambiguously clear" (p. 423).

When Ferenczi died on May 22, 1933, Freud wrote an obituary that praised his loyal friend's contribution to psychoanalysis, singling out for special praise his work of 1924, *Versuch einer Genitaltheorie*, the work we know as *Thalassa: A Theory of Genitality*. *Thalassa* was, Freud says, "his most brilliant and most fertile achievement," and "perhaps the boldest application of psychoanalysis that was ever attempted" (*SE*, 1933c/1991, p. 228). This work of "bio-analysis" was of course the silent partner to Freud's own *Beyond the Pleasure Principle* – so of course Freud admired it. Freud was, however, very ungenerous about Ferenczi's turn to active therapy in the years after *Thalassa*. "After this summit of achievement," Freud says of *Thalassa*, "our friend slowly drifted away from us" (p. 229). "Signs were slowly revealed in him," Freud asserts, "of a grave organic destructive process which had probably overshadowed his life for many years already" (p. 229). Freud's claim couldn't be more ironical or, as we will see, more typical: Ferenczi's attempt to love his patients was evidence of a degeneration made possible by the death drive. "Shortly before completing his sixtieth year," Freud wraps up, "he succumbed to pernicious anemia." "Pernicious anemia": Freud's retrospective diagnosis was that his friend suffered from impaired neurological functioning. It took Freud no more than nine days to produce this diagnosis, since the date of the obituary reads "May, 1933" (and Ferenczi died on the 22nd).

Freud's other loyal follower, the far less kind and gentle Ernest Jones, similarly piled on the poor Ferenczi (Clark, 1980, p. 459). But according to the analyst Michael Balint, who met with Ferenczi many times during his final months, the claim that the dying Ferenczi was "deluded, paranoid or homicidal" is simply false. So what justifies Freud's final act of betrayal? The answer is very simple: Ferenczi's turn away from the metapsychology was proof enough that his old friend had lost his mind, and precisely in the terms of the metapsychology that they had both created, namely the death drive. Ferenczi had unwittingly performed the death drive, and so proved Freud right. The other reason: Freud was ruthless when faced with threats to the future of psychoanalysis, even from a close friend.

2   Origins of the Death Drive Theory

Just as a stretched rubber band has the tendency to assume its original shape, so all living matter, consciously or unconsciously, craves to regain the complete and absolute inertia of inorganic existence.

(Freud in Viereck, 1930, p. 32)

Scholars and analysts provide many internal and external reasons for why Freud wrote and then published *Beyond the Pleasure Principle*. According to the internal explanation, Freud had always been a gloomy fellow, uncommonly consumed by thoughts of death and mortality; was even more so inclined in the wake of the First World War, partly because of the fresh spectacle of barbarism and partly because his sons, Martin and Ernst, risked their lives as soldiers serving the Republic of German-Austria; and was, in early 1920, depressed by the deaths of key people in his life, notably his friend and benefactor Anton von Freund and his favorite daughter Sophie. Another consideration: by the time *Beyond* appeared Freud was already in his mid-60s and even more inclined toward misanthropy. All of this is true.

According to the external explanation, Freud was obliged in 1920 to establish a new, more robust dualism between life and death drives because the problem of narcissism had undermined the old dualism of ego and sex instincts. Why? Because the existence of narcissism or self-love collapses the difference between love of one's self and love of an other. One loves one's self *as the other*; or, in the lingo of psychoanalysis, one takes one's self as an "object" of love. Freud was philosophically wedded to dualism and so took steps to reinforce it in 1920. This is also true.

Yet things are more complicated than what these two poles of interpretation suggest. Take the internal interpretation. Freud's lifetime of brooding was hardly unusual for Europeans living in the wake of postrevolutionary France, witnesses to the decline of the Habsburg Empire, and at times personal casualties of social and political conflicts that erupted in war. As the world-weary Goethe is to have quipped, "I thank Heaven that I am not young in so thoroughly finished a time." Freud's pessimism was not, therefore, just a symptom of personal psychopathology. Nor is it fair to cast his pessimism as a reflection of collective psychopathology. Arguably Europeans like Freud had earned their pessimism the hard way – by the actual deprivations of everyday life. Gloom about human nature and about the future was simply realism. Life was hard. As that great prophet of gloom Arthur Schopenhauer (1851/1893) once wrote, "Unless *suffering* is the direct and immediate object of life, our existence must entirely fail of its aim" (p. 11).

By the same token we should not overstate the importance of the external interpretation for Freud's new dualism. For while it is true that a more robust form of dualism was a theoretically useful expedient to repair the weakened dualism, it cannot be claimed that the death and life drives were the only possible solution to that problem; or, more simply, that a fundamental dualism was justified by empirical observation. Freud's commitment to a dualist worldview functions instead as an unexamined first principle or, less charitably, a prejudice. Why not monism? Why not a triadic structure? Part of the answer is that Freud believed that only dualism correctly captures the conflictual reality of the psyche. It was a given, a biological imperative, and not just a consequence of social conditions. Yet because this belief is insufficiently rationalized by observation we are inevitably led back toward internal interpretations. One might rightly ask, for example, why Freud proposed the new dualism in 1920 and not earlier.

Other analytic colleagues, not to mention earlier thinkers like Gustav Fechner and Schopenhauer, had in fact already considered ideas similar to the death drive. Freud's two earliest and at the time most talented followers, Alfred Adler and Wilhelm Stekel, also came close. Adler's theory of a "drive for power" strikes a similar note and even harkens back to a shared source, Nietzsche's will to power. And Stekel was perhaps the first analyst to speak about the influence of "Thanatos," even as he argued that human nature was "bipolar," for example, was split between love and hate (Stekel, 1950, p. 132). "Freud later adopted some of my discoveries," Stekel complains in his autobiography, "without mentioning my name. Even the fact that in my first edition [of *Causes of Nervousness*, 1907] I had defined anxiety as the reaction of the *life instinct* against the upsurge of the *death instinct* was not mentioned in his later books, and many people believe that the death instinct is Freud's discovery" (p. 138; see also Stekel, 1925/1975, p. 138). And then there is the Russian Sabina who, in November 1911, presented a version of "Destruction as the Cause of Coming into Being" at a meeting of the Vienna Psychoanalytic Society (Nunberg & Federn, 1975, pp. 329–35, 316). According to Spielrein sexuality necessarily implies its opposite – a claim she explicitly derives from the contemporary works of Freud, Bleuler, Stekel, and Jung (Spielrein, 1994, p. 173), and also on what she calls "the biological facts" (p. 184). "The reproductive drive," Spielrein argues, "consists psychologically of two antagonistic components, a destructive drive as well as a drive for coming into being" (p. 184). It is worth mentioning that Theodor Reik also presented, in late 1911, an essay to the Society called "On Death and Sexuality."

Years later Freud admitted his "own resistance when the idea of the destructive drive first arose in psychoanalytic literature, and how long it took before I became receptive to it" (*SE*, 1930/1991, p. 119). Already in 1909 Freud felt obliged to register his disagreement in print, stating that "I cannot bring myself to assume the existence of a special aggressive instinct alongside of the familiar instincts of self-preservation and of sex, and on an equal footing with them" (*SE*, 1909/1991, p. 140). A footnote added in 1923 registers his eventual change of heart. "Since then," Freud admits, "I have been obliged to assert the existence of an 'aggressive instinct,' but it is different from Adler's. I prefer to call it the 'destructive' or 'death instinct'" (*SE*, 1909/1991, p. 140, n. 2). Freud preferred to coin his own terms. The same holds for Stekel. Even years after Freud came to believe in the existence of a "death drive" he still refused to utilize the word "Thanatos," god of death, as the logical counterpart to his Eros, god of love. After introducing the new dualism he only referred to Thanatos in conversation, not in print (Jones, 1957, p. 273). Stekel would get no recognition at all, not even by dint of holding a word in common (Roazen, 1976, p. 218). As for Spielrein, Freud took a different tack. In a footnote in *Beyond the Pleasure Principle*, Freud duly acknowledged her role in conceiving of "primary masochism," an idea he admits may have merit: "A considerable portion of these speculations have been anticipated by Sabina Spielrein in an instructive and interesting paper which, however, is unfortunately not very clear to me" (*SE*, 1920a/1991, p. 55, n. 1). That's typical of Freud. But actually Spielrein's essay is not so very unclear, including her argument on behalf of a fundamental yet paradoxical will to, and wish for, "self-injury" (1994, p. 160). In 1924, four years later, the "new" idea of primary masochism is simply assumed by Freud – only now without any attribution at all to Spielrein's work (*SE*, 19: 156–70). Under the circumstances one can perhaps be forgiven some word play: Freud's characteristic anxiety over priority about the death drive idea seems like a petty game or, if you will, *ein reines Spiel* – an act of pure gamesmanship.

As for the timing of the new theory, one plausible explanation is that Freud intended the new dualism to reestablish the darker foundation of psychoanalysis against Carl Jung's alternate view that, from Freud's perspective, flirted with a Pollyanna form of monism. More about Jung later. The point is that the external interpretations of *Beyond the Pleasure Principle*, although partly true, fail to tell the whole story of the genesis of the late dualism. It is therefore bootless to ignore the many personal, political, and psychological motivations for the appearance and, indeed, the meaning of the death drive theory of 1920. Theory always has a context. This means that when attempting to understand the significance of *Beyond* it is insufficient to reduce things to either Freud's subjectivity or to idealistic norms about scientific objectivity; to internal or external explanations. It is far more productive, if not more accurate, to tread a middle path, as the twin dangers of naivety and dogmatism lay at either end of the spectrum of possible interpretations.

* * *

Of course one can speculate about internal and external motives forever. It is therefore fortunate that Freud himself provides evidence for his death drive theory, and that we can assess it on this uncontroversial basis. Among the ten different kinds of evidence that he considers, the first is easily the most persuasive. During the First World War many psychoanalysts served their countries as medically trained psychotherapists, a fact that greatly accelerated the global brand recognition of psychoanalysis. The greatest challenge for such practitioners was the phenomenon of war trauma or "shell shock." Why a challenge? Because traditional psychoanalysis dictates that all dreams are expressions of pleasure, no matter how disguised or perverted in their aim; all dreams obey, in Freud's terms, the pleasure principle and, as such, aim to fulfill repressed wishes. The challenge of war trauma, as with other industrial examples of "traumatic neuroses" (e.g., train derailments, steam ship explosions), was that sufferers often relived in their dreams the event that traumatized them. In other words, the trauma was repeated, a phenomenon Freud refers to as "fixation to the trauma." The war had impelled Freud to account for these traumas in the language of psychoanalysis. And so he asked: Can dreams ever fail to be wish fulfillments? Can affect ever go "beyond the pleasure principle" and beyond the interpretation of sexuality?

Freud's discussion of trauma is one of the most controversial yet influential aspects of *Beyond the Pleasure Principle*. Put very summarily, he concludes that mechanical or physical trauma overwhelms the delicate interior of the psyche, and thereby "floods" the defenses. As a neurologist, Freud means this literally: traumatic energy invades the outer layer of the brain, the cerebral cortex, and causes damage to the interior. What he adds to this mechanistic etiology is a second form of traumatic energy that originates from the inside of the brain, what we could call the death drive proper. Not able to defend oneself from this internal enemy, one is forced, psychologically, to treat it as though it too arises from the outside world of traumatic stimuli. This is what Freud calls the origin of "projection" (1920/2011, pp. 69–70; *SE*, 1920a/1991, p. 29). Put otherwise, one inevitably treats this *silent* energy inside as a part of *noisy* reality outside.

Had Freud stuck to the problem of the traumatic neuroses, he could have avoided dealing with something that was strictly exceptional. But instead he goes on to consider other kinds of evidence in favor of the death drive theory, thereby forcing the question of how relevant the death drive is to everyday life and, therefore, to psychoanalysis. To this extent Freud brings metapsychology and speculation into contact with psychoanalysis and science – making them overlap. So while death belongs to metapsychological speculation and life belongs to the science of psychoanalysis, the two are in fact locked together as the late dualism that grounds everything Freud says after 1920.

Let's turn to the other nine examples that Freud considers, always provisionally, as evidence for the existence of a drive to nonexistence. In addition to the traumatic neuroses, Freud proffers the following examples: the "fort/da" game, according to which a child plays at absence/presence; transference neurosis, a centerpiece of analytic therapy and interpretation; salmon spawning; migratory patterns of birds; embryology, which is an allusion to Haeckel's theory of recapitulation; compulsions of fate, a discussion linked to Freud's own disappointments with erstwhile followers; cellular biology; ancient mythology, derived from the poet Aristophanes, concerning the origin of sexual difference; Schopenhauer's philosophy, mentioned directly; and Nietzsche's doctrine of eternal recurrence, mentioned in quotation marks but unattributed. With the exception of Freud's reference to Schopenhauer, each example hinges directly upon the role that *repetition* plays in undermining the dominance of psychoanalysis and its pleasure principle. The same holds for Freud's interpretation of the traumatic neuroses.

The idea of repetition compulsion, first introduced in "The Uncanny" in 1919, functions in *Beyond* as the means by which the death drive is realized in everyday life. Compulsive repetition, *Wiederholungszwang*, is fundamental to Freud's argument. Here is how it works in the case of the nine examples (the argument from Schopenhauer being discussed in the next section). The traumatized soldier repeats in his dreams the precipitating experience, a phenomenon not easily reduced to the drive for pleasure. A child's play with a bobbin, repeatedly thrown out (made-gone, "fort") and then wound up again (there, "da"), is a game without pleasure that implies a demonic force at work. The patient's transference neurosis (irrational identification with the analyst) during treatment is an unconscious repetition of past experiences, a kind of irruption of unreason and death into the analysis of life. Salmon spawn down a stream and die from the effort, as though compulsively and instinctually, thus showing how death is intimately tied to life. Migrating birds follow invisible pathways over and over again, possibly guided by an instinct that goes beyond the pleasure principle. All life is patterned and structured to follow a course dictated in advance by embryology, including a repetition of all the external conditions that made life possible across evolution – including even those conditions once unfavorable to life. Again and again ungrateful students are driven by self-destruction to betray their mentors and benefactors. Cellular biology discovers that organic material, left to its own devices and cut off from any new infusions of energy or matter, always dies after a few generations. Greek mythology posits that human sexuality was once doubled and only subsequently torn apart by the gods, a trauma that drives the separated parts (biological male and female) to desire reunion again and again. And Schopenhauer's great heir, Nietzsche, posited that humankind's "greatest burden" was the thought of the "eternal return (or repetition) of the same."

That, in sum, is the totality of Freud's evidence scattered across seven unequal chapters. Freud wasn't convinced by any of it. *Beyond* begins as thought experiment, gathers momentum as speculation, and concludes with the wistful figure of a limping man. "Concerning the slow advances of our scientific knowledge," Freud writes, "we are also comforted by the words of a poet [al-Hariri, in Friedrich Rückert's German translation]: "What one cannot fly to one must limp to ... The scripture says that limping is no sin" (1920/2011, p. 99; *SE*, 1920a/1991, p. 64). Freud understood that his evidence was inconclusive, figuratively no better than a kind of limping forward. But this conclusion comes into better focus only in the years after *Beyond the Pleasure Principle*. For although the repetition compulsion was enshrined in psychoanalysis after 1920 – even by analysts who rejected *Beyond* – Freud never again made any real effort to find empirical support for the death drive theory. In *Civilization and Its Discontents*, he admits the following: "Since the assumption of the existence of the [death] instinct is mainly based on theoretical grounds, we must also admit that it is not entirely proof against theoretical objections" (*SE*, 1930/1991, pp. 121–2). Freud would add the "negative therapeutic reaction" and primary masochism to the list of examples of the death drive, but they don't come close to providing conclusive evidence.

Ultimately Freud took a different tack altogether: he came to believe that the death drive only did its work in silence. Consequently the many possible instances of the death drive, including all of the evidence outlined earlier, were knowable only because they were tinged, fused, or "alloyed" with Eros, with life (*SE*, 1933b/1991, p. 209). This means that, after *Beyond*, the death drive operates as a theoretical postulate, impossible to demonstrate or prove but nonetheless *required* by the metapsychology of psychoanalysis. In this sense Freud's death drive theory has a status analogous to what theoretical physics attributes to unseen but mathematically necessary entities – like invisible black holes known only because of their gravitational pull on visible objects. And actually this sounds just about right: the death drive theory is Freud's black hole, a force that exerts itself from beyond psychoanalysis, beyond life, and beyond empirical verification. Its reality is deduced, as a matter of principle, by the effect it has on everyday life; but it is assumed, as a matter of fact, as an exigency of metapsychological speculation.

3   Speculation and Philosophy

Freud himself worried about the style of argumentation in *Beyond the Pleasure Principle*, twice declaring his aversion to "mysticism." In the chapter on the traumatic neuroses, discussed above, Freud writes, "The emerging discussion may seem like 'false profundity' or mysticism, but we know we have not striven for any such thing" (1920/2011, p. 76; *SE*, 1920a/1991, p. 37). And then, having seemingly established the necessity for a death drive in the next chapter (six), Freud admits that "this view is far from being easily comprehensible, and makes a perfectly mystical impression" (1920/2011, p. 91; *SE*, 1920a/1991, p. 54). A third instance is more indirect, but connects to Freud's growing distrust of a kind of mysticism associated with introspection and intuition – an issue I discuss in Chapter 2. During a fascinating discussion at the end of chapter six, Freud broaches the "figurative language" of his metapsychology. One consequence of the slow drift away from observation and toward so-called intuitions is that certainty has been compromised. "One may have made a lucky guess," he writes, "or may have gone terribly astray. In this type of research I do not attribute much to so called 'intuitions'" (1920/2011, pp. 95–6; *SE*, 1920a/1991, p. 59). As Freud says, it is difficult to be impartial "when dealing with the ultimate questions – the great problems of science and life" (1920/2011, p. 96).

But if metapsychology isn't mysticism or mystical intuition, then what is it? One answer is that it is a species of "philosophy." Certainly *Beyond the Pleasure Principle* is often considered to be Freud's most philosophical text, or at least his most obtusely theoretical. Yet Freud kept his distance from philosophy and philosophers. In a preface written for Theodor Reik in 1919, Freud equates hysterics with artists and obsessional patients, all of whom have "created a private religion for themselves" (Reik, 1931/1958b,

p. 9; *SE*, 1919/1991, p. 261). "The delusions of the paranoic," Freud continues, getting to his real target,

> show an unwelcome external similarity and inner relationship to the systems of our philosophers. We cannot get away from the impression that patients are making, in an asocial manner, the same attempts at a solution of their conflicts and an appeasement of their desires which, when carried out in a manner acceptable to a large number of persons, are called poetry, religion, and philosophy. (p. 10)

It is really quite an indictment: the clinical diagnoses of hysteria, obsessive compulsion, and paranoia are different from poetry, religion, and philosophy only because one is private and the other is shared. Consequently, instead of "mysticism" or "philosophy" or "metaphysics" Freud engaged in "metapsychology." So although *Beyond* marks a return to cultural issues, it assiduously avoids the history of philosophy as it concerns, for example, pleasure and love.

However, despite Freud's inflated rhetoric, the death drive theory does seem like a scientist rendering of some suspiciously familiar, even old-fashioned metaphysics. "We have unwittingly sailed," Freud admits in chapter six of *Beyond*, "into the harbour of Schopenhauer's philosophy" (1920/2011, p. 87; *SE*, 1920a/1991, pp. 49–50). To Schopenhauer's declaration in *The World as Will and Representation* that "death is the real aim of life," Freud merely adds that life is a detour on the path of death. Freud, always ready to downplay his retrograde attraction to Schopenhauer, later defends himself in the *New Introductory Lectures on Psychoanalysis* (*SE*, 1933a/1991):

> You may shrug your shoulders and say: "That isn't natural science, it's Schopenhauer's philosophy!" But, Ladies and Gentlemen, why should not a bold thinker have guessed something that is afterwards confirmed by sober and painstaking detailed research? Moreover, there is nothing that has not been said already, and similar things had been said by many people before Schopenhauer. (p. 107)

Freud's approach is entirely characteristic: he accepts and rejects his debt to philosophy in nearly the same breath. Indeed, a similar double operation opens *Beyond*, where Freud's debt to philosophy is immediately recognized, *da*, only to be sent far away, *fort*. The history of philosophy, Freud claims, is no help with an investigation of the pleasure principle (1920/2011, p. 51; *SE*, 1920a/1991, p. 7). When Freud goes on to discuss Plato later on, it is only to invoke and then ignore and even denigrate him. Such is Freud's *dismissive interest* in philosophy. In a delightfully facetious passage in his "Autobiographical Study" of 1925, Freud chortles his position as follows:

"Even when I have moved away from observation, I have carefully avoided any contact with philosophy proper. This avoidance has been greatly facilitated by constitutional incapacity" (*SE*, 1925c/1991, p. 59). A similarly grand denunciation of philosophy-metaphysics is made in a private letter to German psychologist Werner Achelis just a couple years later.[4]

> What I have to say about your argument will not surprise you, as you seem familiar with my attitude toward philosophy (metaphysics). Other defects in my nature have certainly distressed me and made me feel humble; with metaphysics it is different – I not only have no talent for it but no respect for it, either. In secret – one cannot say such things aloud – I believe that one day metaphysics will be condemned as a nuisance, as an abuse of thinking, as a survival from the period of the religious *Weltanschauung*. I know well to what extent this way of thinking estranges me from German cultural life. (Freud, 1939/1960b, pp. 374–5)

Moments later Freud, adopting a tone very apropos the cultural works, adds that "it is certainly simpler to find one's way in 'this world' of facts than in the 'other world' of philosophy." The later Freud is always on the side of objective facts and reality.

In other contexts, however, Freud could strike a very different tone. In a letter of August 1, 1919, Freud tells his friend and analytic colleague (also Nietzsche's would-be love interest), Lou Andreas-Salomé, "For my old age I have chosen the theme of death; I have stumbled on a remarkable notion based on my theory of the instincts [*Triebe*, drives], and now I must read all kinds of things relevant to it, e.g., Schopenhauer, for the first time" (Freud & Andreas-Salomé, 1966, p. 99). Official recognition of a kind followed in a 1935 postscript to the "Autobiographical Study," cited at the outset, where Freud finally concedes that the theories of *Beyond* returned him not just to his oldest ideas about mental life, but to his earliest interest in philosophy. He writes: "Threads which in the course of my development had become inter-tangled have now begun to separate; interests which I acquired in the later part of life have receded, while the older and original ones become prominent once more" (*SE*, 1935/1991, p. 71). And again: "My interests, after making a lifelong *détour* through the natural sciences, medicine, and psychotherapy, returned to the cultural problems which had fascinated me long before" (p. 72). How long before? To his fiancée, Martha Bernays, Freud had in August of 1882 admitted his illicit attraction to cultural problems and to philosophy.

---

[4] In the 1930s Achelis would become director of the public relations department of the Göring Institute (Cocks, 1985/1997, pp. 159–60).

"Philosophy," the twenty-five-year-old writes, "which I have always pictured as my goal and refuge in my old age, gains every day in attraction" (in Jones, 1957, p. 41).

Freud's theory: Every organism, having repeated all the historically acquired conditions that made it possible and having completed the many practical detours required of the reality principle (reflecting law, society, the horde – *Kultur*), merely wishes to "die in its own way," to at last achieve the pleasure of nonexistence. Freud's translation of that theory into autobiography – his regressive return to cultural problems and to philosophy – is evidence of a drive to end things on his own terms, to be done with the detour called life (and its psychoanalysis), and to finally become the inorganic nothing from whence he came. What has been "acquired" will have finally been overcome, not by what is new but by what is ancient. Or as he writes to Andreas-Salomé in a fascinating letter of May 1925, "A crust of indifference is slowly creeping up around me; a fact I state without complaining. It is a natural development, a way of beginning to grow inorganic" (Freud & Andreas-Salomé, 1966, p. 154). As always, Freud's life is subject to the theory of psychoanalysis, or in this case to its recent metapsychology.

The aging Freud had rediscovered a philosophy with an ancient pedigree: philosophy as preparation for dying. But the truth is, the botched metabiology that Freud in *Beyond* lifts, holus-bolus, from the *Project for a Scientific Psychology* of 1895, and before that from Gustav Fechner and others, is of a piece with the unbridled philosophical speculation of his youth. Despite Freud's many protestations to the contrary, we know that he was very interested in philosophy as a young man. He took formal classes in philosophy with Franz Brentano at the University of Vienna, where they discussed the unconscious; corresponded and passionately debated philosophy with his friend, Eduard Silberstein; in a letter expressed interest in completing a PhD in philosophy and zoology; read works by Plato, Aristotle, David Hume, Kant, Schopenhauer, Eduard von Hartmann, Ludwig Feuerbach, Nietzsche, Franz Brentano, Theodor Gomperz, and Henry Thomas Buckle; translated into German (for Gomperz) an essay on women by John Stuart Mill; was almost certainly aware of and likely influenced by a work on Aristotle and catharsis written by his wife's uncle, Jakob Bernays; and was obviously influenced, not just by Schopenhauer's thoughts on death, but by Nietzsche's ideas, such as the "id" (*das Es*), the "will to power," and by the "eternal return of the same," the last appearing, as noted, in quotation marks in passages about repetition compulsion in *Beyond*.

Those in Freud's inner circle were well aware of his interests, if not his intellectual debts, and were not always shy about saying so. Freud's friend, the respected novelist Arnold Zweig, gushed the following compliment to Freud in a letter of late 1930:

> To me it seems that you have achieved everything that Nietzsche intuitively felt to be his task, without his really being able to achieve it with his poetic idealism and brilliant inspirations. He tried to explain the birth of tragedy; you have done it in *Totem and Taboo*. He longed for a world Beyond Good and Evil; by means of analysis you have discovered a world to which this phrase actually applies. Analysis has reversed all values, it has conquered Christianity, disclosed the true Antichrist, and liberated the spirit of resurgent life from the ascetic ideal. (Freud & Zweig, 1970, p. 23)

Similar sentiments are recorded in the *Minutes of the Vienna Psychoanalytic Society* in April 1908. Ernst Federn, who would later coedit the *Minutes*, is claimed to have remarked, "Nietzsche has come so close to our views that we can ask only, 'Where has he not come close?' He intuitively knew a number of Freud's discoveries; he was the first to discover the significance of abreaction [reenacting and purging a past act], of repression, of flights into illness, of the instincts – the normal as well as the sadistic" (Nunberg & Federn, 1962–1975, 1: p. 359). Freud himself, in an uncharacteristic flourish, once claimed that "Nietzsche was one of the first psychoanalysts" (in Viereck, 1930, p. 38). Yet the invocation of Nietzsche's name was double-edged. Years after their falling-out, analyst Otto Rank sent a gift on Freud's seventieth birthday that apparently wasn't appreciated: Nietzsche's complete works, bound in white leather (Roazen, 1997, p. 15).

Yet even if the death drive theory sounds like Schopenhauer warmed over with a dash of Nietzsche, the same cannot be said about Freud's *methodology* in *Beyond the Pleasure Principle*. There really is no precedent for it in the history of philosophy – even less so in the history of science. It best resembles the experiments of avant-garde literature. Arguably this method is the single best excuse Freud had for refusing to call his metapsychology a kind of metaphysics – although at a high cost to "science." There really is no name for this method, although for convenience we could just call it "speculation," a term Freud uses often in *Beyond*.[5]

[5] Borch-Jacobsen and Shamdasani argue that Freud's penchant for wild speculation lands him in the camp of positivism as practiced by Ernst Mach: one is permitted speculation precisely because one relies on observation; observation that puts speculation to the test and so challenges and modifies it. The problem is that psychology is notoriously compromised by "looping effects," essentially the input of the human subjects being observed, which undermines any challenge and only leads to false

Speculation, an activity located somewhere between play and philosophy, allows Freud to put forth the death drive theory as just one hypothesis among others. As he says in chapter four, "The following is speculation, often far-fetched speculation, which each person will appreciate or disregard according to his or her particular interests" (1920/2011, p. 65; *SE*, 1920a/1991, p. 24). Speculation makes no claims on belief. "It would be reasonable to ask me," Freud writes, "whether and to what extent I am convinced of the hypotheses developed here. My answer would be the following: neither am I convinced myself, nor do I seek to convince others to believe in them" (1920/2011, p. 95; *SE*, 1920a/1991, p. 59).

Probably the most useful discussion of Freud's method is offered by French philosopher Jacques Derrida, who demonstrates convincingly how Freud treats his speculation the same way that his grandson Ernst treats the bobbin on a string: he repeatedly tosses out an idea and then reels it back again. In short, he plays. At one point Derrida rightly calls Freud's writing "a kind of discourse on method" (1980/1987, p. 406). Of course such a method gets Freud nowhere with his argument, at least nowhere beyond its own performativity. For this reason, the most apt figure of Freud's methodology is the devil's advocate.

And yet it must be remembered: the cool dispassion of the devil's advocate quickly gave way to Freud's abiding faith in his own theory – perhaps already in *Beyond*, where Freud's own rhetoric of nonchalance ("you can take it or leave it") shouldn't be accepted at face value. Freud is more forthcoming in later works. "I can no longer think any other way," Freud writes in 1930 (*SE*, 1930/1991, p. 119), and then adds a few lines of derision aimed at his critics:

> For little children do not like to hear it when mention is made of the inborn human inclination to "evil," to aggression and destructiveness, and thus to cruelty as well. God made them in the image of His own perfection, and no one wants to be told how hard it is to reconcile the existence of evil . . . with His omnipotence or His all-goodness. (SE, 1930/1991, pp. 119–20)

Simply put, the death drive theory became the dominant theory of psychoanalysis in the late period because at some point Freud came to fully believe in it. And this is what provokes, for Derrida, an interesting paradox: Freud's playful method in *Beyond* gets nowhere beyond itself, and yet this very activity manages to produce big changes within psychoanalysis. The play

confirmations (see Borch-Jacobsen & Shamdasani, 2012, pp. 116–45). I don't disagree, but see the appeal to Machian positivism as a cover for a more covert attachment to late Romanticism.

begets institutional effects; effects realized in the objective world. *Play exists.*
As such, play seeks no justification beyond itself, or at least beyond its own
authority. But, once again, it comes at a cost – the cost of seriousness,
perhaps, and the cost of science.

4　Much Ado about Nonexistence

Freud's playful (non)method, his speculation, is nonetheless a play with
and through biology – a feature that many philosophers, including
Derrida, fail to appreciate. This is important enough to warrant
a categorical statement: without a proper appreciation of the bio-logic of
the death drive theory, one does not understand anything about the
cultural works of Freud's final period. In this respect, and to stretch it
just a little, *Beyond* is the Rosetta stone of Freudian theory – the key that
unlocks the psychological theories of the late works precisely because it
provides a translation of the biological theories of the earliest. As for the
third side of the stone, to continue the analogy, that would have to be the
partially legible script in *Beyond* devoted to Schopenhauer, Nietzsche, and
the suppressed history of philosophy.

In this context, three kinds of misunderstanding of Freud's *Beyond* are
worth noting. The first kind is highly motivated or willful, which in the
best case signifies an authentic *critical* reckoning. A fair portion of the
interpretation of *Beyond* fits into this camp. For example, the philosopher
Herbert Marcuse repairs and remakes Freudian theory in his own Freudo-
Marxist image, and is to that extent perfectly justified – despite the
uselessness of his work as a faithful commentary on Freud's own claims
and arguments. Another example is Derrida's deconstruction: again, this
work is often interesting in itself and can be highly clever, but it's nearly
useless as a commentary on Freud and psychoanalysis. The second kind of
misunderstanding is driven by ideology. The resulting scholarship often
appears sound, as judged, for instance, by the number of references cited.
But that is a pleasant illusion. At best this work represents an authentic
political reckoning, the references themselves just ideology parading as
scholarship. Let's return to this issue in a moment, because it's important.
The third basic kind of misunderstanding is neither critical nor political.
It is merely ignorant – the accumulation and regurgitation of sausage-
insights produced by a century of moonlighting by amateur scholars, chief
among them psychoanalysts and their former patients.

These three basic misunderstandings of *Beyond*, which are often alloyed
with each other, have in turn generated misperceptions about the essential

meaning of the cultural works and the epistemological status of ego psychology. With rare exceptions, such as Norman O. Brown and Paul Ricoeur, almost no one has attended carefully to the connection between *Beyond the Pleasure Principle* and Freud's late analysis of *Kultur*. This is unfortunate, since the reasoning of *Beyond* dictates that the cultural works are really asocial if not anticultural in orientation; or again, they are elaborate refutations that culture in any way trumps Freud's biologically driven, and therefore irrefutable, psychology. If psychoanalysis has anything to say about culture, it is that it always plays second fiddle to the radical depths of a tragic metapsychology as elaborated in these late works (see Dufresne, 2000, pp. 145–83).

The second misunderstanding fails to address the connection between the metapsychology of *Beyond* and the ego psychology that follows. Either the logical and intellectual coherence of the metapsychology is downplayed, as in Erich Fromm, or its singular radicality is vastly overplayed (and fundamentally misunderstood), as in Jacques Lacan. But to the chagrin of both Fromm and Lacan – and by extension to the chagrin of American and French traditions of psychoanalysis – works like *Group Psychology and the Analysis of the Ego* of 1921 and *The Ego and the Id* of 1923 are in fact continuous with *Beyond*, reflections of the metapsychology and not exemplars of a simple paradigm shift toward ego psychology. *Group Psychology*, partly composed at the same time as *Beyond* and with a foot in both camps (ego psychology and cultural works), actually provides the logical flipside of Freud's analysis of the death drive: namely, an analysis of group love and Eros. Similarly, Freud explicitly conceived of *The Ego and the Id* of 1923, the work most closely associated with the advent of ego psychology, as a continuation of ideas begun in *Beyond*. "I am occupied with something speculative," the vacationing Freud tells Ferenczi in July 1922, "which is a continuation of 'Beyond,' and will either become a small book or nothing" (Freud & Ferenczi, 2000, p. 84). He repeats the claim near the beginning of *The Ego and the Id*. Nothing could be plainer: the late works are grounded upon the death drive theory of 1920.

The majority of analysts were right, however, to complain that metapsychology subverts psychoanalysis. On this score the political reckoning with Freud can't be ignored. For institutional psychoanalysis after *Beyond* is nothing if not the exorcism of this unwanted metapsychology, whether by theorizing the conformist ego of a presentist and pragmatic psychology or by theorizing the nonconformist id of a utopic and aspirational psychology. In effect, institutional psychoanalysis after Freud perfectly reflects a crisis that begins with *Beyond* and, frankly, never ends – the battle between idealized versions of American and French psychoanalysis merely echoing, critically *and* politically, the eternal battle of life and death that Freud left them with. Ironically, then, even when psychoanalysts rejected *Beyond* (by minimizing it or transforming metabiology into a symbol of something else) they ended up perpetuating it – compulsively, of course, as though driven by the death drive that Freud injected into psychoanalysis. If so, they are themselves the overall shape of the death drive that Freud had trouble proving, the concrete and very noisy examples he himself created even as he stumbled, in *Beyond*, to find instances of it at work in the everyday world of mechanical trauma and child's play.

The unavoidable conclusion: *Beyond the Pleasure Principle* is itself the name of the trauma Freud inflicted on psychoanalysis from a position inside psychoanalysis. In Freud's terms it is unbound endogenous energy, energy from the inside, masochistic energy, which was only secondarily projected onto the world of others. The history of this trauma's reception – interpretation after interpretation, book after book – is therefore the history of its compulsive drive, not for mastery, but for nothingness.

As for what follows in *The Late Sigmund Freud*, I am far more interested in how Freud's own later works reflect and extend the basic thinking of *Beyond the Pleasure Principle*; in how the trauma plays out, so to speak. Let's begin with Freud's famous attack on religion, *The Future of an Illusion*, which on the surface looks like a very poor candidate for thinking deeply about the death drive theory in Freud's work. For in no work is Freud's recourse to positivism, science, and objectivity made so aggressively and, it must be admitted, so differently from what we find in *Beyond the Pleasure Principle*. But for this reason it is the perfect test case to see if, or to what extent, my claim holds true about the importance of the death drive theory to Freud's thinking about culture.

CHAPTER I

Positivism and the Specter of Nonexistence
The Romantic Depths of Freud's The Future of an Illusion

> What will they do with my theory after my death?
> Will it still resemble my basic thoughts?
> (Freud in Choisy, 1963, p. 5)

The Future of an Illusion is an unusual work within Sigmund Freud's oeuvre. First of all, it seems like a throwback to eighteenth-century critiques of religion, a redux of Enlightenment values in the twentieth century. To Voltaire's plea for liberty and reason in the face of religious intolerance – *écrasez l'infâme*, "crush the infamy" – Freud adds his own plea for "my god, Logos" in his diatribe against religious belief. To Kant's description of Enlightenment as "man's emergence from his self-incurred immaturity" (1784/1970, p. 54), Freud adds, "People cannot remain children forever; they must ultimately go out, into 'hostile life'. One may call this *'education to reality'*" (Freud, 1927/2012, p. 108; *SE*, 1927b/1991, p. 49). Freud's essential contribution is to update Enlightenment critiques with diagnostic insight gleaned from psychology: religion, the therapist declares, is "the universal obsessional neurosis" (1927/2012, p. 103; *SE*, 1927b/1991, p. 43).

It's not just that Freud's pose as eighteenth-century philosopher is strangely anachronistic in 1927. It is rather that this pose runs against the grain of Freud's other public and private pronouncements – from the pre-psychoanalytic essays of the 1880s to his last works in 1939, and throughout his thousands of letters to friends and colleagues. For scholars, therefore, the positivistic side of the *Future* is puzzling, Freud's arguments an unconvincing paean for reason by the last great figure of the counter-Enlightenment.

Far from being a Voltaire or Kant for the twentieth-century Freud was our greatest Romantic. Like Schopenhauer, Dostoevsky, and Nietzsche before him, Freud embraced the irrational facts of human suffering, masochism, and overwrought conscience, and reveled in the underground current of human nature that Nietzsche dubbed *das Es*, i.e., the "it" or "id." In similar fashion Freud's thought echoed the nineteenth-century fascination with fractured and divided consciousness, from debates about medical hypnosis and spirit possession to literary case studies such as Stevenson's *The Strange Case of Dr Jekyll and Mr Hyde* (1886) – phenomena Freud understood as uncanny harbingers of death that pointed the way toward "thought transference" or telepathy. In other words, like other late Romantics before him, Freud understood that the diabolical discourses of the unconscious challenged the philosophy of consciousness and the presumed supremacy of reason.

The late works of Freud mark a dramatic return to and reinvestment in this late Romantic heritage. The key text in this regard is *Beyond the Pleasure Principle* of 1920, the masterwork responsible for inaugurating this phase in the history of psychoanalysis. In it Freud offers metabiological and metaphysical speculations about the death drive and the repetition compulsion, thereby effecting the wholesale reconstruction of the foundations of psychoanalysis. The result: the lifelong dualist married the traditional territory of psychoanalysis – life, sex, and love – to death, destruction, and hate. The Freud of *Beyond* thus returned psychoanalysis to its roots as an id psychology infused with the dark overtones of nineteenth-century Romantic philosophy, literature, and biology. As remarked in the Introduction, even his late interest in "ego psychology" is caught in the undertow of *Beyond*, often to the great annoyance and incomprehension of later ego psychologists.

Consequently, the positivistic aspects of *The Future of an Illusion* don't fit well with the historical development of psychoanalysis, most especially with its final expression in works written between 1920 and 1939. This includes Freud's other famous cultural work of this period, *Civilization and Its Discontents* (1930). For, unlike the *Future*, *Civilization* is an unambiguous product of Freud's darkest ruminations about *Kultur* – and precisely in terms established in *Beyond*. Scholars therefore have three good reasons for their continued interest in the *Future*: first, as an uncompromising, old-fashioned instance of the rationalistic critique of religion, albeit updated in terms of depth psychology; second, as an aberrant example of positivism in the context of Freud's counter-Enlightenment raison d'être; and third, more pointedly, as an intellectual puzzle on account of its seemingly groundless status in the context of the "late Freud," a work in some ways set apart from the theories of *Beyond the Pleasure Principle* and the contemporaneous cultural observations of *Civilization and Its Discontents*.

Freud provided his own harsh assessments of the *Future*. In October of 1927, referring to the advance proofs of his manuscript, Freud admitted to his friend and colleague, Hungarian analyst Sándor Ferenczi, that the *Future* "already strikes me as childish, I basically think differently, [and] consider this work analytically frail and insufficient as a confession" (Freud & Ferenczi, 2000, p. 326). Later, when speaking to former analysand René Laforgue, Freud quashed his admiration for the *Future* by declaring: "This is my worst book! It isn't a book of Freud. It's the book of an old man" (in Choisy, 1963, p. 84). In 1927 Freud was seventy years old.

It would be churlish and uncharitable to leave it at that, since Freud's self-deprecating irony is very nearly his natural fallback position – most especially in his private correspondence. And Laforgue isn't the only one to express admiration for the book. Neo-Freudian psychoanalyst Erich Fromm refers to the *Future* as "one of [Freud's] most profound and brilliant books" (1950, p. 10; see Burston, 1991). Yet I think Freud's own damning remarks about the *Future* are basically correct. The book isn't very good. It's not only derivative historically and an aberration concep-tually, but is sloppily argued, repetitive, unfocused, and at times confused. To take one example, Freud only spells out a thesis for the book – a rationale – at the end of chapter nine. The thesis concerns our "education to reality," cited above, about which he adds the following: "Must I still make it clear to you that the sole purpose of this publication of mine is to show the need for progress of this sort?" (1927/2012, p. 108; *SE*, 1927b/1991, p. 49). The answer is "yes"; he should have said as much in chapter one – or two or three. Arguably *The Future of an Illusion* would not get published today, at least not without extensive revisions. In fact, it was probably not publishable in Freud's own time were it not for Freud's reputation and the fact that Freud and Freudians operated their own publication venues.[1]

This perhaps surprisingly negative verdict doesn't mean that the *Future* isn't interesting or doesn't warrant close examination. On the contrary, given Freud's stature as one of the most significant thinkers of the twentieth century, everything he wrote rewards close scrutiny – perhaps most especially those works that Freud himself recognized to be

---

[1] Like many of his longer works, *Die Zukunft einer Illusion* was originally published in the *Internationaler Psychoanalytischer Verlag* for which Freud was one of a handful of directors after its inception in January 1919. According to analyst and biographer Ernest Jones, the *Verlag* [press] appealed to Freud's "strong desire for independence," about which he adds: "The idea of being completely free of the conditions imposed upon him by publishers, which had always irked him, and of being able to publish just what books he liked and when he liked, made a forcible appeal to this side of his nature" (Jones, 1957, p. 30).

insufficiently Freudian. Certainly the specter of the book's "childish insuf-ficiency even as a confession" begs the question: Why this book at this time? And then another: Why this apparent love letter to "my god, Logos," and, by extension, to classical philosophy?

In what follows I will sketch three plausible answers to these two questions, as I expand upon the general reasons, outlined above, for our continued interest in *The Future of an Illusion*. But let's first consider a bit more closely the late Romantic philosophy that informs Freud's work, even in the *Future*.

1.1   The Nietzschean Critique of Reason

Psychoanalysis was devised as a corrective to and critique of the philosophy of consciousness advanced during the Enlightenment and then entrenched in philosophy and academic psychology. Psychoanalysts claim that reason, consciousness, and ego are only one part of the story of human psychol-ogy – and not the most interesting or important part. As Freud variously analogized, the relation of ego to id is like that of rider to horse (*SE*, 1923/1991, p. 25; *SE*, 1933a/1991, p. 77); and the relation of present to past is like that of the buildings of contemporary Rome to the ancient ruins literally buried in layers deep beneath the surface (*SE*, 1930/1991, pp. 69–70). Such was, for Freud, the singular promise of his "archeology of the mind," namely, the methodical restoration of the repressed and forgotten at both individual and group levels (since for Freud the latter is determined by the former). The human condition is therefore Romantic, even if Freud reserved for his own practice the outward vestiges of a science. According to Freud's Romantic science, only psychoanalysis can cast light onto this psychic hell; only psychoanalysis can restore a semblance of reason in a situation structured by unreason.

Above all it was Nietzsche who taught Freud the critical power of late Romantic philosophy, including the critique of religion. Following Schopenhauer and Feuerbach, Nietzsche argued that classical philosophy and Christian thought invented the ideals of truth and God, and then mistakenly subjected a world of differences to those concepts. Such is the cornerstone of Nietzsche's indictment of the history of philosophy as nihilism, as the denial of everyday existence. Railing against this Platonism, this "history of the error" – what we nowadays call "essentialism" – the early Nietzsche writes,

> What is truth? A mobile army of metaphors, metonyms, and anthropo-morphisms: in short, a sum of human relations which have been poetically

and rhetorically intensified, transferred, and embellished, and which, after long usage, seem to a people to be fixed, canonical, and binding. Truths are illusions which we have forgotten are illusions – they are metaphors that have become worn out and have been drained of sensuous force, coins which have lost their embossing and are now considered as metal and no longer as coins. (1873/1974a, pp. 46–7)

"All that philosophers have handled for thousands of years," Nietzsche continued twenty-five years later in *Twilight of the Idols* (1888), "have been concept-mummies; nothing real has escaped their grasp alive" (1888/1974b, p. 479). For Nietzsche the faculty of reason is a compensation derived of human weakness vis-à-vis other animals, a means by which we preserve and enhance our lives. In this respect reason is driven by what he eventually calls the "will to power," the everyday expression of which lies in the art of simulation: "deception, flattery, lying and cheating, talking behind the back, posing, living in borrowed splendor, being masked, the guise of convention, acting a role before others and before oneself" (1873/1974a, p. 43). If so, the history of philosophy is the history of this will to power, that is, of lies – the history of the effacement of the role that reason actually plays in the world of human beings.

This is of course a wickedly perverse conclusion, where philosophers lie about reason, inflating it beyond comprehension, in order to cover up reason's affinity with – lying. The abstract world of philosophy is therefore, Nietzsche writes, "a refuted idea: let us abolish it!" (1888/1974b, p. 201). Consequently, just as a certain kind of "fixed, canonical, and binding" truth is found dead in the late nineteenth century, so too is the Christian conception of God. This is the conclusion for which Nietzsche, self-declared "anti-Christ," is best known: "God is dead."

This, simply put, was the godless philosophy of the mid to late nineteenth century that Freud inherited from Nietzsche and, before him, from Schopenhauer, philosophies he read and admired as a young man (see Lehrer, 1995, pp. 13–18), studied in formal classes in philosophy (including one on the existence of God) with philosopher Franz Brentano during his time as a medical student at the University of Vienna, and adapted to his own theories of death, repetition, and guilt and then disowned when constructing his own creation myths of psychoanalysis (Sulloway, 1979, pp. 467–8; Roazen, 1997). Consequently, Freud's frequent attacks and rants against philosophy and philosophers must be understood as the continuation of criticisms that Nietzsche had already made – and which took decades for institutional philosophy to forgive, if partially and begrudgingly.

Arguably, then, Freud's attitude toward the illusion of religion is informed, not just by the old Enlightenment critiques of religion, but by Nietzsche's attitude, well known in Freud's midlife, toward the "illusion of truth" and its expression in classical philosophy and Christianity. Yet it must be conceded that neither the Enlightenment philosophes nor the late Romantics provide an occasion for the appearance of the *Future*. They are necessary but are not *sufficient* causes. That role is left, in part, to Karl Marx. Although he is never named, which is typical of Freud's treatment of philosophers, his work and impact is repeatedly gestured toward in the opening two chapters of the *Future*. It forms the first answer to the question: Why this book now?

1.2   Freud's Alternative Theory of Political Revolution

I don't think that Communism is the salvation of the future [*Ich glaube nicht dass der Kommunismus das Heil der Zukunft ist*].
(Freud to Wortis [in Wortis, 1954, p. 162; adjusted])

In the early years of the new century Freud was surrounded by a disparate group of followers, none of whom matched his sparkling intellect and ambition. As Freud's reputation increased, most especially after psychoanalysis was utilized as a treatment for war trauma in the First World War, the quality of his followers also increased. However, "Herr Professor" Freud did not always appreciate the competition, which he read as proof that the growing psychoanalytic society was just an echo of everyday society – and so subject to natural selection and patricide. What does this have to do with *The Future of an Illusion*? The best students, sometimes as talented and ambitious as Freud, were liable to disagree with aspects of Freud's thinking. Consequently, the works of Freud's middle and late periods were opportunities to correct the record, but also to admonish, discipline, erase, and blacklist his wayward disciples. Hence the brooding, self-reflecting tone of *Totem and Taboo*, which was in part a response to a "parricidal" Carl Jung, and *Civilization and Its Discontents*, which was in part a response to a "parricidal" Wilhelm Reich (Roazen, 1976, p. 504). "The son-religion," Freud writes in *Totem*, "displaced the father-religion" – a theory Freud described in 1912 even as he resisted its actualization in the analytic horde (*SE*, 1913b/1991, p. 154).

It is likely that Reich's activities were in part related to the appearance of the *Future* in 1927. From the beginning Reich disliked the death drive theory of *Beyond*, focusing instead on Freud's early view that neurosis is caused by dammed-up libido (see Dufresne, 2000, pp. 94–101). In this respect Reich drew the obvious inference: if neurosis is caused by the inhibited discharge of sexual energy ("libido"), then mental health must be improved by its free release, that is, by orgasm. Freud disagreed with but indulged Reich's so-called *Steckenpferd*, his "hobby-horse" (Reich, 1969, p. 13), since it was indeed based on his own work. But Freud certainly did not approve of Reich's other hobbyhorse, Marxism, which became explicit in the late 1920s and early 1930s. In the late 1920s Reich went on a lecture tour of Russia, where, according to Paul Roazen, "he claimed that unless there was a sexual revolution Communism would deteriorate into a bureaucratic state" (1976, p. 504). Then, in 1930, Reich left Vienna for Berlin and founded Sexpol, the German National Association for Proletarian Sexual Politics. In 1931 he published "The Masochistic Character," which effected an early (possibly the first) synthesis of Marxism and psychoanalysis (in Freud, 1992, p. 119) – which very much displeased Freud. On January 1, 1932, Freud records the following in his *Diary*: "Step against Reich" (Freud, 1992, p. 119). By 1933 Reich was lecturing in Vienna about psychology and politics at gatherings of communists.

The Freud scholar Michael Molnar connects Freud's annoyance with Reich not only to disagreement about Marxism, but about *Realpolitik* – specifically of the Austrian variety. According to Molnar, "Freud considered that in the unstable, proto-fascist political situation at that time," Reich's views were "harmful and irresponsible" (in Freud, 1992, p. 285, n.). But irresponsible to whom exactly? Molnar cites Anna Freud for the answer: "My father's remark on this [situation] is: if psychoanalysis is to be forbidden, let it be forbidden as psychoanalysis, but not as the mixture of politics and analysis that Reich represents" (p. 285). So really there were two problems: as Molnar says, Marxian politics jeopardized "scientific neutrality" (p. 119); but just as important, fascist politics in Austria made Reich's kind of synthesis foolhardy for the future of psychoanalysis itself.

And so Reich fell out of favor during the second half of the 1920s and into the early 1930s. "While Freud developed his death-instinct theory which said 'the misery comes from inside,'" Reich would recall, "I went out where the people were ... *I had drawn the social consequences of the [early] libido theory. To Freud's mind, this was the worst thing I did*" (1952, p. 51; his emphasis). By "social consequences" Reich meant his own Marxist commitments, which were concretely reflected in his work at a free outpatient clinic or "Ambulatorium" for workers unable to afford psychoanalysis.

Historians often insist that the *Future* reflects a trend in Freud's thinking that goes back to "Obsessive Actions and Religious Practices" of 1907 and *Totem and Taboo* of 1912–13. And this is obviously true. But arguably the appearance of the *Future* in 1927, so different in tone from Freud's other works, is at least in part explained by Freud's pressing need to distinguish psychoanalysis from Marxism in light of the growing cachet of the communist worldview in the 1920s. In other words, it is the specter of Karl Marx that Freud attempts to exorcise in the introductory chapters of the *Future*. This is an unusual claim, so let's turn to the first two chapters of the *Future* now.

Psychoanalysis is the interpretation of individual (and collective) history as filtered through the distorting conditions of the present. And so, for example, Freud utilizes a patient's "free associations" as a way to disrupt linear reason and break through to the latent (historical) meaning of dreams. In the *Future of an Illusion* Freud sets his sights on a very different goal: insight into "the future," not the past. "When one has lived for a long time in a particular culture," Freud begins the book, "and has often tried to determine the nature of its origins and developmental path, one is sometimes tempted to cast one's gaze in the other direction and to ask what further fate awaits this culture and what changes it is fated to undergo" (1927/2012, p. 73; *SE*, 1927b/1991, p. 5). This first sentence is highly strategic. For with it Freud establishes his singular credentials for providing a prediction about the future: first of all, as an old man at the end of his life, someone who has gained critical distance from what he calls "the naïve present"; and, second, as the first psychoanalyst, someone intimate with the repressed past.

Long consumed with his own legacy, Freud in the 1920s thought he was near death and thus removed from the vagaries of everyday life (see Jones, 1957, p. 42; Dufresne, 2000, pp. 20, 39–41). He was diagnosed with cancer of the jaw in 1923 and, after the removal of parts of his upper palate, was given a poorly fitting and painful prosthesis. Freud survived, but the experience changed him. Recall his remarks to Lou Andreas-Salomé in May 1925, which invoke the theories of *Beyond the Pleasure Principle*: "A crust of indifference is slowly creeping up around me; a fact I state without complaining. It is a natural development, a way of beginning to grow inorganic. The 'detachment of old age', I think it is called" (Freud & Andreas-Salomé, 1966, p. 154). This peculiar yet characteristic way of positioning himself influenced the production of the *Future* and his own assessment of the book. Consider the entirety of Freud's critical remarks in response to Laforgue's praise for the *Future*:

> This is my worst book! It isn't a book of Freud. It's the book of an old man.
> Besides, Freud is dead now, and believe me, the genuine Freud was
> a really great man. I am particularly sorry for you that you didn't know
> him better. (in Choisy, 1963, p. 84)

Not incidentally, this "dead" Freud perfectly meets the conditions he
describes in the *Future*. "[T]here is the remarkable fact," Freud writes,
"that people generally experience the present naively, so to speak, without
being able to appreciate its content; they must first gain some distance from
it, i.e., the present must have become the past before one can derive from it
clues for making judgments about the future" (1927/2012, p. 73; *SE* 1927b/
1991, p. 5). Suitably mortified, Freud in 1927 had become a classic anti-
subject, a Romantic figure of death against whom nothing critical could be
said. For his pronouncements on the future were oracular, truths delivered
at the end of life – if not beyond it.[2]

Of course "the future" is precisely what interests Marxists, especially
those "scientific socialists" who predicted the future communist utopia out
of the resolution of the contradictions of capitalism. From Freud's
perspective, however, they could not possibly know a future that is determined by a repressed prehistory that is revealed only through psychoanalysis; is conditional upon the psychoanalytic resolution of individual
neuroses (of the would-be historian) today; and is, in any case, limited to
those who occupy a critical distance from the present.

Having met these three exclusionary conditions – publicly and obliquely
in the *Future*, and privately and explicitly in his various asides – Freud
begins his indirect discussion of Marxism. "Human culture," he says, has
"two sides":

> It includes on the one hand all the knowledge and power that people have
> acquired in order to master the forces of nature and gain material wealth for
> the satisfaction of human needs, and on the other hand it includes all the
> institutions necessary to regulate the relations of humans to each other,
> especially the distribution of the attainable material wealth. These two
> orientations of culture are not independent. (1927/2012, p. 73; SE, 1927b/
> 1991, pp. 5–6)

Freud goes on to discuss the difficulties of "communal existence," one that
is fatally compromised by a dark realization central to the late Freud:

---

[2] In *Beyond*, Freud argues that one chooses one's own path to death once all the stages of development
have been exhausted, that is, when the detour of life, ontogenetically stored, has finally been spent.
In this sense one is finally free from deterministic biology, i.e., one is "beyond" it. Freud often implies
that his late return is just such a freedom.

individuals must choose between sadism (destroying others) and masochism (destroying oneself). "A sad disclosure indeed," Freud chortles elsewhere, "for the moralist!" (*SE*, 1933a/1991, p. 105; see Fromm, 2011, p. 275). Freud therefore concludes that all aspects of culture – specifically "organizations, institutions, and laws" – must defend against this innately destructive individual. He adds,

> These [goals of culture] aim not only to effect a certain distribution of material wealth, but also to maintain that distribution. Indeed, they must protect against people's hostile impulses all those things that serve for the conquest of nature and the production of material wealth. Human creations are easy to destroy. (1927/2012, p. 74; *SE*, 1927b/1991, p. 6)

Freud then wonders if "a reorganization of human relations" – he avoids naming it, but he means communism – could ever "nullify the sources of dissatisfaction with culture" that he associates with our raging drives. Although "that [reorganization] would be a golden age," Freud insists that human nature is not equal to the ideal. "On the contrary," he adds, "every culture must be based on coercion and the renunciation of drives," drives that are for Freud the sine qua non of human biology (p. 74). The upshot, delivered as a "psychological fact," is that some individuals will always remain "anti-social and anti-cultural." In this respect Freud perfectly echoes Schopenhauer's sentiments from "Sufferings of the World." "If all wishes were fulfilled as soon as they arose," Schopenhauer writes,

> how would men occupy their lives? What would they do with their time? If the world were a paradise of luxury and ease . . . men would either die of boredom or hang themselves; or there would be wars, massacres, and murders; so that in the end mankind would inflict more suffering on itself than it has now to accept at the hands of Nature. (1851/1925, p. 13)

Freud's opinion about *Massenpsychologie* owes everything to the influence of Hobbes, Schopenhauer, Nietzsche, and Gustave Le Bon – the French psychologist responsible for work on the "psychology of the crowds" and influential for Freud's *Group Psychology and the Analysis of the Ego* (1921). Like Le Bon, but owing as much to the others, Freud agreed that the *Masse* – the mass or mob – would always need a leader, *der Führer*. "For the masses," Freud concludes, "are lazy and stupid," uninterested in work and insensible to reasoned argument (1927/2012, p. 75, translation adjusted; *SE*, 1927b/1991/ p. 7). *Kultur*, therefore, is what Freud means by the force that keeps our Manichean, practically unchangeable and essentially antisocial, biology in check: a thin veneer, recently acquired, that only partially covers over our innate, and therefore ancient, destructive ids. This is why Freud speaks of deterministic "fate" rather than freedom and change when he predicts "the future."

Marxists, however, will have none of this pessimism. Marx thought that psychology merely described epiphenomena of a more fundamental economic reality; that the masses had been stupefied by *nurture*, not *nature*; and that, therefore, any significant change to the economic structure would result in a change to human *Kultur*, including its mass psychology. Because his thought is dialectical rather than dualistic, Marx assumes a level of change and progress that reflects the ideals of human and social perfectibility common to the Enlightenment. Indeed, Marx is a nineteenth-century optimist, which is precisely why people such as Reich – and, over two decades later, Freudo-Marxists such as Herbert Marcuse (1955/1966, 1970/2011) and Norman O. Brown (1959) – thought that a dash of Marxism would repair an unduly pessimistic Freud.

Obviously, this Marxist perspective on psychoanalysis entails a serious critique of psychoanalytic praxis qua therapy. For how can a therapy so intrinsically resigned to fate and biology, so stuck in the past, so much a product of brooding late Romanticism, ever make room for change, hope, progress – for the future? How could a Freudian psychoanalysis ever claim to "cure" patients, since cure is based on the possibility of breaking with old patterns? Similarly, how could Freud's instrumental and wholly defensive conception of culture square with its constructive aspects? "I can only feel stupefaction," huffs the poet T. S. Eliot, "on reading such a course of argument" (1928, p. 351; in Kiell, 1988, p. 576).

* * *

It is no accident that Freud's newfound interest in "the future" is connected to his newfound interest in the conditions of "material wealth." But just in case the reader misses his meaning about the ideal of "communal existence" and the "reorganization of human relations," Freud spells it out at the end of chapter one – albeit negatively, in relief, disowning the very territory he just covered. Freud concludes,

> I do not want to create the impression that I have wandered far off the path envisioned for my investigation. I shall therefore expressly affirm that I have no intention of assessing the great cultural experiment currently underway in the vast country between Europe and Asia. I have neither the expertise nor the ability to determine its practicability, to test the appropriateness of the methods applied, or to measure the width of the inevitable cleft between intention and execution. What is being prepared there remains incomplete

and eludes the examination for which our long-consolidated culture provides the material. (1927/2012, p. 76; *SE*, 1927b/1991, p. 9)

Freud speaks of a "path," one that he has "wandered" away from, although not far; apparently the thesis or rationale for the book remains close at hand. The truth is, however, that Freud has yet to spell out a thesis for *The Future of an Illusion* – at least beyond his opening remarks that he is interested in looking at the future of *Kultur*, that is, of culture, society, and civilization. Consequently, Freud can't wander "off the path envisioned for [his] investigation" when wandering itself verily describes the process of his investigation thus far – unless, of course, wandering *is* the path, a path Freud doesn't so much follow as make up as he goes along. A new reader of the *Future* could therefore be forgiven for thinking, at this point, that the book has nothing at all to do with religion, since the opening chapters function as primers of psychoanalysis in 1927, the critical foil played by the theory of communism associated with Karl Marx. Then again, the future at stake in the *Future*, as elsewhere in Freud's work, is always the future of psycho-analysis defined against its many enemies.

Chapter two of the *Future* offers more of the same: Freud returns to psychology but quickly wanders back into a discussion of economics. The key paragraph concerns what Freud calls a "crude and unmistakable situation." Under repressive conditions the "lower classes" are unable to discharge the "excess of privation" (1927/2012, p. 78; *SE*, 1927b/1991, p. 12), *Mehr von Entbehrung*, that are its lot in life. When people suffer such over-privation they lose the capacity to identify with the aims of culture, to wit, to absorb the prohibitions of law that enforce civility. In the case of political revolution, the "excess of privation" floods the defensive barrier influenced by *Kultur* and formed by psychology, namely, the superego of each individual of the lower classes. Conscience is thus weakened to its breaking point and the destructive energy of the *Masse* is released. The situation is analogous to the etiology of trauma that Freud describes in 1895 and again in 1920, where a "surplus of excitation," *Überschuss an Erregung*, floods or breaches the defenses of the mental apparatus (Freud, 1920/2011, p. 70; *SE*, 1920a/1991, p. 29). On this analogy, however, it is not the *lower classes* that are traumatized, for example, by the "energy" of culture; culture is, on the contrary, the force that dams up the energy, and so causes neurosis and unhappiness. The direction of energy is otherwise: it's the *state apparatus* that is over-whelmed and traumatized by the release of hostile energy from the now un-repressed, un-coerced *Masse*. In short, freed of the ego and superego functions of culture that Freud associates with "organizations, institutions, and laws," the lower classes revolt; the state apparatus is breached, flooded, traumatized by the frenzied and pleasurable release of tension in the *Masse*. This is the realization of Rousseau's "state of nature" which Freud mocks as untenable at the beginning of chapter three, and which necessitates "the chief task of culture": defense against nature (1927/2012, p. 81; *SE*, 1927b/1991, p. 15). As Freud says, civilization is "easy to destroy." "It is hardly necessary to say," Freud concludes, "that a culture that leaves so many of its members unsatisfied, driving them to insurrection, has no prospect of perpetuating itself. Nor does it deserve to do so" (1927/2012, p. 79; *SE*, 1927b/1991, p. 12).

And so ends the lesson. Freud may agree with some Marxist conclusions about religion, but he can't accept their reasoning. Consider Marx's sensible criticism of religion in his "Introduction" to *A Contribution to the Critique of Hegel's Philosophy of Right* (1843):

> Religion ... is the opium of the people. The abolition of religion as the illusory happiness of the people is a demand for their true happiness. The call to abandon illusions about their condition is the call to abandon a [materialist, economic] condition which requires illusions. Thus the critique of religion is the critique in embryo of that vale of tears of which religion is the halo. (1843/1982, p. 131)

Marx claims that revolution is based on the internal contradictions of capitalism, on economics, while Freud claims that it is really all about the psychological conflict between our ancient, innate, biologically expressed drives and the more fragile forces of our recent, nurture-based, sociologically expressed laws. Simply put, Freud believes that Marx mistakes the mob, the *Masse*, of present-day capitalist society for "the people," the *Volk*, of a very distant, idealized utopia of the future – and on this basis has expectations for human reason that ignore our animal origins, thus inflating the actual achievements of *Kultur*. So, in a way, the conflict between Freudism and Marxism is a conflict about the present. Such is the essence of Freud's psychoanalytic theory of political revolution – the masses revolt when their animal origins and needs are not adequately tended – which he proposes as an alternative theory to the kind we associate with the "cultural experiment currently underway in the vast country between Europe and Asia." Freudo-Marxism is therefore incoherent, indeed oxymoronic.

It would seem that the Soviets, at least, got the message – since *The Future of an Illusion*, published in Russian in April 1930, was the last work of Freud's published in the Soviet Union. The Soviets declared psychoanalysis a doctrine of "bourgeois-individualism" (in Freud, 1992, p. 67).

Freud was not shy about sharing his own political beliefs. To his friend and colleague Arnold Zweig, Freud described himself in 1930 as "a liberal of the old school" (1970, p. 21). And to Joseph Wortis in 1935 he stated that "I find capitalism quite satisfactory. I think the discovery of money was a great cultural advance" (1954, p. 164). And again, this time connecting his views to Reich: "[Marxism] is not compatible with psychoanalysis because it is too dogmatic. Reich, a talented psychoanalyst, will probably have to leave the movement, because he has turned Communist and altered his views. He believes, for example, that the aggressive instinct and sex problems are products of the class struggle, instead of products of inborn drives." Freud then spoke of the necessity of having a private room and the right to be alone occasionally. "That in itself is enough to make Communism impossible for me" (1954, p. 165).

Like Virginia Woolf, Freud just wanted a room of his own – a private clinic wherein he could see his patients, make a little money, smoke cigars, store his antiquities, and write his letters, essays, and books. Capitalism made this all possible. And so Freud never warmed to Marxism or Bolshevism, claiming in print in 1933 that "although practical Marxism has mercilessly cleared away all idealistic systems and illusions, it has itself developed illusions which are no less questionable and unprovable than the earlier ones" (*SE*, 1933a/1991, p. 180; cf., *SE*, 1933b/1991, p. 211).

Yet for those outside of psychoanalysis, it was still possible to mistake Freud's work as complicit with Marxism. For example, a prominent anthropologist, Father Wilhelm Schmidt, complained in a public lecture in Vienna in November 1928 that psychoanalysis and Marxism enjoyed "an entente cordiale" – a formal alliance (Yerushalmi, 1991, p. 28). In the *Future* of 1927 Freud wasn't quite ready to spell out his political views and instead challenged Marxism and the Russian "cultural experiment" by an indirection appropriate to his procedural wandering. It is only in chapter five of *Civilization and Its Discontents*, three years later, that Freud finally discusses the principles of communism (e.g., the abolition of private property) that he alludes to and sometimes skirts in the *Future*; and where he finally names "Russia" and "the Soviets" rather than gestures toward them in an incredibly awkward locution ("between Europe and Asia").

As for religion, the theme for which the book is primarily known, it arrives only in chapter three of the *Future*.

1.3   Dialogical Thought, Science, and the Trial of Religion

The common man cannot imagine this Providence other than in the person of an immensely exalted father ... All of this is so obviously infantile, so far from reality, that it is painful to anyone with convictions friendly toward humanity to think that the great majority of mortals will never be able to rise above this view of life.

(*SE*, 1930/1991, p. 74)

Between June and September of 1926 Freud quickly wrote and published *The Question of Lay Analysis*. In it he defends the rights of "lay" or nonmedical analysts to practice psychoanalytic treatment; a right challenged in the Vienna courts by an American patient who charged Freud's colleague, Theodor Reik, with "quackery."[3] Freud returned to the subject again in June 1927 in a "Postscript" to a fresh debate about lay analysis among psychoanalysts. These defenses of psychoanalysis in 1926 and 1927 help determine *The Future of an Illusion*, in particular its dialogical style and aberrant positivism.

These, too, are unusual claims, so let's compare and contrast relevant passages from *Lay Analysis* and the *Future* – even as we attend to Freud's rhetoric.

In *Lay Analysis* Freud rationalizes the theory and practice of psychoanalysis to an "Impartial Person" of his own imagination, purportedly based on a "high official" of the Vienna courts (*SE*, 1927a/1991, p. 251), from whom he hopes to win "a just judgment" concerning the legitimacy (and thus the legality) of nonmedical analysis in Austria (*SE*, 1926/1991, p. 208).[4] Consequently this latest "trial" of psychoanalysis (p. 207) is loosely structured like a Socratic dialogue – where the give-and-take of question and answer propels the argument forward. As Freud puts it to the Impartial Person, "interrupt me whenever you feel inclined, if you cannot follow me or if you want further explanations" (p. 191).

Freud introduces a similar style of presentation at the beginning of the fourth chapter of the *Future*: another faux dialogue, this time with "an imaginary opponent" – *einen Gegner*, an enemy. About these proceedings, he writes as follows:

---

[3] In a letter of March 1925, Freud indicates that Reik "has been prohibited from practicing psychoanalysis by the Municipal Council of Vienna as of February 24, 1925" (Freud, 1960b, p. 359).

[4] To his colleague Karl Abraham, Freud identifies the "Impartial Person" as the physiologist and "senior medical official" Arnold Durig, and claims that Durig requested the "expert opinion" (Freud & Abraham, 2002, p. 525). This chapter adds a wrinkle to this claim.

> An investigation that proceeds uninterrupted, like a monologue, is not completely free of danger. One may too easily yield to the temptation to push aside thoughts that seek to interrupt, and end up instead with a feeling of uncertainty, which in the end one tries to overpower through excessive assertiveness. I will therefore imagine an opponent who attends to my arguments with mistrust; here and there I will let him express himself. (1927/2012, p. 85; *SE*, 1927b/1991, p. 21)

While Freud very often entertains likely criticism the better to defeat it, thereby winning the reader's confidence, the personification of criticism only becomes a *method* in *The Question of Lay Analysis* and *The Future of an Illusion*. Nowhere else does Freud structure his works in this unusual way, and it behooves us to wonder why.

Consider for a moment Freud's rhetoric. He has identified a "danger," one he implies is already at work in the *Future*. Apparently monological enquiries are threatened by self-criticism. Freud's claim is that "interruption" in the guise of "thoughts which threaten to break into it," that is, into the monologue, are pushed aside. Note the negative form of his claim: monological enquiry "is not altogether free from danger." Freud could have emphasized the positive side of this equation by claiming that monological enquiry is in fact *mostly safe* from danger. But Freud emphasizes the negative, presumably because the impulse to push thoughts aside, to repress or censor them, is always a temptation. Indeed, the enquiry is "too easily tempted" in this regard. Note also that Strachey has Freud adopt the first-person singular – "One is too easily tempted" – which perfectly reflects the fact that, even as he acknowledges it, Freud is still dangerously at work within the monological structure of the *Future*. This can't last, however, since this opening paragraph of chapter four is above all an explanation, if not an apologia, for what lies ahead in the *Future*. It's just this: the danger of monological enquiry, although small, will be studiously avoided. Freud is unwilling to pay the price for remaining strictly monological. What price? "In exchange" for producing soliloquies, *ein Monolog*, "one is left with a feeling of uncertainty [*Unsicherheit*]." The monological has not yet finished paying the price, since Freud adds that this is a feeling of uncertainty or insecurity that "one tries to keep down by overdecisiveness," *allzu große Entschiedenheit übertönen will* (*GW*, 1948a/1991, p. 342). Once again Freud's verdict is essentially negative: one *tries* to keep it down.

The upshot couldn't be more clear or, for that matter, more classically Freudian: what was once "pushed aside" must now be "kept down," a reiteration of the old chestnut (from the 1880s) about "the return of the repressed." No matter what we do, Freud claims, critical voices will be heard. The unified subject is a haunted subject, and it's bootless to pretend otherwise. In this regard the Hebrew word for 'adversary' – Satan, the Devil – is rather telling. For as we will see, the genesis of psychological haunting takes us back to the Christian battle with spirit possession.

In this brief apologia to the rest of the *Future*, Freud is diagnosing a psychological problem, namely the problem of *defensive over-decisiveness* in the face of self-critical doubt. It is a common enough problem among writers, especially intellectuals, who do their work in isolation, and it is through writing that Freud seeks to address it. Enter the imaginary opponent. He is called upon by Freud to ward off the threat of danger. "I will therefore imagine," Freud says, "an opponent who attends to my arguments with mistrust; here and there I will let him express himself" (1927/2012, p. 85; *SE*, 1927b/1991, p. 21).

So who is Freud's imaginary opponent, his enemy, *Gegner*? The answer brings us back a few years, a millennia in fact, but 1923 will suffice. The imaginary opponent is none other than Freud's own superego, the product of human evolution or, more prosaically, of Freud's late topography of the mind (id/ego/superego) as announced in *The Ego and the Id*.

Through the divided and dialogical structure of *Lay Analysis* and the *Future*, Freud enacts the late Romantic theory of the divided self. As Freud characterizes the divided self in *Lay Analysis*, one carries secrets "that one would not care to admit to oneself" – closely echoing the insights of Dostoevsky's *Notes from Underground* (1864). Or as Freud clarifies, this time echoing Stevenson's *The Strange Case of Dr Jekyll and Mr Hyde* (1886/1945): "It looks as though his own self were no longer a unity which he always thought it to be, as though there were something else as well in him that could confront that self" (*SE*, 1926/1991, p. 188). That "something else" is the Impartial Person of *Lay Analysis* and the imaginary opponent of the *Future*, both of whom play the role of prosecutor, conscience, and superego to Freud's two defenses of psychoanalysis. Of course it is Freud, at this point in his life (literally) silenced by the painful prosthesis in his mouth (Jones, 1957, p. 292), who plays both parts himself, who decides if and when the voice interrupts and what it has to say, and who dramatizes the proceedings – presumably staging it all for the theatrical, cathartic, and juridical benefit of his readers. Assuming, of course, that Freud is able to keep the two voices (of Freud) apart, and that the dialogical approach still follows the dictates of reason and consciousness. For just who directs whom has yet to be decided, which is probably the quintessential question of "the future"; i.e., the question of who should speak for Freud when he can no longer speak for himself, namely when he is dead. To this end *Lay Analysis* is all dress rehearsal.

So Freud attempts the impossible: he promises to write the *Future* in two voices. One will give, the other (which is the same) will take away; one will hypothesize and the other (which is the same) will criticize; one will construct and the other – I won't say deconstruct, because that's too easy – one will construct and the other (which is the same) will observe, direct, instruct, inspire, restrict, demand, threaten, humiliate, hector, admonish, judge, and censor.

The contest is not just dramatic, but melodramatic. For at the individual level the conflict between two voices, ego and superego, is nothing less than a conflict between reality and fantasy, outer world and inner world. "Whereas the ego is essentially the representative of the external world, of reality," Freud declares in *The Ego and the Id*, "the super-ego stands in contrast to it as the representative of the internal world, of the id" (*SE*, 1923/1991, p. 36). Moreover, the conflict between ego and superego is an idealized conflict about ego psychology and id psychology, about the future institutionalization of psychoanalysis, one where the father of psychoanalysis himself gives voice to the two basic choices: the-future-driven-rationalistic-ego-Freud versus the-past-driven-irrational-superego-Freud.

On the one hand, the melodramatic encounter of ego and superego in the *Future* has all the significance of an identity crisis in and for psycho-analysis. Its future is well known: after Freud's death the (internal) division crystalizes around American and French analytic cultures. On the other hand, the seriousness of this crisis is all the more incredible since the attempt to write the *Future* in two voices not only is imaginary, as Freud puts it, but is so obviously scripted and staged. In this respect there is a jarring disjuncture between artifice in the *Future* and what quickly escalates into a serious matter; between simulated judgment, part of a still uncertain rhetorical strategy, and judgment itself, part of a frankly bizarre self-confession.

Recall again what Freud in the *Future* says of his internal enemy: "I will *let him* express himself" – will let him get a word in here and there, *und lasse ihn von Stelle zu Stelle zu Worte kommen* (*GW*, 1948a/1991, p. 342). It is Freud, an author, who directs and is in control of this fiction. Clearly we are not in the presence of Freud's actual superego in chapter four (which would never accept these terms), but with its imaginary, fantastical double. Why does this matter? Because the danger of the monological, of unwisely repressing self-criticism – a danger as old and, for Freud, as real as any in psychoanalysis – is by no means averted by this practiced, if surreal, gesture. Just the opposite. For where could we hope to find a more perfect instance of defensive over-decisiveness than with someone pretending to defend himself from *fake* self-criticism? What could be more illusory than counterfeiting judgment in the name of judgment itself? And what, in the service of certainty and Logos, could be more absurd or, as it turns out, more effective? These questions haunt, and even possess, *The Future of an Illusion*.

* * *

The theme of "judicial authority" – driven by the dialogical and divided structure, and essential to the future of psychoanalysis after the death of Freud – is already floated in chapter three of the *Future*, and not long after Freud has introduced a straightforward thesis about religion. The crux of Freud's argument: religion is an infantile desire for Daddy's protection from a world of natural threats and, later on, from "the inadequacies and hurts of culture" (1927/2012, p. 83; *SE*, 1927b/1991, p. 18). "Thus a store of ideas is created," Freud continues, "born of the need to make human helplessness bearable, and constructed with the material of recollections of. . . the helplessness of one's own childhood and that of the childhood of the human race." Of course *Totem and Taboo* provided Freud's foundation for understanding the "childhood of the human race," and it is never far from his mind. In 1919 he summarizes his position perfectly:

> If we submit the prehistoric and ethnological material relating to this archaic heritage to psychoanalytical elaboration, we come to an unexpectedly definite conclusion – namely, that god the father at one time walked incarnate on the earth and exercised his sovereignty as leader of the hordes of primitive men until his sons combined together and slew him; and further, that the first ties, the basic moral restrictions, and the oldest form of religion – totemism – originated as a result of, and a reaction against, this liberating misdeed. Later religions are filled with the same content. . . As a result we can recognise in myths the echo of that occurrence which throws its gigantic shadow over the whole development of mankind. (in Reik, 1931/1958b, pp. 11–12; *SE*, 1919/1991, p. 262)

What Freud adds in *The Future of an Illusion* is the idea that God represents the protective force of culture writ large on the stage of the universe – a "supreme juridical authority [*höchsten richterlichen Instanz*] with incomparably more might and consistency" (Freud, 1927/2012, p. 84; *SE*, 1927b/ 1991, p. 19; *GW*, 1948a/1991, p. 341). The goal of religion is therefore to allay our (reasonable) anxieties about the dangers of the external world, and to compensate us for the inadequate balm that is civilization. "These [religious] ideas," Freud concedes, "are deemed the most precious possession of culture, as the most valuable thing it has to offer its members" (1927/2012, p. 85; *SE*, 1927b/1991, p. 20).

By contrast, the specter of religion arrives in *Lay Analysis* in chapter one, immediately following Freud's discussion of the therapeutic "magic" of words and his invocation of the divided self (*SE*, 1926/1991, p. 187–8). More precisely, it arrives when the Impartial Person of his faux dialogue notices the similarity between Freud's cathartic therapy and that of the "Confession, which the Catholic Church has used from time immemorial in order to make secure its dominance over people's mind" (p. 189). Freud rejects the charge, after which the Impartial Person raises the stakes: "as an analyst you gain a stronger influence over your patient than a Father Confessor over his penitents"; and this is because "the miraculous results of your treatment are the effect of hypnotic suggestion" (p. 189). The connection between word magic, the divided self, and the problem of suggestion is not incidental. Freud studied hypnosis, translated the work of a hypnotherapist (Hippolyte Bernheim), and in his early practice utilized hypnosis with patients; hypnosis evokes trance states that were thought to confirm the reality of divided consciousness; hypnotic trances are very often effected through the magic of words; and, finally, hypnosis is connected historically with discourses of spirit possession that go back to Mesmerism, animal magnetism and, before that, to early Christianity (Crabtree, 1993; Dufresne, 2003, p. 4–52). Dig deeply enough and you always find the Devil.

Freud, therefore, had very good reasons for contesting the criticism that psychoanalysis not only was compromised by suggestion, as many of his early critics had already claimed, but had indeed perfected the therapeutic successes of the Catholic Confession. This is of course a very common suspicion. A few years later, the English sexologist Havelock Ellis would plainly link "the catharsis process of yielding up and bringing to the surface suppressed elements of consciousness and so relieving the tension caused by the suppress" with the "process of self-confession" utilized by Freud (Ellis, 1933/1948, p. 5). Self-confession is then linked with religion. Ellis continues: "The religious process, so completely developed in Catholicism of confession and absolution, rests psychologically on this same basis, and (though it has other reasons for existence) it tends, without doubt, to produce the same beneficial results" (p. 6). In *Lay Analysis* Freud lays out his defense against this charge as follows:

> Our Impartial Person cannot be either so ignorant or so perplexed as we thought to begin with. There are unmistakable signs that he is trying to understand psychoanalysis with the help of his previous knowledge, that he is trying to link it up with something he already knows. The difficult task now lies ahead of us of making clear to him that he will not succeed in this: that analysis is a procedure *sui generis*, something novel and special, which can only be understood with the help of *new* insights – or hypotheses, if that sounds better. (*SE*, 1926/1991, p. 189–90; his emphasis)

Freud saves psychoanalysis from the Impartial Person's (arguably fatal) charges by refusing the inheritance of it all, and by insisting on the originality of his findings: psychoanalysis cannot be linked to the confession, or to the suggestive authority of the priest, because it is "novel and special," "new," a "procedure *sui generis*," utterly unique. Of course the desperate lengths of this alibi – demonstrably false in every way, as even our cursory review of late Romantic thought shows – are commensurate with the seriousness of the criticism. Clearly Freud has no good answer to the charges, neither here nor anywhere. Instead he offers a schoolyard assertion about the divine revelation that is psychoanalysis: psychoanalysis cannot be hypnosis because hypnosis is old and psychoanalysis is new. Same thing holds for confession. Of course the defense of psychoanalysis on these grounds only strengthens its ties with religion, where the word of Freud functions like dogma for disciples.

Perhaps Freud realizes as much, because in chapter two of *Lay Analysis* he quickly invokes the scientificity of psychoanalysis; an invocation and rhetorical strategy repeated in the *Future*. Psychoanalysis is not complete or tidy, "like a philosophical system," but evolves and changes over time. Freud continues:

> Science, as you know, is not a revelation; long after its beginnings it still lacks the attributes of definiteness, immutability and infallibility for which all human thought so deeply longs. But such as it is, it is all that we can have. If you will further bear in mind that our science is very young, scarcely as old as the century [i.e., twenty-six years old], and that it is concerned with what is perhaps the most difficult material. . . you will easily be able to adopt the correct attitude toward my exposition. But interrupt me whenever you feel inclined, if you cannot follow me or if you want further explanations. (p. 191)

The incompleteness of psychoanalysis is itself a feature of its scientificity, and also of its difficult subject matter and relative youth. In this context the invitation to "interrupt me whenever you feel inclined" is an invitation to "adopt the correct attitude toward my exposition," which Freud equates with the spirit of scientific inquiry, openness, and youthfulness. Freud is showing us how it's done: he interrupts himself in the service of the scientific ideal. As in the *Future*, the false certainty of the monologic will be avoided in *Lay Analysis*.

Freud echoes these views about science in *The Future of an Illusion*, but also vastly inflates his commitment by invoking empirically based reality. In fact the status of reality has already been debated with respect to the challenge of Marxism, but is explicitly taken up again (at the beginning of chapter five) in the context of religion. Freud asks himself (not in the guise of an imaginary opponent, but as himself, *sans* italics) how he should categorize the psychological significance of religious ideas. His answer: "After eliminating various formulations, we will stand by just one: religious ideas are teachings and pronouncements about facts and states of external (and internal) reality that convey something one has not discovered for oneself and which assert the right to be believed" (1927/2012, p. 88; *SE*, 1927b/1991, p. 25). Just as Freud had, in the past, reduced child's play to proto-scientific research about sexuality (e.g., Little Hans), he reduces religion to a primitive form of reality testing – to a kind of botched science. As he clarifies elsewhere, the religious phase lies between the phases of primitive animism and mature science (*SE*, 1913b/1991, p. 90).

Freud goes on to investigate the status of our variously acquired beliefs: arguments from authority, from tradition, and from prohibitions (1927/2012, p. 88; *SE*, 1927b/1991, p. 17). But since our religious beliefs and doctrines are "not residues of experience or the final result of thought," they are "illusions – fulfillments of the oldest, strongest and most fervent wishes of humanity" (1927/2012, p. 89; *SE*, 1927b/1991, p. 26). In short, they are like dreams, Freud's classic example of wish fulfillment; or again, as he adds in *Civilization*, they are like "mass delusions," that is, illusions shared with others (*SE*, 1930/1991, p. 81). Since religion, cut off from experience, is a form of wish fulfillment, Freud says "we disregard its relation to reality, just as the illusion itself abjures confirmations" (1927/2012, p. 94; *SE*, 1927b/1991, p. 31). Science is another matter: "Only slowly do the riddles of the universe unveil themselves to our investigations; for many questions, science still cannot provide answers today. But scientific work [*wissenschaftliche Arbeit*] is the only path that can lead us to knowledge of reality outside ourselves" (p. 94; p. 31). Or as Freud already said in *Totem and Taboo*, "the scientific phase has its complete counterpart in the stage of maturity in which individuals have renounced the pleasure principle, and, adjusting themselves to reality, seek their object in the external world" (*SE*, 1913b/1991, p. 90). In the *Future* Freud's procedural wandering leads to dialoguing, and dialoguing to science – "the only path that can lead to knowledge of reality outside ourselves."

Freud's constant recourse to the "reality outside ourselves," to the external world of "experience" (and by implication to empiricism), has him align psychoanalysis to this end. Anything less risks illusion. Yet this alignment results in a remarkably un-Freudian claim. Freud continues:

> Again, it is merely illusion to expect anything from intuition and introspection; these can only give us information about our own mental life – information difficult to interpret – never information about the questions that religious doctrine answer so effortlessly. It would be criminal to let one's own arbitrary opinion enter the void and, according to one's own personal estimation, to declare one aspect or another of the religious system more acceptable or less so. For such an approach, these questions are too significant – one might even say too sacred. (1927/2012, p. 94; *SE*, 1927b/1991, pp. 31–2)

Let's unpack Freud's meaning. "Religious doctrine," based on "intuition and introspection," may tell us something about our inner lives, but nothing at all about the external world. Consequently only "arbitrary opinion" could decide which religious beliefs are right and which are wrong. The significant questions concern "knowledge of reality outside ourselves," questions that are, ironically, "too sacred" for any "religious system." In fact, the questions are "sacrilegious," *frevelhaft* (*GW*, 1948a/ 1991, p. 354).

By the end of the chapter Freud will claim that "the truth value [*Wahrheitswert*] of religious doctrine is not within the plan of this investigation" (1927/2012, p. 95; *SE*, 1927b/1991, p. 33; *GW*, 1948a/1991, p. 356). But this is an empty gesture, similar in tone and effect to Freud's earlier disinclination to discuss the Russian experiment with communism, since Freud has already found the truth value of religion utterly lacking; a finding, or verdict, that he repeats again a few pages later (1927/2012, p. 98; *SE*, 1927b/1991, p. 37). But the prosecution of religion comes at the very high price of denigrating, first, "intuition and introspection" – operations central to the foundation myth of psychoanalysis – and, second, the presumed connection between mental and physical realities, internal and external experiences, individual and collective truths, present and past events. In this sense *The Future of an Illusion* vitiates the findings of *The Interpretation of Dreams* of 1900, nullifying the (Romantic) basis of Freud's famous self-analysis: introspection and self-discovery as a basis for scientific insight into the object world. In this sense the *Future* really doesn't seem like a book of the genuine Freud at all, but of an imposter.

If true, this is a radical conclusion, since it means that what began as a dramatization of the voice of an imaginary opponent, what began as *fiction*, quickly became reality: the Freud of the *Future* really does become divided against himself, unable to know which agency, which voice of Freud, is directing the other. "Freud" loses his way, the way of psychoanalysis.

Freud must realize that he is lost, or worse, that he has slid down a slippery slope of his own making. For at the outset of chapter seven he openly asks (of himself, *sans* italics) what "other cultural assets" are caught in the undertow of his critique of illusion. "Once our suspicions have been stirred up," Freud continues, "we shall not shrink back from asking also whether the basis is any better for our conviction that we can learn something about external reality through the application of observations and rational thought in scientific work. Nothing should hold us back from approving the turning of our observation to our own being, from approving the application of thought to criticism of thought itself" (1927/2012, pp. 95–6; *SE*, 1927b/1991, p. 34). Nothing *should* hold us back from "such a comprehensive task" of critical self-examination, of critique in the Kantian sense, especially since Freud acknowledges the need. The problem is Freud's own inadequacies to this end: "the capabilities of the author do not extend to such a comprehensive a task; of necessity, he must restrict his work to pursuing just one of these illusions – that of religion" (1927/2012, p. 96; *SE*, 1927b/1991, p. 34).

To his credit "the author" – Freud awkwardly refers to himself, *des Autors*, in the third person – doesn't un-ask the tough questions, doesn't erase or edit them, but leaves them for us to ponder. The upshot is that Freud and the reader are both fully aware that Freud has flirted with and then preserved an enduring suspicion: perhaps even that cultural asset called psychoanalysis is an illusion. The suspicion hangs over the *Future* and its mise-en-scène.

Later on, in chapter eight, Freud moves on to the idea that religion is not just a wish fulfillment, but contains "significant historical reminiscences" (1927/2012, p. 103; *SE*, 1927b/1991, p. 42). In effect he moves from religion's dubious "truth value" as it concerns external reality to what he calls its "historical value" (1927/2012, p. 104; *SE*, 1927b/1991, p. 43). This is the positive value of religion that Freud, in retrospect, admits he underplayed in the *Future* (see *SE*, 1925c/1991, p. 72): namely, the idea that our wishes, dreams, or religious beliefs are a distant echo of our archaic past; a past he decodes more fully in his final work on religion, *Moses and Monotheism* (see Jones, 1957, pp. 362–9; Zilboorg, 1958, pp. 19, 34, 44). In this sense Freud (but which one?) is nearly back on the path of psychoanalysis, for the primary task of psychoanalysis is just this recovery of repressed truth; a task that goes well beyond questions of therapy and medicine. Which is why Freud, not incidentally, argues in favor of the purely *intellectual* merits of lay analysis, for if anything, the medical analysts, with their narrow "practical" and "professional" concerns, are a drag on the future progress of psychoanalysis. Invoking the "royal we" (*Wir*), Freud in *Lay Analysis* delivers a lengthy salvo that resonates with the themes of the *Future* (including its unusual concern with "the future"):

> We do not consider it at all desirable for psychoanalysis to be swallowed up by medicine. . . It deserves a better fate and, it may be hoped, will meet one. As a "depth-psychology," a theory of the mental unconscious, it can become indispensable to all the sciences which are concerned with the evolution of human civilization and its major institutions such as art, religion and the social order. It has already, in my opinion, afforded these sciences considerable help in solving their problems. But these are only small contributions compared with what might be achieved if historians of civilization, psychologists of religion, philologists and so on would agree themselves to handle the new instrument of research which is at their service. The use of analysis for the treatment of the neuroses is only one of its applications; the future will perhaps show that it is not the most important one. (*SE*, 1926/1991, p. 248)

Freud is clearly bullish about a future that belongs to the historians, psychologists, philologists,[5] and lay analysts, but not really to medical analysts or even analytic treatment. "I have often said," Freud says privately, "that the purely medical importance of analysis is outweighed by its importance to science as a whole, and that its general influence by means of clarification and the exposure of error exceeds its therapeutic value to the individual" (Freud & Pfister, 1963, p. 120). In his own life Freud always favored pure research, preferring the company of students, researchers, and intellectuals to patients. The advancement of "science as a whole" was his life's work. "This prospect of scientific gain," Freud repeats in the "Postscript" of 1927, "has been the proudest and happiest feature of analytic work" (*SE*, 1927a/1991, p. 256).

Arguably, this is the future that Freud stakes his reputation on in *The Question of Lay Analysis* – a future when psychoanalysis will function as the indispensable key to all disciplines. The alternative, he says elsewhere, would be a "gloomy future," one caused by the failure of psychoanalysis to

---

[5] Freud doesn't include "philosophers." But Nietzsche, of course, was trained as a philologist.

create "an abode for itself outside of medicine" (in Jones, 1957, p. 297). And so Freud in 1926 proclaims that lay analysts aren't quacks at all but are legitimate practitioners of psychoanalysis; moreover, they are an *essential* part of the authentic (Freudian) future of psychoanalysis.

It can't be surprising that medical analysts weren't pleased by Freud's defense of lay analysis, fearful that Freud was stripping away the science from psychoanalysis. When Reik won his suit in May 1927, *The New York Times* duly reported, "AMERICAN LOSES SUIT AGAINST FREUD: Psychoanalysis Discoverer Says It Can Do Good Regardless of Medical Science" (in Gay, 1988, p. 491).

Of course Freud and Reik may have won this particular battle over lay analysis but they lost the war with medical analysts. Nearly one year after the court win Freud, dejected, would remark that he was a "Commander-in-Chief without an army" (in Jones, 1957, p. 297). Hence *The Future of an Illusion*, which repairs the impression that Freud is insufficiently devoted to science (as expressed in *Lay Analysis*) by trumpeting the scientificity of psychoanalysis. In other words one PR campaign led to another, one wherein Freud pursues the un-Freudian path of positivism for the sake of the institutional and pragmatic present of Freudianism; where Freud "out-sciences" his colleagues on their own terms. Eliot was the first reviewer to see through the ruse, turning psychology back on psychoanalysis, writing, "it is naturally the adepts of the parvenu sciences, in their anxiety to affirm that their science really is a science, who make the most exaggerated claims for science as a whole" (1928, p. 353; in Kiell, 1988, p. 577).

As for Freud's uncharacteristic optimism in the *Future*, it is also prefigured in *Lay Analysis* where he concludes, first, that child analysis is "an excellent method of prophylaxis" (prevention of neuroses); second, that adult analysis might work as a "corrective" to the sacrifices we face in civilization; and third, that the future might even see "Aha! A new kind of Salvation Army!" run by "social workers" that help prepare humanity for the aforementioned "corrective" (*SE*, 1926/1991, pp. 249–50). About this lattermost remark Freud actually says: "Aha, eine neue Art von Heilsarmee." Strachey adds the two exclamation marks, presumably to make Freud's remark appear more jocular than it is – and less out of character. Freud was usually lukewarm toward such schemes, but they served his (exclamatory) purposes in the two books. All of this brings us full circle to the thesis that Freud provides only belatedly in chapter nine of the *Future*: "the sole purpose of this publication of mine," he says, is to show people the need to grow up and "go out, into 'hostile life'" (1927/2012, p. 108; *SE*, 1927b/1991, p. 49). Freud calls this "education to reality," by which he means education to the external world of others, of the *Masse*, and to the *Kultur* that regulates their psychology. On this score, *Lay Analysis* and the *Future* are of one mind: the future belongs to an education influenced by psychoanalysis.

Facetious mockery greets Freud's un-Freudian optimism at the beginning of the final chapter of the *Future*. The voice of the imaginary opponent declares:

> *That really sounds marvelous! A human race that has renounced all illusions and has thereby become capable of making life on earth bearable for itself! However, I cannot share your expectations. Not because I am the stubborn reactionary you may take me for. No, because of my prudence. It seems to me that we have now switched roles: you prove yourself the enthusiast, who allows himself to be carried away by illusion, and I argue for the claims of reason, the right of skepticism. (1927/2012, p. 109; SE, 1927b/ 1991, p. 51)*

The voice concludes its lengthy and overdue criticism by charging Freud with having attempted "to replace a well-tested and affectively valuable illusion" – religion – "by another one, untested and indifferent" – the science of psychoanalysis (p. 110; p. 52).

Freud is receptive to the criticism since the voice of the opponent is now the genuinely Freudian one. As the imaginary opponent says, the two voices have indeed "switched roles." "Maybe the hopes I have confessed," Freud admits, "are also illusory." If so, then the real and "sufficient" confession missing from the *Future* is the one voiced by the imaginary opponent, Freud's ventriloquist dummy.

Freud is not quite there, not yet, and so takes pains to distance himself and his science from the conclusion that psychoanalysis is just another illusion. Freud summarizes his response as follows: "We believe it is possible for scientific work to learn something about the reality of the world; through such knowledge we will be able to increase our power, and in accord with it we will be able to arrange our life. If this belief is an illusion, then we are in the same position as you are [i.e., the imaginary opponent, enemy, defender of religion], but through its numerous and significant successes science has given us proof that it is no illusion" (1927/ 2012, p. 112; *SE*, 1927b/1991, p. 55). In this passage Freud takes steps to counter the (by definition hysterical) fear that his findings are illusory by tying psychoanalysis to science, science to proof, and proof to reality. For if psychoanalysis is science, and science is reality, then, QED, psychoanalysis isn't illusion. He continues,

> Science has many open enemies and even more hidden ones among those who cannot forgive her for having weakened religious faith and for her threat to overthrow it. People reproach her for how little she has taught us and for the incomparably greater amount she has left in darkness. But in doing so, they forget how young she is, how difficult were her beginnings, and how infinitesimally short has been the period of time since the human intellect has had the strength for scientific tasks.

This passage, which echoes *Lay Analysis*, is crucial. In it Freud compares the "infinitesimally short" time of science in general, and of psychoanalysis in particular, with the deep time of evolution. His argument is brilliant, if diabolical: if psychoanalysis, like science, can boast only modest results, it is because its development has been "infinitesimally short" – as he already points out in 1926, psychoanalysis is scarcely twenty-six years old. "Are we not wrong," Freud therefore asks, "to base our judgments on excessively brief periods of time?" (1927/2012, p. 112–13; *SE*, 1927b/1991, p. 55). Freud's answer, insufficiently appreciated in the secondary literature, is classically Freudian in its total pessimism: "We should take geologists as our example." This dark conclusion marks the moment, more dramatic than the faux drama of the dialogue, when the two voices of the *Future* collapse; when the tension between narrator and imaginary opponent is dropped; and when Freud regains his genuine Freudian voice.

Marx believed that the future had already arrived, or had very nearly arrived, with industrial capitalism, and that the *Masse* was nearly a *Volk*, a people; the experience of oppression and alienation had forged a unit, a whole. With his appreciation of Darwinian evolution and Lamarckian inheritance, Freud knew better: humanity's relatively recent experiences of science and *Kultur* could only become a part of nature, of biological inheritance, once they have been (compulsively) repeated for millennia. Freud said as much to Joseph Wortis during an analytic session:

> Freud acknowledged the force and importance of Communism. "It will take centuries, though," he said, "before its value can be extracted and enjoyed. Communism, like Christianity, always promises the people a better world in the future, to repay them for their misery. The only difference is that Christianity promises it in another world." (1954, p. 165)

The conflict between Freudism and Marxism is a battle for the present – not the distant future. In the geologically distant future, a utopia of reason may indeed entail radically different forms of social relations. But, for Freud, it is only our distant descendants that will be able to speak of a *cultural drive*, of an innate drive to create and foster and protect; that is to say, only the future – "far, far ahead, but probably not infinitely far" (1927/2012, p. 111; *SE*, 1927b/1991, p. 53) – could benefit from the accumulated experiences of the life drive. Until that probable time we should certainly speak out in favor of the future of science and culture, of the battle to master the external world. And arguably the same holds for would-be radicals, who should insist on a future based on equality and social justice. But in the meantime we must more carefully (and reasonably) attend to the psychology of everyday life in our conflictual present, since it is still governed by our animal past.

And that is how Freud, after ten chapters, suspends the tension between Enlightenment and Romanticism, between the dream of progress and the devil of regress, between life and death drives. Simply put, life and culture are for the future, death and nature are for the present. *The Future of an Illusion* is therefore very much a product of *Beyond the Pleasure Principle* and the death drive theory. Indeed, the greatest illusion generated by the *Future* is the commonplace belief that its surface rationalism is derived from Enlightenment critiques and values, whereas it is part and parcel of Freud's brooding late Romanticism. In this sense, it is not quite the case, as Erich Fromm has it, that Freud's theories are "the fruitful synthesis of rationalism and romanticism" (1970, p. 37). Nor is it quite the case, as W. W. Meissner has it, that Freud has "second thoughts" about his scientific claims toward the end of the *Future* (1984, p. 101). It is rather the case that Freud in the *Future* indulges (plays with) but ultimately suspends, or destabilizes, the scientific rationalism that is its Other. Indeed, the importance of Enlightenment thought to the *Future*, and to Freud's thought more generally, is very nearly a red herring, one that has misled readers from the moment the *Future* was published in 1927 – beginning with Oskar Pfister.

1.4 Pastoral Work and the Cure of Souls: Philosophy against the Positivistic Freud

> A powerful-minded opponent of religion is certainly of more service
> to it than a thousand useless supporters.
> (Oskar Pfister to Freud [in Freud & Pfister, 1963, p. 110])

Let's summarize the argument thus far. Freud in the 1920s worries about the future of psychoanalysis, and so takes pains to distinguish it from medicine, from Marxism, and finally from religion. Freudian psychoanalysis is none of these things. "Science" becomes the site where the battle is waged on all three fronts, and in *The Question of Lay Analysis* and *The Future of an Illusion* Freud flirts with a positivism that is not just old fashioned but is remarkably un-Freudian: only empirical knowledge of the external world is real, thus rendering religion and even introspection an illusion. Freud escapes the implications of his positivism, however, by invoking the deep history of evolution with which he predicts the development of the future. This way he has his cake and eats it too: positivistic science remains the hope of a "geologically" distant future, even though we are governed by our animal pasts today. The master key in these respects is the death drive theory, which reveals that supposed progress in our present lives is a kind of illusion; that biology and death will win out over culture and life for the foreseeable future. And so the future he predicts for humanity (and for psychoanalysis) in the *Future* is ultimately the same as the one he pitches in *Beyond*. There is no contradiction between the two works.

There is, however, at least one more significant piece of the puzzle that helps account for the appearance of the *Future* in 1927, and for its unusual positivism: namely, Freud's relationship with the world's first lay analyst. Let's turn to Pfister now.

It is often claimed that the formal argument between psychoanalysis and religion that is dramatized in the *Future* repeats the informal argument between a "godless" Freud and his devout friend, the lay analyst and Swiss pastor Oskar Pfister (Meissner, 1984, pp. 64, 73, 82; Roazen, 1993a, p. 557). On this reading the "imaginary opponent" in the *Future* is a personification of Pastor Pfister, the voice of opposition delivered from within psychoanalysis itself. Freud himself certainly admits that he had Pfister in mind when composing the book. "In the next few weeks," Freud tells him, "a pamphlet of mine will be appearing which has a great deal to do with you. I had been wanting to write it for a long time, and postponed it out of regard for you, but the impulse became too strong" (Freud & Pfister, 1963, p. 109).

By 1927 Freud had known Pfister for nearly twenty years, the two sharing a bond over psychoanalysis, friendly exchanges, and family. In 1909, Pfister began utilizing psychoanalysis with his Protestant (Lutheran) parishioners in Zurich, especially young adults, a practice he called "pedagogic psychoanalysis (paedanalysis)" – the application of analysis to education (p. 78; see Meissner, 1984, pp. 73–4; Irwin, 1973a). That is not all. In addition to his many articles and books on psychoanalysis, in late 1912 Pfister sided with Freud against that other Swiss, Carl Jung, seven years later helping to establish the Swiss Society for Psychoanalysis.

Freud rewarded Pfister for his loyalty, writing a short "Introduction" to Pfister's *The Psychoanalytic Method* in February 1913; not incidentally, this "Introduction" is the first defense of lay analysis ever published. In a rehearsal of arguments outlined in greater depth in *The Question of Lay Analysis*, Freud's "Introduction" already entertains the optimistic idea that psychoanalysis could be a prophylactic against future neuroses. To this end he favorably compares psychoanalysis to education and the kind of pastoral work that Pfister practiced with young adults (*SE*, 1913a/1991, p. 330). "Let us hope that the application of psycho-analysis to the service of education," Freud concludes, "will quickly fulfill the hopes which educators and doctors may rightly attach to it. A book such as this of Pfister's, which seeks to acquaint educators with analysis, will then be able to count on the gratitude of later generations" (p. 331). Freud's hopes were borne out. In a letter to Pfister in 1926, Freud writes that "of all the applications of psychoanalysis the only one that is really flourishing is that initiated by you in the field of education" (Freud & Pfister, 1963, p. 106).

Pfister insisted on the relevance of psychoanalysis to "all those who come into the field of the cure of souls" (p. 104), from alcoholics to frustrated artists, a feature he thought was missing from *The Question of Lay Analysis*. Surprisingly, Freud agreed:

> I am glad that on the whole you like my pamphlet. But do not judge it as an objective, scientific piece; it is a piece of polemics written for a special occasion. Otherwise I should certainly not have omitted the application of analysis to the cure of souls. I considered doing so, but in Catholic Austria the idea of a "churchman's" working with analysis is totally inconceivable, and I did not wish to further complicate the issue. (p. 105)

Freud's "Postscript" (to *Lay Analysis*) of the following year was an oppor-tunity to correct (and "complicate") the public record concerning "the cure of souls," and once again register his favorable views about pastoral work. In it Freud writes:

> A professional lay analyst will have no difficulty in winning as much respect as is due to a secular pastoral worker. Indeed, the words, "secular pastoral worker," might well serve as a general formula for describing the function which the analyst, whether he is a doctor or a layman, has to perform in his relation to the public. Our friends among the protestant clergy, and more recently among the catholic clergy as well, are often able to relieve their parishioners of the inhibitions of their daily life by confirming their faith – after having first offered them a little analytic information about the nature of their conflicts. (*SE*, 1927a/1991, p. 255–6)

In the *Future* Freud admits that religion can be psychologically effective against neuroses, something he mentions in his "Obsessive Actions and Religious Practices" of 1908 and again in the Wolf Man case study of 1918: "it may be said that in the present case religion achieved all the aims for the sake of which it is included in the education of the individual" (*SE*, 1918/1991, p. 114). And to Pfister Freud conceded the "possibility of sublimation to religion" (Freud & Pfister, 1963, p. 63). Freud is therefore far from distancing analysis from the religious context altogether, especially in its connection to Pfister's Protestantism. He even embraces the words "secular pastoral worker," *Seelsorger*, as central to the identity of psychoanalytic practice. Freud is careful, however, to qualify his remarks in the "Postscript" – and he throws "socialism" (still used interchangeably with "communism" in some circles) into the mix as well:

> We who are analysts are set before us as our aim the most complete and profoundest possible analysis of whoever may be our patient. We do not seek to bring him relief by receiving him into the catholic, protestant, or socialist community. We seek rather to enrich him from his own internal sources, by putting at the disposal of his ego those energies which, owing to repression, are inaccessibly confined in his unconscious, as well as those which his ego is obliged to squander in the fruitless task of maintaining those repressions. Such activity as this is pastoral work in the best sense of the words. (*SE*, 1927a/1991, p. 255–6)

I have taken pains to expose the textual and thematic connections between *Lay Analysis* (and its "Postscript") and the *Future*. But the truth is that Freud himself reveals what he calls the "the secret link" between *Lay Analysis* and the *Future* in a letter to Pfister. "In the former," Freud writes in November 1928, "I wish to protect analysis from the doctors and in the latter from the priests. I should like to hand it [psychoanalysis] over to a profession which does not yet exist, a profession of *lay* curers of the souls who need not be doctors and should not be priests" (Freud & Pfister, 1963, p. 126; his emphasis).

In a way Freud holds out Pfister as a rough model of the future analyst, which is a remarkable tribute to the man and his commitment to the "cure of souls." Certainly he held Pfister in high esteem, almost uniquely so in the history of the movement. Their mutual respect is much in evidence in the correspondence, each man outdoing the other in praise – Pfister is praised for his integrity, enthusiasm, and optimism[6] while Freud is praised

---

[6] In a letter to Pfister on June 1, 1927, Freud writes about his earliest recollection of Pfister: "Your picture rose before me as you had been then, with all your winning features, your enthusiasm, your

for his genius and generosity with his work. Each seems to function as the other's ego ideal, the kind of person one gladly invites to family dinners. In this respect, at least, Pfister was obviously not Freud's "enemy" or "opponent."

Pfister's private criticisms of the *Future* came as no surprise to Freud, who agreed with Pfister's suggestion that he formalize them in an essay for the psychoanalytic journal *Imago* – where "The Illusion of a Future" was indeed published in 1928. Naturally, though, a number of criticisms were first floated in the correspondence. For example, in a long letter of November 24, 1927, Pfister challenges Freud's recourse to "'pure' experience" as a "fiction," insisting that "there can be no such thing as a pure empiricism" (Freud & Pfister, 1963, p. 114). Pfister was also the first person to see in Freud's *Future* an echo of Enlightenment ideals. "Your substitute for religion," Pfister tells Freud, "is basically the idea of the eighteenth-century Enlightenment in proud modern guise" (p. 115).

As for Pfister's formal response to the *Future*, it is a work balanced between *pro forma* praise and informed criticism. After an opening declaration of his affection, the essay is divided into two sections: "Freud's Criticism of Religion" and "Freud's Scientism." In the first Pfister quickly outlines Freud's charges against religion and then begins his defense. He accepts the evolutionary grounds that Freud favors, but with a twist: "just as tadpoles offer up their tails" to become frogs, so too has mature religion left behind its admittedly neurotic origins to become a culturally significant force of love, community, and ethics (Pfister, 1928/2012, p. 119). Religion is therefore a part of the "biological-ethical progress of humanity," a claim that informs Pfister's entire critique. Next he criticizes Freud's reduction of science to experience, and delivers a Nietzschean-sounding charge: all concepts "were long ago invented by epistemology as rather clumsy, if indispensable, anthropomorphisms" (p. 128). Consequently, "why should religion and theology form an exception?" The problem, mentioned in the correspondence, is that even if we grant "a surplus of pure objectivity" to the "exact natural sciences, they are lacking just what empirical criticism sought so passionately and unsuccessfully: pure experience." Here as elsewhere Pfister implicitly invokes Kant's Critical Philosophy, even as he offers a backhanded compliment to American

exuberant gratitude, your courage to face the truth, your blossoming out after the first contact with psychoanalysis, also the blind confidence you placed in human beings who were to disappoint you so soon" (Freud, 1960b, p. 377).

pragmatism (p. 129). The upshot: religion is neither so bad, nor science so perfect, that we should invest our "entire fortune in the single bank of science" (p. 131).

To Freud's charge that religion stupefies people, Pfister lists off the achievements of brilliant believers of the past, from Descartes and Newton to Goethe and Schiller (pp. 133–4, 146). To Freud's hope that a secular education is a healthier choice, Pfister points to neurotic atheists and communists and declares that "history has thus far pronounced another verdict" (p. 135). Later on Pfister adds, mischievously, that we should be careful assuming that nonbelieving intellectuals are necessarily morally superior to regular believers. "Hasn't Alexander von Öttingen [the Baltic German statistician and theologian] demonstrated that the highly educated include proportionately more criminals than do those of average intelligence? Do we not sometimes encounter an incredible meanness of spirit among academics?" (p. 147). Touché. Freud felt the same way about psychoanalysts, and Pfister knew as much.

Section one ends with a persuasive critique of Freud's reduction of culture, and of religion therein, to the "police-like mission" of taming our hostile instincts. Like Eliot, Pfister reminds us of the positive and creative side of culture: mature religion elevates humanity, "calling to life a higher, inwardly richer humanity, better corresponding to the true demands of human nature and ethics" (p. 137; cf., Meissner, 1984, pp. 71–2). This recognition of progress in and through religion is for Pfister "genuine realism," against which he contrasts "bad realism" – a term he associates, implicitly, with Freud's thinking.

Pfister's discussion of Freud's "scientism" in section two is philosophically informed, fairly sophisticated, and deepens the charges leveled in section one. According to Pfister, Freud invokes a particular notion of "science" but avoids posing the question of its epistemology. Pfister makes a virtue of Freud's avoidance of philosophy, but then he delivers a wallop: "Freud is a positivist and for that we can thank God. Without his concentrated dedication to the empirical he would not have become the great pioneer that he is. With such a successful and pioneering genius, one can make allowances if at the moment when he attempts to smother religious illusion, he sets up science as the Messiah, without observing that this belief too is permeated with illusion" (Pfister, 1928/2012, p. 20; cf., p. 26). The charge that Freud overvalued science is of course telegraphed in the title of Pfister's essay: Freud's "illusion of a future" perfected by science (cf., Reik, 1942, p. 123).

Pfister praises Freud's self-criticism about his faith in science, but utterly fails to recognize it as an empty gesture in the *Future*. As for Freud's "dedication to the empirical," Pfister takes Freud's professed positivism at face value. How it resonates, or fails to resonate, with Freud's other works is never explored. In fact Pfister's innocence on this score is nearly laughable, since no well-regarded scientist in the history of science has been *less* dedicated to "the empirical" than Freud; no well-regarded scientist has so brazenly over-determined his observations through preexisting theories, as Freud did, for example, when positing the truth of childhood sexuality years in advance of the confirming "observations" of children in analysis.

On the other hand, Pfister at least spells out the latent epistemological tenets of the *Future* and so holds Freud to account. Such clarity allows Pfister to go beyond the minimalist claim that *The Future of an Illusion* echoes Enlightenment critiques of religion, to actually compare Freud with other empiricists. On this score Pfister is useful, not least because he notes a major difference between Freud and the early empiricists. "His [Freud's] empiricism differs completely from that of the English empiricists," Pfister explains, "who seized the world of experience with the greatest precision but simultaneously, in the realm of action, left control to natural instinct and to the conscience – no longer to science" (Pfister, 1928/2012, p. 139). If anything Pfister reveals a Freud that is a more radical, or more naive, empiricist; someone totally uninterested in the ethical accommodations offered by positivists such as Mill, Comte, Strauss, and Dietrich.

Pfister, therefore, underscores and rejects Freud's unthinking disregard for the epistemological debates of modern philosophy. In what may be the most important passage of "The Illusion of a Future," the pastor delivers a quick history lesson and an informed warning:

> May one ignore the entire history of modern philosophy, which begins with Descartes and his absolute skepticism; then goes on to Hume, who destroys the illusion of guaranteed causality; to Kant, who overturns the illusion of empirical knowledge as a conception of the world in itself; and then to the most recent natural science that invokes a veritable twilight of false gods? Has no one yet realized what sort of scientific labyrinths one enters into when epistemological and metaphysical concepts are carelessly included under the descriptive label of natural science?... Natural science without metaphysics does not exist... The world is accessible to us only through our mental organization and indeed not only through the gates of the senses, which of course still yield no knowledge. Our categories of thought, whether understood in Kant's way or otherwise, are always involved. Therefore, we must develop a critical theory of knowledge. (pp. 141–2)

"Thoughts without content are empty," as Kant famously argues in the *Critique of Pure Reason* (1781), "intuitions without concepts are blind" (1993, p. 93). And that really is the crux of Pfister's criticism of Freud's "scientism" in the *Future*: Freud's dubious embrace of empirical science and positivism is conceptually blind, a "negative dogmatism" offered "in the muddled manner of an amateur" (Pfister, 1928/2012, p. 142; cf., Meissner, 1984, p. 93). Or as commentator John Irwin surmises, "The criticism here is that Freud is unconscious of his metaphysical assumptions, and that they are in any case invalid" (1973b, p. 322).

The difficult part for Freud, no doubt, is that this fair and accurate portrait of his reasoning in the *Future* doesn't do justice to the long history of Freud's freewheeling speculation, his wild abandon with the facts of "experience," and his fundamental disregard for therapeutic efficacy and clinical observation. The truth is that Freud never let the facts get in the way of what he called his "Witch Metapsychology" (*SE*, 1937/1991, p. 225); and he was often quite aware, as poststructuralists insist, of the analogical and metaphorical status of his own ideas. So yes, Freud was a blind dogmatist – just not the kind that Pfister diagnoses in his essay on the basis of one work, *The Future of an Illusion*.

And not even then. Like many others, Pfister fails entirely to account for the role of the death drive theory in the *Future*, and so fails to register the dark irony of Freud's closing remarks about the science he champions. Of course Pfister may have purposefully avoided this discourse, since engagement with Freud's death drive theory would only help validate a discourse that Pfister (implicitly but quite obviously) rejects. Perhaps that explains why Pfister often speaks of love but not of "Eros," a word Freud used interchangeably with the life drive, *Leibenstrieb*.

* * *

Let's summarize once again. Pfister believes that religion is a part of culture, like art, that moves humanity forward; is the basis of ethics, justice, love, and communal feeling; and is an "objective" and realized, justified, and "realistic" part of our store of knowledge today. Religion is therefore no illusion at all, but "an educator" (Pfister, 1928/2012, p. 149) – precisely the role Pfister himself, the "paedanalyst," plays in the history of psychoanalysis. As we've seen, Freud is surprisingly receptive to Pfister's work, indeed would like to "hand [psychoanalysis] over to a profession which does not yet exist, a profession of lay curers of the souls" (Freud & Pfister, 1963, p. 126). Freud even suggests that analytic work is a kind of "secular pastoral work" (*SE*, 1927a/1991, p. 256). But they part company on the foundations of Freud's late work: a pessimistic theory of human nature and progress based on the death drive theory. "In instinctual theory," Pfister privately tells Freud, "you are a conservative while I am a progressive" (Freud & Pfister, 1963, p. 131).

As for "illusions," Pfister convincingly turns the tables on Freud: Freud's positivistic future, stripped of ethics and philosophy, is the real illusion. And it is an illusion on the grounds that Freud himself suggests: as a species of wishful thinking, where science plays the role of Messiah. Pfister thus counters Freud's Logos, the god of "intellect" derived from Greek reason, with one derived from the Christian *Gospel of John*, the god of "divine wisdom and love" (1928/2012, p. 151) – where Jesus is the incarnation of Logos. But with this last formula an insurmountable difference between the two men is revealed, since clearly the atheistic Jewish theoretician of the "son-religion" is not going to accept the pastor's preaching about love and Jesus Christ.

Freud's only explicit response to "The Illusion of a Future" appears in a private letter to Pfister. This letter of February 24, 1928, is worth citing in full:

> Some of your arguments seem to me to be poetical effusion, others, such as the enumeration of great minds who have believed in God, too cheap. It is unreasonable to expect science to produce a system of ethics – ethics are a kind of highway code for traffic among mankind – and the fact that in physics atoms which were yesterday assumed to be square are now assumed to be round is exploited with unjustified tendentiousness by all who are hungry for faith; so long as physics extends our dominion over nature, these changes ought to be a matter of complete indifference to you. And finally – let me be impolite for once – how the devil do you reconcile all that we experience and have to expect in this world with your assumption of a moral world order? I am curious about that, but you have no need to reply. (Freud & Pfister, 1963, p. 123)

Freud, the late Romantic, rejects the ethics of Christian humanism that Pfister requires; ethics are like the rules of the road, totally conventional. One year later Freud repeats himself in another letter: "ethics are not based on an external world order but on the inescapable exigencies of human cohabitation" (p. 129). As for the supposed evolution of our finer feelings, Freud sees little evidence of it in the world of the late 1920s. In this sense Freud rejects Pfister's optimism as itself illusory – a criticism of Pfister echoed by an otherwise sympathetic scholar like Irwin (1973a, pp. 193–4; 1973b, pp. 323–4).[7]

---

[7] About Pfister's "overarching idealism," Irwin writes: "This enabled him to see Freudian eros as one step toward Christian love, and Freud's goal of therapy the first step toward the soul care practiced by Jesus" (1973a, p. 193).

It can't be surprising that many of the same disagreements return in 1930 with the publication of *Civilization and Its Discontents*. As before, Pfister rejects the narrow role that Freud assigns to *Kultur*. It would be a mistake, Pfister writes to Freud, "to identify with civilization its existing horrors, to which its magnificent achievements stand out in contrast" (Freud & Pfister, 1963, p. 131). Freud's frank response of February 7, 1930, which doubles as a response to utopians of all stripes, acknowledges the fundamental importance of the death drive theory to his thinking in the late period:

> If I could, I should gladly do as others do and bestow upon mankind a rosy future, and I should find it much more beautiful and consoling if we could count on such a thing. But this seems to me to be yet another instance of illusion (wish fulfilment) in conflict with truth. The question is not what belief is more pleasing or more comfortable or advantageous to life, but of what may approximate more closely to the puzzling reality that lies outside us. The death instinct [*Trieb*, drive] is not a requirement of my heart; it seems to me to be only an inevitable assumption on both biological and psychological grounds. *The rest follows from that.* Thus to me my pessimism seems a conclusion, while the optimism of my opponents seems an *a priori* assumption. I might also say that I have concluded a marriage of reason with my gloomy theories, while others live theirs in a love-match. I hope they will gain greater happiness from this than I. (p. 133; my emphasis)

Freud imagines himself a tough-minded realist unwilling to indulge the illusions of others, who bases his "findings" on "biological and psychological grounds." In this respect everything, as he says, follows from the death drive: "The rest follows from that." Freud's pessimism is therefore earned, while the rosy optimism of his opponents is merely asserted, a wish "in conflict with the truth."

As for happiness, like love, it is left to those under its delusive, essentially pathological spell. And, of course, it is left for those ascetics and would-be saints like his dear friend Pfister, who are clearly better people than the rest of us. More about them in the next chapter.

1.5   The Future in Retrospect: Closing Remarks

While the late Freud begins with tentative speculation in *Beyond the Pleasure Principle*, he becomes more dogmatic over the years. As he says in *Civilization*, ten years after *Beyond*, the death drive has "gained such a hold over me that I can no longer think in any other way" (*SE*, 1930/1991, p. 119). In this respect *The Future of an Illusion* is indeed a peculiar text, since the evidence of Freud's "gloomy theories" is buried under the weight of its un-Freudian calls for reason and science. But the subtext of the *Future* maintains the essence of Freud's dark views, subtly undoing all of his apparent optimism – which properly belongs to his "opponents," including medical analysts, communists, and idealistic humanists (e.g., Lutheran pastors) of various stripes.

This conclusion helps us understand, once again, Freud's remark that the *Future* "isn't a book of Freud," since what is genuinely Freudian is mostly absent. There is no mystery here; we know what constitutes the genuine Freud. This is the Freud who rejects simple-minded progress; rejects optimism about human nature, morality, and ethics; and rejects the "poetical effusion" that mistakes religious illusion for a "genuine realism" with dubious philosophical overtones. Or, if you prefer, this is the Freud who embraces the discourse of the unconscious; embraces the divided self; and embraces a notion of a psychoanalysis that is predisposed to lay contributions, even from pastoral figures like Pfister. In short this is the Freud who knows perfectly well that the positivistic empiricism of the *Future* is false – knows it even before the book is published, as we know from his remarks to Ferenczi – and amuses himself by telling a clueless admirer as much. So while Laforgue may not have found the genuine Freud in the *Future*, he obviously found him in person. Freud spoke the genuine Freud, or performed it, for Laforgue's personal benefit; a benefit, however, that had very little to do with therapeutics and fuzzy sentiment.

Obviously Freud does not speak in one voice in the *Future* – or even two. One voice speaks for religion, one speaks against it, and one speaks for the death drive. And sometimes the voices speak all at once. Appropriately, the voice of the death drive is the faintest; by 1927 Freud had come to believe that it did its work in silence. Yet it is also the most insistent and significant voice, or whisper, since it's the one that directs all the action. So what, then, to make of the elaborate show that Freud puts on in *The Future of an Illusion*? The answer is simply this: the *Future* is a portrait of the great man's *Realpolitik* in the face of his backsliding, myopic, and sometimes dense followers – a *Masse*, like any other, that was unable to see into the distant future, mired as they were in the ugly present. The *Future* is therefore just like *The Question of Lay Analysis*, namely, "a piece of polemics written for a special occasion" (Freud & Pfister, 1963, p. 105). To benefit his followers, Freud holds his nose and stages a positivism that is merely strategic – good enough, perhaps, to placate medical analysts still angry about his defense of that "pastoral" pursuit called lay analysis. The *Future* thereby establishes Freud's bona fides as a legitimate scientist, even as he whispers the truth to those, as Nietzsche says, with ears big enough to hear: *find me elsewhere*. . .

That "elsewhere" is far closer to philosophy than Freud could ever admit. The late Romantic thought of Freud's youth gave him his lifelong convictions and even his opponents: the philosophy of consciousness and reason. Blissfully unaware of the truth of the unconscious, Enlightenment philosophy remained a lingering threat to the new thinking. As such it always functioned as Freud's Other – which of course isn't nothing. In this respect Freud perfectly understood a Nietzschean truism that his friend, the good and faithful Pfister, delivered as a generous throwaway remark in their correspondence: a good opponent is always worth a thousand useless supporters (p. 110). And so the agonistic Freud sides with philosophy against philosophy, just like the other counter-Enlightenment thinkers of the late nineteenth century.

Freud was well aware that the tone of his work had undergone a "significant change" in the final phase – what in 1935 he calls a "regressive development," a subtle, ironical, and characteristic invocation of the theories of *Beyond the Pleasure Principle* (*SE*, 1925c/1991, pp. 71–2). "My interest," Freud reflects, "after making a lifelong *détour* through the natural sciences, medicine and psychotherapy, returned to the cultural problems which had fascinated me long before, when I was a youth scarcely old enough for thinking" (p. 72). Freud's acknowledgment of this return is as close as he comes to spelling out his debt to the thinking of late Romanticism.[8] What he doesn't say is that this return is a public reckoning with an influence that exists from the beginning as an otherwise inexplicable metabiology and metaphysics – i.e., as the "metapsychology." As such, the late works are the official commentary on Freudianism by Freud himself, the culmination of everything that is most genuine in his thinking.

Arguably it is the critic's task to make sure that we adequately respect this return and find Freud where he belongs – not in the illusory future he sometimes imagined for psychoanalysis, nor in the stale bureaucracy that psychoanalysis quickly became for others.

With his thoughts on the future, Freud wondered what would become of psychoanalysis after his death, asking: "Will it still resemble my basic thoughts?" (in Choisy, 1963, p. 5). The answer is yes and no. Freudian

---

[8] In a letter of 1929 to Andreas-Salomé, Freud mentions Thomas Mann's new essay on Freud, "Freud's Position in the History of Modern Thought," which makes a strong case for Freud's connection to Romantic philosophy. Freud doesn't quite agree, but does concede that "whenever Mann has something to say it is pretty sound" (Freud, 1960b, p. 390).

psychoanalysis survives as an immortal contribution to the history of philosophy that Freud, like Schopenhauer and Nietzsche before him, tried his best to revalue and overcome. Freud did not embrace this future let alone love it, but it belongs to him as the essence of his late return to "cultural problems." As for the scientificity of psychoanalysis, the privilege of retrospection permits a harsh verdict on Freud's own terms: it belongs entirely to the history of wishful thinking, illusion, and mass delusion. Today the "scientific Freud" survives only as a particularly complex expression of the philosophical Freud, that is, as a fascinatingly baroque attempt to translate late Romanticism into the more acceptable language of science. And while the history of this error tells us a lot about psychoanalysis, it tells us nothing at all about the external world that intrigued Freud in *The Future of an Illusion* and elsewhere.

Psychoanalysis began with autobiography and, as Freud sometimes feared, never really got beyond it. Instead it sucked others into its reality, which is a terrifying yet magnificent realization – one might say objectively so – about the function, and perhaps even the truth value, of human *Kultur*. If so, then Freud and Freudianism still has the power to teach us something exceedingly important about what it means to be a social animal. Let's turn directly to society now by way of Freud's most famous work, *Civilization and Its Discontents*.

CHAPTER 2

Mysticism, War, Love, and Religion
Civilization and Its Discontents, *Reality,* and Romain Rolland

The death of each of you is certain, mine obviously in a shorter time, and you don't let yourself be disturbed by this. Seven years ago I was told that I would have a maximum of five years to live, and since I took it pretty well, I can also tell mankind the most unpleasant things; it does not touch them.

(Sigmund Freud, March 20, 1930 [Freud, 1992, p. 292])

In the summer of 1929 Freud began work on *Civilization and Its Discontents*, finishing it off –"as far as possible," the vacationing Freud says, "without a library" (Freud, 1960b, p. 389) – on July 28, 1929. "In a way," Freud says, *Civilization* is "the continuation of *The Future of an Illusion*" (in Burnham, 1983, p. 229). The book was sent to the printer in early November and appeared in December 1929. As he did with *The Interpretation of Dreams*, Freud advanced the publication date on the title page to the next year, 1930. It is Freud's first major work after *The Future of an Illusion*, a hiatus of about eighteen months that James Strachey chalks up to his illness from cancer (*SE*, 1927b/1991, p. 59).

The original title of this, Freud's most famous work, was "Unhappiness in Civilization," *Das Unglück in der Kultur*, a fair description of a major theme in the book. But Freud's switch from the word "unhappiness" (*Unglück*) to "discontents" (*Unbehagen*) better captures the overall mood. For while Freud examines the surprising unhappiness of civilized (Western) life in the early twentieth century, his real target is bigger, grander: the innermost unease or, better, dis-ease that human beings experience being a part of society (Jones, 1957, p. 158). Hence the "discomforts of culture," or "civilization and its discontents," or even "society and its discontented."

The work is remarkable for its breadth, Freud discussing mysticism, love, interpretation, narcissism, religion, happiness, science and technology, beauty, justice, work, the origin of civilization and phylogenetic development, Christianity, the Devil, communism, the sense of guilt, remorse, and ethics. To this list we should also add Freud's discussions of key ideas in psychoanalysis such as sublimation, ego psychology, the superego, identification and group psychology, the death drive, and the destructive drive. Appropriately, Freud compared *Civilization* to "Trajan's Tropaeum of Adamklissi – a small monument built on a vast base" (Molnar in Freud, 1992, p. 62). Consequently, although *Civilization* is ostensibly about happiness or the lack thereof – at the beginning of chapter three Freud refers to "Our inquiry concerning happiness," and so names his theme explicitly – it is also, simultaneously and repeatedly, about everything else on this laundry list and more.

In many ways *Civilization* continues with and expands upon the procedural indirection that we find in *The Future of an Illusion*. It is probably too much to say that Freud "free associates," but not too much to say that he freely engages, sometimes with the slightest justification, all of the major threads of the late period. *Civilization* is therefore more expansive than the *Future*. It is also a better and more successful book – just as politically savvy as the *Future*, but intellectually risky, playfully charming, and at times thought provoking. The public was certainly drawn to it, the book selling 12,000 copies in its first year in print (Kiell, 1988, pp. 589, 607).

In this chapter I follow the trail of one theme discussed in *Civilization and Its Discontents*, mysticism and the "oceanic feeling" – with the proviso that it connects up, in any case, with most of the other themes. This theme of the book's introductory chapter is particularly rich, evocative, and at times peculiar, owing everything to Freud's correspondence with the French novelist and peace activist Romain Rolland. It also foreshadows an important work that Freud dedicates to Rolland in 1936. In what follows I begin with Rolland's discussion of a quasi-religious, mystical feeling that he calls "oceanic," and quickly outline Rolland's international reputation as a man of peace; examine the limitations and strategic importance of Freud's attempt to represent the psyche in pictorial terms, even as he aims for the true origins of civilization in his rebuttal of Rolland's view; review Rolland's informal and formal responses to Freud and psychoanalysis in the correspondence of the period and in two more or less forgotten books written in the late 1920s; explicate how Freud's investments in death and the origin of guilt, discussed late in *Civilization*, provide his deepest reasons for dismissing the oceanic feeling; and, finally, wrap up with a consideration of Freud's autobiographical "Letter to Romain Rolland (A Disturbance of Memory on the Acropolis)," a work of 1936 written for a Festschrift on the occasion of Rolland's seventieth birthday. The thread that runs through it all: Freud's consuming interest in science, objectivity, and the external world.

2.1   Romain Rolland and the "Oceanic" Hypothesis

The emerging discussion may seem like "false profundity" or mysticism, but we know we have not striven for any such thing. We are seeking the unadorned results of research, or of reflections based on it, and we wish to lend these results nothing but the character of certainty.

(Freud in *Beyond the Pleasure Principle* [1920/2011, p. 76; cf., p. 91; *SE*, 1920a/1991, p. 37])

It was Freud who reached out to Romain Rolland – distinguished man of letters, social critic, and peace activist. On February 9, 1923, Freud received a letter from Eduardo Monad-Herzen, mutual friend and French scientist, and in response asked him to pass along a message to Rolland. To Monad-Herzen Freud writes, "Since you are a friend of Romain Rolland, may I ask you to pass on to him a word of respectful veneration [*der respektvollen Verehrung*] from an unknown admirer" (Freud, 1960b, p. 341; Freud, 1960a, p. 359; translation adjusted). Rolland, happy to receive Freud's unsolicited admiration, responds in turn with effusive praise. "Allow me to take this opportunity to tell you," Rolland writes, "that if your name is now among the most illustrious in France, I was among the first Frenchman to know you and read your work. It was about twenty years ago that I found one of your books in a Zurich bookstore (*The Interpretation of Dreams*), and was fascinated by your subliminal visions which articulated several of my intuitions" (in Parsons, 1999, p. 170). Rolland was being kind; Freud's name was not "among the most illustrious in France" in 1923. During Freud's life France was uniquely indifferent to psychoanalysis, establishing the Psychoanalytic Society in Paris only in 1926 (Parsons, 1999, p. 31). French xenophobia meant that it was Pierre Janet's work – for example, on "subconscious" rather than unconscious mental processes (associated with Schopenhauer and von Hartmann, and later with Freud) and on somnambulic influence rather than transference (Ellenberger, 1970, p. 407) – that held court with everyone but the surrealists, a group that made Freud uneasy. Rolland adds, "You were the Christopher Columbus of a new continent of the spirit." Rolland also mentions the Great War in Europe. As in his published work during and after the First World War, Rolland's letter proffers guarded optimism about the future. "I do not give up hope," Rolland writes, "even if the political ruin of western Europe seems to me inevitable. But humanity has a hard life, and I'm convinced that from these convulsions the spirit will renew itself" (in Parsons, 1999, pp. 170–1). A few years later Rolland would announce that renewal through the teachings of Indian mysticism.

Beyond the miseries of everyday postwar Austria, Freud had in early 1923 been diagnosed with "a leucoplastic growth" on his jaw; over the next months it became impossible to avoid a diagnosis of cancer (see Schur, 1972, pp. 347–66). In fact, his first letter to Rolland is written just days after the first worries, but before the surgeries that would remove parts of his jaw and upper palate. It is tempting to think that the confirmation of the cancer diagnosis hastened Rolland's decision to visit Freud in person in 1924. But in fact Freud read about Rolland's visit to Vienna in the newspaper, which reported that he was attending the Richard Strauss Festival. And so, for the second time, it was Freud who initiated contact with Rolland, this time physical, through Stefan Zweig. Freud's tone is that of a fan. To Zweig he writes:

> On reading in the paper that Romain Rolland is in Vienna I immediately felt the desire to make the personal acquaintance of the man I have revered from afar. But I did not know how to approach him. I was all the more pleased to hear from you that he wants to visit me, and hasten to submit to you my suggestions. (in Fisher, 1976/1991, p. 31)

So on May 14, 1924, the men met for the first and only time at Freud's house on 19 Berggasse in Vienna. By then Freud had undergone the removal of part of his upper palate, and was fitted with an uncomfortable prosthetic device. Consequently his speech was garbled, most especially when he attempted French. "My prosthesis," Freud is said to have quipped on a different occasion, "doesn't speak French" (in Jones, 1957, p. 108). Consequently, at Freud's request Zweig, a mutual friend and one of Rolland's first biographers (in 1921), played translator at the meeting (see Vermorel & Vermorel, 1993, pp. 235–40). French historian Elisabeth Roudinesco sets the scene: "In Vienna, at 9:00 P.M., on a Thursday in March 1924, Freud and Rolland sipped a China tea and sampled chocolate pastries in the presence of the ladies of the house, Anna and the rest" (1990, p. 81). Their hour-long discussion is reported to have included the role of epilepsy in famous figures from history (Flaubert, Dostoevsky, Caesar, Alexander, Napoleon), and Rolland's own anti-fascist novel *L'Ame enchantée* (*The Soul Enchanted*) – most especially the first volume, *Annette and Sylvia* (1922), which Freud admired – and Rolland's forthcoming biography of Gandhi (1924).

Freud was delighted by the encounter. Reflecting on the visit in a brief tribute to Rolland in 1926, Freud would later write: "Unforgettable man, to have soared to such heights of humanity through so much hardship and suffering! . . . When I finally came to know you personally I was surprised to find that you hold strength and energy in such high esteem, and that you yourself embody so much will power" (in Parsons, 1999, p. 172). Or as he confided to Rolland in a letter of June 15, 1924: "When I am alone in my study, I often think of the hour that you gave me and my daughter here, and I imagine the red chair which we set out for you" (in Parsons, 1999, p. 172). Rolland was just as impressed. To his friends Rolland wrote about how pleased he was to learn that the "scientific experiences" of this "great confessor of souls" had confirmed his own experiences; and how "the old prof. Freud," seriously ill and surrounded by his antiquities ("little monsters" and "hallucinatory projections of religious and erotic dreams of the human race"), impressed him with a feisty spirit and an "admirable lucidity" (Vermorel & Vermorel, 1993, p. 238; my translation). Some scholars, such as Henri Vermorel (2009, p. 1241), claim that Rolland was even inspired to create a personal journal devoted to introspective examination of his life history, in which Rolland says that "I should like to throw some light on the mystery of my existence" (1947, p. ix). The journal was unfinished – "halfway through, it was interrupted" (p. x) – and posthumously published in 1947 as *Journey Within*. But Rolland boasted a "sixty-year habit" of keeping notebooks with personal observations (Fisher, 1988, p. 16), so it is hard to attribute a late introspective turn to meeting Freud. Moreover, as we will see it was Rolland, not Freud, who kept the faith as it concerns the value of introspection.

The relationship between the two men exhibits all the hallmarks of a deep emotional attachment, what Freud calls "transference," based on mutual admiration and idealization. Certainly ambivalence and hostility are also at work from the beginning, as when Rolland praises Freud but is careful to qualify that Freud's "subliminal visions" articulate "several of my intuitions" (in Parsons, 1999, p. 170) – a misunderstanding he repeats after their face-to-face meeting. Freud is just the same, only more so. In his first letter to Rolland, written on March 4, 1923, Freud begins: "That I have been allowed to exchange a greeting with you will remain a happy memory to the end of my days. Because for us your name has been associated with the most precious [*köstlichsten*] of beautiful illusions, that of love extended to all mankind" (Freud, 1960b, p. 341). We are immediately back to the subject of illusion, and also the future of humankind, themes that came to dominate Freud's discussions in works published after 1920, but which are very clearly present at least as early as Freud's "Thoughts for the Times on War and Death" of 1915.[1] The rest of Freud's letter is worth citing in full:

> I of course belong to a race which in the Middle Ages was held responsible for all epidemics and which today is blamed for the disintegration of the Austrian Empire and the German defeat [in WWI]. Such experiences have a sobering effect and are not conducive to make one believe in illusions. A great part of my life's work (I am 10 years older than you) has been spent [trying to] destroy illusions of my own and those of mankind. But if this one hope cannot be at least partly realized, if in the course of evolution we don't learn to divert our instincts from destroying our own kind, if we continue to hate one another for minor differences and kill each other for petty gain, if we go on exploiting the great progress made in control of natural resources for our mutual destruction, what kind of future lies in store for us? It is surely hard enough to preserve the continuation of our species in the conflict between our instinctual nature and the demands made upon us by civilization. (Freud, 1960b, pp. 341–2)

Beginning with the history of racism toward Jews, Freud draws a self-portrait that is surprisingly candid – and very much tailored to Rolland's interests. Freud's "hope" is wrapped up in destroying illusions, his own and those of humankind. The failure to realize this hope is then linked, audaciously, to other hopes, collective hopes: if we don't curb our instincts, and if we continue to hate and kill and squander our technology on war, then the future itself is risked. Put otherwise, if psychoanalysis fails, then so much the worse for the future of civilization. Note that Freud is essentially claiming that destroying illusions (with psychoanalysis) is part of the project of destroying, or at least curtailing, hatred and war, or again, that a kind of destruction is capable of destroying human destructiveness. This is of course a "hope" of a radically different sort than the one espoused by people like Rolland: "love extended to all mankind."

Beyond these characteristic features of irony and romanticism, Freud's letter ends with startling condescension. In a third paragraph Freud adds:

> My writings cannot be what yours are: comfort and refreshment [*Labsal*: solace] for the reader. But if I may believe that they have aroused your interest, I shall permit myself to send you a small book which is sure to be

---

[1] It is therefore implausible to claim, as Vermorel does, that Freud's interest in the theme of illusion, including *The Future of an Illusion*, grows out of his correspondence (which begins in 1923) with Rolland (Vermorel, 2009, p. 1238).

unknown to you: *Group Psychology and the Analysis of the Ego*, published in 1921. Not that I consider this work to be particularly successful, but it shows a way from the analysis of the individual to an understanding of society. (Freud, 1960b, p. 342; Freud, 1960a, p. 360)

One wonders at Rolland's reaction to having had his creative, intellectual, and humanitarian efforts summarily reduced to entertainment, to "comfort and solace." Like his love for humankind, the work is illusory; like religion, however "precious and beautiful," it is merely compensatory, a balm or refreshment.

Actually we know how Rolland responds. He immediately (March 1923) sends Freud a copy of his play of 1919, *Liluli*, in which he inscribes the following remark: "To Freud, the Destroyer of Illusions" (in Vermorel, 2009, p. 1240). About the play, Stefan Zweig tells us, "At the culminating point ... we behold the two friends who are misled by Liluli, the mischievous goddess of illusion (for her name signifies 'L'illusion'), wrestling to their mutual destruction" (Zweig, 1921, p. 336). Through absurdist laughter, Rolland's point is to satirize the dire conditions of war in Europe – the pointless, illusory nature of it all. Freud gets the message, and on March 12, 1923, he thanks Rolland for *Liluli* and adds, "I have of course been long familiar with its terrible beauty. I find the subtle irony of your dedication well deserved since I had completely forgotten Liluli when I wrote that silly passage in question in my letter, and obviously one ought not to do that" (in Parsons, 1999, p. 171). Chastened, Freud would in the future be more careful about his expressions of contempt for the unabashed lover of mankind. He closes the letter with rapprochement: "Across all boundaries and bridges, I would like to press your hand." In the second edition of *Civilization and Its Discontents* Freud dutifully adds a footnote mentioning *Liluli* and its author by name.

Civilization begins where Freud left off in *The Future of an Illusion*: namely, with a discussion of the external world. Freud's excuse is a personal anecdote derived from his famous correspondent. In a letter of December 5, 1927, Rolland commended Freud for *The Future of an Illusion*, which Freud had sent along, but challenged him with a pantheistic idea (a "perennialist" position, in more technical terms [Parsons, 1999, pp. 6–7, 61–3]) gleaned from Indian mysticism and from the philosophy of Baruch Spinoza (Vermorel & Vermorel, 1993, p. 306): the source of religious sentiment comes from a fundamental "oceanic" feeling of eternity and oneness, not from infantilism (as Freud argues). Rolland writes,

Your analysis of religion is right. But I would have liked to see an analysis of spontaneous *religious sentiment* or, more precisely, religious *feeling*, which is different than religion proper and a lot more durable.

I mean: [a feeling] that is altogether independent of dogma, Credo, and any organization of the Church, Holy Book, hope for personal salvation, etc. – the simple and direct fact of a *feeling of "the eternal"* (which may very well not be eternal, but simply without perceptible limits and so somewhat oceanic) . . .

I think that you will classify it [the feeling] also under the *Zwangsneurosen* [obsessive compulsive disorders]. But I have often had occasion to observe its rich and beneficent power . . .

I am myself familiar with this feeling. Throughout my life it has never failed me, but has been a vital source of renewal. In this sense I am deeply "religious," without this abiding state . . . interfering in any way with my critical faculties and freedoms – even as it concerns the intimacy of this inner experience.

Let me add that this "oceanic" feeling has nothing to do with my personal aspirations . . . And as I recognize the same feeling (allowing for shades of difference) among many living souls, it has allowed me to comprehend that this was the true underground source of all religious energy – which is gathered, channeled, and dried up by the churches. (Vermorel & Vermorel, 1993, p. 304; my translation)

Rolland's enthusiasm is characteristic of his letters to Freud, which freely invoke his personal feelings even as he frames them as viable hypotheses about life more generally. In this sense he shares with Freud a predilection for utilizing introspection to creative and universal ends. But ultimately, as with Pfister, Freud differs with Rolland about how this introspection relates to the external world, to reality.

Freud neglects to respond to Rolland's letter for over *nineteen months*. When he does respond, it is to secure Rolland's permission to reference his remarks about the oceanic hypothesis in a new work, *Civilization and Its Discontents*. In other words, Freud gives Rolland the analysis he thought was missing from *The Future of an Illusion*, the analysis Rolland "would have liked to see." In this sense *Civilization* is itself Freud's response to Rolland's letter, a formal raising of the stakes as it concerns their disagreement about the true origins of religion. "Your remark about a feeling you describe as 'oceanic,'" Freud writes in a letter of July 14, 1929, "has left me no peace" (1960b, p. 388). He adds,

It happens that in a new work which lies before me still uncompleted I am making a starting point of this remark; I mention this "oceanic" feeling and am trying to interpret it from the point of view of our psychology. The essay moves on to other subjects, deals with happiness, civilization and the sense of guilt; I don't mention your name but nevertheless drop a hint that points toward you.

And now I am beset by doubts whether I am justified in using private remarks for publication in this way.

Freud drops "a hint" in the work or, better, gives a wink, *einen Wink*, that the idea being discussed originates with Romain Rolland, and so is obliged to drop him a letter. As always with Freud, the work and the life, the theory and the practice, reflect and reinforce each other. For in light of a new work largely concerned with the sense of guilt, Freud is guiltily worried for having used Rolland's remark without permission. "I therefore ask," Freud writes, awkwardly, "that you hold me back from any abuses with a kind word if you are not releasing this remark to me completely without restrictions" (Freud, 1960a, p. 406; my translation). *Ich bitte Sie also, mich durch ein freundliches Wort von solchem Missbrauch zurückzuhalten, wenn Sie ihn mir nicht ganz ohne Einschränkung freigeben.* Although happiness and civility are at stake, Freud puts a reverse onus on his friend: having already written the remark into a chapter, Rolland is then asked to approve it – without reading it – "completely" and "without restrictions." Freud says that he could replace the introduction since "perhaps it is not altogether indispensable." Perhaps. But the implication is that it is already a vital part of Freud's argumentation in the book.

To put Rolland, if not his own conscience, at ease, Freud ends the letter with an assurance: "Please bear in mind that I always think of you with feelings of the most respectful friendship" (1960b, p. 388). On the one hand, this closing assurance of friendship is merely an echo of the florid (but actually conventional) salutations utilized in French. In letters after December 5, 1927, Rolland's typical salutations are *"Cher ami respecté,"* Dear respected friend, or *"Cher grand ami,"* Dear great friend, while his complimentary closings are *"Veuillez croire, cher ami, à mon affectueux respect,"* Please believe, dear friend, in my affectionate respect, or even *"Veuillez croire, Cher grand ami, à mon respectueux et affectueux dévoument,"* Please believe, Dear great friend, in my respect and affectionate devotion (Vermorel & Vermorel, 1993, pp. 303–10, 349). On the other hand, Freud's exchange of his "feelings of the most respectful friendship" for Rolland's letter about the oceanic and eternal feeling is just another instance of the way the men mirror each other in the epistolary love transference. One feeling deserves another – and yet another, as we will see later in Freud's essay of 1936.

Within a week Freud is able to thank Rolland for his belated permission. As always, Rolland is enthusiastic: "I am much honoured to learn that the letter I wrote to you at the end of 1927 has prompted you to new researches, and that in a new work you will reply to the questions I had posed to you" (in Parsons, 1999, p. 175). Perhaps in light of Rolland's enthusiasm, Freud reassures him yet again. "But please don't expect from it," Freud replies, "any evaluation of the 'oceanic' feeling; I am experimenting only with an analytical diversion [*einer analytischen Ableitung*] of it; I am clearing it out of the way, so to speak" (Freud, 1960b, p. 389). It remains for us to wonder what this "experiment" with Rolland means for the rest of *Civilization* and, by way of beginning, why the oceanic feeling must indeed, "so to speak," be cleared away, *aus dem Weg*, thrown out, made gone, *fort* – implying that the idea blocks the way to a proper psychoanalysis of civilization. It certainly does block the way to "our inquiry concerning happiness," which is to say, to chapters two and three. In fact, the "analytical diversion" that is chapter one does and does not belong to *Civilization*. First, as a self-described "diversion" and "clearing away," it is at best a preface to work that doesn't begin until chapter two or even three; second, it could in principle be replaced with something else, albeit at a cost; and third, the chapter functions as a self-contained essay in its own right. As we learn from Strachey, the introductory chapter was first published as a stand-alone essay in *The Psychoanalytic Movement*, a less technical periodical introduced in 1929, a few weeks in advance of the publication of *Civilization* in December 1929 (*SE*, 1930/1991, p. 59).

And so, with his belated permission, Freud is (guilt-)free to take up Rolland's challenge in the opening pages of *Civilization*. The experiment, diversion, abuse, clearing away, begins.

Of course, as "diversions" go Romain Rolland is not just anyone. He represents "the exceptional few" that Freud invokes in the first paragraph, someone who manages – in a way we have yet to understand; a Freudian way – to win admiration even from the masses (*SE*, 1930/1991, p. 64). In this sense Freud's invocation of Rolland in chapter one is not innocent. For by beginning with one of the exceptional few no one can accuse Freud of invoking the example of psychopathology – or even of normal psychology, as he does when he sets up the example of a very average Little Ernst in *Beyond the Pleasure Principle* – when discussing the supposed discomfort we experience as ambivalent subjects of *Kultur*. Instead Freud starts with the best that human culture has produced, a doctor of history, former professor at elite French universities, controversial peace activist and humanitarian, and, in 1915, a Nobel Prize winner in literature.

The Nobel Prize was awarded for Rolland's novel of 1912, the acclaimed ten-volume, 1,600-page *Jean-Christophe* that launched Rolland's international reputation and secured his financial independence thereafter. But the substance of the novel, the reconciliation of German and French cultures in the characters of Jean-Christophe and Olivier Jeannin, is obviously not unconnected to Rolland's peace activism. As the historian and lay analyst David James Fisher suggests, "The Nobel Prize symbolically legitimized his humanitarian antiwar stance, and was widely regarded by Europeans as a surrogate Peace Prize" (1988, p. 44). In fact, the novel is activism by another name, Rolland's prescient *cri de coeur* in advance of the coming war. In his biography of Rolland, Stefan Zweig puts it this way:

> No one had been more perfectly forearmed than Romain Rolland. The closing chapters of *Jean-Christophe* foretell the coming mass illusion. Never for a moment had he entertained the vain hope of certain idealists that the fact (or semblance) of civilization, that the increase of human kindliness which we owe to two millenniums of Christianity, would make a future war, comparatively humane. Too well did he know as historian that in the initial outbursts of war passion the veneer of civilization and Christianity would be rubbed off; that in all nations alike the naked bestiality of human beings would be disclosed; that the smell of the shed blood would reduce them all to the level of wild beasts. (1921, p. 271)

As for Rolland, he worried that the Nobel Prize (awarded in November 1916, well into the war) would compromise his independence (Fisher, 1988, p. 44) and so he donated the proceeds "to the mitigation of the miseries of Europe, that he might suit the action to the word, the word to the action" (Zweig, 1921, p. 270).

Rolland was disappointed, although not surprised, that neither his prescience nor good counsel did anything to influence or prevent the war. "I feel at the end of my resources," Rolland records in his diary on August 3, 1914, less than a week after the outbreak of war. "It is horrible to live when men have gone mad, horrible to witness the collapse of civilization" (in Zweig, 1921, p. 265). Inspired by his own novel, Rolland reached out to successive German figures to bridge their differences, but failed. And so, in September 1914, having decamped to the mountains of French Switzerland (Fisher, 1988, p. 13), Rolland publishes the impassioned essay for which he would become best known, *Au-dessus de le mêlée, Above the Battle* – what Zweig calls a "declaration of war against hatred" (1921, p. 293), and an attack on "the ideology of war, the artificial idolization of brutality" (p. 298). "Love of my country does not demand that I should hate and slay those noble and faithful souls who also love theirs," Rolland the moralist writes, "but rather that I should honor them and seek to unite with them for our common good" (p. 295).

The public, however, did not agree with Rolland's dispassionate stand for unity and common good – the oceanic sentiment rendered political. Intellectuals were no great support, either. In the context of war, few intellectuals would rise to Rolland's level of independence and abhorrence of nationalism (see Fisher, 1988, pp. 40–3). Worse, many intellectuals abandoned altogether the ideals of peace by lending their thought to the "militarization of the intellect," in short, to rationalizing war, destruction, and hatred (in Fisher, 1988, p. 42). "With criminal self-confidence," Rolland declares, "they have driven millions to death, sacrificing their fellows to the phantoms which they, the intellectuals, have created" (in Zweig, 1921, pp. 299–300; Rolland, 1916, pp. 117–18, 152).

In 1919 Rolland wrote *Liluli*, satirizing his spineless peers, and drafted a manifesto for peace and internationalism called "Declaration of Independence of the Mind." The "Declaration" attracted hundreds of signatories, including international figures such as Albert Einstein, August Forel, Georges Matisse, Heinrich Mann, and Bertrand Russell, and offended and/or alienated many others (see Fisher, 1988, pp. 62–3). When Bernard Shaw privately mocked Rolland's manifesto, deriding the pretense of standing "above the battle," Rolland won his respect by sending along *Liluli* (Fisher, 1988, p. 70) – the very same strategy he would later employ to rebuff Freud's own condescension. In 1919, however, Freud was conspicuously absent among the world's leading figures asked to sign the manifesto, a fact Freud would have known, at the very least, from his contact with Stefan Zweig, who was asked.

In 1915 Freud, too, responded to a war that imperiled his everyday livelihood and put his two sons in harm's way by publishing "Thoughts for the Times on War and Death." If Rolland was a "pessimistic idealist," as Fischer characterizes his thought, then Freud was a pessimistic pessimist. In the essay Freud argues that the illusions we share about civilized altruistic society are stripped away by war. "We welcome illusions because they spare us unpleasurable feelings." But psychoanalysis points us toward the truth, if not toward disillusionment: civility is far less secure than we had assumed. As Freud repeats again in "On Transience" (1916), war "revealed our instincts in all their nakedness and let loose evil spirits within us which we thought had been tamed by centuries of continuous education by the noblest minds" (*SE*, 1916/1991, p. 307). The upshot is that our former illusions have "come into collision with some portion of reality, and are shattered against it" (*SE*, 1916/1991, p. 280). So while Rolland called for unity and harmony, Freud invoked *Totem and Taboo* and described the dangers of what he calls our "blood-guilt," *Blutschuld* (pp. 292, 295). His conclusion could not be more severe: we are all of us "a gang of murderers" (p. 297), or again, "the history of the world which our children learn in school is essentially a series of murders [*Völkermorden*, genocides] of peoples" (p. 292). The death drive theory is still five years away, but is already lurking.

   While war made talk of reconciliation difficult if not impossible to imagine for most, the prospect was marginally improved in the war's immediate aftermath. But, frankly, Freud's rejection of the oceanic hypothesis has nothing to do with his own political views, which were not especially developed. It was more simply the case that Freud, at times a no-nonsense rationalist, failed to find any oceanic feeling in his own life. As he admits to Rolland, "To me mysticism is just as closed a book as music" (Freud, 1960b, p. 389); music, not incidentally, was another Rolland specialty. As a consequence Freud attempts to "open a book" on the oceanic hypothesis the only way he knows how, namely, by lending it the rigor of psychology. "It is a feeling of an indissoluble bond," Freud clarifies, "of being one with the external world as a whole" (*SE*, 1930/1991, p. 65). The strangeness of Rolland's claim for this primal feeling – it "sounds so strange [*fremdartig*] and fits in so badly with the fabric of our psychology" – is enough to justify a psychoanalytic interpretation. Freud continues,

> The following line of thought suggests itself. Normally, there is nothing of which we are more certain than of our own self, of our own ego. This ego appears to us as something autonomous and unitary, marked off distinctly from everything else. That such an appearance is deceptive, and that on the contrary the ego is continued inwards, without any sharp delimitation, into an unconscious mental entity which we designate as the id and for which it serves as a kind of façade – this was a discovery first made by psychoanalytic research, which should still have much more to tell us about the relation of the ego to the id. But towards the outside, at any rate, the ego seems to maintain clear and sharp [*klare und scharfe*] lines of demarcation. (*SE*, 1930/ 1991, pp. 65–6; 1930/2016, pp. 46–7)

Freud has not yet turned to abnormal psychology to find exceptions to the rule that the ego appears "autonomous and unitary" (*selbständig, einheitlich*) from "the outside." As with the exceptional example of Rolland, he sticks carefully to the most agreeable evidence. And so he moves on to the example of love, "an unusual state, but not one that can be stigmatized as pathological." As Freud puts it, "At the height of being in love the boundary between ego and object threatens to melt away" (p. 66). Hence the oceanic feeling of oneness, of a "feeling of 'the eternal'" – and with it the dissolution of the difference between internal and external worlds.

With the turn to love Freud returns not only to a lifetime of discussion about love and sexuality, but more specifically to conclusions about group love, and about society, as formulated in *Group Psychology and the Analysis of the Ego* of 1921. But that is saying too little. The turn to love, in 1929 as in 1921, is simultaneously a return to death, to 1920, since love or Eros is the logical flipside of Freud's metapsychological speculations about the death drive as advanced in *Beyond the Pleasure Principle*. Which is no surprise: *Group Psychology* was conceived and in part written during the same period as *Beyond*. We might even say that the boundary between these two works is by no means *klar und scharf*, clear and distinct – no less so in the case of the death and life drives themselves, which is one of the mysteries of existence that the late Freud reveals. Love always implies its opposite, and in chapter one of *Civilization* Freud is already laying the groundwork for that discussion. In fact death, as we will see, already haunts Freud's discussion of love and oceanic feeling.

In chapter one Freud claims that love forms a non-pathological exception to the apparent unity of the ego. Love thereby demonstrates in the external world a truth that psychoanalysis knows only too well about the internal world: sometimes human beings confuse themselves, their egos, with what is other. Or again, sometimes human beings fail to differentiate between internal and external stimuli. And so the lover loses herself in an identification, a merging of egos, with her partner. Enter pathology – which shows us the same thing as love, and just as dramatically. Freud writes,

> Pathology has made us acquainted with a great number of states in which the boundary lines between the ego and the external world become uncertain or in which they are actually drawn incorrectly. There are cases in which parts of a person's own body, even portions of his own mental life – his perceptions, thoughts and feelings – appear alien to him and as not belonging to his ego; there are other cases in which he ascribes to [*zuschiebt*, blames] the external world things that clearly originate in his own ego and that ought to be acknowledged by it. Thus even the feeling of our own ego is subject to disturbances and the boundaries of the ego are not constant [*nicht beständig*, not stable]. (*SE*, 1930/1991, p. 66)

Thus, even though Freud himself has no personal experience of the oceanic feeling, it is admittedly a fairly common experience. Mystics, lovers, and neurotics have some claim on it. Freud's knowledge of it all is purchased, presumably, from the outside – as a scientist focused on clear and distinct objects against which he can measure the stability and instability of subjects. Judgment and valuation are at stake, as is the certainty of science.

Freud is not done with exploring the idea of the oceanic feeling in *Civilization*, and turns to early ego development to better understand it. Here Freud invokes Baby who makes no differentiation between self and breast. This breast, Freud opines, is the first object to frustrate Baby's emersion in this oceanic oneness with the external world. In this sense, the breast – or rather, the absent breast, what Melanie Klein (following Abraham, 1924/1979, p. 463; Ferenczi, 1926/1952, p. 371) calls the "bad breast" (Klein, 1981, p. 291; see also Klein, 2011; Dufresne, 2000, pp. 71–3) – is the first affective representative of *Kultur* for the developing ego. The next feature that provokes the developing ego to acknowledge the existence of an external world is the "manifold and unavoidable sensations of pain and pleasure." Baby learns to dispense with unpleasure by "throw[ing] it outside," by clearing it away, only to realize that pain and pleasure exist in both internal and external states. The recognition of a difference between internal and external states is finally facilitated by what Freud calls "a deliberate direction of one's sensory activities and through suitable muscular action" (*SE*, 1930/1991, p. 67). One thus takes a "first step" toward the recognition of the reality principle, the idea that we defer pleasure – plan for it, wait for it – to better secure pleasure. The reality principle is a pragmatic "detour" around the pleasure principle, but in service of the pleasure principle. Eventually Baby will learn how to adjust itself to and manipulate this external reality, an approach later taken up by "object relations" theorists.

The upshot is that what begins as an undifferentiated contact between self and object, inside and outside, becomes ever more refined as a feeling of autonomy and unity, a "shrunken residue" of our original sense of oneness with the external world. This is what Freud, influenced by the work of his friend Sándor Ferenczi (1913), calls "the development of the sense of reality." As for those adults who, like Rolland, persist in this feeling of oceanic oneness – akin to what Ferenczi calls a "thalassal" regression to the womb (1924/1968, p. 20) – Freud has very obviously rendered them case studies in narcissism.

Freud, however, is careful to avoid diagnosing narcissism until the end of the first chapter; a diagnosis interrupted by an attempt to represent pictorially the palimpsest of old and new memories that is Freud's model of the psyche. About this detour, this digression within the digression about Rolland, more in a moment. For now let's stick to Freud's diagnosis of narcissism so that we don't lose the thread of his argument.

Three paragraphs from the end of the chapter, Freud finally clears away Rolland's attempt to usurp the thesis that the origin of religion – "the *fons et origo*," the fount and origin, "of the whole need for religion" (*SE*, 1930/ 1991, p. 65) – is found in an infantile relationship with Daddy. Freud says that the findings of psychoanalysis are "incontrovertible," *unabweisbar.*

> The derivation of religious needs from the infant's helplessness and the longing for the father aroused by it seems to me incontrovertible, especially since the feeling is not simply prolonged from childhood days, but is permanently sustained by fear of the superior power of Fate. I cannot think of any need in childhood as strong as the need for a father's protection. (p. 72)

The oceanic feeling is thus trumped by another feeling, the fear of Daddy and, later, of Fate. Freud, not comfortable with feelings any more than with mysticism, closes the book on Rolland with reason: he can't *think* of anything more basic than this fear.

Immediately following this passage, Freud continues:

> Thus the part played by the oceanic feeling, which might seek something like the restoration of limitless narcissism, is ousted from a place in the foreground. The origin of the religious attitude can be traced back in clear outlines as far as the feeling of infantile helplessness. There may be something further behind that, but for the present it is wrapped in obscurity. (72)

While there may be something even deeper than infantile helplessness as an explanation of the "origin of the religious attitude," it is too obscure for chapter one. Freud leaves these depths for the last chapters of *Civilization*, so let's do the same. For now it is enough for Freud to add that the oceanic feeling gets tacked on later as a "religious consolation, as though it were another way of disclaiming the danger which the ego recognizes as threatening it from the external world." It is important to note that Freud will make no such mistake. He recognizes the dangers originating from the external world, including, in this particular context, dangers presented by the unsettling idea of mystical union with the universe. A narcissistic idea. An illusion.

The truth is that Rolland's idea of the oceanic feeling is *doubly* narcissistic, first as a subtle piece of individual psychopathology and second as a presumptuous contestation of Freud's authority as the father of psychoanalysis. In this respect Rolland's letter to Freud about *The Future of an Illusion* is received as a Trojan horse delivered to the very source of psychoanalysis. No wonder Freud waits over a year and a half to respond. Freud, discontented, did what is required: at the very outset of his psychoanalysis of *Kultur*, before he could provide an inquiry concerning human unhappiness, he clears away Rolland's alternative theory of religion. The oceanic feeling is "ousted" from the foreground. Peace of mind that was disturbed over a nineteen-month period is restored. The experiment of thinking through the meaning of Rolland's oceanic feeling, like the diversion it required, is over. The idea of a more original feeling, the oceanic, however beautiful and comforting, is destroyed; the objective reality of the pleasure principle, and so of psychoanalysis proper, is defended. Science is defended.

In short, the future of civilization is given another chance. Freud, lost, is found again, while Rolland is cleared away. *Civilization and Its Discontents* proper can finally begin.

2.2   Of Right and Representation

Of course the diversion required to make Rolland *fort* also places him right at the beginning of *Civilization and Its Discontents, da*. And so, like the chapter as a whole, Rolland's presence violates the unity of *Civilization* from the outset, as we used to say, "always already." As a result the chapter functions, despite itself, as a confession of failure in advance of its declaration of victory. Freud will and will not get beyond Rolland and the oceanic hypothesis, at least not here. One consequence is that *Civilization* – as a book or essay with a thesis or theses – never really begins, or rather, never stops beginning. At least not until it's almost over.

It is fairly obvious that the uncivil diagnosis of Rolland's limitless or unrestricted narcissism, *des uneingeschränkten Narzißmus*, reflects back onto Freud himself, one great man's presumption matching the other's. It is certainly true that the "abuse," masturbatory or otherwise, goes on and on with Rolland, and with it the lingering sense of guilt that implicates other works and other letters at other times.

The abuse continues in *Civilization* as a diversion inside the analytic diversion, *mise en abyme*, about Rolland's oceanic hypothesis. It intervenes the moment Freud could have diagnosed narcissism but does not, and lasts until he does diagnose it at the end of the chapter. Arguably it is the (inherently pleasurable) specter of his diagnosis of narcissism, and the guilty conscience it provokes, that has Freud abruptly change direction part way through chapter one of *Civilization*. Let's turn to this interior fold to see how it relates to Freud's rejection of Rolland's alternative hypothesis concerning the true origin of religion.

Freud has just noted that there are "many people" who, as adults, continue to access the infantile "bond with the universe – the same ideas with which my friend [Rolland] elucidated the 'oceanic' feeling" (*SE*, 1930/1991, p. 68). Instead of concluding this paragraph with a diagnosis of limitless narcissism, Freud changes direction. To better telegraph this fact, Strachey introduces a paragraph break not found in the German original; in English the last sentence of Freud's discussion of the oceanic feeling gets pushed into the next paragraph as a new beginning. And again this makes sense since, conceptually, Freud has moved on. But it reveals a shift that Freud had, one supposes, buried purposefully under the cover of his discussion about the oceanic feeling.

The sentence, conceptually and structurally an orphan, deserves to be treated as such. It comes in the form of a question, the relevance of which is not immediately obvious: *"But have we a right to assume the survival of something that was originally there, alongside of what was later derived from it?"* (p. 68; my emphasis).

The answer Freud provides is *"Unzweifelhaft,"* undoubtedly (*GW*, 1948b/1991, p. 425): what is originally present in the psyche can still exists "alongside" what is later derived from it; or as he says in the previous paragraph, it exists "like a kind of counterpart to it." The importance of this indubitable claim of psychoanalysis cannot be exaggerated. For, indeed, it is essential to the great epistemological conundrum of *Civilization and Its Discontents*, the paradoxical conclusion that the super-ego is both derived from the guilt of *committing* murder and from the guilt of *not committing* murder (*SE*, 1930/1991, p. 137). Either way: guilt. Freud's discussion of the oceanic hypothesis in chapter one is his first attempt at addressing this conundrum about the "origin of the sense of guilt"; it is one of the "troublesome *détours*," literally "dreary and tedious detours" (*öder Strecken und beschwerlicher Umwege*), for which he will apologize to the reader at the beginning of the last chapter of *Civilization*. But apologies are for later.

For now the guilty author has great difficulty explaining the idea of an origin (in this case, the origin of the religious attitude or feeling) that is known only through the representation of its derivatives, and stumbles repeatedly over his own examples. Recall his opening bluff. Does he have "a right," *ein Recht*, to assume the origin and its counterpart? "Undoubtedly," Freud begins: "There is nothing strange in such a phenomenon, whether in the mental world or elsewhere" (p. 68). Note that while Rolland's claim about the oceanic feeling is strange, *fremdartig*, Freud's claim is not strange or disconcerting, *befremdend*, at all (*GW*, 1948b/1991, pp. 423, 425).

To make his point he gives the example of a modern crocodile that exists as a "true representative" of "the great saurian" – *Saurier*, the dinosaurs – only to qualify, almost immediately, that this example isn't very good. "The lower species which survive," he concedes, "are for the most part not the true ancestors of the present-day more highly developed species. As a rule the intermediary links have died out and are only known to us through reconstruction." So much for the crocodile example which, long cut off from its dinosaur origin, still requires reconstruction. Freud pushes ahead, this time pursuing another strategy meant to validate his assertion that there is "nothing strange in such a phenomenon" (i.e., knowing the original by means of the derivative):

> In the realm of the mind, on the other hand, *what is primitive is so commonly preserved* alongside of the transformed version which has arisen from it *that it is unnecessary to give instances of evidence.* When this happens it is usually in consequence of a divergence in development: one portion (in the quantitative sense) of an attitude or instinctual impulse has remained unaltered, while another portion has undergone further development. (SE, 1930/1991, pp. 68–9; my emphasis)

The upshot is that Freud has no evidence at all, aside from asserting the utter obviousness of it all: his claim is *not* strange, and in any case the "primitive is so commonly preserved ... that it is unnecessary to give instances of evidence." Where is it preserved? "Alongside the transformed version." The uncomfortable conclusion is that Freud's evidence – e.g., about the origins of religion in our primitive, infantile need for and fear of Daddy and, later, of Fate – is actually bound up with and preserved by forms of thought that are derivative of this need. One is therefore obliged, as Freud says of crocodiles, to reconstruct after the fact ("the intermediary links ... are known to us only through reconstruction") precisely on the basis of evidence that is secondary, derivative.

And this, of course, is what Freud does with Rolland's evidence of an oceanic feeling of oneness with the universe. It points the way back by preserving, alongside it, a still older and more original representation; a preservation that will have to suffice as evidence of that which is *beyond* oceanic feeling, which is finally to say, *beyond representation.*

If the evidence is amazingly weak, if nonexistent, for Freud's (strange?) belief in "the survival of something that was originally there, alongside of what was later derived from it," his next step is just as dubious. He provides an analogy. His goal in this regard is to take up the "more general problem of preservation in the sphere of the mind." He continues, moving on to a new paragraph: "The subject has hardly been studied as yet; but it is so attractive and important that we may be allowed to turn our attention to it for a little, even though our excuse is insufficient." Freud finally admits it: he has an insufficient excuse for this latest discussion. It is enough that "the problem of preservation" is "so attractive and important." We are beginning to see why. Freud continues:

> Since we overcame the error of supposing that the forgetting we are familiar with signified a destruction of the memory-trace – that is, its annihilation – we have been inclined to take the opposite view, that in mental life nothing which has once been formed can perish – that everything is somehow preserved and that in suitable circumstances (when, for instance, regression goes back far enough) it can once more be brought to light. (SE, 1930/1991, p. 69)

In practical terms this means that evidence of memories that are literally prehistoric, that is, memories from before recorded history (or before Baby's speech), can be accessed through the neurotic regressions of patients today. Here comes the analogy: "Let us try to grasp what this assumption involves by taking an analogy from another field. We will choose as an example the history of the Eternal City" (p. 69). Thus does Freud rummage Hugh Last's entry for *The Cambridge Ancient History*, "The Founding of Rome," for myriad details from the ancient history of Rome. Although Freud barely cites Hugh's entry, it suits him perfectly: "Roman history," the Oxford University lecturer in Roman history begins, "does not begin at Rome" (1928, p. 333). Against all the "dubious," "misleading," and simply "false" claims about "Italian pre-history" circulated in the nineteenth century, Last appeals instead to the recent "sphere of archaeology" for his conclusions.

The rabbit hole deepens, however, since Freud's turn to "argument from analogy" is in its turn analogical; its meaning lies elsewhere, alongside the argument. For it is no accident, not in the context of a wayward psychoanalysis of Romain Rolland, that Freud chooses an analogy based on Rolland's namesake (Fisher, 1988, p. 263; Vermorel, 2009, p. 1245). After all, Romain or Roman is the Latin name for a citizen of Rome. It therefore follows that the archeology of ancient Rome is simultaneously a veiled testament about the validity of the operation Freud seeks to justify with evidence that is always derivative: he does indeed have a *right* to assume the survival of something that was originally there, alongside what was later derived from it. Archeology has this right, as we learn from the prehistory of Rome provided by Last; evolutionary theory has this right, as we know from our Darwinian understanding of human and natural history; and psychoanalysis has this right, too. Consequently this abrupt shifting of gears to Rome and the problem of preservation remains a crucial, if diabolical, part of Freud's response to Rolland. It is the *justification* for his (uncivil) psychoanalysis, and he appeals to this right or law, this indubitable *Recht*, before he declares what is older and deeper than the oceanic feeling: the diagnosis of Rolland's limitless narcissism.

Freud has not yet provided the equivalence needed for his analogy, the Romain side of the Rome analogy. Having raided Last's article for details about ancient Rome, Freud continues:

> Now let us, by a flight of imagination, suppose that Rome is not a human habitation but a psychical entity with a similarly long and copious past – an entity, that is to say, in which nothing that has once come into existence will have passed away and all the earlier phases of development continue to exist alongside the latest one. (SE, 1930/1991, p. 70)

The result is one of the most potent, best-known images of psychoanalysis: the psyche, like an archeological site, is subject to an archeology of the mind, to psychoanalysis. As Freud put it in his "first full-length analysis of a hysteria," back in 1892, the "procedure was one of clearing away [*Ausräumung*] the pathogenic material layer by layer, and we [Freud and his patient 'Elisabeth von R.,' Ilona Weiss] liked to compare it with the technique of excavating a buried city" (*SE*, 1895b/1991, p. 139; *GW*, 1925/1991, p. 127).

Analogies have limits, however, and Freud reaches it in a paragraph that spins out the comparison of psyche to city, Romain to Rome. "There is clearly no point," Freud says, "in spinning out our phantasy any longer" (*SE*, 1930/1991, p. 70). For the analogy to work, the position of all buildings and structures must exist at the same time and in the same space. Without this equivalency, the analogy is useless. But as Freud concedes, the analogical substitution of space (buildings) for time (memories) "leads to things that are unimaginable and even absurd." Interestingly enough, Freud had already concluded as much years before in "Thoughts for the Times on War and Death" (1915). Consider his remarks about what he calls "the extraordinary plasticity of mental developments":

> [T]he development of the mind shows a peculiarity which is present in no other developmental process. When a village grows into a town or a child into a man, the village and the child become lost in the town and the man. Memory alone can trace the old features in a new picture; and in fact the old materials or forms have been got rid of and replaced by new ones. It is

otherwise with the development of the mind. Here one can describe the state of affairs, which has nothing to compare with it, only by saying that in this case every early stage of development persists alongside the later stage which has arisen from it; here succession also involves co-existence . . . (*SE*, 1915/1991, p. 285)

So none of this analogical terrain is new for Freud, not the uselessness of the city analogy or, in this case, the town, for understanding the plasticity of mental developments, and not the incomparable uniqueness of the mind as a site that preserves the earliest stages of history. As he adds, "the primitive mind is, in the fullest meaning of the word, imperishable." And so his conclusions about this in chapter one of *Civilization* are not surprising, least of all to Freud. As he repeats in *Civilization*, "If we want to represent historical sequence in spatial terms we can only do it by juxtaposition in space: the same space cannot have two different contents. Our attempt seems to be an idle game. It has only one justification" (*SE*, 1930/1991, pp. 70–1).

Stretched too far, analogies break; they become unimaginable, absurd. But at least the "idle game," a gimmick, *Spielerei*, has one justification, *hat nur eine Rechtfertigung*, and so won't be wasted. We already know what it is: Freud is justified, by right, subjecting derivative representations to a psychoanalytic interpretation, one that reveals its hidden but preserved origins; and Freud is justified, by right, to do the same with Romain Rolland's letter about the real origins of religion in the oceanic feeling. The game of positing an analogy between psyche and city, Romain and Rome, has a payoff, is worthwhile, *justified*. It has, he says, *one* justification. But in fact Freud does not provide the justification we expect of the analogy: "It shows us," Freud says of the failed analogy, "how far we are from mastering the characteristics of mental life by representing them in pictorial terms" (p. 71).

The analogy at the limits, unimaginable and absurd, has Freud conclude with an unimaginable and absurd realization: the diversion into analogy has produced nothing beyond the realization that the analogy itself is flawed; that pictorial representation is unequal to the model of mind Freud champions. What remains alongside the limit of the analogy is only the base assertion of Freud's right – an *argument from authority* that Freud launders, or fails to launder, through an *argument by analogy* that goes nowhere beyond itself. The attempted justification really is a gimmick, then, an excuse that puts distance and the appearance of argumentation between Freud's psychoanalysis of Rolland's oceanic feeling and his inevitable diagnosis: the origin of oceanic feeling in limitless narcissism.

Freud continues to vitiate his own analogy, *fort*, agreeing (with himself, now an ideal reader) that the attempt to model the psyche on a city is a bad idea. Cities, for example, demolish and remove buildings even in peace-time, and so they are not even, by analogy, akin to a mind that is damaged by trauma. "A city is thus *apriori* unsuited for a comparison of this sort" (p. 71). "We bow to this objection," Freud concedes, "and, abandoning our attempt to draw a striking contrast." The diversion inside the diversion about the oceanic hypothesis is nearly over – abandoned, like an unprofit-able archeological dig. Freud moves on to what may be a more promising analogy, the comparison of the mind to "the body of an animal or human being." But we already know that this is no better than the crocodile/dinosaur example. "The fact remains," Freud repeats, "that only in the mind is such a preservation of all the earlier stages alongside its final form possible, and that we are not in a position to represent this phenomenon in pictorial terms."[2]

Strictly speaking, however, this is not true. In 1925 Freud had published "A Note upon the 'Mystic Writing Pad'" in which he provides a clever analogy meant to depict aspects of the conscious, preconscious, and perceptual-conscious systems (*SE*, 1925a/1991, pp. 227–32). The "*Wunderblock*" or "mystic writing pad" is a common toy, employing a clear plastic sheet, a thin sheet of waxed paper, and a wax slab below. The pad allows one to write on the plastic sheet with a stylus, and then "erase" the sheet by simply lifting it away from the wax slab. In this toy Freud finds a ready analogy for how the mental apparatus receives stimuli from the external world and then stores it, like a palimpsest, in the wax below. So after erasing or clearing the top sheet – by analogy the conscious system – one has merely to lift the sheet and study the marks left in the wax underneath – by analogy the unconscious. "If one examines it [the toy] closely, one will find in its construction," Freud remarks, "a remarkable correspondence with the structure of our perceptual apparatus as I have conceived it, and will be convinced that it can really deliver both compo-nents: an always receptive surface and lasting traces of the notations below"

---

[2] Freud expresses an interest in "pictorial representation" in other works, most notably in *The Ego and the Id* (1923) and again in *New Introductory Lectures* (1932/1933). In both instances he depicts "the structural relations of the mental personality," i.e., the late structural or "topographical" model mind that consists in superego, ego, and id. Despite Freud's misgivings about contemporary painting, he writes: "We cannot do justice to the characteristics of the mind by linear outlines like those in a drawing or in a primitive painting, but rather by areas of color melting into one another as they are presented by modern artists" (*SE*, 1933a/1991, p. 79). And then he sounds a familiar note: "You must not judge too harshly a first attempt at giving a pictorial representation of something so intangible as psychical processes" (*SE*, 1933a/1991, p. 79; see also *SE*, 1923/1991, p. 24).

(Freud, 1920/2011, p. 129; cf., *SE*, 1925a/1991, p. 228). Obviously Freud could have adapted this rich analogy about perception to his ends in chapter one of *Civilization*. For the mystic writing pad really is a simple and effective means of demonstrating, by analogy, how unconscious traces will always exist alongside any new conscious scribbling on the surface of current experience. By merely looking beneath the surface, akin to archeology, one can decipher and reconstruct the oldest, most effaced, entirely forgotten "memories" of past activity with the pad. The pad is certainly a more effective, less absurd analogy than his Rome analogy. That Freud doesn't invoke the pad in *Civilization* lends credence to the suspicion that he has other, highly contextual and personal reasons for exploring the admittedly failed example of Rome/psyche, Rome/Romain. One further, perhaps not incidental, benefit: the Rome analogy has none of the baggage that would attend to an analogy derived from a *mystic* writing pad. For clearly a "mystical" toy is not fit for helping Freud clear away a mystical feeling.

The internal diversion is nearly over: it is left for Freud to declare his diagnosis upon the oceanic feeling and upon the mystical hypothesis that declares it the *fons et origo* of religion. To this inevitable end Freud first considers a possible limitation on his claim that the past is always preserved in our mental lives: maybe it is just *mostly* preserved; and maybe at times it is even degraded beyond the possibilities of retrieval. "It is possible," Freud says, "but we know nothing about it," conceding nothing since it is of course impossible to know either way. But somehow Freud does know, immediately declaring that such loss or degradation is the exception to the rule; that the past is nearly always preserved alongside its derivative representations (*SE*, 1930/1991, p. 72).

From this (meaningless) qualification, Freud returns to the oceanic feeling. Recall that Strachey has Freud begin his paragraph "Thus . . ." as though anything that transpired over a three-and-a-half-page diversion warrants the hallmark of an argument with a definitive conclusion. Again, there is no argument, no justification; there is only right. Strachey's Freud: "Thus we are perfectly willing to acknowledge that the 'oceanic' feeling exists in many people, and we are inclined to trace it back to an early phase of ego feeling." But Freud's German isn't nearly as certain or declarative. He twice employs the conditional "if": "If we are so thoroughly prepared to acknowledge that there is an 'oceanic' feeling, and if we are inclined to derive it from an earlier phase in the sense of self, then the question arises as to what claim this feeling has to be regarded as the source of religious needs" (*GW*, 1948b/1991, p. 430; my translation).

Of course, *if* we grant everything that Freud claims about the derivative status of the oceanic feeling, *then* the answer about the origins of religion is obvious. Yet it is precisely this *if* that Freud has been debating, that he fails to establish – but that he asserts nonetheless as a conclusive *then*. And so if Strachey squares the circle, making a *thus* out of an *if*, it is only because Freud himself has already squared the circle. In this sense, the derivative translation validates the very theory that Freud cannot perform and validate himself: it deftly points the way back to the original German source, Freud.

Freud's response brings us back, finally, to the diagnosis of narcissism. Here the "undoubted" matches up with the "incontrovertible," both assertions justifying Freud's right. Let's cite the passage one more time:

> To me the [Rolland] claim does not seem compelling. After all, a feeling can only be a source of energy if it is itself the expression of a strong need. The derivation of religious needs from the infant's helplessness and the longing for the father aroused by it seems to me incontrovertible, especially since the feeling is not simply prolonged from childhood days, but is permanently sustained by fear of the superior power of Fate. I cannot think of any need in childhood as strong as the need for a father's protection. Thus the part played by the oceanic feeling, which might seek something like the restoration of limitless narcissism, is ousted from a place in the foreground. The origin of the religious attitude can be traced back in clear outlines as far as the feeling of infantile helplessness. (*SE*, 1930/1991, p. 72)

Detour completed, Freud pulls his punch for the sake of civility and at the price, no doubt, of unmediated happiness (glee, *Schadenfreude*, sadistic joy): the oceanic feeling "might seek something like the restoration of limitless narcissism." Might – meaning that it might not.

In fact Freud gives Rolland a way out of his patronizing diagnosis altogether. To this end he invokes "another friend" whose merits include an "insatiable craving for knowledge," a penchant for "unusual experiments," and the acquisition of "encyclopedic knowledge" (p. 72). This Faustian friend, never named, has examined yoga and assured Freud that there is a "physiological basis" for the "wisdom of mysticism." Maybe, Freud concedes, this physiological basis even helps explain "trances and ecstasies," mental states of certain interest to psychoanalysis (p. 73; cf., p. 79).

Loyalist French historian and psychoanalyst Henri Vermorel claims, citing a personal communication with Ernst Federn, that Freud's unnamed friend is Frederick Eckstein, a former monk (Vermorel, 2009, p. 1245). This is possible. But it is just as likely that the unnamed friend is once again

Romain Rolland, as William Parsons argues in detail (1999, pp. 45–6; cf., Roudinesco, 1990, p. 82), a proposition supported by a simple review of their correspondence around the time of *Civilization*. Rolland, learning that Freud is preparing to publish on the oceanic hypothesis, informs Freud that he too has worked up a study: the first of a three-part, two-volume "study of mysticism and action in living India," *The Life of Ramakrishna*. Recall that Rolland, in December of 1927, had responded to *The Future of an Illusion* with a letter about the oceanic feeling. On July 17, 1929, having given Freud permission to use his remarks about the oceanic hypothesis, Rolland adds the following remark: "Since 1927 I have been able to delve deeply into that 'oceanic' sentiment, innumerable examples of which I find not only among hundreds of our contemporary Asians, but also in what I might call *the ritualistic and multi-secular physiology* which is codified in treatises on *yoga*" (in Parsons, 1999, p. 175; my emphasis).[3] Freud's response: "I cannot imagine reading all the literature which, according to your letter, you have studied" (p. 175).

In any case, this parting gesture further mitigates the diagnosis of limitless narcissism. For it would mean that Freud, at the last moment, allows for Rolland's alternate, perfectly coherent, *Weltanschauung*. It is a possibility he essentially repeats in one of the *New Introductory Lectures* written in 1932, albeit with unsurprising qualifications (see *SE*, 1933a/1991, p. 80; cf., Parsons, 1999, pp. 79–80). Civility does not prevent Freud, however, from having the last word in chapter one of *Civilization*, ending it with a reference to fresh air amidst the waves of mystical profundities. "But I am moved to exclaim," Freud concludes, "in the words of Schiller's diver: 'Let him rejoice who breathes up here in the roseate light'" (*SE*, 1930/1991, p. 73). Yoga and Eastern mysticism get an indulgent, condescending nod from Freud, but rationalism, as always, gets the final word.

Back to the beginning of *Civilization*: Why is it that the masses love Romain Rolland, one of the "exceptional few" that Freud mentions in the first paragraph? It is obviously not because he is right; even less because he reveals difficult truths. It is rather because Rolland tells the masses what they want to hear, to wit, bedtime stories about peace, love, and understanding. In short, he preaches illusions about oceanic sentiment. In this

---

[3] In *The Life of Ramakrishna*, Rolland twice, in footnotes, points to phenomena that he says warrants the interest of "European psycho-physicalists" (see 1930, p. 169, n. 1; and p. 299, n. 1). The French original also includes a long appendix ("Note 1"), excluded from the translation, devoted to "La physiologie de l'ascèse Indienne" (1929, pp. 293–9), "The Physiology of the Ascetic Indian." Freud, however, did not have access to this work while composing *Civilization*, only to Rolland's promise of it in the letters.

sense it is not true, as one historian contends, that Freud "recognized that Romain Rolland's idealism was not sentimental, passive, or mystified" (Fisher, 1988, pp. 8–9). The truth is Freud never took the oceanic hypothesis seriously at all; he took *the man*, the icon, seriously. And again, it is not true not that "Freud's deepest acknowledgment of Romain Rolland was in taking seriously his critical perspective" (Fisher, 1988, p. 9).[4] In a way Freud didn't care about Rolland's "critical perspective," which, like the radical politics, was incidental to Freud. Freud was totally unmoved by Rolland's arguments *qua* arguments; his peace was broken by the *source* of the arguments, by the danger they posed to psychoanalysis as a movement. It was all about authority and right. For this reason William Parsons's "sociological" interpretation of Freud's motives, which see in the late cultural works a reflection of Freudian politics (the "movement"), is a less naive and far more compelling approach (1999, p. 29).

Ultimately it did not matter to Freud that the masses had in fact turned on Rolland for his seemingly traitorous advocacy of peace during and after the First World War (Fisher, 1988, p. 43; Fisher, 1976/1991, p. 39). In 1929, long after the French masses and much of the intelligentsia had blacklisted Rolland, Freud continued to characterize Rolland as one of the "few men from whom their contemporaries do not withhold admiration" (*SE*, 1930/ 1991, p. 64). It was more than enough for Freud that Rolland was a Nobel laureate for his literature *qua* peace activism, and that his fame, or notoriety, only rose in the wake of his uncompromising politics of reconciliation. By contrast, psychoanalysis "cleared away" the illusions that made Rolland a lightning rod for the beautiful sentiments of European brotherhood espoused in *Above the Battle*. As Freud reiterated yet again in a letter to Rolland on May 13, 1926, "Unlike you, I cannot count on the love of many people. I have not pleased, comforted, edified them" (in Parsons, 1999, p. 173).

From Freud's perspective it was no wonder that he himself had been passed over by the Nobel Committee, despite the efforts of influential people like Marie Bonaparte and, indeed, Romain Rolland (Fisher, 1976/ 1991, pp. 63, 71); no wonder that he himself was not universally loved by the masses; and no wonder that he himself was ambivalent about the achievements of his dear friend. Psychoanalysis was deeper, more original, truer than anything Rolland had ever produced, and so more disturbing and less popular, too. That, in essence, was the story Freud told himself and indeed told Rolland. That Rolland put up with it is a testament to his good

---

[4] For more flagrant examples of the misreading and loyalist over-reading of Freud, see Fisher, 1982.

humor, tolerance, and belief in the ideal of reconciliation. However, as we will see in a moment, Rolland was by no means the pushover that Freud first imagined.

2.3 Coarse Methods, Greek Harmony, and the "Function of the Real"

> My European companions, I have made you listen through the Wall, to the blows of the coming one, Asia . . . Go to meet her! She is working for us. We are working for her. Europe and Asia are the two halves of the soul. Man *is not* yet. He *will be*. God is resting and has left to us . . . to free the sleeping forces of the enslaved soul; to reawaken God in man; to recreate the Being itself. R.R. (October 9, 1928)
> (Final words of *The Life of Vivekananda and the Universal Gospel* [Rolland, 1931, p. 366])

Against the backdrop of the disastrous First World War, Rolland turned to Indian thought for a radical alternative to Western rationalism, and in 1924 published his biography of Gandhi. The book was a key moment in the Western recognition of "the Mahatma's" critique of capitalist imperialism and the philosophy of nonviolence (Fisher, 1988, p. 116). It also helped Rolland rethink his own assumptions. "Rolland's Gandhism," Fisher writes, "permitted him to absorb the immediate postwar trauma without despair, cynicism, crackpot realism, or irony and to search for a nonviolent alternative" (1988, p. 144). After the Gandhi book Rolland moved on to a loving biography of two Indian mystics, the Hindu saints Ramakrishna and Vivekananda.

In January 1930 Rolland sent Freud his completed three-part, two-volume "study of mysticism and action in living India." Published in France in 1929 and 1930, *The Life of Ramakrishna* and *The Life of Vivekananda and the Universal Gospel* explore Indian mysticism as a much-needed palliative for the pressing ills of Western civilization. As Parsons puts it, Rolland's thought had evolved from an "unchurched mysticism to the advocacy of a mystical psychology" (1999, p. 57), or again, evolved from a Jungian-inspired, "philosophical-poetic" mysticism to a more sophisticated psychological perennialism (pp. 108–19, 102). Rolland's serious turn to mysticism was part of a wave of interest that began in the nineteenth century and peeked in the 1950s and 1960s, when the teachings of these two gurus would influence a generation of Western readers interested in Eastern thought – including the rise of yoga as a philosophy, meditation, body discipline, and, ultimately, a fashion.

The two books also reveal just how far Rolland was from accepting the findings of psychoanalysis. It is not just that Rolland rejected psychoanalysis as the latest misstep in the history of Western reason. It is also that he quite emphatically rejected the substance of Freud's own interpretations of him as made in their private correspondence. In this sense the *Ramakrishna* and the *Vivekananda* are in part formal responses to Sigmund Freud, just as *Civilization and Its Discontents* is in part a formal response to Romain Rolland. They both began with the correspondence and raised the stakes with major publications.

Freud acknowledged receipt of the *Ramakrishna* and the *Vivekananda* in a letter of January 19, 1930. He also responded to some of Rolland's charges buried within.

What he does not do is send Rolland a copy of *Civilization*, as would be expected, first, because in it he critiques Rolland's idea of the oceanic feeling; second, because he procured Rolland's permission to this end; and third, because Rolland had just sent Freud his own works that take off from the same idea, the oceanic feeling. Freud only sends *Civilization* fifteen months after its original appearance, on March 18, 1931 (Parsons, 1999, p. 222, n. 24), when the second edition duly reveals Rolland's name in a footnote. The delay, uncivil on its face, demands an explanation, and an explanation demands that we turn to Rolland's two works of the late 1920s.

* * *

Rolland opens the *Ramakrishna* with an "Avertissement au lecteur d'Occident" – Notice to My Western Readers – dated Christmas 1928, wherein he declares "the fruit of a new autumn" (1930, p. 14) even as he prods Western thinkers to get with the program. "Of course I soon discovered the section of the book most interesting to me," Freud writes in the letter of January 1930, "the beginning, in which you come to grips with us extreme rationalists" (in Parsons, 1999, p. 176). In the *Ramakrishna*, Rolland refers to those "who are or who believe they are free from all religious belief, but who in reality live immersed in a state of super-rational consciousness" (1930, pp. 5–6) – *un état de conscience suprarationnelle* (1929/1952, p. 14) – "which they term Socialism, Communism, Humanitarianism, Nationalism – or even Rationalism" (1930, p. 6; translation amended with reference to Rolland, 1929, p. 15). Rolland's invocation of the *conscience suprarationnelle* is a subtle intimation of Polichinelle, literally "Punch," the over-rationalistic character from his old play *Liluli*. "Polichinelle, the dialectician of the piece, the rationalist in cap and bells," explains Stefan Zweig, "is reasonable to excess; his laughter is cowardly, being a mask for inaction"

(1921, p. 337). The search for truth, Rolland continues, could even be called "religious": "Scepticism itself when it proceeds from vigorous natures true to the core, when it is an expression of strength and not of weakness, joins in the march of the Grand Army of the religious Soul" (1930, p. 6). Freud takes this generic passage in the book personally, and in his letter responds: "That you call me 'grand' here I have taken quite well; I cannot object to your irony when it is mixed with so much amiability" (in Parsons, 1999, p. 176). But Freud also closes the letter by denying the charge. "Just one more thing: I am not an out-and-out skeptic. Of one thing I am absolutely positive: there are certain things which we cannot know now" (p. 177). Freud says "cannot know *now*" and not, more emphatically or indeed "mystically," "cannot know." Freud most pointedly does not cite Shakespeare's *Hamlet* according to which "There are more things in heaven and earth, Horatio, / Than are dreamt of in your philosophy."

A central theme of the two volumes is Rolland's claim that a new way of thinking must overcome the partiality or narrowness of conventional Western thought. Once again addressing his "European friends," this time in the *Vivekananda*, Rolland claims that "I am not trying to prove to you the truth of a system, which, like all others, being human, is only hypothesis. But what I have shown you is the loftiness [*grandeur*] of the hypothesis, and that . . . in the realm of fact it is not contrary to the most recent findings of modern Western science" (1931, pp. 296–7). Rolland asserts that his "hypothesis" – influenced especially by Brahmin and Hindu thought (Starr, 1971, pp. 203–4) – is not contrary to Western science, since Indian mysticism consciously incorporates scientific findings. Mysticism bridges oppositions in a new unity. As Rolland puts it in the *Vivekananda*: "With science and religion (as Vivekananda understood the word), the foundation is the same, namely, reason; there is no essential difference between them, only a difference in use" (1930/1948, p. 80, sec. 2, vol. 2, my translation; 1931, pp. 274–5).

This "universal gospel" is a reflection of Rolland's belief, expressed to Freud in a letter of July 24, 1929, that he "did not suffer from a conflict between" faith and reason; it is a criticism he forcefully repeats almost two years later in his letter of response to Freud's *Civilization*. Both this letter and the chapter (of the *Vivekananda*) called "The Universal Science-Religion" end on the same note and with the same referent. The sentiment is borrowed from Heraclitus. "The sovereign balance is realized," Rolland exclaims, in "the ideal of the [Bhagavad] *Gîtâ* and of Heraclitus!" (1930/1948, p. 325). Then he invokes Heraclitus in the original Greek: ἐκ τῶν διαφερόντων καλλίστην ἁρμονίαν. The same words close out his letter to Freud, also in Greek, to which he adds, "The great words of Heraclitus that I have made mine" (in Parsons, 1999, p. 176). The message works as a motto for Rolland's philosophical position: "the harmony between opposing forces is that which is the most beautiful" (in Parsons, 1999, p. 176) or, in its more literal rendering, "from differences, best harmony." Rolland's point is that the West and the East must finally come together: "The union of Europe and Asia must be ... the most noble task of mankind" (in Starr, 1971, p. 200).

Like many intellectuals of the time, Freud does not get, or does not accept, Rolland's message of harmony and synthesis – Greek or otherwise. In his copy of *Civilization* sent to Rolland in March 1931, he inscribes a playful greeting that reaffirms the essential difference between rationalist and mystic, land dweller and ocean dweller: "The Landtier to his great Oceanic Friend," *Seinem Grossen, ozeanischen Freund, das Landier* (in Fisher, 1976/1991, p. 40). Rolland sends a response on May 3, 1931, on the occasion of Freud's seventy-fifth birthday (May 6). After thanking Freud for associating his name with *Civilization*, Rolland takes the opportunity to address the inscription as a way of addressing their differences once more:

> Your kind dedication juxtaposes with an affectionate irony, the "Landtier" with the "Oceanic" friend. This opposition does not materialize, (not) only between two men, but neither in one man, in me. I am also a *Landtier* from the French countryside, from the core of old France, who seems best protected from the ocean breezes! And I am also an old Frenchman who is able to see through illusions, who is able to bear life without them, who no longer needs them. (in Parsons, 1999, p. 177)

As in his letter of December 5, 1927, Rolland continues to remind Freud that he too contests illusions. One of the greatest illusions, Rolland claims, is the artificial separation of reason and mysticism, land dweller and ocean dweller. As he says in *The Life of Ramakrishna*, "In our days an absurd separation has been made between these two halves of the soul, and it is presumed that they are incompatible. The only incompatibility lies in the narrowness of view, which those who erroneously claim to be their repre-sentative, share in common" (1930, p. 4).

Rolland continues his letter:

> If you would allow me, for documentary purposes, to expound upon the psychological curiosity in my case, I distinguish very clearly in myself:
> (1)   what I *feel*;
> (2)   what I *know*;
> (3)   what I *desire*.

What I *feel*, I have told you [on May 5, 1927], and I have explained it in
the introduction to the *Ramakrishna*: it is the *Oceanic*. What I *know*, it is
the: "What do I know?" of Montaigne. And what I *desire* is: *Nothing* . . .
(Nothing, *for me*). As for others, may their desires be fulfilled! (in Parsons,
1999, p. 177)

That Rolland feels compelled to correct the record – for "documentary
purposes" – is telling. Rolland is clearly aware of the risk he took in sending
Freud his ideas about the oceanic feeling. Recall that Rolland had already,
as a defensive strategy, guessed at Freud's likely diagnosis: the oceanic
hypothesis betrays a *Zwangsneurosen*, an obsessive compulsive disorder.
He was also careful to say that "this 'oceanic' feeling has nothing to do with
my personal aspirations" (in Vermorel & Vermorel, 1993, p. 304). It would
therefore seem that Rolland was prepared for the interpretations he found
in chapter one of *Civilization*. And so Rolland, seemingly nonplussed,
responds with good humor. He reaffirms the feeling of eternity associated
with the oceanic feeling; praises the knowledge of skepticism contained in
Montaigne's famous refrain, *Que sais-je?*;[5] aligns his desire with Eastern
precepts and the nascent existentialism appropriate to his age; and leavens
it all with his characteristic regard for the aspirations of other people. A few
sentences later he adds: "I am therefore telling you that my feeling . . . is
absolutely disinterested! I state it, but I am not particular about it. It (the
feeling) is a psychological fact, a vital trait of my character" (in Parsons,
1999, p. 178). Rolland is repeating himself. In his letter of 1927 on the
oceanic feeling he already states that the feeling is "a fact. It is a *contact*"
(p. 174).

According to Rolland, good analysis begins with an acknowledgment of
this "psychological fact." As he says in the *Ramakrishna*, "The first
qualification for knowing, judging, and if desirable condemning a religion
or religions, is to have made experiments for oneself in the fact of religious
consciousness" (1930, p. 5). Or as he says in the *Vivekananda*, "each person
comes back in the last resort to this argument: 'I feel that it is so. Do you
not feel the same?'" (1931, p. 295). Rolland's response: "Yes, I do." It is at
this point, precisely, that Rolland adds a footnote calling for a "new science
of the mind": "How is it possible to estimate the value of such [mystical]
experiences [found cross-culturally and across history]? Perhaps by a new
science of the mind, armed with a more supple, and finer instrument of

---

[5] To Max Eastman in late 1919, Rolland writes, "I am not a believer in a faith, religious or Marxist. I am
from Montaigne's country that doubts eternally but that searches eternally. I search for the truth.
I will never reach it" (in Fisher, 1988, p. 71).

analysis than the incomplete and coarse [*grossières*] methods of psycho-analysis and its derivatives" (1931, p. 295, n. 1; translation adjusted).[6]

In the letter, as in the two volumes, Rolland adds that others have confirmed his observations of the "invisible forces that act in secret when they are not made manifest by explosions in broad daylight," forces that "go as far back as I can drive my borer into the past centuries of Europe and Asia" (in Parsons, 1999, p. 178). Clearly Freud is not the only one who can play the origins game and plunder, as Rolland says, "my subterranean city, my Herculaneum, sleeping under its lava" (1930, p. 11). The big difference is that Rolland plays the game with two great civilizations, while Freud sticks with only one.

In closing the letter, Rolland makes a curious but important distinction, one that is meant to underscore the partiality, indeed absurdity, of Freud's self-conception as rationalistic land dweller. Rolland claims that the "existence" of the invisible forces, such as the oceanic feeling, "does not establish . . . their *truth*. It only establishes their *reality*." It is a distinction Rolland learned from Vivekananda, namely, between the metaphysical and the physical, the internal and the external. "Religion deals with the truths of the metaphysical world," Vivekananda says, "just as chemistry and the other natural sciences deal with the truths of the physical world" (1931, pp. 275–6). The implication is that Freud's rationalistic concern for external truth – the truth of the external world – comes at the expense of the lived reality of internal truth, which is essentially a mystical experience. Rolland already said as much in the *Ramakrishna*: "The confusion created by our rationalists between the outward expression and the power of thought seems to me as illusory as the confusion common to the religions of past ages of identifying magic powers with the words, the syllables, or the letters whereby they are expressed" (1930, p. 5). As Rolland therefore warns Freud in the letter, "It would be dangerous for the philosopher and man of action to ignore [the invisible forces]." Between the lines of his apparent goodwill, Rolland is perfectly able to match Freud's condescension with his own.

---

[6] Among other infelicities, the English translator of Rolland's two volumes, Elizabeth Frances Malcolm-Smith, botches things by inflating Rolland's rhetoric against psychoanalysis. For example, in *The Life of Ramakrishna*, she has Rolland say: "Let the learned men of Europe, who are preoccupied by *the problem of mystic psychoanalysis*, put themselves in touch with these living witnesses [Indian Gurus] while there is yet time" (1930, p. 246, n. 1; my emphasis). Rolland actually writes about "ces problèmes de *psycho physiologique mystique*," the problem of psycho-physicalistic mysticism (1929/1952, p. 226; my emphasis). This error has since been repeated throughout the secondary literature. When necessary, I have simply provided alternative translations.

Rolland's most explicit and sustained discussion of the "coarse methods" of psychoanalysis appears in an appendices to *The Life of Vivekananda and the Universal Gospel.* Unfortunately, "Concerning Mystic Introversion and Its Scientific Value for the Knowledge of the Real" betrays a limited understanding of the history of psychoanalysis – or is intentionally and mischievously lax in its command of detail. Relying heavily on Ferdinand Morel's book of 1918, *Essay on Mystic Introversion*, Rolland rather egregiously refers to "the psychoanalysis of Freud, Janet, Jung, Bleuler, etc." (1931, p. 384).[7] But what Rolland lacks in accuracy he makes up for in vigor. He is also rightly focused on an issue that consumes the later Freud, and that informs the thinking of chapter one of *Civilization*: the question of the external world.

According to Rolland, the problem with the current science of the mind is that it denigrates, according to a hierarchy, the "whole realm of mind" (p. 385) associated with "'religious' spirit" (p. 384). Such scientists are often "lacking in every kind of 'religious' inclination, and so are ill-equipped for the study, and involuntarily prone to depreciate [*déprécier*] an inner sense that they do not themselves possess" (p. 384). The result is an overvaluation of reason, a recent acquisition, and a concurrent under-valuation of religion, an ancient acquisition. "Freud, with customary energy," writes Rolland, "asserts that reverie and all that emerges from it is nothing but the debris of the first stage of evolution" (p. 386). From the scientific mind-set, an appeal to religious sentiment is therefore interpreted as "a retrogression in a backward sense, a fall of the mind" (p. 386), or, similarly, a "return to a primary stage, to an intra-uterine state" (p. 389). In effect, the oceanic feeling betrays a fundamental "introversion," Ferenczi's "thalassal regression" to the maternal womb (Ferenczi, 1924/1968, pp. 20, 73–80).

A few pages later Rolland complains that "The mistrust shown by some masters of psychoanalysis toward the free natural play of the spirit, which enjoys its possession of itself – and the stigma [*la flétrissure*] they heap on this play, calling it 'narcissism' and 'autoeroticism' – shows, without their knowing it, a kind of backwards asceticism and religious renunciation" (Rolland, 1930/1948, p. 209; my translation). This is a remarkable passage.

---

[7] Morel studied philosophy in Paris and Geneva, and in 1918 earned a PhD in philosophy for his *Essay on Mystic Introversion* at the University of Geneva (Tsai, 1968, pp. 105–6). In 1921, increasingly dissatisfied with what he had learned from Jung and Freud, Morel turned to the rigors of medicine and, in 1929, became a medical doctor; a decade later he was a professor of psychiatry at the university. As Tsai rightly surmises, the direction of Morel's career "was the opposite" of that of Freud's (p. 107). See Silberer's review (1922b, pp. 121–3).

For in it Rolland anticipates exactly Freud's diagnosis of narcissism in *Civilization and Its Discontents*, and takes steps to contest it *in advance*. Unlike Freud, however, Rolland doesn't bother to hide the identity of the major representative of the introversion interpretation; Rolland imputes it all to Freud and psychoanalysis.

Freud responds to Rolland's charges in a letter acknowledging receipt of the *Ramakrishna* and the *Vivekananda*. His tone is remarkably restrained. He begins by correcting only one aspect of Rolland's misunderstanding of psychoanalysis. "Concerning the criticism of psychoanalysis," Freud begins, "you will permit me a few remarks: the distinction between *extrovert* and *introvert* derives from C. G. Jung, who is a bit of a mystic himself and hasn't belonged to us for years. We don't attach any great importance to the distinction and are well aware that people can be both at the same time, and usually are" (in Parsons, 1999, p. 176; emphasis in original). As we will see later, Jung used the terms extroversion and introversion to describe the different temperaments of Stekel and Freud, respectively. So it is certainly true – Freud didn't much appreciate those terms. But when Rolland speaks of introversion he is just referring to the turning inward that begins with introspection. So it is not actually a new idea to the author of the *Dream Book*. Moreover, Freud's concept of "regression" covers some of the same territory as introversion. Consider "Thoughts for the Times on War and Death," where Freud discusses how the impact of war undermines the civility of both states and individuals. He argues that war strips away the illusions that fool us into thinking the state and individual had ever truly surpassed a stage of incivility. "Bedazzled" by war, regression or involution (used interchangeably) takes us back to primitive states of mental development. "The essence of mental diseases," Freud insists, "lies in a return to earlier states of affective life and of functioning" (*SE*, 1915/1991, p. 286).

One implication is pretty clear: Rolland's version of oceanic oneness is just like the many other pathological reactions to the war, namely, a regression to a primitive, pathological state of mind. In other words, Freud's opening invocation of Rolland as moralist and lover of humankind was indeed a subtle, ironic recourse to abnormal psychology and psycho-pathology. As Freud put it in the essay of 1915, "most of our sentimentalist, friends of humanity and protectors of animals have been evolved from little sadists and animal-tormentors" (p. 282). It is a view he repeats later on in *Civilization* – to which we will return in a moment.

In his letter Freud does not correct Rolland's impression that Janet and Bleuler are psychoanalysts. Janet, a French philosopher and physician known for work on hypnotism and subconscious mental processes, was a famous competitor with Freud in the field of psychopathology and was openly critical of psychoanalysis (publishing a critique in 1911). Bleuler, a well-regarded Swiss psychiatrist known for his work on schizophrenia, introduced Jung to psychoanalysis and was involved in institution-building in Zurich, but became openly skeptical of psychoanalysis by 1911–13 – the same period that Jung broke from Freud and psychoanalysis. Nor does Freud bother contesting Rolland's depiction, at one point, of the priority issue as running "Janet, Freud, et leur '*succédanés*'" (1930/1948, p. 201; 1931, p. 386), their "substitutes." Freud was very sensitive about such things and would not have failed to notice the mistake – or to think it was innocent. And perhaps it wasn't. Rolland lived in French Switzerland, knew some members of the Swiss contingent of psychoanalysis, such as Charles Baudouin, and appears to have read the psychoanalytic investigations of Swiss researchers such as Ferdinand Morel and Alphonse Maeder (Parsons, 1999, pp. 33, 65). Rolland would have had at least passing familiarity with Jung's work and, no doubt, would have known something about the debates between rival theorists such as Pierre Janet.

Freud's letter moves on to the delicate issue of his diagnosis of Rolland's narcissism. "Our terms such as regression, narcissism, pleasure principle are of a purely descriptive nature," Freud assures him, "and don't carry within themselves any valuation" (in Parsons, 1999, p. 176). "Even reflecting is a regressive process without losing any of its dignity or importance in being so" (p. 177). The truth is, however, that psychoanalysis does depreciate or disparage, *déprécier*, all forms of mental activity, and to that extent no one gets away undiagnosed. That is the crux of Freud's late Romanticism, which Rolland, a guarded optimist, clearly rejects.

Next Freud deals a bit more carefully with the question of valuation. "Finally, psychoanalysis also has its scale of values," Freud says, changing tack, "but its sole aim is the enhanced harmony of the ego, which is expected successfully to mediate between the claims of the instinctual life (the 'id') and those of the external world; thus between inner and outer reality" (p. 177). Freud, too, is concerned with harmony. But the harmony psychoanalysis seeks has nothing to do with mysticism (or, by extension, a politics of reconciliation). An inner life unmoored by contact with reality is a delusional, pathological life; reality provides the many objects against which we can (and must, as realists) test the truth of our innermost thoughts. Or again, introversion without reality testing is delusion.

Rolland had a very different understanding of the right balance between inner and outer realities, spirit or mind and external world. In his very early reflections on Spinoza, Rolland contested altogether the existence of the external world, which he reduced to a kind of illusion (see Starr, 1971, p. 211). And this tendency is still at work in "Concerning Mystic Introversion and Its Scientific Value for a Knowledge of the Real." For example, Rolland contends that Western science presumes that the "supreme function of the mind" is caught up with assessing something Janet calls "la fonction du réel" (in Rolland, 1930/1948, p. 201), "the function of the real" (1931, p. 386). This presumed equivalency between mind/reality is critical to Rolland's critique of science as partial and unbalanced.

We also know what Freud thought: the religious worldview cannot tell us anything about the external world. Freud repeats this claim from *The Future of an Illusion* in his letter in response to the *Ramakrishna* and the *Vivekananda*. "We seem to diverge rather far," Freud writes, "in the role we assign to intuition. Your mystics rely on it to teach them how to solve the riddle of the universe; we believe that it cannot reveal to us anything but primitive, instinctual impulses and attitudes – highly valuable for an embryology of the soul when correctly interpreted, but worthless for orientation in the alien, external world" (in Parsons, 1999, p. 177). Freud repeats himself in a formal declaration in the *New Introductory Lectures*, written in 1932. According to Freud, science "asserts that there are no sources of knowledge of the universe other than the intellectual working-over of carefully scrutinized observations – in other words, what we call research – and alongside of it no knowledge derived from revelation, intuition, or divination" (*SE*, 1933a/1991, p. 159). "Intuition and divination," Freud continues, "may safely be reckoned as illusions, the fulfillments of wishful impulses." For the late Freud introspection is *not* a potential source of knowledge about "reality." In this sense Rolland, like Pfister before him, is right to be concerned about the rationalism of Freud's late works: dogmatic recourse to the "function of the real," an idea from Janet that Freud explicitly invokes in his early work (see Ellenberger, 1970, p. 407), renders intuition and inner feeling utterly worthless for science.

Rolland may have picked up Freud's commitment to objective reality from reading the *Future* in late 1927; it is certainly not typical of Freud's earlier works. In any case he contests Freud's rationalism in strong terms in "Concerning Mystic Introversion":

> If a scientist maintains that such a knowledge of psychic profundities teaches us nothing about exterior realities, he is really, though perhaps unwittingly,

obeying a prejudice of proud incomprehension as one-eyed as that of religious spiritualists who set up an insurmountable barrier between spirit and matter. What is the "function of the real" of which scientific psychology claims to be the standard-bearer? And what is the "real"? . . . There are not two realities. That which exists in one exists equally in the other. The laws of the inner psychic substance are of necessity themselves of outside reality. And if you succeed in reading one properly, the chances are that you will find the confirmation and if not, the presentiment of what you have read or will read in the other. (1931, pp. 392–3)

We are back to Heraclitus: "from differences, best harmony." As Rolland states toward the end of "Concerning Mystic Introversion," "I maintain that the principle whereby we ought to attempt to satisfy the operations of the mind is that of proportion, of equilibrium between the diverse forces of the mind" (p. 396). Or as Ramakrishna teaches, "You must be all-sided" (in Rolland, 1930, p. 82). Rolland was surely frustrated that the wisdom of harmony, unity, synthesis, reconciliation, and oceanic feeling (see Fisher, 1988, p. 12) found in ancient Greek thought had been thoroughly misunderstood or forgotten by educated Westerners. By contrast, Indian mystics were far more open-minded and ecumenical than "extreme rationalists" like Freud.

The key to a "new science of the mind" is therefore well at hand. "The judicious use of deep introspection opens to the scientist unexplored resources," Rolland says, "for it constitutes a new method of experiment, having the advantage that the observer identifies himself with the object observed" (1931, p. 393). Hence the primacy of religious sentiment, including the "psychological fact" that Rolland calls the "oceanic feeling," or again, "*the feeling of the 'eternal'*" (in Parsons, 1999, p. 173). For Rolland, it is crucial that the West rediscover this power, not of regression, with its negative valuations, but of an "active and creative" introversion (1931, p. 397). From the perspective of the interwar period, the very survival of the human species depends on it. As for the "extroverts" and rationalists, if they continued on their narrow and close-minded path then there isn't "much hope for the future. Their gigantic technical knowledge, far from being a source of protection, will bring about their annihilation" (p. 397). Of course the idealist in Rolland cannot leave his reader with such a foreboding, pessimistic despair for the future. Rolland is not Freud. Instead he imagines that the positive forces of introversion will right the imbalance – and the West will be saved. Rolland's final, consoling words: "Mais je ne suis pas inquiet. Les même sources dorment au fond de l'âme d'Occident. A l'avant-dernière heure, elles ressurgiront" (1930/1948, p. 211);

"But I'm not worried. The same [positive] sources are sleeping in the depths of the Western soul. At the last minute they will resurface."

Freud also knew his Greek and would cite approvingly the thought of Empedocles and Heraclitus. And like Rolland, he was a committed dualist. Unlike Rolland, however, he did not believe in a synthesizing moment above and beyond the interminable dualism of opposites. Life, like analysis, was conflictual, interminable – and tragically so. Yet the dualism of life and death drives still allowed Freud to end *Civilization and Its Discontents* on an uncharacteristically upbeat note. The first edition ends as follows: "And now it is to be expected that the other of the two 'Heavenly Powers', eternal Eros, will make an effort to assert himself in the struggle with his equally immortal adversary [the death drive, Thanatos]" (*SE*, 1930/1991, p. 145). Unfortunately things had changed in the nearly two years that Freud had written those lines. With the rise of National Socialism things were decidedly worse. Freud had also had a chance to read Rolland's final lines from the *Vivekananda*. So in the second edition of *Civilization* Freud takes the opportunity to amend his closing optimism, which must have struck him in 1931 as another precious but hopelessly "Rollandian" illusion. To the old conclusion, *fort*, he adds another, *da*. "But who can foresee," Freud writes of the promised Eros, "with what success and with what result?" The pessimistic ending effectively doubles as a warning to readers, including (perhaps most especially) to his friend Rolland – who of course only received the second, chastened edition. And so the optimism of the *Vivekananda* is met with a dose of reality, namely, a recognition of the innate death drive and its derivative, the aggressive drive. Events in the real world would quickly reveal which thinker was better equipped to predict the future – and which thinker was the better "realist" about human nature.

So how does Freud respond to Rolland's long letter about *Civilization* and, along with it, the private details that elaborate, "for documentary purposes," upon Rolland's own psychology? He doesn't take the bait. Freud dutifully thanks Rolland for "the most precious information about your own person," and concludes with a touching tribute that in some way harkens back to his early letters. "Approaching life's inevitable end, reminded of it by yet another operation [for cancer of the jaw] and aware that I am unlikely to see you again, I may confess to you that I have rarely experienced that mysterious attraction [*die geheimnisvolle Anziehung*] of one human being for another as vividly as I have with you; it is bound up, perhaps, with the awareness of being so different" (Freud, 1960b, p. 406; Freud, 1960a, p. 424). With Freud's final "Farewell!," *Leben Sie Wohl!*,

"Live Well!," the correspondence is brought to an end. The epistolary transference is over.

* * *

Let's summarize what we have learned. Chapter one of *Civilization* tries to "clear away" Rolland's alternative theory of the origin of religion – ironically, just as the baby narcissist clears away unpleasant sensations that interfere with its happiness. But *The Life of Ramakrishna, The Life of Vivekananda and the Universal Gospel*, and Rolland's letter of May 3, 1931, make it perfectly clear that Freud did not get the last word; he certainly did not get the sweet satisfaction, the happiness, of converting his famous interlocutor to psychoanalysis. On the contrary. Their debate, and consequently the "mysterious attraction," was at an impasse well before 1931 when Freud finally – no doubt hesitantly – sent along the second edition of *Civilization and Its Discontents*. It could not have been easy for Freud to ignore Rolland's characterization of psychoanalysis as a "coarse method" – ignorant of the facts, arrogant in its condemnation, narrow in its argumentation – that devalued what it could not understand, religious sentiment. Or Rolland's attack on Freud's impaired sense of reality, purportedly built on a form of extreme rationalism that was itself "religious" – an illusion. Rolland had confirmed Pfister's critique of Freud's illusory form of rationalism, but this time the criticism issued from outside psychoanalysis – out in an external world of facts, truth, and science. In short, Rolland had become a critic and as such could do serious damage to the cause.

By the end of 1931 Freud's relationship with Rolland only confirmed everything he knew to be true about civilization and its discontents: *Homo homini lupus*, "man is a wolf to man" (*SE*, 1930/1991, p. 111), a remark Freud lifted from Hobbes. As always the uncanny truths of psychoanalysis were best demonstrated by the experiences of psychoanalysis itself, the inside always reflecting back exactly what it expected of the outside. As a critic Rolland was a piece of external reality that argued on behalf of mystical intuition and "deep introspection" – a position that casual readers will attribute to Freud himself. But Rolland's thought doesn't fit with Freud's views of the late period, which is determined by an ego psychology under the sway of *Beyond the Pleasure Principle*, and so must be cleared away. Ultimately Freud is obliged, out of love for psychoanalysis and respect for his correspondent, to accept a friendship based on irreconcilable differences.

Consequently Freud's failure to send Rolland a copy of *Civilization and Its Discontents* when it was first published makes perfect sense. It is not just because Rolland vigorously *defends* himself from the charge of narcissism even before Freud rushed chapter one into print in his journal, *The Psychoanalytic Movement*, in late 1929.[8] It is also because Rolland vigorously *attacks* Freud and psychoanalysis. Freud had once again misjudged his interlocutor, as he did at the beginning of their epistolary exchange, and received a stern rebuke in response. Recall that in 1923 Rolland simply responded to criticism by sending Freud his *Liluli* with an ironical inscription "To Freud, Destroyer of Illusions." By the late 1920s Rolland couldn't afford to be subtle, since Freud didn't get or accept the message. Moreover, Rolland obviously understood that Freud would use his confession of the "oceanic feeling" against him, and even guessed at the correct diagnosis, narcissism. Imagine Freud's shock when he received the *Ramakrishna* and the *Vivekananda*: Rolland, the lover of humanity, may have hoped for peace but he prepared for war.

The truth is Rolland was never a naive idealist. His well-known *bon mot*, delivered in a review of a novel by Raymond Lefebvre, was "pessimism of the intelligence, optimism of the will" (in Fisher, 1988, pp. 7, 88–9, 299–302). It is a characteristic that David Fisher quite rightly calls "pessimistic idealism" (p. 21). So of course Freud held off sending a copy of *Civilization*, which would only confirm everything Rolland had guessed about the "coarse methods" of psychoanalysis. As for Freud's silence in the face of Rolland's published criticism, it is not just a feature of an epistolary transference having run its course. It is the *détente* that followed their open declarations of hostility in their works of the late 1920s.

2.4   "Battle of the Giants": Death and the "Fatal Inevitability" of Guilt

The oceanic feeling persists long after Freud stops discussing it in *Civilization and Its Discontents*. It is therefore necessary to turn a page on chapter one to confront those later chapters where Freud introduces his keystone insight concerning the development of civilization, the origin of the sense of guilt, and its metapsychological rationalization, the death drive theory. For there we find death and guilt more than a match for oceanic feeling, love, and group cohesion.

---

[8] On December 30, 1929, Rolland says in a letter to Stefan Zweig that he was the "unnamed friend" in chapter one (in Fisher, 1976/1991, p. 53). It is possible that Rolland read the chapter in *The Psychoanalytic Movement*; or read it in *Civilization and Its Discontents*; or didn't read it at all and just passed along information to Zweig that he gleaned from Freud's letters. It seems the only certainty is that Freud himself did not send him a copy of the first edition in late 1929.

The secondary literature is hardly aware of the role that death and guilt play in Freud's overall rejection of the oceanic hypothesis. Everyone understands that Freud undercut Rolland's alternative hypothesis about the true foundation of religion by rendering it pathologically narcissistic. Freud insisted that the turn to the oceanic is actually a return, a regression to a womb-like merging with Mommy, an idea Ferenczi introduced (with Freud's enthusiastic blessing) to psychoanalysis in *Thalassa: A Theory of Genitality* (1924). But Freud does not stop with a diagnosis of narcissism. Indeed, the raison d'être of chapter one is to clear Rolland's hypothesis away and make room for what is properly psychoanalytic. That is why Freud spends considerable effort, however botched, trying to establish the legitimacy of his claim that there must exist alongside the derivative affect (the oceanic feeling) a truth that is older than and independent of narcissistic union with Mommy.

Everyone also understands that what is supposedly older than and independent of the oceanic feeling is fear of Daddy and his substitute, fear of Fate. Daddy comes before Mommy, always. But lest we get carried away with a necessary but oversimplified critique of Freud's dated misogyny, it must at once be observed that Freud doesn't care too much about Daddy either – at least not from the perspective of his metapsychology. In this context gender is a means to an end that exceeds questions about patriarchy. For what is truly older than and independent of gender difference, oceanic feeling, and the pleasure principle – in short, what is older than and independent of psychoanalysis – is precisely the fundamental metapsychological discovery of Freud's late works: the anti-cultural, radically amoral death drive. Let's turn to it now as it functions in *Civilization and Its Discontents* and sketch an answer to the question that animates much of Freud's discussion: Why are individuals discontented with civilization?

After publishing chapter one of *Civilization* in the November–December issue of *The Psychoanalytic Movement*, about one month ahead of the book itself, Freud does the same with chapter five: it appears in the January–February issue of the same journal. Thus does Freud hive off and orphan a second chapter in the book, which is just as prefatory and disposable as chapter one. Chapter five bridges Freud's myriad discussions of the previous chapters – happiness, sublimation, group psychology, technology, beauty, justice, work, family, prehistory, and more besides – with the death drive theory that is finally introduced in chapter six proper. And so while the first half of chapter five is taken up with a discussion of Christian love, a theme that harkens back to Oskar Pfister and *The Future of an Illusion*, the second half explores what Freud calls the innate "inclination to aggression," *Aggressionsneigung* (*SE*, 1930/1991, p. 112; *GW*, 1948b/1991, p. 471).

> The existence of this inclination to aggression, which we can detect in ourselves and justly assume to be present in others, is the factor which disturbs our relations with our neighbour [about whom Christianity asks us to "love as we love ourselves"] and which forces civilization into such a high expenditure [of energy]. In consequence of this primary mutual hostility of human beings, civilized society is perpetually threatened with disintegration [*vom Zerfall*].

It is in this context that Freud contests the communists for believing that property ownership under the conditions of industrial capitalism is to blame for this "primary mutual hostility" (*SE*, 1930/1991, pp. 112–13). Freud writes: "I am able to recognize that the psychological premises on which the [Communist] system is based are an untenable illusion" (p. 113). He repeats himself in more general terms in his 1933 response to Einstein, "Why War?" "The Russian Communists," Freud says, "hope to be able to cause human aggressiveness to disappear by guaranteeing the satisfaction of all material needs and by establishing equality in other respects among all members of the community. That, in my opinion, is an illusion" (*SE*, 1933b/1991, pp. 211–12). Freud insists that aggressivity is older than property ownership, showing itself "in the nursery almost before property has given up its primal, anal form" (*SE*, 1930/1991, p. 113). For Freud, of course, psychology is older and more fundamental than economics; economics is a derivative effect of psychology and, in the case of communism, the realistic measure of its mistaken view of human nature. And so, trapped between the rock of a repressed sexuality and the hard place of innate and primary hostility, Freud gives slim odds for revolutionary escape from individual unhappiness in civilization.

All of which brings Freud to his "turn," *Wendung*, to the death drive in chapter six. Freud provides a quick genealogy of the death drive, the effect of which is to reaffirm explicitly the conclusion that he already drew in chapter five. "In all that follows," Freud writes, "I adopt the standpoint, therefore, that the inclination to aggression is an original, self-subsisting instinctual disposition in man, and I return to my view [expressed in chapter five] that it constitutes the greatest impediment to civilization" (p. 122). The truth is Freud doesn't add much to this conclusion in the remaining chapters, where it is repeated and unpacked again and again. The life drive builds up, gathers, binds, and unifies, while the death drive tears down, destroys, negates, and scatters. The two forces, Freud says grandly, share "world-dominion," *Weltherrschaft* (p. 122; *GW*, 1948b/1991, p. 481). His conclusion echoes his private remarks about the life and death drive accounting for "all the riddles of life":

> And now, I think, the meaning of the evolution of civilization is no longer obscure to us. It must present the struggle between Eros and Death, between the instinct of life and the instinct of destruction, as it works itself out in the human species. This struggle is what all life essentially consists of, and the evolution of civilization may therefore be simply described as the struggle for life of the human species. And it is this battle of the giants that our nurse-maids try to appease with their "lullaby about Heaven"! (*SE*, 1930/1991, p. 122; adjusted slightly, with reference to *GW*, 1948b/1991, p. 481)

Freud claims that the "battle of the giants," this struggle of Eros and Death (*Eros und Tod*),[9] is precisely what we mean by "life," a tragic conclusion that effectively demotes one of the giants, Eros, to junior status in the partnership. For the life struggle is always waged under the influence of something older than and independent of love. As Freud already claimed in "Instincts and Their Vicissitudes" (1915), "hate, as a relation to objects, is older than love" (*SE*, 1915/1991, p. 139). Or as he put it in "Thoughts for the Times on War and Death" from the same year, "everyone owes nature a death and must expect to pay that debt" (*SE*, 1915/1991, p. 288). This quip, inspired by Shakespeare's *Henry IV* – "Thou owest God a death" – gets to the heart of Freudian metapsychology. Psychoanalysis, the interpretation of sexual life, must bow before metapsychology, the interpretation of Death.

But, again, this discussion of drive theory is old news – and Freud, passing time on his summer vacation, knows it. At best it is, as Freud says, "a matter of bringing into sharper focus a turn of thought arrived at long ago and of following out its consequences" (*SE*, 1930/1991, p. 117). At worst it is simply redundant, repetition for the sake of repetition. It is perhaps not surprising, then, that work on the theory of the drives has "felt its way the most painfully forward," *mühseligsten vorwärts getastet*, that is to say, it has "laboriously groped forward" (*GW*, 1948b/1991, p. 476). Such is Freud's subtle irony: one "limps forward," as he says at the close of *Beyond the Pleasure Principle* (*SE*, 1920a/1991, p. 64), but in the service of an idea of Death and regression that makes a mockery out of evolutionary progress or forward motion. Progress in this area is therefore painful, always in the

---

[9] Only in this passage does Strachey capitalize the word "Death," which I will do without comment in later passages.

service of Death, since anything pleasurable, purposeful, and confident would by definition have missed its mark. That said, Freud does try to shift gears and nudge his treatise on human happiness forward. It is to this eventuality that he finally turns in chapter seven of *Civilization and Its Discontents*, the most conceptually adventurous and difficult of the entire book. This is the moment Freud finally examines the relationship between the death drive, guilt, conscience, and the superego.

* * *

> I wrote the book [*Civilization*] with purely analytic intentions, based on my former existence as an analytic writer, in brooding contemplation, concerned to promote the concept of the feeling of guilt to its very end.
>
> (Freud to Max Eitingon; Freud, 1992, p. 62)

Chapter eight begins with an apology. "The author," Freud writes at the outset, "must ask his readers' forgiveness for not having been a more skillful guide and for not having spared them empty stretches of road and trouble-some *détours*" (*SE*, 1930/1991, p. 134). This isn't mere irony. As interesting as it is, *Civilization and Its Discontents* is not very well composed – perhaps on account of its painful labor. "There is no doubt," Freud continues, "that it could have been done better." Even so, Freud is clearly not willing to edit or otherwise improve the work. Instead he offers atonement to the reader: "I will attempt, late in the day, to make some amends [*etwas gutzuma-chen*]." Chapter eight, the last of the book, is that atonement. Its content is the purposeful repetition of what just came before it – chapter seven.

Freud's guilt, or more precisely his guilty paranoia, is focused on the theory of guilt introduced in chapter seven. In other words the "sense of guilt" is performed, and therefore confirmed, by the author's own admis-sion of guilt. "In the first place," Freud conjectures, "I suspect the reader has the impression that our discussions on the sense of guilt disrupt the framework of this essay: that they take up too much space, so that the rest of its subject-matter, with which they are not always closely connected, is pushed to one side." Of course, for guilt to have disrupted the "framework" of *Civilization* – Freud says *Rahmen*, the "frame" or "scope" – means that it must indeed have a frame. But if it has a frame, then the opening apology about "empty stretches and troublesome *détours*" is either gratuitous or disingenuous. The same point holds for his invocation, not just of a "frame," but of an "essay" or "article," *Aufsatzes*, as though a freewheeling discussion of multiple themes across eight chapters, two of which are published separately, still counts as one essay or even three. For now, though, let's bracket this concern and move on. Freud is not done. Having invoked the "framework of this essay," he goes on to assert a claim about its "structure," *Aufbau*, its construction: "This [discussion of guilt] may have spoilt the structure of my paper," Freud writes, "but it corresponds faithfully to my intention to represent the sense of guilt as the most important problem in the development of civilization and to show that the price we pay for our advance in civilization is a loss of happiness through the heightening of the sense of guilt" (*SE*, 1930/1991, p. 134). The structure is spoiled, but not without an important gain. In place of a compromised structure, Freud is finally able to reveal the intent of *Civilization and Its Discontents*: it aims to demonstrate that guilt is "the most important problem in the development of civilization."

If readers are perhaps irritated with Freud's circuitous, cumbersome, and tedious discussions, *beschwerlicher Umwege*, or are baffled by the long diversion about guilt in chapter seven, then chapter eight promises to set us straight. The scattershot essay has lost its structure but gained a thesis; to that extent both the framework and the painful labor have been salvaged, along with the reader's trust. But note that Freud has delayed providing the single best rationale for *Civilization* until the book (essay, article, treatise, freewheeling exploration, or whatever it should be called) is nearly complete – just as he did in *The Future of an Illusion*. In short, the security of knowing exactly where we are going has once more been strangely suspended; swapped out, perhaps, for the pleasure of playful wandering. That said, the declaration of a thesis so late in the work has all the hallmarks of an ad hoc declaration.

What demands clarification and atonement, but also elevation by declaring a thesis, is chapter seven. As in chapter one, Freud is concerned to establish a psychoanalytic origin, in this case the origin of the sense of guilt and, by extension, its role in the origin of civilization. Freud teaches that guilt arises in response to human aggression, which is a biological given. The deployment of guilt, Freud says, is "the most important" method employed by civilization against the "primary mutual hostility" of individuals (*SE*, 1930/1991, p. 123). The next point he makes is somehow both "very remarkable," *sehr Merkwürdiges*, curious, and "quite obvious," *naheliegt*, natural:

> What happens in him [the hostile individual] to render his desire for aggression innocuous? Something very remarkable, which we should never have guessed and which is nevertheless quite obvious. His aggression is introjected, internalized; it is, in point of fact, sent back to where it came from – that is, it is directed towards his own ego. (p. 123)

Aggression sent away, *fort*, becomes aggression brought back, *da*. It has returned. A part of the ego is thereupon hived off to form the superego, the "over-I," which is "ready to put into action against the ego the same harsh aggressiveness that the ego would have liked to satisfy upon other, extraneous individuals" (p. 123). Curiously, instead of turning on others one turns on one's own self. Freud characterizes the shift as "natural," presumably because it's a biological given, i.e., it comes before culture.

As for the "sense of guilt," it is a by-product of friction between ego and superego. Civilization, Freud says, has set up "an agency within" the ego to police aggression, "like a garrison in a conquered city" (p. 124). At the same time, Freud claims that this friction or conflict is not quite the *origin* of the sense of guilt. To this lattermost end Freud invokes a now well-worn claim of psychoanalysis: guilt is not only derived from wrong acts, but from acts that are imagined or intended. Why? Because from the perspective of the superego, "the intention is regarded as equal to the deed." Or as Freud qualifies in the next chapter, "a sense of guilt could be produced not only by an act of violence that is carried out (as all the world knows), but also by one that is merely intended (as psychoanalysis has discovered)" (p. 137).

Yet how can the ego differentiate, in the first instance, between acts that are good and acts that are bad? How can the naive ego, before directing aggression away from others and toward itself, conceive of an ethics beyond pure egoism? More simply yet, where does goodness (altruism, love, and so on) come from, especially given the claims of a primary hostility? It is here that Mommy and Daddy influence the development of the self-involved baby narcissist. In this way chapter seven returns to the essential territory introduced in chapter one: the development of a sense of reality. "There is," Freud begins, "an extraneous influence at work, and it is this that decides what is to be called good or bad [*Gut und Böse*, good and evil]. Since a person's own feelings would not have led him along this path, he must have had a motive for submitting to this extraneous influence" (*SE*, 1930/1991, p. 124; *GW*, 1948b/1991, p. 483). A force of the external world – a "foreign influence," *fremder Einfluß* – is the "motive" for ethics. In fact, it is the motive for any sense of reality whatsoever, which is why "hate, as a relation to objects, is older than love": namely, because "It derives from the narcissistic ego's primordial repudiation of the external world with its outpouring of stimuli" (*SE*, 1915/1999, p. 139). "Such a motive" for conscience, Freud goes on, "is easily discovered in his helplessness and his dependence on other people, and it can best be designated as fear of loss of love" (*SE*, 1930/1991, p. 124).

It is notable that this fundamental "fear of loss of love" (*als Angst vor dem Liebesverlust*) is rather different than those other fears that Freud addressed in chapter one. Recall the developmental importance that Freud assigns to Baby's fear of Daddy and, later on, of Fate. He is building up to that point again, which is essential to the psychological development of the individual. But the emphasis in chapter seven is different: not fear of Daddy's aggression, but fear of loss of Mommy's love. It is at this point that Freud undercuts Mommy's role in the development of the individual. He continues:

> If he loses the love of another person upon whom he is dependent, he also ceases to be protected from a variety of dangers. Above all, he is exposed to the danger that this stronger person will show his superiority in the form of punishment. At the beginning, therefore, what is bad [*Böse*, evil] is whatever causes one to be threatened with loss of love. For fear of that loss, one must avoid it. (p. 124)

Freud is strangely evasive in these passages, never actually naming Mommy or Daddy, so let's spell it out again in terms that resonate more clearly with his discussions in chapter one. Civilization begins when Baby, wrapped in oceanic love with Mommy, confronts the reality of a stronger, foreign influence, namely Daddy, who threatens to take that love away and even punish the child. Daddy is a force of evil that wrenches Baby from Mommy's breast and demonstrates a power that demands recognition. Daddy is *culture*, or more precisely, is a force of *enculturation* that threatens the oceanic narcissism that is Baby's original milieu.

There is a simple, if lazy, heuristic value in laying things out so neatly according to these commonplace binaries: good/evil, mother/father, Eros/Death, nature/culture, inside/outside. But while the sexism is blatant and breathtaking, it is not decisive. This is because the influence of the *Masse* on the individual is mechanical, a force that cannot be reduced to gender – even though it plugs so nicely into culturally relative narratives about parenting. The tension between the mechanistic and the cultural interpretations results in a lack of clarity: in chapter seven Freud often neglects to discuss the etiological significance of Mommy or Daddy, and when they are mentioned they are generalized as "parents." Consider two examples. Speaking of Baby's "fear of loss of love" or "social anxiety," Freud says that it persists in some adults, where "it has only changed to the extent that the place of the father *or the two parents* is taken [over] by the larger human community" (*SE*, 1930/1991, p. 125; my emphasis). A similar elision occurs in the next paragraph. If the origin of the sense of guilt originates with the fear of loss of love, Freud argues, then it is maintained and heightened by a second phase: the internalization of authority called the superego. "The phenomena of conscience then reach a higher stage" (p. 125). In fact, only at this second stage can we speak, properly, of guilt or conscience – in part because no thought, no evil intent, can be hidden from this agency. "Nothing can be hidden from the superego, not even thoughts." Fate, too, makes an appearance at this point in the form of "misfortune" (*daß Mißgeschick*) or "external frustration" (p. 126; *GW*, 1948b/1991, p. 485). Freud already connected such fateful misfortune to fear of Daddy in chapter one but now says rather more broadly and ambivalently that Fate is "regarded as a substitute for the *parental agency*" (my emphasis).

Freud is less circumspect about the role of gender in Baby's developing sense of reality in chapter one. But even there the role of fear and loss complicates things. Freud acknowledges that loss is built into life and love, into enculturation, and this is always experienced by Baby as a harbinger of harsh reality, an external force that is by definition "evil." And so Mommy is never a "good enough mother," in Winnicott's term; and the breast is inevitably a "bad object," in Klein's term. Mommy will fail the baby narcissist no less than Daddy, and she will, abstractly, be the first representative of culture and, thus, of evil (Dufresne, 2000, pp. 70–7, 149–52). Consequently, from the perspective of the development of a sense of reality, and also of the sense of guilt, there is nothing special about Mommy's relationship with Baby. Ultimately she is a "foreign" force like any other, albeit one that is particularly able (in this classic, patriarchal version to which Freud always returns) to sustain Baby's oceanic self-involvement to a greater degree than others. Thus does Freud preserve classic (culturally relative) views about Mommy's connectedness to nature, even as he undermines its etiological importance from a mechanistic or functional perspective. (More about this in the Coda.)

The upshot: what is developmentally crucial is not Mommy or Daddy as individual agents or subjects, but as impersonal forces that activate the child's fear or anxiety, *Angst*. But this fear is innate, given *before* culture, and abiding, given *to* culture. As Freud says, "Thus we know of two origins of the sense of guilt: one arising from fear of an authority, and the other, later on, arising from fear of the superego" (*SE*, 1930/1991, p. 127). What was a periodic threat from outside becomes a permanent threat on the inside. The external authority who threatened "loss of love," figuratively the Daddy, is "exchanged for a permanent unhappiness," namely, the "sense of guilt" (p. 128).

This dark conclusion brings Freud to an idea that finally "belongs entirely to psychoanalysis," and promises to clear up "subject-matter [that] was bound to seem so confused and obscure to us," *verworren und undurchsichtig*, "convoluted and opaque" (p. 128; *GW*, 1948b/1991, p. 488). *Angst* about the threatened loss of love is the cause of instinctual renunciation and is what causes Baby to curb its innate narcissistic feelings. Or again, Daddy threatens Baby's feelings of oceanic bliss by bringing reality, the external world, to bear on its existence. The resulting *Angst* is the prototype of conscience in its most basic form. In Freud's tentative and "paradoxical" formulation, this means that instinctual renunciation causes conscience and conscience causes instinctual renunciation. Or again: *Angst* feeds conscience and conscience feeds *Angst*.

This formula for a paradoxical double bind amounts to a third interpretation of the origin of conscience, one that best captures the tragic romanticism of the Freudian subject in the wake of the death drive theory. For it is with this thoroughly compromised subject that Freud accounts for human unhappiness. It also requires, most importantly, that he "postulate a different derivation for the first instalment of the superego's aggressivity" (p. 129), in short, a different origin of the sense of guilt. According to this revised scenario, derived from the assumption of innate aggression, Baby is not just fearful of Daddy, like a passive victim, but comes equipped with a "considerable amount of aggressiveness" toward this authority figure. Innate aggressiveness inhibits Baby's would-be oceanic pleasure from the beginning, or rather, from *before the beginning*. But because of Daddy's "superiority," Baby cannot properly vent this aggression: "he is obliged to renounce the satisfaction of this revengeful aggressiveness" (p. 129). The way out of this "economically difficult situation" is identification: Baby "takes the unattackable [*unangreifbare*, incontestable] authority into himself." This tale of identification is also the alternate origin of the superego, where Daddy's superiority is introjected – but under the impress of a primary masochism that is only possible after the death drive theory of 1920. Freud is not quite done. Baby's recourse to masochism is the occasion for a typical Freudian reversal, since for Freud Baby's aggression toward self is just a cover for its basic aggression, its sadism, toward the "incontestable" Daddy. "If this is correct," Freud says, "we may assert truly that in the beginning conscience arises through the suppression of an aggressive impulse, and that it is subsequently reinforced by fresh suppressions of the same kind" (p. 130). This is why Freud can speak, in chapter one, about Baby's "helplessness and longing for the father," i.e., why he is able to glide over the difference between Baby's innate *fear of* and *longing for* Daddy.

As for the two basic theories of the origin of the sense of guilt, psycho-analytical and metapsychological, Freud wonders which one is correct: "The earlier one, which genetically seems so unassailable, or the newer one, which rounds off the theory in such a welcome fashion?" (p. 130). The answer is both. It is not a question, Freud says, of "contradiction" between competing views or between "history" and "theory" (p. 138), but of tracking a phylogenetic disposition that is older than and independent of life and its psychoanalysis; that is "beyond" the pleasure principle. And so Freud claims:

> It can also be asserted that when a child reacts to his first great instinctual frustration with excessively strong aggressiveness and with a correspond-ingly severe superego, he is following a phylogenetic model and is going beyond the response [*über die Annahme hinaus*] that would currently be justified; for the father of prehistoric times was undoubtedly terrible, and an extreme [*äußerste*] amount of aggressiveness may be attributed to him. (p. 131; GW, 1948b/1991, p. 490)

What is revealed through Baby's *over*reaction (to a life of loss, to Others) is the phylogenetic truth of the death drive and the Oedipus complex. "We cannot get away from the assumption," Freud says, "that man's sense of guilt springs from the Oedipus complex and was acquired at the killing of the father by the brothers banded together" (p. 131). Not inciden-tally, the same "obscure memory of that primal event" is what drives the story of Christ's death on behalf of the original sin of humankind (p. 142); He is killed so that we can live, and so that Christianity can be institutionalized.

With patricide in mind, Freud is now able to solve "the part played by love in the origin of conscience and the fatal inevitability" – *die verhängnisvolle Unvermeidlichkeit*, the fateful or ominous inevitability – "of the sense of guilt" (p. 132). The key, as always, concerns the ambivalent tension between Eros and Death.

> Whether one has killed one's father or has abstained from doing so is not really the decisive thing. One is bound to feel guilty in either case, for the sense of guilt is an expression of the conflict due to ambivalence, of the eternal struggle between Eros and the instinct of destruction or death. *This conflict is set going as soon as men are faced with the task of living together.* (p. 132; my emphasis)

Group dynamics are forged out of the interminable conflict between Eros and Death. What exists at the beginning of life is an innate predisposition toward aggression that is breached by the "fatal inevitability" called guilt, born out of dependency upon Mommy and Daddy, made possible by a force of *Kultur* given to life and group dynamics, epistemologically grounded by an external world of impersonal mechanical forces, and endured as a feature of Fate to which humankind is thereafter subject.

It is therefore naive to impute to oceanic feeling a privileged access to the depths of the psyche; oceanic feeling cannot be the origin of religion. Such love, not unlike Christian love, is a delusion based on its opposite: an extreme *over*reaction to a developmentally original experience of hate, aggression, and hostility to others. That is to say, oceanic feeling is simply the *repetition* of Baby's narcissistic conflict with Eros, to wit, is Baby's *over*reaction to a life and love defined by loss and absence. Hence the development of our moralists, as noted earlier, who cannot hide what must be the most hostile, aggressive, and uncivil thoughts (pp. 126, 128); who fear the loss of love that makes docile subjects of us all; and who identify with what they are not, namely, Daddy, Fate, Eros, God. Presumably people like Pastor Pfister and the laureate Rolland. This is, of course, a droll conclusion: the existence of saints only demonstrates the noisy truth of the death drive, an overinvestment in love and Eros that betrays the original silent overinvestment in hate and Death that defines the Freudian subject. Hence Freud's scientistic rendering of Shakespeare's most clever and celebrated quip: "The lady doth protest too much, methinks." In effect, moralists are the most ironic proof imaginable of the truth of the death drive theory.

Once we acknowledge the *coercive others* – technically a redundancy, since to speak of "others" is to already imply their coercive influence – we are in a better position to state that Freudian individual psychology is conditioned by reaction formation to the external world, that is, to *Kultur* and its mass psychology. "What began in relation to the father," Freud repeats, this time naming the traditional parental figure responsible, "is completed in relation to the group," the *Masse* (p. 133; *GW*, 1948b/1991, p. 492). The sense of guilt is thereafter the glue that ensures sociality, even as it measures the impossibility of individual happiness. The mass subject is therefore a discontented subject, unable to recapture the ideal pleasure of hate that is the very price of admission to the group. But it bears repeating: unhappiness as such is unavoidable practically from the time of birth. "Integration in, or adaptation to, a human community," Freud repeats in chapter eight, "appears as a scarcely avoidable condition" (p. 140). Or as Freud says elsewhere, "Our life is necessarily a series of compromises, a never-ending struggle between the ego and his environment" (in Viereck, 1930, p. 31). Consequently the most egoistic aims of happiness are pushed aside when one becomes a mass subject: "It is true that the aim of happiness is still there, but it is pushed into the background" (*SE*, 1930/1991, p. 140). One could even say it is "cleared away," made gone, by mechanical forces stronger than any individual, namely, by society. Consequently the question of happiness as the fulfillment of a narcissistic self-sufficiency – "the true aim of happiness" – is itself a red herring, at least as it concerns life, the pleasure principle, and the developing sense of reality.

Why a red herring? Because happiness is just another illusion. Pure happiness, like egoism, is reserved for Death and nonexistence, while unhappiness, like altruism, is left for Life and existence. As Freud put it very early in his career, the aim of therapy is to convert "hysterical misery into common unhappiness" (*SE*, 1895b/1991, p. 305). The metapsychology of *Civilization* explains why this is so.

Freud, however, is not quite willing to draw this logical conclusion to his arguments. "This struggle between the individual and society," he insists, "is not a derivative of the contradiction – probably an irreconcilable one – between the primal instincts of Eros and Death" (*SE*, 1930/1991, p. 141). So what causes the struggle between individual and society? "It is a dispute within the economics of the libido," Freud says, "comparable to the contest concerning the distribution of libido between ego and objects" (p. 141). But this doesn't follow. Just as Freud refuses to choose between the genetic (or historical) accounts and the theoretical accounts – saying that they are not in contradiction (p. 130), just like the relationship between psychoanalysis and metapsychology – he cannot now choose Eros and libido over the death drive and its "destrudo" or "mortido" (to borrow words coined by Freud's contemporaries for the energy of the death drive [see Dufresne, 2000, p. 24]). Or rather he can, but the choice is arbitrary, a good example of trying to have one's cake and eat it too.

Let's return to the passage cited earlier about the "dispute within the economics of the libido." Freud continues: "and it does admit of an eventual accommodation in the individual, as, it may be hoped, it will also do in the future of civilization, however much that civilization may oppress the life of the individual today" (*SE*, 1930/1991, p. 141). And there we have it. With this last remark Freud takes us back to the diabolical but facetious conclusion of *The Future of an Illusion*. In *Civilization and Its Discontents* the accumulated impact of sociality and altruistic feeling is relegated to a hoped-for "future of civilization" – *hoffentlich auch in der Zukunft der Kultur* – just as in *The Future of an*

Illusion the accumulated impact of reason, of enlightenment, is relegated to the geological future. Let's restate our conclusion (from chapter one) once more: contentment with civilization lies not in the psychoanalytic present, but in what Freud in *The Future of an Illusion* (1927) calls "geological" time; to wit, the distant future where the totality of minuscule (ontogenetic) advances, not of decades or even centuries but of millennia, finally adds up to something discernibly better for human beings, both individually and collectively. There can be no doubt that Freud in 1929 has in mind this same long view from 1927, one that diagnoses the necessary, fateful conditions of irrationality, unhappiness, and the oppression of "the life of the individual today." Discontent and unhappiness are from the past and remain still in the present, while happiness is an illusion left to the "future of civilization." In fact, in "Why War?" of 1932, Freud could not be any clearer: although a "dictatorship of reason" over instinct might be ideal, it is very likely a "Utopian expectation" (*SE*, 1933b/1991, p. 213).

To his colleagues on March 20, 1930, Freud complained that he forgot to provide the conditions of *happiness* in *Civilization and Its Discontents*, so intent was he on laying out the argument for *unhappiness*. The "omission," Freud says, "is a gigantic disgrace" (in Sterba, 1982, p. 114). Freud is reported to have said:

> This possibility of happiness is so very sad. It is the person who relies completely upon himself. A caricature of this type is Falstaff. We can tolerate him as a caricature, but otherwise he is unbearable. This is the absolute narcissist. This unassailability by anything is given only to the absolute narcissist.

The prototype for Daddy's unassailability is precisely the original unassailability of the Baby narcissist or "absolute narcissist." This uncompromising form of self-love and disregard of Others is quite simply what Freud means by "happiness." True, he doesn't quite spell it out in *Civilization*, but it is implied everywhere (see Dufresne, 2000, pp. 145–83). For example, having characterized "integration" and "adaptation" to society as a "scarcely avoidable condition" of existence under the domination of the pleasure principle, Freud adds, "If it could be done without that condition, it would perhaps be preferable" (*SE*, 1930/1991, p. 140). The "preferable" state is the absolute narcissism he holds up as a twisted, "so very sad" ideal – *and the polar opposite of Romain Rolland's oceanic feeling*, of meaningful connectedness with others.

Yet obviously Freud's ideal of human happiness is no less illusory than Rolland's oceanic feeling of eternity. The one reifies a state of complete connectedness with others (Rolland), while the other reifies a state of complete isolation from others (Freud). They mirror each other just as the death drive mirrors the life drive, the silent drive providing the context for the noisy work of sociality. Hence Leo Bersani's (2002) perceptive remark that "Aggression is beginning to sound bizarrely like – of all things – the oceanic feeling" (p. xv); and again, "human love is something like the oceanic aggressiveness which threatens to shatter civilization in the wake of its own shattering narcissistic pleasure" (p. xvi). It is certainly interesting that Rolland's first guess at Freud's interpretation of the oceanic feeling was *Zwangsneurosen*, an obsessive compulsive disorder. For that was exactly the clinical behavior that Freud thought best proved the noisy truth of the death drive.

Freud always imagined himself in splendid isolation, unloved and ignored – as silent and inconspicuous as Death – just as he imagined Rolland at the center of social and political issues, loved and celebrated – as noisy and conspicuous as Life. Arguably Freud's attitude to Rolland was determined by these grandiose fantasies, which helped rationalize their relationship, just like everything else, according to the complex dictates of psychoanalytic theory.

2.5   Unfinished Business: Fate, Fame, and Wonderment

> Outside experience merely brought me the realization of my own mind, the state of which I had noted but to which I had no key. Neither Shakespeare nor Beethoven nor Tolstoy nor Rome, the masters that nurtured me, ever revealed anything to me except the "Open Sesame" of my subterranean city, my Herculaneum, sleeping under its lava.
>
> (Romain Rolland, *The Life of Ramakrishna* [1930, p. 11])

In late 1935, the poet Victor Wittkowski asked Freud to consider contributing to a celebration of Rolland's seventieth birthday. Freud, however, was disinclined to participate and, in a letter of January 6, 1936, provided three excuses. First excuse: "A few months after our revered friend Romain Rolland has reached his 70th birthday, I shall be 80. I am afraid this must be my answer to your suggestion" (Freud, 1960b, p. 426). He adds that he might have contributed a recent work "of special interest to R.R.," but that it still "suffered from one defect." The work in question was *The Man Moses: A Historical Novel*, a work that would become chapter one ("Moses: An Egyptian") of his last book, *Moses and Monotheism.* To Stefan Zweig, Freud more simply admitted that "historical evidence for my theory is lacking" and so was not yet publishable (in Jones, 1957, p. 222). It would have been a fitting gift, though, since Rolland himself had published numerous historical portraits of great men (for example, of Beethoven and Tolstoy). Second excuse: since writing the Moses essay, "my ability to produce has dried up again. It is probably too late for it to revive again." Freud, seriously ill since 1923, had slowed his formerly prolific output of new works, most especially after 1934. Third excuse: "If there is something that makes this refusal easier for me," Freud writes, "it is that 'all reference to politics' has to be excluded. Under this paralyzing restriction ... I couldn't do anything, even if I were in my prime." This is the most mysterious excuse, since Freud only rarely addressed politics in any case.

In lieu of a proper contribution, Freud indicates by way of closing that "On January 29 I shall tell him in a few lines that I am thinking of him with affection." And then comes a revealing remark: "Thanks to your letter I now know the date." Clearly Freud was not given much advance notice of a January birthday. It is therefore possible that his three excuses paper over his annoyance at being asked, like an afterthought, to contribute a new work with only three weeks' notice.

Freud changed his mind and in the following week composed a tribute for Rolland. On January 15, 1936, Freud wrote a second letter to Wittkowski: "I have yielded to your insistence and finished a contribution for R.R" (in Vermorel & Vermorel, 1993, p. 402). As Freud says to Arnold Zweig, "I have been greatly importuned to contribute something written to Romain Rolland's 70th birthday, and I have finally yielded" (in Schur, 1972, p. 460). And so, on Rolland's birthday on January 29, 1936, Freud did as promised, first of all sending along his minimal best wishes: "Best wishes from your faithful friend, Sigmund Freud" (in Parsons, 1999, p. 178). No elaborate "complimentary close" this time. And he also included "Letter to Romain Rolland (A Disturbance of Memory on the Acropolis)," a substantial new work of Freud's later period (Fisher, 1988, p. 48; Parsons, 1999, p. 222, n. 26).

The "Letter" is not only Freud's last significant epistle to Rolland; it begins with an exclaimed greeting, "Dear Friend!" It is also the last substantial self-analysis that Freud ever published. Without reducing it – doggedly and at times absurdly – to what commentators variously call "the structure of an analytic session" (Vermorel, 2009, p. 1246),[10] let's turn now to Freud's "Letter to Romain Rolland."

* * *

In the "Letter" of 1936 Freud picks up exactly where the two men left off in 1931: debating the external world. To this end Freud turns not to the example of ancient Rome and Romain Rolland but to classical Greece and Sigmund Freud – to the cradle of Western civilization and its incarnation in contemporary Vienna. And so while Freud's *"Brief an Romain Rolland (Eine Erinnerungsstörung auf der Akropolis)"* does not belong to *Civilization and Its Discontents* in fact, it nonetheless belongs to it in spirit – not in truth, as Rolland might put it, but in reality.

Actually the relationship is less circuitous: the "Letter" runs alongside *Civilization* by way of Freud's late work on religion, *The Future of an Illusion*, the subject matter of chapter two of *Civilization* and the cause of the debate that opens chapter one of that book. The theme of the "Letter" first appears in the *Future* as Freud's wonderment over an experience he recalls from a single visit to the Acropolis in 1904 (*SE*, 1927b/1991, p. 25; *GW*, 1948a/1991, p. 347). What was remarkable to Freud, then forty-eight years old, is the realization that the famous Acropolis really exists. Freud writes:

> I was already a man of mature years when I stood for the first time on the hills of the Acropolis in Athens, between the temple ruins, looking out over the blue sea. A feeling of astonishment mingled with my joy. It seemed to say: "So it really *is* true, just as we learnt at school!" How shallow and weak must have been the belief I then acquired in the real truth of what I heard, if I could be so astonished now! (SE, 1927b/1991, p. 25)

So much of what we know about the world we accept on a faith won from books, or from those who communicate the findings of books, namely teachers. We do not have the time or, in most cases, the inclination to see

---

[10] The literature on the "Letter" is vast, most of it bent on analyzing Freud from various analytic perspectives. See the 1969 winter issue of *American Imago* for examples. A good overview of mid-century interpretation is provided by Maynard Solomon (1973), and updated by Vermorel and Vermorel (1993, part 4). Some fair representations include Mark Kanzer's (1969) Oedipal interpretation and an analysis of Freud's brother Alexander; Harry Slochower's (1970) invocation of the primal scene with Mommy, the sea, and Freud's travel phobia; and Irving Harrison's (1966) reorientation away from traditional defense to an analysis of identity. Arguably the richest, most useful analytic approach is initiated by Max Schur (1969), an analyst and Freud's personal physician during his final decade; Schur assisted with Freud's ultimate suicide in 1939. Schur untangles the historical connections between Fliess and the disturbance of memory on the Acropolis, beginning with the fact that the trip of August 1904 happens soon after Freud's break with Fliess, who had accused Freud of plagiarizing his doctrine of human bisexuality.

for ourselves the many things we accept secondhand from others. In other words, much of our knowledge of the world is the derivative testimony of others. The same holds for "religious assertions," which Freud says are "teachings and assertions about facts and conditions of external (or internal) reality which tell one something one has not discovered for oneself and which lay claim to one's belief" (p. 25). So the framework here is epistemological: How can we possibly distinguish between claims that exhibit the hallmarks of true justified belief and claims that do not? Or again, more simply, how can we be sure that our beliefs are not illusions or even delusions?

It is perhaps no accident that Freud's language concerning his "disturbance of memory" on the Acropolis is hyperbolic. So, too, is the punctuation, which in the space of one paragraph occasions two exclamation points. In the *Future* he recalls "a very remarkable experience," *sehr merkwürdiges Erlebnis* – a very surprising experience (*GW*, 1948a/1991, p. 347). Upon seeing the Acropolis he is overcome by "a feeling of astonishment," *ein Gefühl von Erstaunen*, amazement or surprise. His faith in these derivative truths must be very weak indeed if he can "be so astonished now!," *so erstaunt sein kann!*, so amazed or surprised. Reading these words we could almost conclude that Freud – amazed, surprised, astonished at this remarkable experience – is bedeviled by doubt. For the fabric of reality itself has been compromised, and the experience (at the time, and later on as a memory) is vertiginous.

Freud retains and even amplifies the hyperbole in the retelling of 1936. Let's ignore the context for a moment and attend only to Freud's hyperbolic rhetoric of wonderment, first in German and then in literal English translation (italics are mine):

> Dies Benehmen war doch sehr *sonderbar*. (*GW*, 1936/1991, p. 251)
> . . . kam mir plötzlich der *merkwürdige* Gedanke: . . . (p. 251)
> . . . beide waren *verwundert*, wenn auch nicht über das gleiche. (p. 251)
> Die andere Person war aber mit Recht *erstaunt* . . . (p. 251)
> . . . der *befremdliche* Gedanke auf der Akropolis . . . (p. 252)
> Aber das bliebe eine sehr *sonderbare* Einkleidung . . . (p. 252)
> . . . aber es ist etwas daran *befremdend*. (p. 252)
> This behavior was very *strange*. (*SE*, 1936/1991, p. 240)
> I suddenly had the *strange, curious, remarkable* idea: . . . (p. 241)
> . . . both were *surprised, amazed*, but not by the same thing. (p. 241)
> The other person was *amazed, astonished* . . . (p. 241)
> . . . the *strange* thought on the Acropolis . . . (p. 241)
> But that would remain a very *strange, peculiar* disguise . . . (p. 241)
> . . . but there is something *strange, disconcerting*. (p. 242)

Freud's language is obviously very rich in its description of wonderment – *sonderbar* (twice), *merkwürdige, verwundert, erstaunt, befremdliche* (twice) – so much so that the words "strange" and "surprise" really don't do it justice. But what is perhaps even more striking, amazing, and astonishing is how very surprised Freud is by an experience that is actually common-place. That is to say, what is striking is less the content of Freud's experience than his *feelings* about it.

Arguably, though, that's the point. In the opening paragraph of the "Letter" Freud recounts his "long efforts" to create something "worthy" of Rolland's commitment to the truth, the courage of his convictions, and his love for humanity; or, failing that, at least something that reflects on the "many moments of exaltation and pleasure" this work has given Freud. Freud is unequal to these lofty goals, not because he disagrees with them (they both know that he has already reduced it all to a grand illusion), but because "my powers of production are at an end" (*SE*, 1936/1991, p. 239). "All that I can find to offer you," Freud therefore says, "is the gift of an impoverished creature, who has 'seen better days.'" The "Letter to Romain Rolland" is in this regard the gift of Freud's own recollection of better days, of a remarkable and surprising disturbance of memory, and of a *feeling* of skeptical doubt on the verge of mysticism. It is, moreover, not just a gift, but a highly personal exchange – the return of Freud's feeling (yet to be defined) for Rolland's oceanic feeling of 1927, and also for the "the most precious information about your own person" of Rolland's previous letter of 1931 (in Parsons, 1999, p. 178). In short, the correspondence continues.

In the *Future* the recollection of the Acropolis was used to introduce Freud's discussion about the claims of religious knowledge, which Freud reduces, with characteristic violence, to a knowledge of the internal and external worlds. We know his conclusion: religious knowledge is illusory. In the "Letter," which was initially called "Disbelief on the Acropolis" (Freud, 1992, p. 196), Freud pauses to add a deep – that is, a psychoanalytic – account of his "incredulity," *Unglaube*, his disbelief about the reality of the Acropolis during his 1904 visit. "Incredulity of this kind," Freud now adds, "is obviously an attempt to repudiate a piece of reality" (*SE*, 1936/1991, p. 242; *GW*, 1936/1991, p. 253). "But why should such incredulity arise in something which," he asks, "promises to bring a high degree of pleasure?" Freud, after all, was not just plagued by a strange feeling but was notably "happy," *Beglückung*, to be standing on the Acropolis (*GW*, 1948a/1991, p. 347). Freud finds the answer with those patients who are "wrecked by success"; those who fall ill "because an overwhelmingly powerful wish of theirs has been fulfilled" (*SE*, 1936/1991, p. 242). Freud writes:

> The sufferer does not permit himself happiness ... But why? Because ...
> one cannot expect Fate [*vom Schicksal*] to grant one anything so good ...
> As has long been known, the Fate which we expect to treat us so badly is
> a materialization of our conscience, of the severe super-ego within us, itself
> a residue of the punitive agency of our childhood. (*SE*, 1936/1991, pp. 242–3;
> *GW*, 1936/1991, p. 253)

Guilt turns an otherwise pleasurable experience into its opposite. Freud, delighted to finally stand on the Acropolis, is overcome by an unpleasant (classically neurotic) feeling.

The "feeling of astonishment" directed at the reality of the Acropolis therefore veils a feeling of guilt about Freud's happiness; a guilt based on a happiness that is undeserved, and thus, as Freud says in English, "too good to be true" (p. 242). Freud, however, has trouble capturing his meaning. "So I will conclude," he clarifies,

> by saying briefly that this whole psychical situation, which seems so
> confused and is so difficult to describe, can be satisfactorily cleared up by
> assuming that at the time I had (or might have had) a momentary feeling:
> "What I see is not real." This feeling is called a "derealization." I made an
> attempt to rid [*erwehren*] myself of it, and I succeeded, at the cost of making
> a false statement about the past. (SE, 1936/1991, p. 244; translation adjusted
> slightly with reference to *GW*, 1936/1991, p. 254)

The "false statement" is the claim about the seeming unreality of the Acropolis. This feeling of derealization, *Entfremdungsgefühl*, of estrangement from reality, is of course a pathological mental state – which is why, in part, it is so very noteworthy, literally remarkable. Freud offers Rolland, therefore, not only the gift of a "feeling of astonishment" or even a "feeing of guilt or inferiority," *ein Schuld- oder Minderwertigkeitsgefühl* (*GW*, 1936/ 1991, p. 253). The deepest, most meaningful gift is a "feeling of derealization," a pathological feeling; or rather, technically, the deeper gift is the psychoanalytic interpretation of Freud's own feeling of derealization while standing in Athens, birthplace of *Logos*. Freud says that these "sensations" – he puts the word in quotation marks, *"Empfindungen"* – "arise very frequently in certain mental diseases, but they are not unknown among normal people, just as hallucinations occasionally occur in the healthy" (*SE*, 1936/1991, p. 244; *GW*, 1936/1991, p. 254). On the other hand, "like dreams" these "sensations" "serve us all as models of psychological disorder, they are abnormal structures" (pp. 244–5).

It was Rolland who spoke to Freud of "*sentiment religieux* spontané ou, plus exactement, de la *sensation* religieuse," religious *sensation* or *feeling*, in his letter of December 5, 1927 (Vermorel & Vermorel, 1993, p. 304). In the passage cited, Freud seems to invoke just this idea. And indeed Freud's *sensation of derealization* is related to Rolland's *sensation of eternity*, albeit as its mirror or obverse – a feeling of alienation from reality rather than an oceanic merging into reality. And that is in fact what Freud goes on to describe. "These phenomena [sensations] are to be observed in two forms," Freud writes, that "are intimately connected" (*SE*, 1936/1991, p. 245). The first, we already know, is called derealization: "the subject feels that a piece of reality . . . is strange [*als fremd*] to him." The second form is called "depersonalization": "the subject feels that . . . a piece of his own self is strange to him" (p. 245). Although Freud admits that his persona was split between the *experience itself* and the *reflection upon the experience*, and that "both [parts of himself] were astonished" (p. 241), he has relatively little to say about the second form of pathology, depersonalization. Freud insists that his experience on the Acropolis is characterized by the first form, derealization.

Having identified these two forms of psychopathology, Freud goes on to discuss "another set of phenomena which may be regarded as their positive counterparts." They include the following:

> "*fausse reconnaissance*," "*déjà vu*," *déjà raconté* etc., illusions in which we seek to accept something as belonging to our ego, just as in the derealization we are anxious to keep something out of us. A naively mystical and unpsychological attempt at explaining the phenomena of *déjà vu* endeavours to find evidence in it of a former existence of our mental self. Depersonalization leads us on to the extraordinary condition of "*double conscience*," which is more accurately described as "split personality." But all of this is so obscure and has been so little mastered scientifically that I must refrain [*mir verbieten*: I must forbid myself] from talking about it any more to you. (p. 245; *GW*, 1936/1991, p. 255)

Freud has to stop himself. He can't go on, it's forbidden, because it's too obscure scientifically to understand these mystical-seeming experiences that somehow confuse the external world with the internal. But there is more going on here. These other illusory phenomena run alongside the two forms that interest Freud – forms that warrant a complex medical taxonomy, namely "derealization" and "depersonalization." But what of these other phenomena? The uncanny feeling of déjà vu, for example, is described in similar terms that Freud, in *Civilization*, describes the oceanic feeling in adults: the oceanic feeling is "wie eine Art Gegenstück an die Seite," "a kind of counterpart [existing] along the side" of mature ego-feeling (*SE*, 1930/1991, p. 68; *GW*, 1948b/1991, p. 425). It is an echo, recall, of a "primary ego-feeling" that Freud calls limitless narcissism. In the "Letter," déjà vu has the same status: it is a "*positiven Gegenstücke*" or "positive counterpart" (*SE*, 1936/1991, p. 245; *GW*, 1936/1991, p. 255) to the dominant forms that interest Freud, derealization and depersonalization. If they are "positive" counterparts, it is because they are consciously felt; they are made known to the subject as uncanny feelings. Both the uncanny feeling and the oceanic feeling run alongside the ego and point the way back, far back, to the primitive origins of mental development. In short, they exist as distorted representations of the deep past; they are derivative of something that still requires depth interpretation. It is the job of psychoanalysis to discover this repressed past.

If Freud mentions this "set of phenomena," it is obviously not to explain them – for he reveals almost nothing about them. But they do work to subtly conjure an old debate about the mechanism of defense taken up in the following paragraph, and to that extent they allow Freud to redress an old wound. That wound concerns Pierre Janet, who Rolland, mistakenly or not, includes with the psychoanalysts, and perhaps even as the first psychoanalyst ("Janet, Freud, and their substitutes"). Recall the passage cited earlier: in the extreme, Freud says, "depersonalization" can lead to what the French call *double conscience*, dual consciousness, but what is "more correctly described as 'split personality'" (p. 245). The theory of double or dual consciousness is associated with Janet's theory of dissociation – a theory Freud and Breuer invoke as early as *Studies on Hysteria* in 1895, but against which Freud seeks to establish (the more correct, independently derived, earlier) theory of defense and repression (see Nemiah, 2000, pp. 300–1).

This old debate about the truth of mental functioning, but also about priority in the history of ideas, is not unconnected to this late debate with Rolland about the existence of the external world. In the pre-psychoanalytic era of the 1880s to 1896, Freud was deeply interested in the question of how the psyche is impacted by the external world. Culminating in (the never completed) *Project for a Scientific Psychology* of 1895, Freud lays out in strict mechanistic terms a psycho-physicalist theory of defense that he not only doesn't abandon, but enshrines in *Beyond the Pleasure Principle* of 1920 – and institutionalizes in *The Ego and The Id* as a shift toward "ego psychology." Here is the idea, quickly put: every organism seeks constancy, ultimately the constancy of nonexistence, death; but life, first in the form of Mommy and then in the form of society more generally, demands otherwise. The organism's existence is henceforth determined by a reactive or defensive response to an external world that demands growth and life. The individual's ultimate defense, the expression of its biologically determined individuality, is to find its "own way to death" amidst all the possible choices available in the external world. Existence is therefore the consequence of a battle between life and death drives – and, by extension, between sociality and primary (or absolute) narcissism, group psychology and individual psychology – the end of which is the termination of this seemingly interminable battle of drives. There is no "synthesis" or final overcoming of these conditions, and hence no room for idealism or even optimism. Life is existential and fundamentally tragic, and is thus subject to psychoanalysis (while death is *beyond*, and so subject to *meta*-psychology).

What Freud's mechanistic theory of defense gives him is a uniquely psychoanalytic answer to the problem of skepticism concerning the existence of the external world. For the very fact of growth and change – which is to say, the fact of evolution – is proof enough that an external world has duly left its mark on organisms. That is why Freud remains a psycho-Lamarckian throughout his career: organisms develop according to the inheritance of acquired characteristics; i.e., they are the ontogenetic (individual) accumulation of a phylogenetic (objectively historical) process. This includes, perhaps especially includes, even the simple elements of the natural world. "In the last resort," Freud says in *Beyond*, "what has left its mark on the development of organisms must be the history of the earth we live in and of its relation to the sun" (*SE*, 1920a/1991, p. 38). The upshot is significant: Freud implicitly updates Descartes' indubitable foundation of modern philosophy, the *Cogito*, with the mechanistic thought of nineteenth-century science: "I *grow*, therefore I exist."[11] In the process he necessarily establishes the incontrovertible existence, not just of himself, but of an outer world of (hostile) stimuli – and of its forgotten (and repressed) history. Nothing could be more clear and distinct, indubitable.

So Freud, in the "Letter," is not really interested in *double conscience* or split personality, with "depersonalization." It is all just an entrée to this prehistory with Janet and dissociation, and to his own (rather more correct, earlier) theory of defense and repression (psychoanalysis). To this end he points to two "characteristics" of the "phenomena of derealization." "The first is that they all serve the purpose of defence," Freud says, adding: "they aim at keeping something away from the ego, disavowing it" (*SE*,

---

[11] For a more substantial discussion of these points, see Dufresne, 2000, pp. 147–57. There I formulate it more strictly as "*I am stimulated, therefore I defend, I grow, I exist*" (p. 154).

1936/1991, p. 245). Freud already provides just such an example in chapter one of *Civilization*: the baby narcissist "throws outside" any feeling of unpleasure. But Freud says that there is a better method: "The most primitive and thorough-going of these methods, 'repression,' was the starting-point of the whole of our deeper understanding of psychopathology" (p. 245). The second characteristic of the phenomena of derealization, Freud goes on to say, is their "dependence upon the past, upon the ego's store of memories and upon earlier distressing experiences which have since perhaps fallen victim to repression" (p. 246). While this second characteristic is not universally accepted, Freud thinks his own experience of a feeling of derealization helps make the connection. He writes,

> But precisely my own experience on the Acropolis, which actually culminated in a disturbance of memory and a falsification of the past, helps us to determine this connection. It is not true that in my schooldays I ever doubted the real existence of Athens. I only doubted whether I should ever see Athens. It seemed to me beyond the realm of possibility that I should ever travel so far – that I should "go such a long way." (p. 247)

The guilt that Freud repressed in 1904, and which expressed itself in a distorted estimation of reality, in derealisation, goes back to "the limitations and poverty of our conditions of life in my youth" (pp. 246–7). To travel to Athens as Freud had done is fantastical, "like a hero who has performed deeds of improbable greatness." If he could have verbalized it to his traveling companion at the time, his aptly named younger brother Alexander, he would have recalled their humble beginnings and added: "And now we are in Athens standing on the Acropolis! We've come really far!" (*SE*, 1936/1991, p. 247; *GW*, 1936/1991, p. 256). Of course it is not just travel that Freud is discussing in this passage, or in the "Letter" as a whole, but the trajectory of his entire life. He has indeed traveled very far; given his humble (actually middle-class) beginnings, Freud's fame is almost too good to be true. It has even permitted Freud the opportunity to exchange personal feelings with the era's most important thinkers, including the recipient of his Festschrift contribution, Romain Rolland. In this sense Freud has exceeded Daddy, and standing on the Acropolis triumphant, like a hero, is in a sense leaving his past, and Daddy, well behind. Freud himself invokes in this respect Napoleon who, upon his coronation as emperor at Notre Dame, is reported to have said to his own brother, "What would *Monsieur notre Père* have said to this, if he could be here today?" (p. 247). Consequently, "what interfered with our enjoyment of the journey to Athens was a feeling of *filial piety*" (pp. 247–8) – a guilt over this symbolic murder of Daddy, someone who had literally passed away only a few years before in 1896. But it is simultaneously the guilt of having so impressively cheated Fate its usual negative effects.

This really is a triumphal conclusion. Recall what Freud says in *Civilization*: religion originates in a fear of Daddy and, later on, "is permanently sustained by fear of the superior power of Fate" (*SE*, 1930/1991, p. 72), *die Angst vor der Übermacht des Schicksals dauernd erhalten wird* (*GW*, 1948b/1991, p. 430). Yet in Freud's interpretation he overcomes both Daddy and Fate, and so overcomes the original causes of fear itself, with a career that is objectively (truly and realistically) spectacular. What is remarkable, surprising, astonishing about Freud's disturbance of memory on the Acropolis is just this sense of having overcome, already in 1904, the conditions of his own history; or, better yet, having overcome "history," for having become a genuine world historical figure (a Napoleon). And what is astonishing is that Freud doubts, not the reality of the Acropolis, but the reality of his own heroic ascent, the reality of his life, and the reality of psychoanalysis. Finally, then, derealization concerns an internal world (Freud's autobiography, psychoanalysis) that has somehow managed to tame the external world – so much so that Freud is right to wonder at the objectivity of it all. For as we have had reason to remark, the inside and the outside realities of Freud's life match up *perfectly*, one could say uncannily, with each other. Thus there really is no need, in Freud's exceptional case, to choose between psyche and reality, the genetic and the theoretical. Why? Because the contradiction is perfectly overcome, sublated, in the heroic ascent of the famous Sigmund Freud.

In the "Letter" Freud finally understands the near-mystical feeling of unreality, of alienation from the real, that he experienced on the Acropolis in 1904. But the memory of it all haunts the older Freud, "an impoverished creature, who has 'seen better days'" (*SE*, 1936/1991, p. 239). "And now you will no longer wonder," Freud concludes his open birthday letter to Rolland, "that the recollection of this incident on the Acropolis should have troubled [*heimsucht*: haunted] me so often since I myself have grown old and stand in need of forbearance [*Nachsicht*: indulgence, tolerance] and can travel no more" (p. 248; *GW*, 1936/1991, p. 257). But of course there is still room to wonder. What haunts the frail and dying Freud about this particular recollection? Is it the realization that he has overcome Daddy and Fate? The memory of the incredible distance he has traveled since a little boy? The realization that his achievements, objectively realized, are now a thing of the past? The dream of travels never made, people never met, conquests never won, in short, the sting of regret? The objective reality of it all, which is bound to seem too good to be true, like a dream? Or is it all somehow connected with Wilhelm Fliess, his mother, Alexander, Greek mythology, Jewish revenge, and everything else that analysts have so creatively (sometimes absurdly, sometimes cleverly) unearthed in the "Letter"? All of the above? Some? None?

The truth is, with Freudian psychoanalysis we cannot pretend to know when or where interpretation originates *or* ends. Instead the competing and sometimes mutually exclusive psychological interpretations are more or less *all plausible, all contenders* in a bid to find the origin, the ground, amidst all the derivative clues, all the ends. As Maynard Solomon remarks, "Commentators of the Acropolis experience have discovered that it points to multiple layers of meaning, indicating perhaps that the Letter permits access to the entire range of Freud's fantasy-life" (1973, pp. 143–4). "The entire range," everything. The "Letter to Romain Rolland" is therefore exemplary. What Solomon doesn't say is that these multiple layers of significance also, and very obviously, represent more than just *Freud's* fantasy life. In the same way that Rolland's existence was a means to Freud's own ends, Freud has become a means to an interpretive culture that never ends. The analysis is interminable. Why? Because the autobiographical depths of Sigmund Freud are obviously beyond representation, and so limitless in their potential for narcissistic projection. In other words we are all of us derivatives, not standing on the shoulders of this giant, Sigmund Freud, but looking over our shoulders at this ur-paranoic, ultimate Daddy figure – with fear, perhaps, but also with surprise, amazement, incredulity, and so on.

* * *

"Letter to Romain Rolland" remains one of the most affecting works Freud ever wrote, a generous gift of one old man to another not so young himself. As for the interpretation Freud offers, the substance of the gift, Freud flirts with the kind of mystical feeling that Rolland cherished but ultimately, appropriately and necessarily, reduces it to the truth of psychoanalysis. In other words, Freud does to himself what he already did to Rolland in chapter one of *Civilization and Its Discontents*: he submits his mental life to psychoanalysis. In this sense he once again shows Rolland how and why it's done. True, Rolland is still left with an uncivil diagnosis of limitless narcissism and illusory contributions to posterity, while Freud is left, through the trial of *de*-realization, with the objective *realization* of his great achievements as the founder of a new science. On the other hand Rolland is easily as famous as Freud during these years, and in this sense

Freud shares an aside about fame and Fate with a fellow traveler for whom he has, finally, nothing but fellowship. Their fame is a shared piece of reality that no amount of debate can clear away; they are peerless, together. And so the "Letter" may be "open" for all to read, but it is nonetheless whispered sotto voce with little fear of being overheard. Or maybe – probably – Freud is simply too old and too sick to care about who over-hears his remarks to Rolland.

In the end Freud finds himself, *da*, in this paragon of virtue, and to this extent Rolland the optimist completes Freud the pessimist. Such is "the mysterious attraction" that binds them together because of, and in spite of, their differences. And such is the harmony they create together, a unity of opposites that, perhaps surprisingly, favors Rolland's optimistic and mys-tical *Weltanschauung* over Freud's pessimistic and rationalistic one. Could it be, then, that the deepest meaning of Freud's gift to Rolland is the universal love and brotherhood that Rolland always demanded of human-ity? Probably not. The "mysterious attraction" felt by Freud was an *uncanny* attraction, one that doesn't fit the idea of submersion of self in an oceanic sameness with the eternal. The uncanny is the measure of a *distance* that cannot be bridged, of a sameness that is never resolved in harmony.

In "The Uncanny" of 1919 Freud theorized that the double is a portent of impending death. That same year Rolland published *Liluli* and then circulated and published his "Declaration of Independence of the Mind" – a process that had Rolland ask dozens of famous world figures to sign, but not Sigmund Freud. Two years later their mutual friend, Stefan Zweig, published Rolland's biography in Austria; it opens with a lavish dedication to its subject, "the most impressive moral phenomenon of our age," about whom "it has been vouchsafed to me to know the miracle of so radiant an existence."

In 1923 Freud took Fate into his own hands and reached out to the miraculous Rolland himself, just days after his initial discovery of a leucoplastic growth on his jaw, and made contact with a worthy double. Rolland's reaction was a great satisfaction that arrived, Freud says, "like a breath of fresh air" (in Schur, 1972, p. 349): Rolland claims to be one of his earliest French readers and confirms Freud's importance as "the Christopher Columbus of a new continent of the spirit."[12] Their friendship

---

[12] Or as he privately remarks in *Journey Within*, Freud is "the pilot who, equal to his great Phoenician ancestors, first ventured into the circumnavigation of the black Continent of the Spirit [*l'Esprit*]" (Rolland, 1959, p. 112, my translation; in Fisher, 1976/1991, p. 36).

is thereafter the realization of the grandiose fantasy of Rolland's great novel *Jean-Christophe* – the reconciliation of French and German cultures, the forestalling of war through mutual understanding, respect, and universal brotherhood (see Fisher, 1988, pp. 33–6). In 1932, Rolland helps organize a new petition against war, an Appeal for the World Congress, and this time Freud is indeed asked to add his signature. But they keep their distance. Rolland may not even have read Freud's "Letter to Romain Rolland" (Fisher, 1976/1991, p. 69). And there is certainly no red chair set out for Rolland when he visits Vienna in 1936 to celebrate Beethoven's centenary – since neither man takes steps to contact the other. As for Wittkowski, the poet who in 1936 importuned Freud to contribute to the Rolland *Festschrift*, he sends Freud a book of his poems in October 1937. "I am very grateful for the gift of your poems," Freud responds. "I suspect they are very nice, but I haven't enjoyed lyric poetry for many years" (in Molnar, 1994, p. 264, n. 18). He suspects they are nice, but he's not willing to find out. He doesn't enjoy poetry and isn't willing to try. Sigmund Freud – *Landtier* till the very end.

The single most important feature of Freud and Rolland's relationship: it is born under the shadow of war, cultural annihilation, illness, and imminent personal death.[13] Consequently it can't be surprising that Freud's letters to Rolland sometimes read like deathbed confessions. What is surprising, no doubt to both men, is that Freud survived such a serious illness for so many years. Longer, perhaps, than the forces that initially propelled their friendship.

Yet whatever one *thinks* about their relationship – about ambition, jealousy, rivalry, mistrust, hostility, condescension, perceived and real slights, revenge, grandiosity, admiration, inspiration, understanding, flattery, love, opportunism, fame, and so on – Freud's "Letter to Romain Rolland" still *feels* like a beautiful song of friendship written by a man proud to be tone-deaf. Which is appropriate. When it came to his great friend, the ironist in Freud always came undone. To this extent their sometimes fractious friendship demonstrates, Freud's pessimism notwithstanding, that hope and reconciliation, love and fellowship, are possible even in a time of war and destruction; and that happiness in civilization, however fleeting, is possible, too. Freud remained intractable in his positions, and yet sought out someone who promised more of life than

---

[13] Both men have a long history of fearing an early death (see Fisher, 1988, p. 16). About Freud, Jones writes: "Even in the early years of our acquaintance [ca. 1910] he had the disconcerting habit of parting with the words 'Goodbye; you may never see me again'" (Jones, 1957, p. 301; Schur, 1969, p. 303; Dufresne, 2000, pp. 39–41).

he ever could. In this respect, Fisher is absolutely right: "Rolland was everything Freud was not" (1976/1991, p. 57; cf., Fisher, 1982, pp. 253, 270–2). But we can nuance this insight a bit more: Romain Rolland was everything Freud was not *in truth* or *in reality*, but was *in spirit*. If so, this Freud is surprisingly Other than what is usually thought of in most traditional portraits.

Divided, ambivalent, conflicted – it is comforting to think that even the pessimistic and rationalistic Freud of the late years could be moved by the charms of sentiment, cheap or otherwise.

CHAPTER 3

"The Audacity Cannot Be Avoided"
Freud and Moses, Reality and Fiction

> The Christian religion is every bit as bad as the Jewish. Jew and Christian ought to meet on the common ground of irreligion and humanity.
>
> (Freud to Joseph Wortis, January 17, 1935 [Wortis, 1954, p. 144])

Moses and Monotheism of 1939 is Freud's last significant work and one of his most controversial. It is the culmination of his thinking about religion and society that begins in earnest with *Totem and Taboo* (1913); that repeats and extends the classic examinations of culture made in *The Future of an Illusion* (1927) and *Civilization and Its Discontents* (1930); and that echoes the theoretical innovations of *Beyond the Pleasure Principle* (1920), *Group Psychology and the Analysis of the Ego* (1921), and *The Ego and the Id* (1923). While *Moses* was being written, edited, and revised between 1934 and 1938, Freud expressed typical reservations about the originality and substance of the work. At the same time he held it in high regard. In March 1937 Freud confessed to Ernest Jones that, while he was unable to "provide adequate historical proof" for his arguments, its "results are very significant" (Freud & Jones, 1993, p. 757). Freud's remarks to other correspondents are similarly enthused.

Posterity has not been kind to Freud's *Moses*. Its main argument – that Moses was an Egyptian killed by the Jews – is widely considered an embarrassment, a fate shared with only one other work of Freud's, *Thomas Woodrow Wilson: A Psychological Study*, cowritten with William C. Bullitt. As a consequence, observers often contend that *Moses* is noteworthy only as a flawed, highly autobiographical investigation of the origins of Jewish identity, and as a fresh excuse to psychoanalyze the founder of psychoanalysis. There is a lot to go on. We know, for example, that while Freud distanced himself and his family from Jewish religion, he always identified himself culturally, intellectually, and even historically as a Jew. As he wrote in a letter to Arthur

137

Schnitzler, "Emotionally, Jewishness is still very important to me" (in Clark, 1980, p. 521). Despite being an ambitious young man, Freud refused to convert to Catholicism, effectively cutting off the possibility of a university post (which he favored) in anti-Semitic Austria; married a Jewish woman, Martha Bernays, from a prominent orthodox family; was for decades an active member of the B'nai B'rith, the Jewish cultural organization, in Vienna; maintained and cultivated his Jewish friendships, playing tarock weekly; and was surrounded by Jewish followers, and not just in the early days of psychoanalysis. In the December 1930 "Preface" to the Hebrew translation of *Totem and Taboo*, Freud says very explicitly that he is Jewish despite disbelief in Judaism. To this end he poses both the question, "What is left of you that is Jewish?," and the answer, "A very great deal, and probably its very essence" (*SE*, 1913b/1991, p. xv). Or as he says in an interview of 1926: "I considered myself German intellectually, until I noticed the growth of anti-Semitic prejudice in German and German Austria. Since that time, I consider myself no longer German. I prefer to call myself a Jew" (in Viereck, 1930, p. 34). Ultimately Freud never denied his Jewishness, and was in his own way proud to be a Jew.

Throughout his life Freud identified with Moses, Jewish leader of men and paragon of ethical responsibility. During vacations to Rome, a place of great ambivalence for Freud, he would often visit San Pietro in Vincoli (Saint Peter in Chains), a titular Catholic church and minor basilica, to contemplate and even draw Michelangelo's sculpture of Moses, created in 1513–15. In 1913 Freud attempted an interpretation of the sculpture, which depicts Moses sitting alert with the tablet of laws in his hands, in a speculative essay called "The Moses of Michelangelo." Three features of the essay stand out. First, Freud was only willing to publish the work anonymously – for the first time in his career. It was only in 1924 that Freud admitted authorship of this orphaned work. "Not until much later," Freud explains to Eduardo Weiss in 1933, "did I legitimize this nonanalytic child" (Freud, 1992, p. 146; cf., Clark, 1980, p. 358). Second, it is not presented under the rubric of psychoanalysis, even applied psychoanalysis (referring to the analysis of culture). The editors of *Imago*, Otto Rank and Hanns Sachs, provide the rationale for its inclusion in the journal: because "the author, who is personally known to them, moves in psychoanalytic circles, and since his mode of thought has in point of fact a certain resemblance to the methodology of psychoanalysis" (in Clark, 1980, p. 357). Third, like *Totem* the essay was written under the influence of Freud's break with Carl Jung; some commentators therefore claim that the interpretation of Moses echoes Freud's own feelings about Jung (Puner, 1947, p. 246; cf., Yerushalmi, 1991, p. 75).

So, yes, there are numerous biographical details of relevance to our understanding of Freud's final work. Yet as Yosef Yerushalmi and Richard J. Bernstein argue, it is also grossly reductive to consider *Moses* as merely the final piece of Freud's interminable self-analysis. Like Freud's "Letter to Romain Rolland," its meaning extends beyond the inevitable, obfuscating, and finally tiresome psychoanalyses of Freud's unconscious. For one thing, *Moses* is continuous with everything else that characterizes the late Freud. Consequently if there is embarrassment about *Moses and Monotheism*, then there should be embarrassment about the other highly speculative works such as *Totem and Taboo* and *Beyond the Pleasure Principle* – and, moreover, about every other essay and book that is based on them.

One underappreciated aspect of the work's inherent significance is especially pertinent to our investigation here: like *The Future of an Illusion* and *Civilization and Its Discontents, Moses* continues to pose the question of external reality. Unlike these other works it confronts this question by explicitly recalling an issue that haunts psychoanalysis from the beginning: the relationship between the objective present and the recovery of the repressed past.

In what follows I provide a quick overview of, first, the genesis of Freud's writing of *Moses and Monotheism*; second, his complex relationship with Judaism; and third, his thesis concerning the origins of monotheistic religion, that is, of Judaism (Yerushalmi, 1991, p. 55). One more qualification: my overall goal is not a full-blown critique of *Moses*, including the debatable arguments and speculations that Freud advances. That work has been done many times already. My goal is to explore the work's continuity with earlier works, including *Beyond the Pleasure Principle*, and with important contemporaneous ideas, such as Freud's late interest in "constructions in analysis." Beyond that I am interested in a crucial and underappreciated innovation of the final period – the concept of "historical truth" – which amounts, I think, to Freud's last word on psychoanalysis. As we will see, constructions in analysis and historical truth also bring us back to the very origins of psychoanalysis. And resolves them, too.

3.1   The Genesis of Freud's *Moses*

During August and September of 1934 Freud completed a draft for a new book called *The Man Moses: A Historical Novel*. In a letter of September 30,

Freud describes the three-part work to his friend Arnold Zweig, the German novelist and progressive writer, and offers two reasons for why it is not ready for publication. First, he is hesitant to publish a psychoanalysis of the origins of monotheism given the political situation in Austria, pointing to the influence of Father Wilhelm Schmidt. Schmidt, an ordained priest, linguist, and prominent ethnologist, had already produced his own work on monotheism; was in 1928 a vocal critic of Freud's earlier work, *Totem and Taboo*; and was, Freud asserts, "a confidant of the Pope" (Freud, 1960b, p. 422; Robert, 1976, p. 147; Vitz, 1988, pp. 197–9; Yerushalmi, 1991, pp. 27–9). In this lattermost regard Freud claims that Schmidt had been involved in banning the *Rivista Italiana di Psicoanalisi*, despite what Freud considered (falsely, according to Roazen [1976, p. 534]) to be Italian analyst Edoardo Weiss' favorable relationship with Mussolini. Freud worried that the Moses book would only stir up similar trouble for Viennese analysts. "Were this danger confined to myself," Freud writes, "it would make little impression on me, but to deprive all our members in Vienna of their livelihood strikes me as too great a responsibility" (Freud, 1960b, p. 422). A year later Freud would add, in a letter to Lou Andreas-Salomé, that it is only "Catholicism which protects us from the Nazis" (in Bernstein, 1998, p. 118) – an ironic realization, given Freud's overall antipathy to Catholicism, that he repeats in a prefatory note of 1938 to the third essay of *Moses and Monotheism* (*SE*, 1939/1991, pp. 55–6). Ultimately, Freud both feared and needed the Catholics and thus refused to publish the Moses work.

Freud's second reason for delaying publication is both more prosaic and, I think, more accurate: it wasn't ready. "The work," Freud admits to Zweig, "does not seem to me sufficiently substantiated" (Freud & Zweig, 1970, p. 92). In a letter of November 6, 1934, Freud is more emphatic. "More important [than politics]," Freud adds, "is the fact that this historical novel won't stand up to my own criticism. I need more certainty and I should not like to endanger the final formula of the whole book, which I regard as valuable, by founding it on a base of clay" (p. 97). Freud repeats himself in December, albeit with a significant change of tone: cautious self-doubt has given way to belief. "Nor is it any inner uncertainty on my part," Freud clarifies, "for that is as good as settled, but the fact that I was obliged to construct so imposing a statue upon feet of clay, so that any fool could topple it" (p. 98).

In March 1935 Zweig, ever the accommodating correspondent, recommends that Freud read Elias Auberbach's first (1932) volume of *Desert and Promised Land*. Auberbach, a German physician, bible scholar, and Zionist, was, like Zweig (in 1933), a transplant to Palestine.[1] Freud reads the book but is dismissive: "his Moses is not my Moses" (p. 104). Even so, Auberbach reconfirms his basic caution. "My opinion about the weakness of my historical construction was confirmed and it was this which rightly made me desist from publishing my work. The rest is really silence" (p. 104).

Although Freud remained obsessed with his Moses book throughout 1935 – "*Moses* will not let go of my imagination"; "So do I now remain fixated on the *Moses*" (pp. 106, 107; cf., Freud, 1992, p. 205) – he was unable to complete it to his own satisfaction. In January 1936 he considers offering the work for a *Festschrift* in honor of Romain Rolland, someone celebrated for his own historical portraits of great men, but declines because it remains unfinished. Two months later Freud admits to Ernest Jones that he has been working on *The Man Moses: A Historical Novel*, and states again why it hasn't been published. "The title already betrays why I have not published this work and will not do so. I lack historical verification for my construction" (Freud & Jones, 1993, p. 751).

During the summer of 1936, Freud edits and rewrites the Moses book (see Jones, 1957, p. 388), and then reads it aloud to Zweig, who was visiting (Freud, 1992, pp. 204–5). Freud then edits the work again in early 1937 (see Clark, 1980, p. 522). On February 3, he records in his *Diary*, "Small Moses finished . . . " On the 5th he tells Max Eitingon that he has managed to free and then finish "a fragment" from the project, but that "the most essential things about it must remain unsaid" (in Freud, 1992, p. 215). Later in July the second essay is also completed. On October 21, Freud signs off on the galley proofs, and the first and second essays of the Moses project are finally published in *Imago* (in Freud, 1992, pp. 220–1). Unlike his Moses essay of 1913, Freud takes authorship of the works and defines them, in the first essay, as "an application of psychoanalysis" (*SE*, 1939/1991, p. 10).[2] As for the third and final chapter, the longest and most important part, Freud is still revising it as late as June 28, 1938 – "I am enjoying writing the third part of Moses," he tells Zweig (Freud & Zweig, 1970, p. 163) – only now from his new home in north London, having finally fled from the "furor teutonicus" of Nazi-occupied Austria (in Burnham, 1983, p. 276).

* * *

As it happened, Freud's late-Romantic world-weariness, so attractive in the abstract, was inadequate for anticipating or even understanding the rise of

---

[1] See www.danielabraham.net/tree/auerbach/elias.
[2] These essays appear in English in July 1938 and January 1939, respectively (see Brill, 1944/1962, p. 225).

National Socialism. True, Freud hardly failed to register the fact that life had gotten decidedly worse after Hitler, especially for Jews. Already in June of 1933 Freud could tell Marie Bonaparte,

> It seems to me that not even in the [First World] War did lies and empty phrases dominate the scene as they do now. The world is turning into an enormous prison. Germany is the worst cell. What will happen to the Austrian cell is quite uncertain. I predict a paradoxical surprise in Germany. They began with Bolshevism as their deadly enemy, and they will end with something indistinguishable from it – except perhaps that Bolshevism after all adopted revolutionary ideals, whereas those of Hitlerism are purely medieval and reactionary. This world still seems to me to have lost its vitality and to be doomed to perdition. (in Jones, 1957, pp. 181–2)

And to Zweig in 1935 Freud could "see a cloud of disaster passing over the world, even over my little world" (Freud & Zweig, 1970, p. 101). Yet Freud badly misunderstood the dangers of institutionalized anti-Semitism. This was understandable in 1930, when Freud told Bullitt that "a nation that produced Goethe could not possibly go to the bad" (in Jones, 1957, p. 151), but much less so with each passing year. For example, in 1937 the French analyst René Laforgue traveled to Vienna to urge Freud to leave and was shocked by Freud's attitude toward the Nazis. "He responded almost with contempt," Laforgue recalled: "'The Nazis? I am not afraid of them. Help me rather to combat my true enemy'. Astonished, I asked him just what enemy was in question, and I heard him reply: 'Religion, the Roman Catholic Church'" (Laforgue, 1956/1973, pp. 343–4).

On May 10, university students, following Goebbels's orders, burned over 20,000 books in the Bebelplatz, a public square in central Berlin. About Freud's "un-German writing," a student representative read out their verdict: "Against soul-disintegrating exaggeration of the instinctual life, for the nobility of the human soul! I commit to the flames the writings of Sigmund Freud" (in Freud, 1992, p. 149). Freud's "smiling comment" to Jones about the book burning was clever, as always. But, in retrospect, it is also cringe-inducing: "What progress we are making," Freud said. "In the Middle Ages they would have burnt me; nowadays they are content with burning my books" (in Jones, 1957, p. 182). People were slowly inured to the constant escalation of danger, and were perhaps invested in a certain blindness when confronted with monstrous reality. Clearly Freud was not alone in failing to anticipate the extremes of anti-Semitism, including the Final Solution, the policy of systematic extermination that came into effect a few years (1942) after Freud left Vienna. But if Freud, committed as he was to parsing reality in his late phase, had such an imperfect understanding of current events, then one is justified in at least wondering about the usefulness of psychoanalysis for understanding the major problems of everyday existence.

On March 12, 1938, the Nazis marched into Austria as Hitler prepared for his speech in Vienna on March 15. In view of the *Anschluss*, the forced unification of the two countries, Freud's diary entry on the 12th simply reads, "Finis Austriae" (Freud, 1992, p. 229). As Michael Molnar sagely observes, Freud was succinctly declaring the end, not just of Austrian political autonomy, but of the rich Viennese cultural and intellectual heritage, largely Jewish, that had prospered even beyond the official end of the Habsburg Empire in the First World War (in Freud, 1992, pp. 229–30).

Freud once remarked that "Austrians are really very kind people so we do not expect any real danger" (in Guest, 1984, p. 212). But in fact Austrians often behaved worse than the Germans (see Gay, 1988, p. 620). Jews were systematically harassed, mistreated, beaten, humiliated, and robbed. Many frightened Austrians chose suicide in the face of maltreatment (Gay, 1988, p. 622) – perhaps as many as 1,300 people killed themselves (in Burke, 2006, p. 322). But when Freud's daughter Anna broached the idea of suicide, Freud blanched: "Why? Because they would like us to?" (in Schur, 1972, p. 499).

Despite such treatment, Jones still had trouble convincing the stubborn Freud to leave Austria. The turning point might have been when Anna was taken into custody by the Gestapo and interrogated (Clark, 1980, p. 507). For not long thereafter Jones and Marie Bonaparte, with the help of the American diplomat William C. Bullitt, managed to arrange for Freud's exit at nearly the last possible moment – and only on account of Freud's fame, the looting of Freud's personal safe, a bogus "exit tax," and Bonaparte's additional "ransom" money (Roazen, 1993b, p. 146). Finally on Saturday, June 4, 1938, the following people gathered on the Orient Express train for Paris: Freud, his wife Martha, daughter Anna, a pediatrician and friend of Anna's named Dr. Josephine Stross, Freud's maid Paula Fichtl, and Freud's beloved dog, Lün. Freud's personal physician, Max Schur, along with his wife and two children, came along later (Freud, 1992, p. 237; Freud, 1960b, p. 445). Freud had been unable to extend his protection any wider (Schur, 1972, p. 501). As a consequence, four of Freud's sisters were left behind in Vienna, all of whom were killed in the Holocaust (see Burke, 2006, pp. 322–3).

After he left Austria for England, there was no longer any reason to hold the completed *Moses* back from the wider public. From his home on Maresfield Gardens in Hampstead, north London, now housing the Freud Museum, Freud took up the third essay on June 21, 1938. "I also work for an hour a day at my Moses," Freud tells Jones, "which torments me like a ghost not laid" (Freud, 1992, p. 240; cf., *SE*, 1939/1991, p. 103). The work was finally completed on July 17, 1938 (Freud, 1992, pp. 240, 243). To Salvador Dali, who visited two days later, Freud is reported to say that the "Moses is flesh of sublimation" (p. 243). The German edition was published in Amsterdam on February 2, 1939, as *Der Mann Moses und die monotheistische Religion: Drei Abhandlungen* – *The Man Moses and Monotheistic Religion: Three Essays* (Clark, 1980, p. 523). The English translation by Katherine Jones, Ernest's wife, was quickly completed, and *Moses and Monotheism* followed on May 19, 1939.[3] Beyond the appearance of the complete book, a five-page selection from within chapter three called "An Advance in Intellectuality" was also published separately in 1939 in the *Internationale Zeitschrift für Psychoanalyse*.

"The Moses," Freud crows from London on March 12, 1939, "made its appearance here today in two copies. Quite a worthy exit, I believe" (Sachs, 1945, p. 184; cf., Freud, 1992, p. 255). By June the German edition had already sold 1,800 copies (Gay, 1988, p. 648).

That summer Freud's health began to decline precipitously. In July Schur found "foul necrotic tissue" and a "fetid odor" around his jaw (Schur, 1972, p. 525), then "necrosis of the bone" (p. 526). Antibiotics had not yet been discovered. At the beginning of August Freud finally stopped seeing patients, having enjoyed in London a "restricted but regular practice" (Freud, 1992, p. 263); this marked the end of a fifty-three-year practice as a therapist. By August the smell intensified; Freud's cheek was gangrenous, opening up a hole to the oral cavity (Schur, 1972, p. 517). Freud's chow, Lün, only out of quarantine seven months, refused to approach his master (in Freud, 1992, p. 252). "Freud knew what that meant," Schur writes, "and looked at his pet with a tragic and knowing sadness" (Schur, 1972, p. 526). On September 21, 1939, Freud reminded his

---

[3] Freud gave the Joneses his Moses in late August 1938 and was anxious to see the English and American versions published – even complaining that Katherine was needlessly delaying (see Molnar in Freud, 1992, p. 260). Freud regretted having to rely upon Jones, complaining to Max Eitingon that Jones "sometimes behaves as if he wanted to sabotage the book" (in Freud, 1992, pp. 242–3). According to Molnar, "American sales were vital" for Freud after he bought his London home (in Freud, 1992, p. 242) – the purchase loan for which concluded on July 28, 1938, with possession occurring in September. Ultimately Freud was grateful for the work and gave Katherine a precious stone to be made into a ring at his own expense (Roazen, 1976, p. 345).

personal physician of their arrangement: "My dear Schur, you certainly remember our first talk. You promised not to leave me in the lurch [*nicht im Stiche zu lassen*] when it's time. Now it's nothing but torture and makes no sense" (Schur, 1972, p. 529; translation modified; cf., p. 408). During this entire period Freud refrained from using barbiturates and opiates, using morphine only "as a last resort" (p. 525). The pain must have been tremendous. The next day Schur administered "a hypodermic of two centigrams of morphine," a small dose that put Freud to sleep; then he repeated the dose about twelve hours later and Freud fell into a coma.

Freud died in the early morning of September 23, 1939. Three days later he was cremated at Golders Green Cemetery in London, where his ashes were interred in a favorite Greek urn from roughly the fourth century BCE (Burke, 2006, pp. 161–2, 340); it had been a gift from Marie Bonaparte. Depicted on the urn were two figures in red: Dionysus, among much else the god of regeneration, and a maenad, a fanatical female follower of Dionysus (p. 162). At the funeral Jones delivered the English eulogy, Stefan Zweig the German. Zweig: "Wherever we seek to advance into the labyrinth of the human heart, henceforth his intellectual light will shine upon our path" (in Freud, 1992, p. 308).

In January 2014 craven vandals badly damaged the funeral urn, possibly in a botched burglary attempt, and in the process scattered the ashes of both Freud and his wife Martha (who died in 1951).

3.2   What's Love Got to Do with It? Inheritance, Character, Anti-Semitism

> Your letter contains the assurance which testifies to your superior intelligence, that everything I write is bound to cause misunderstanding and – may I add – indignation. Well, we Jews have been reproached for growing cowardly in the course of the centuries. (Once upon a time we were a valiant nation.) In this transformation I had no share. So I must risk it.
>
> (Freud to Charles Singer, October 31, 1938 [Freud, 1960b, p. 453])

Moses and Monotheism was widely criticized – most of all by Jewish readers.

Such criticism was not entirely new for Freud, or unexpected. In January 1938 Freud wrote, "I don't anticipate a friendly reception from the scientific circles – Jewry will be very offended" (Freud, 1960b, p. 440). Abraham Arden Brill, Freud's first American translator, reports that over the years he personally fielded many letters of complaint from Jewish readers. "Jewish scientists," Brill says, occasionally accused Freud of "crypto anti-Semitism" (1962, p. 195). One reader sent him an angry missive about Freud's frequent recourse to Jewish humor in *Jokes and Their Relation to the Unconscious* (1905). And a "Jewish medical biographer" even claimed, upon reading *Moses and Monotheism*, to have ripped up his unpublished manuscript on Freud's life.

In early 1936, Freud's Moses project had been mentioned by Stefan Zweig in a newspaper article for the London *Sunday Times* (in Freud, 1992, p. 190).[4] By June of that year Freud began to receive letters from Jewish correspondents, as he says, "imploring me not to deprive our poor unhappy people of the one consolation remaining to them in their misery" (Freud & Zweig, 1970, p. 163). The special pleading followed him to London. After he arrived in June 1938 at his rental house on Elsworthy Road, Freud's very first visitor was a neighbor, the Jewish Bible scholar Abraham Shalom Yahuda, who urged him to reconsider publishing the book (Freud, 1992, p. 240; cf., Clark, 1980, p. 523). Freud's response no doubt echoed his written remarks made to Charles Singer, the British historian of science: "Needless to say, I don't like offending my own people, either. But what can I do about it? I have spent my whole life standing up for what I consider to be the scientific truth, even when it was uncomfortable and unpleasant for my fellow men" (Freud, 1960b, p. 453). A similar sentiment opens the first essay of *Moses and Monotheism* (*SE*, 1939/1991, p. 7).

Freud was obviously aware that he was contesting pieties, breaking taboos, and courting bad taste, including his controversial decision to focus not on anti-Semitism but on Jewish character. Already in his first long letter about the Moses project, in September of 1934, Freud tells Arnold Zweig,

> Faced with the new persecutions, one asks oneself again how the Jews have come to be what they are and why they have attracted this undying hatred. I soon discovered the formula: Moses created the Jews. So I gave my work the title: *The Man Moses, a historical novel* (and with more justification than your Nietzsche novel). The material fits into three sections: The first part is like an interesting novel; the second is laborious and boring; the third is full of content and makes exciting reading. The whole enterprise broke down on this third section, for it involved a theory of religion – certainly nothing new for me after *Totem and Taboo*, but something new and fundamental for the uninitiated. (Freud & Zweig, 1970, pp. 91–2)

---

[4] Interestingly enough, Ernest Jones was only alerted to the Moses project because of Zweig's article. Possibly out of consideration for Jones, who must have chaffed at being denied this information, Freud (March 3, 1936) tells him that he began his *Moses* "last year" when the first draft was actually completed before September 1934 (Freud & Jones, 1993, p. 751).

The timing of the work was determined by the "new persecutions" of Jews after the election in 1932 of the National Socialists and subsequent appointment of Hitler as chancellor of Germany in January 1933. Institutionalized anti-Semitism was the end result of the collapse of liberal policies going back to the 1880s and 1890s and the decline of the Habsburg Empire. If Freud's response to the Nazis was especially provocative, it was because he seemed to blame Jews for their own victimization: Why had Jews, he says to Zweig, "attracted this undying hatred?" "It seemed extraordinary," the historian Henri Ellenberger writes, "that at a moment when the physical existence of the people of Israel was threatened, a Jew should publish a book contending that Moses was an Egyptian and had been killed by the Hebrews" (1970, p. 862). Most historians agree. Helen Puner: Freud "took from the Jews two great things which had traditionally characterized them: a great national hero, and a worldwide cultural achievement. These he gave to the Gentiles" (1947, p. 256). Marthe Robert: the effect of Freud's argument "was to declare a whole people illegitimate" (1976, p. 151); Ronald Clark: "the book could easily be classed as intellectual treason" (1980, p. 520); Peter Gay: "Freud seemed to be intent on wounding Jews instead of defending them" (1988, p. 604).

Freud not only repeats the old canard that Jews killed Jesus Christ, but adds to that another: Jews also killed their own prophet, Moses. In *Moses* Freud writes,

> If Moses was this first Messiah, Christ became his substitute and successor, and Paul could exclaim to the peoples with some historical justification: "Look! The Messiah has really come: he has been murdered before your very eyes!" Then, too, there is a piece of historical truth in Christ's resurrection, for he was the resurrected Moses and behind him the returned primal father of the primitive horde, transfigured and, as the son, put in the place of the father. (*SE*, 1939/1991, pp. 89–90; cf., p. 136)

And again:

> The poor Jewish people, who with their habitual stubbornness continued to disavow the father's murder, atoned heavily for it in the course of time. They were constantly met with the reproach "You killed God!" And this reproach was true, if it is correctly translated. If it is brought into relation with the history of religions, it runs: "You will not *admit* that you murdered God . . ." There should be an addition declaring: "We did the same thing, to be sure, but we *admitted* it and since then have been absolved." (*SE*, 1939, pp. 89–90; Freud's emphasis)

And so the historic differences between Christian and Jew was a matter of *admission* and *denial* of murder, a difference cashed out, of course, as the acceptance or rejection of Jesus as the son of God. This was Freud's first explanation for the existence of anti-Semitism, one that, he claims, has at least some kind of "justification" (p. 90). More about this in a moment.

It would therefore seem that indignation over *Moses and Monotheism* is very much deserved. Yet the situation is more complex than these judgments allow. Critics fail to appreciate that the Moses book is *an expansion* upon Freud's previous claims; and on claims made by others. Consider the following. (1) The charge that ancient Israelites killed an Egyptian nobleman named Moses, the very man who brought them safely out of the wilderness, was partly motivated by Freud's late interests in mass psychology, the leadership–discipleship relationship, and the deep origins of ethical responsibility. The key works in this regard are *Group Psychology and the Analysis of the Ego* (1921) and *Civilization and Its Discontents* (1930), works hardly ignored or denigrated in the secondary literature. (2) Freud was not alone in advancing speculation about the Egyptian origins of Moses. Such speculation, however shocking to nonspecialists, had already been published by others – including someone with impeccable credentials, the Jewish scholar and journalist Asher Hirsch Ginsberg, better known by his Hebrew pseudonym Ahad Ha'Am (Gay, 1988, pp. 606–7; Yerushalmi, 1991, p. 5). In fact, revisionist studies of the Bible were entirely common at the turn of the nineteenth century (Yerushalmi, 1991, pp. 23–4). Although characteristically unimpressed by these biblical authorities, Freud knew about them, thanks to Zweig (see Freud & Zweig, 1970, pp. 128–9, 131). (3) The application of the Oedipus complex to ancient history was very well known to analysts after 1912–13. As Freud himself put it in a letter of October 1938, *Moses* "is essentially a sequel to and an expansion of another work which I published twenty-five years ago under the title *Totem and Taboo*. New ideas do not come easily to an old man; there is nothing left for him to do but repeat himself" (Freud, 1960b, p. 453). He says the same thing elsewhere, including in his *Moses*: "It is not as though there were an absence of conviction in the correctness of my conclusions. I acquired that a quarter of a century ago when in 1912 I wrote my book *Totem and Taboo*, and it has only grown firmer since" (*SE*, 1939/ 1991, p. 58). There is no doubt at all. *Moses and Monotheism* repeats the bloody origins of society, the "secret of tragic guilt," described in *Totem and Taboo* – albeit tweaked to suit his present purposes concerning the origins of Judaism (Freud & Ferenczi, 1993, p. 281). (4) And finally, most important of all, *Moses* only reconfirmed Freud's lifelong Lamarckian convictions. If anything, *Moses and Monotheism* is Freud's most significant reaffirmation of his fundamental psycho-Lamarckianism (Yerushalmi,

1991, pp. 30–1). As Strachey acknowledges in a substantial footnote, Freud's discussion of "archaic inheritance" in *Moses* is "the longest in Freud's writings" (in *SE*, 1939/1991, p. 102, n. 1).

Frankly there is no mystery here: evidence of Freud's belief in Lamarckianism is readily available, not because of newfound letters and the recovery of lost texts, but directly in Freud's published works. In the third essay of *Moses* Freud writes emphatically, if unequivocally, about the importance of phylogenesis and "archaic heritage" (*archaische Erbschaft*) to his overall argument. Having already discussed the "constitutional factor" – those "things that were innately present in him at his birth, elements with a phylogenetic origin," namely "an *archaic heritage*" (*SE*, 1939/1991, p. 98; his emphasis) – Freud makes a signal declaration in subsection E, appropriately called "Difficulties":

> On further reflection I must admit that I have behaved for a long time as though the inheritance of memory-traces of the experience of our ancestors ... were established beyond question. When I spoke of the survival of a tradition among a people or of the formation of a people's character, I had mostly in mind an inherited tradition of this kind and not one transmitted by [conscious] communication. Or at least I made no distinction between the two and was not clearly aware of my audacity in neglecting to do so. My position, no doubt, is made more difficult by the present attitude of biological science, which refuses to hear of the inheritance of acquired characteristics by succeeding generations. *I must, however, in all modesty confess that nevertheless I cannot do without this factor in biological evolution.*
>
> If we assume the survival of these memory-traces in the archaic heritage, we have bridged the gap between individual and group psychology: we can deal with these peoples as we do with an individual neurotic ... *If this is not so, we shall not advance a step further along the path we entered on, either in analysis or in group psychology. The audacity cannot be avoided.* (*SE*, 1939/1991, pp. 99–100; my emphasis)

Freud's psychoanalysis of ancient history is founded entirely upon Lamarckian assumptions, assumptions that oblige Freud to very consciously leave behind the best practices of biological science. As he once said to a patient in the early 1930s, "We can't bother with the biologists. We have our own science" (in Wortis, 1954, p. 84). And Freud was right. Without the assumption of a repressed but still preserved archaic memory, there could be no analytic work at all, let alone analytic work on ancient history. This is obviously true of works like *Totem and Taboo* and *Moses and Monotheism*. And so, as Freud says, "The audacity [of invoking Lamarckianism] cannot be avoided." This is why Brill quite perceptively refers to Freud as a "paleopsychologist of the mind" (1962, p. 225). The bridge between the present and repressed past, and between individual and collective prehistory, is made possible *only* on the condition we accept Lamarck's claim about the inheritance of acquired characteristics as run through the pro forma recapitulation theory (or "biogenetic law") of Haeckel, ontogeny repeats phylogeny.

Like many others, Ernest Jones cringed at Freud's speculative "audacity." Francis Galton's research on genetics had been rediscovered and widely accepted after 1900. As a result, Lamarck's theories had fallen into disrepute long before 1939. Freud's open reliance on them in *Moses* was therefore an embarrassment – at least among those identified with the norms of science, which would include nearly all medically trained analysts at the time. Jones regularly contested Freud's most sensational beliefs, such as his belief in telepathy (aka "thought transference"), and pressured him to hold the results back from the public. Indeed, this is probably why Freud neglected to tell Jones at all about the Moses project until Stefan Zweig's newspaper article of 1936 made it impossible to avoid. In his official biography of Freud, Jones nonetheless gets the last word. In a chapter on "Biology" he writes,

> Freud never gave up a jot of his belief in the inheritance of acquired characteristics. How immovable he was in this matter I discovered during a talk I had with him in the last year of his life over a sentence I wished him to alter in the Moses book in which he expressed his Lamarckian view in universal terms. I told him he had of course the right to hold any opinion he liked in his own field of psychology, even if it ran counter to all biological principles, but begged him to omit the passage where he applied it to the whole field of biological evolution, since no responsible biologist regarded it as tenable any longer. All he could say is that they were all wrong and the passage must stay. And he documented this recalcitrance in the book with the following words: "This state of affairs is made more difficult, it is true, by the present attitude of biological science, which rejects the idea of acquired qualities being transmitted. . ." (Jones, 1957, p. 313)

"Begging" notwithstanding, Freud refused to remove the offending sentence; he was "immovable." Even more striking is Jones's claim that Freud's most explicit statement about Lamarckian inheritance in *Moses* (cited above) may have been *added* as a stubborn and very explicit reaffirmation of his views. So we should have known about Freud's Lamarckianism from reading his original works, long available; and if that didn't work, then we should have known because of the third volume of Jones's biography published in 1957; or if that failed to register, then from Sulloway's big book on the "biologist of the mind" of 1979. Consequently, the continuing "debate" about Freud's embarrassing Lamarckianism by influential scholars like Jacques Derrida (1996) and Richard J. Bernstein (1998) is not just remarkably tone-deaf; it is an unwitting and regrettable kind of whitewashing (cf., Dufresne, 2000, pp. 142–4; 2003, pp. 72–83).

Freud's Lamarckianism is just as evident in his private letters, sometimes in subtle ways. Consider his remarks to the psychiatrist Jan Ehrenwald. Between 1932 and 1937, Ehrenwald had delivered six lectures to the B'nai B'rith in Bratislava, then a part of Czechoslovakia. These lectures became a ninety-four-page book called *Über den sogenannten jüdischen Geist: eine Aufsatzfolge* (*On the So-Called Jewish Spirit: A Series of Essays*), which the author sent to Freud just before its publication in 1938. Here is Freud's reply of December 14, 1937:

> I must add a few words to my thanks for sending me your valuable little book . . . Several years ago I started asking myself how the Jews acquired their particular character, and following my usual custom I went back to the earliest beginnings. I did not get far. I was astounded to find that already the first so to speak embryonic experience of the race, the influence of the man Moses and the exodus from Egypt, conditioned the entire further development up to the present day – like a regular trauma of early childhood in the case history of a neurotic individual. To begin with. . . (Freud, 1960b, p. 439; cf., Gay, 1988, p. 605, n.)[5]

Translation: Freud had found the acquired characteristics of Jews, much like the neurotic symptoms of individuals informed by early trauma, in the "embryonic" experiences that began with the trauma of Exodus, of Moses leading the enslaved Israelites out of Egypt to the Promised Land. Despite what Freud says to Ehrenwald, the new "findings" were really not very "astounding" at all; they were determined by everything Freud had already theorized under the banner of psychoanalysis and its metapsychology. What *is* new is Freud's willingness to confront present-day Judaism and Jewish character with the same critical approach with which he had already confronted Christianity. But ultimately modern Christians and Jews share the same failings – as Freud exclaims, "Caught together, hanged together!"

---

[5] Ehrenwald (1900–88) was a Czech-born, Prague-trained psychiatrist who worked in London and then the United States. He is best known for his work on telepathy, sometimes discussing it alongside psychoanalysis, and the history of psychotherapy. A highly abridged version of the book appears under the same title in *The Jews of Czechoslovakia: Historical Studies and Surveys* (1938/1971, vol. 2, pp. 455–68).

(Freud, 1960b, p. 453) – and are subject to the same metapsychology, including its questionable metabiological assumptions.

Freud connects contemporary Jewish character to the history of the distorted reception of Moses's life – to myth – and to that life itself as revealed by depth psychology, that is, to the actual "man Moses." Jewish character was created, Freud argues, by the murder of Moses, first messenger of a monotheism once propounded by the Egyptian leader, Akhenaton. The "catastrophic" impact of this murder, to use Ferenczi's language, was thereafter inherited as a "growing sense of guilt" (*SE*, 1939/1991, p. 86) and passed along until a second Moses, a Jewish Moses, could finally sell the message to the Chosen People. So what does this ancient experience teach Freud about Jewish character? "To begin with," Freud says to Ehrenwald, "there is [in Jewish character] the temporal conception of life and the conquest of magic thought, the rejection of mysticism, both of which can be traced back to Moses himself and – although not with all the historical certainty that could be desired – perhaps a little further" (Freud, 1960b, p. 439). These remarks are repeated in the crucial third essay of *Moses*: monotheistic religion "was bound to leave a permanent imprint on their [Jewish] character through its rejection of magic and mysticism, its invitation to advances in intellectuality [*Geistigkeit*] and its encouragements of sublimations" (*SE*, 1939/1991, pp. 85–6).

It is worth noting that the development of Jewish *Geistigkeit*, a word that means both spirituality *and* intellectuality, was enhanced by the Mosaic "prohibition against making an image of God." The prohibition generated a new compulsion, namely "the compulsion to worship a God whom one cannot see" (p. 112–13). Such a dematerialized God, Freud argues, "has helped curb brutality and the inclination to violence which are usually found where the development of muscular strength is the popular ideal" (p. 115; and Jones, 1957, p. 147; translation adjusted). Later Freud adds that "progress in intellectuality" is connected to an "enhancement of self-consciousness" (*der Hebung des Selbstbewußtseins*) and of "the higher intellectual processes – that is, memories, reflections, and inferences" (pp. 117–18; translation modified; Freud, 1939, p. 207). Freud accepts that Jews have never achieved the harmony of body and mind as achieved in "muscular" ancient Greece. But Freud is undaunted just the same: "Im Zwiespalt trafen sie wenigstens die Entscheidung für das Höherwertige" – historically Jews have chosen the higher (*Höherwertige*) of the two options, intellectuality (Freud, 1939, p. 204).

That Freud felt these speculations were significant is evidenced by his decision, not only to publish his brief discussion of "The Advance in

Intellectuality" separately after the publication of *Moses and Monotheism*, but to have his daughter Anna deliver this discussion as a brief lecture at the Fifteenth International Psychoanalytic Congress in Paris in August of 1938 (Yerushalmi, 1991, p. 51).[6] One has to think Freud had carefully directed these remarks at anti-Semites everywhere during an era of institutionalized anti-Semitism.

Clearly, then, Freud enumerates *positive*, not simply negative, characteristics about the phylogeny of Jewish identity; characteristics he associates with himself and his own creation, psychoanalysis. Freud is therefore very far from disowning "Jewish character." For what does psychoanalysis promise but an understanding of deep time and the (however incomplete) triumph of reason over magical and mystical thinking? The result is sobering, and for some perhaps a bit surprising: intellectually and spiritually, Jews are more highly evolved than either Christians or mystics. Consequently Jews are better prepared – historically and biologically – for the truths of psychoanalysis. This is why Freud, already in 1908, could advise a Jewish colleague, Karl Abraham, to "tolerate" the Christian Carl Jung:

> since to begin with you are completely independent, and then you are closer to my racial kinship, while he [Jung] as a Christian and a pastor's son finds his way to me only against great inner resistances. His association with us is therefore all the more valuable. I was almost going to say that it was only by his emergence on the scene that psychoanalysis was removed from the danger of becoming a Jewish national affair. (Freud & Abraham, 2002, p. 38)

Two months later Freud repeated himself, saying that "On the whole it is easier for us Jews, as we lack the mystical element" (p. 52). As for Abraham, he happily conceded that "the Talmudic way of thinking cannot disappear in us just like that" (p. 40; cf., Wortis, 1954, p. 146).

As Dennis Klein insists in *Jewish Origins of the Psychoanalytic Movement* (1985), it is no accident that the first psychoanalysts were Jews – some of whom openly championed "Jewish pride" and nationalism in the face of rising anti-Semitism, and some of whom championed Jewish exceptionalism, not necessarily for the purpose of isolationism, but as the key for renewing tolerance and liberal humanism in the West. This is in fact one of

---

[6] During the Congress the Association debated the existence of lay analysis, with Americans against it, and Europeans for it (Burnham, 1983, p. 276). To Smith Ely Jelliffe, an American analyst, PhD, and physician, Freud on August 23, 1938, issued a familiar complaint: "I feel hurt by the behavior of the American analysts in the matter of Lay Analysis" (p. 276). Freud's grievance goes back to the 1920s. See Chapter 1, above.

Ehrenwald's messages in the little book of 1938 that he sent to Freud: "The traumatic experience of the two millennia of the Diaspora has raised this experience to the level of a compelling new political insight, to the insight that, in its final reckoning, it is universal humanistic values – transgressing national, ethnic, racial, and religious boundaries – which will carry the day" (Ehrenwald, 1938/1971, p. 467). Freud's thinking was part of this belief system, which explains why the first audience for many of his ideas between 1897 and 1917 was the B'nai B'rith – where Freud delivered numerous lectures. And so Freud, obviously self-conscious about "the Jewish origins" of psychoanalysis, was committed to reaching out to and accommodating well-placed gentiles like Jung in Switzerland and Ernest Jones in Canada and England. The goal was never isolationism, but rather the advancement of universal science.

As a consequence, the first Jewish analysts were obliged (by Freud, mostly) to ignore the casual anti-Semitism of gentile colleagues (Lieberman, 1985, pp. 64–5, 120, 220–1, 407). In this respect, Yerushalmi wonders aloud what Freud would have thought had he overheard the crude discussion between James Strachey, Ernest Jones, and Joan Riviere about the propriety of using the Latinate word "id" for Freud's original "*das Es*," the "it": apparently the concern was whether the word "id" might conjure up an unfortunate association with the word "Yidd" (see Yerushalmi, 1991, pp. 54–5). Jones in particular has come in for criticism for being anti-Semitic. He once incensed Otto Rank at a congress in 1923 by implying that he was something like a "swindling Jew" (Jones considered this a "gross exaggeration" of his words) (Lieberman, 1985, pp. 189–90); in 1934 Jones was so aggrieved by a manuscript of Isidor Sadger that he suggested (in a letter to Paul Federn) that Sadger be interned in a concentration camp (Roazen, 1976, p. 351); and in 1945 Jones wrote an essay, "The Psychology of the Jewish Question," that James Lieberman (among others) calls "startlingly anti-Jewish" (Lieberman, 1985, p. 407; cf., Yerushalmi, 1991, pp. 54–5). To be sure, Jones comes off badly in these accounts. At the same time accommodation runs both ways, since gentile analysts were also obliged to ignore the presumed superiority of their Jewish colleagues. Take the case of Theodor Reik, the lay analyst well known for his own highly developed sense of superiority. About Jones's biography of Freud he is reported to have said the following to psychologist David Bakan: "It's a good book. But there are two things that Jones doesn't understand. He doesn't understand the Jews, and he doesn't understand the Viennese. Jones is like a porter: he carries your bags but has no idea what's in them" (Bakan, 1996). The baggage Reik carried, by contrast, was the baggage of Jewishness, which the oddball Welshman was ill-equipped to fathom.

* * *

> I nurse a suspicion that the suppressed anti-Semitism of the Swiss that spares me is deflected in reinforced form upon you. But I think that we as Jews, if we wish to join in anywhere, must develop a bit of masochism, be ready to suffer some wrong. Otherwise there is no hitting it off.
>
> (Freud to Abraham, July 23, 1908 [Freud & Abraham, 2002, pp. 53–4])

In *Moses* Freud reveals a world historical father who, after being murdered, returns again in the form of a second Moses; together they give birth to the future of Judaism in the form of a band of brothers whose "growing sense of guilt" about the original patricide thereafter binds, and so creates, the Jews as one mass, one people; a people historically conditioned for a high level of *Geistigkeit*, of spirituality or intellectuality. These are the traumatic conditions that made strict monotheism possible, a monotheism characterized by a deep commitment to truth and justice.

As for Christians, Freud says that they took a different path after the murder of Jesus Christ: "the delusional disguise of the glad tidings," according to which "'we are freed from all guilt since one of us has sacrificed his life to absolve us'" (*SE*, 1939/1991, p. 135). True, Christians do not quite claim absolution for having "murdered" God, "but a crime that had to be atoned by the sacrifice of a victim [the son of God] could only have been a murder" (p. 135). In the place of yet another repression of this latest repetition of the murder of the primal father, Christians have "the somewhat shadowy conception of original sin" (p. 135; translation adjusted with reference to Freud, 1939/1967, p. 175). But in some ways, Freud says, the Christian path of salvation – of forgiveness and love rather than guilt – represents an advance over the "father religion," Judaism. Why? Because Christians acknowledge, albeit in disguised form, the very thing that ails humankind: the primal guilt for having murdered the father, ultimately God the father. For Jews, by contrast, it all remains repressed. And so the new "son religion," Freud says, helps makes Judaism a "fossil" (*SE*, 1939/1991, p. 88). Recall that Freud characterizes the Christian rationale as follows: "'They [Jews] will not admit it as true that they murdered God, whereas we admit it and have been cleansed of that guilt'" (p. 136). Jews pay for their repression with "a tragic load of guilt" (p. 136). For clearly, historically speaking, they were not willing to "join in this forward step" (*den Fortschritt mitzumachen*) of Christian confession for the murder of God in the form of his chosen son (p. 136; Freud, 1939, p. 241). Christianity is therefore triumphant, precisely the conclusion that grates on Freud's Jewish readers.

But not so quick. We already know from *Civilization and Its Discontents* that the foundation of culture is precisely repressed or unconscious guilt; a guilt, unforgiven because still unacknowledged, that actually *protects Jews* from the magical, ritualistic, inherently pagan thinking that returns to thwart the intellectual and cultural progress of Christendom. "After the Christian doctrine had burst the framework of Judaism," Freud argues, "it took up several components from many other sources, renouncing a number of characteristics of pure monotheism and adapting itself in many details to the rituals of the other Mediterranean peoples" (p. 136). Given this regression to paganism, Christianity was only an advance in *accessibility*, not *intellectuality*. It is therefore an appropriate spirituality, Freud implies, for those cultures who have taken muscles as their ideal, appropriate, let's be blunt, for dummies. Only Judaism maintains the moral stricture of a "pure monotheism." The upshot: Jewish monotheism is an older, deeper, and more intellectually demanding religion than the one associated with Greece, Rome, and Christianity. So yes, we are all of us bloody murderers – Christian and Jew alike. But the Christian belief in an original sin that is absolved through the death, resurrection, and forgiveness of a loving Jesus Christ circumvents the hard truths known (inherited and stubbornly repressed) most especially to Jews: an interminable guilt beyond the promise of forgiveness, the "delusional disguise of glad tidings." And so once again: The son religion called Christianity is a far cry, psychologically speaking, from the truth of *Kultur*, a truth better comprehended by the children of the father religion called Judaism. And that is why, to come full circle now, the teachings of Christianity in particular are singled out as *pathetic* illusions in both the *Future of an Illusion* and *Civilization and Its Discontents*. For although Judaism is also an illusion, it is not in its essence *pathetic*; it maintains within its traditions the weight of culture, dignity, discipline, learning, and civility. It maintains the weight, indeed, of *the future* – for these are the very qualities of *Geistigkeit* that drive forward the cause of reason and science. In short, as Jonathan Lear perceptively argues, *Moses* "in fact offers Jews a way of leapfrogging ahead of Christianity" (2000, p. 151).

If so, it is not entirely fair to charge the author of *Moses and Monotheism* with simple Jewish self-loathing. Strip away the political insensitivity of his project, set aside the racist biology, and Jewish psychology is actually rationalized and, in a way that is admittedly perverse, privileged. So too is Freud's own special role in history. For while Freud is a proud but secular Jew, and is therefore heir to a tradition of intellectual and ethical refinement, he is also, like Moses, a world-historical figure – a secular Moses no longer delivering the laws of God unto his Chosen People, but a father who gives birth to a future based upon the laws of psychoanalysis. Let's put this programmatically. The Egyptian Moses, having led the Exodus, was killed trying to convert the polytheistic Israelites to monotheism; a second Jewish Moses, many generations later, made good on the promise of founding a higher ethical and spiritual existence with "Mosaic" law, institutional Jewish monotheism, Judaism; and a third Moses, Sigmund Freud, gave to the entire Judeo-Christian world the even more refined, universal truths of the unconscious, psychoanalysis. Thanks to Freud, in other words, *religion finally becomes science* – that is to say, becomes real, an objective part of the external world.

And so Freud asks why *Jews* are hated. Obviously it would have been less distasteful to ask hard questions of anti-Semites. Why are some gentiles hateful? Why are the powerful obliged to fuel racism and utilize scapegoats? Why did the Germans and Austrians bend so willingly to Hitler's evil schemes? These are good and fair and necessary questions. But the truth is that we already know Freud's answers to these and similar questions from works written well before *Moses and Monotheism*. Civilization is a recent, fragile, superficial accomplishment. Hatred, aggression, and sadism are dictated by events in ancient history and forever encoded in our biology. Hitler was just the latest in a line of leaders to mobilize the masses through an identification that necessitated the existence of scapegoats. In other words, the substance of Freud's theoretical work before 1938 contains all the basic answers to the riddle of evildoing. Contemporary German social and political life was a dramatization of everything psychoanalysis had discovered about the life and death drives; about the limited possibilities for happiness in civilization; and about the destruction of pleasant illusions, shared by Jew and gentile alike, concerning the inevitability of progress, peace, love, and civility. This is why Arnold Zweig, in a letter of February 1939, found comfort in the explanatory power of *Civilization and Its Discontents* (conspicuously omitting to mention *Moses and Monotheism*). "I have discovered," he writes, "that the explanation of the pile of ruins on which we and the dictators now live like rats, is to be found in your work – in your *Civilization and Its Discontents*. Your ideas alone explain the hatred and indifference to everything that culture has achieved and signified since Moses" (Freud & Zweig, 1970, pp. 176–7).

As late as December 1927 Freud claimed to have no interest at all in explaining anti-Semitism, claiming instead a "wholly non-scientific belief that mankind on the average and taken by and large are a wretched lot" (Freud & Zweig, 1970, p. 3). It was only the arrival of Hitler that obliged Freud to subject his own feelings about anti-Semitism to his science. And so Freud does enumerate, in passing, the deeper motives for *Judenhass*, for "hatred of Jews" – motives beyond the historically "justified" complaint about the repressed and so unforgiven murder of the father in the symbol of His son, Jesus Christ (discussed above). These deeper motives, Freud says, are jealousy of Jews for claiming to be the Chosen People, the mark of circumcision, and a "grudge" from recent history (*SE*, 1939/1991, pp. 91–2). About the origin of this lattermost grudge or resentment (*Groll*), Freud basically tweaks the findings of *Civilization*: if some Christians are hateful it is because they are poor Christians, that is to say, are only recent converts to Christianity; given that they were "often driven to [conversion to Christianity] by bloody coercion" (p. 91), they remain superficially civilized. As a good Lamarckian, Freud understood that the acquisition of civility takes millennia. Consequently, the racist "hatred of Jews is at bottom a hatred of Christians" (p. 92). Self-loathing motivates anti-Semitic Christians.

But anti-Semitism just wasn't a very interesting question for Freud. He was far more interested in a perplexing and indeed perverse question, the question appropriate to a *depth* psychology: namely, the uncomfortable, repressed, monstrous fact of an inborn or, better yet, acquired sense of *Jewish* self-hatred, self-destruction, and primary masochism. Far from being an aberration in Freud's thinking, these are the exact same issues that always motivated his thinking about patients: the "secondary gain from illness," and during his last phase, the "negative therapeutic reaction," "moral masochism," and "primary masochism." Take his remark, just as offensive as anything he says about Jewish character, about childhood sexual abuse in essay three of *Moses*: "A girl who was made the object of a sexual seduction [*sexuellen Verführung*] in her early childhood may direct her later sexual life so as to constantly provoke similar attacks" (*SE*, 1939/ 1991, pp. 75–6). In *Moses* as elsewhere in the late Freud, the deeper question of inborn masochism belongs to metapsychology, not psychoanalysis, and to the logic of the death drive. Arguably it is a deeper, more tragic question than what we usually associate with everyday Jewish "self-loathing." Self-loathing is a question of integrity, a moral question. By contrast, the death drive is a question of *metaphysical* discontent, a question *beyond* good and evil actions.

So, then, why do Jews attract so much hatred? Quite simply because Jews are guilty – or, more precisely, are *the most guilty of all*. And being the most guilty, a trait inherited over centuries, they are also the most civilized. Translation into the stark language of the death drive: the contest between Christian and Jew is nothing less than the battle of love and hate, saved and chosen, forgiveness and guilt, life and death, Eros and Thanatos – a contest of worldviews written in the passage of religious history and owned, because they were acquired and then repeated, in the psyche of every individual. The Christian doctrine of salvation through forgiveness (for original sin, for murder) introduces love into the picture, while the origins of Judaism remain in contact with a primal urge for nonexistence and death. What is difficult to appreciate in these respects is Freud's guiding assumption: the claim that this older impulse is effectively the truth of culture, the truth of love – or, actually, their untruth, their undoing – that reveals every Christian impulse as a pathetic illusion.

Put a bit starkly, the metapsychology is fundamentally Jewish.

According to Yerushalmi, Freud's *Moses* provides a "countertheology of history," one that swaps out the "Chain of Tradition" common to biblical lore with "the chain of unconscious" (1991, p. 35). And he's right, so far as it goes. Repetition reaching back to what is unconscious is critically important for Freud. But it is actually *compulsive repetition* that sets everything in motion, and not just in *Moses and Monotheism*. The raped girl later repeats the circumstances that led to the rape. The victimized Jew later repeats the circumstances that led to his or her victimization. It is "from such discoveries about the problems of neurosis," Freud claims, that "we can penetrate [*vordringen*] to an understanding of the formation of character in general" (*SE*, 1939/1991, p. 76; Freud, 1939, p. 136). This approach may be offensive, but it is also a core belief of psychoanalysis and a capstone of the late metapsychology. The upshot: we are haunted by history, tormented by the death drive; but, thanks to Freud, we are now "penetrated" by the insights of psychoanalysis. What has been repressed and repeated is finally brought to consciousness – and, in the ideal, remembered.

Let's turn now to repetition, this time as it functions in Freud's *Moses*.

3.3 Repetition and Construction in *Moses*

James Strachey, ever attuned to Freud's telegraphic, colloquial, and even comic dimensions as a writer – albeit in the negative, since he tends to purge these features as a translator – is clearly bemused by *Moses and*

Monotheism. In an introductory note to his translation in the *Standard Edition*, Strachey writes,

> What is perhaps likely to strike a reader first about *Moses and Monotheism* is a certain unorthodoxy, or even eccentricity, in its construction: three essays of greatly differing length, two prefaces, both situated at the beginning of the third essay, and a third preface situated half-way through that same essay, constant recapitulations and repetitions – such irregularities are unknown elsewhere in Freud's writings, and he himself points them out and apologizes for them more than once. (*SE*, 1939/1991, p. 4)

Strachey follows Jones and blames these "irregularities" on the book's long gestation, the political climate in which it was composed, and the disruption of relocating to England (Jones, 1957, p. 362). And lest the reader attribute the eccentricities of *Moses* to Freud's diminishing powers as an old man – as Freud himself sometimes did, and as critics after Freud have often insisted – Strachey rightly reminds us that Freud's next long (unfinished) work, *An Outline of Psychoanalysis* (1938/1940), was "among the most concise and well-organized of Freud's writing" (*SE*, 1939/1991, p. 5). The "construction" of *Moses* is therefore puzzling, and Freud's many "apologies" for it obviously double as Strachey's own.

With this observation about *Moses*, Strachey is actually highlighting two features of its presentation: its unorthodox "construction," and its recourse to "constant recapitulations and repetitions." Let's consider both features, but in reverse order.

3.3.1   Repetition in Moses and Monotheism

Strachey notices that Freud repeats himself. Others have said the same thing. The loyalist Freud scholar Ilse Grubrich-Simitis, for example, speaks of "the book's deficiencies of content" (1997, p. 56) and adds, "Repetitions make for circular arguments." Acclaimed literary critic Edward Said agrees, arguing that "Moses seems to be composed by Freud for himself, with scant attention to frequent and often ungainly repetition, or regard for elegant economy of prose and exposition" (2003, p. 28).

It would be simple enough to demonstrate these claims, the collection of example after example constituting a major flaw in the work's composition. But there is more than one kind of repetition at work in *Moses*, and the charges of circularity and inelegance don't begin to comprehend it. Sometimes Freud (1) repeats a specific claim more than twice, (2) summarizes and therefore repeats previous remarks,

(3) reflects upon and even apologizes for his own repetition, and (4) reflects upon repetition itself, as a theory and as a clinical phenomenon. Because of the reflexive nature of (3) and (4), the many instances of repetition in *Moses* can be gathered up and related. For what Freud *does* with repetition is inevitably subject to what he *says about* repetition.

Consider, for a moment, those meta-commentary asides where Freud reflects upon and even apologizes for the fact that he is repeating himself.[7] We have seen this before, most dramatically at the beginning of chapter eight of *Civilization and Its Discontents*. Recall what Freud says: "Having reached the end of his journey, the author must ask his readers' forgiveness for not having been a more skillful guide" (*SE*, 1930/1991, p. 134). A similar remark from *Moses and Monotheism* is also the book's most rhetorically fascinating. It occurs during Freud's brief discussion of repetition at the beginning of the second half of the third essay, what Strachey informally refers to (above) as the work's "third preface." The book's first translator, Katherine Jones, calls this discussion a "Summary" and assigns it the Roman numeral "I." Strachey calls it "Summary and Recapitulation" and doesn't assign it a number at all. As for Freud, he calls it "Zusammenfassung und Wiederholung" and it appears with no number at all; it is only the next section, "Das Volk Israel" (The People of Israel), that is assigned, not a number but the letter "a" (Freud, 1939, p. 183). Of the two translations, Strachey's is obviously the more faithful. For "Zusammenfassung und Wiederholung" does mean "summary and repetition" or "summary and recapitulation." That Jones effaces altogether the conjunction and noun, *und Wiederholung*, is telling. For the word "recapitulation" evokes the outdated biology that her husband Ernest regretted and had "begged" Freud to minimize in this very work. Ironically or not, Katherine does just that – she minimizes it. By contrast, Strachey's attention to the full title follows his long footnote about Freud's biological commitments that closes out Part I of *Moses and Monotheism* (*SE*, 1939/1991, p. 102, n. 1). And, speaking of circularities, in that very note Strachey discusses in detail the theory of recapitulation that Katherine Jones erases in the title; Strachey even ends that note with a nod to Ernest Jones's discussion of Freud's Lamarckianism in the official biography.

---

[7] Yerushalmi offers another explanation that does not contradict the one I am developing here. He shows how the "Summary and Recapitulation" echoes "the development of biblical texts," at least according to Freud's own explanation. Yerushalmi's claim is that Freud is deliberately allowing for "inartistic" repetitions the better to avoid a biblical tradition that glosses over differences (Yerushalmi, 1989, p. 390).

Arguably Freud's title already hints at the serious humor that is to come. For the brief discussion that follows the title is a playful invocation of a theory of recapitulation that helps rationalize all the flaws that Strachey mentions: the unorthodox organization of the book and most especially its irregular repetitions. In this regard it is essential to note that Freud does *not* call "Summary and Recapitulation" a "Preface" or "Introduction," *Vorbemerkung*, the word that appears before the two brief sections that open Part I. More intriguing yet, it is not even certain that Freud's title refers strictly to the four paragraphs that follow. That is certainly the assumption, reasonable on its face, of both Jones and Strachey, who reduce the opening four paragraphs to one section among the ones that follow: Jones by assigning it Roman numeral "I," a decision that obliges her to make the next section start at Roman numeral "II"; and Strachey by effacing the difference between the four opening paragraphs and the section that follows it, "The People of Israel." For in the German original, the former appears in full caps as ZUSAMMENFASSUNG UND WIEDERHOLUNG – which is also how the printers treat the aforementioned Prefaces, VORBEMERKUNG – while the latter (the following section) is printed in regular type. In Strachey both this opening title and the section that follows are printed in the same regular type.

The upshot is that "Summary and Recapitulation" is neither outside the work as a preface, nor inside the work as a section warranting a number (i) or letter (a). Arguably that is because it functions as a meta-commentary and "confession" that stands apart from the rest of the book; and because it does double duty as the uncertain title, or even theme, for the *entirety* of Part II of the third essay. If so, it is not just a "summary" of what came before; it is instead a "summary to come," a promise about what is to follow. Which would make sense, since the overarching theme of Part II concerns precisely "summary and recapitulation."

These are unusual claims, so let's just cite the first two paragraphs in full, interjecting here and there our own meta-commentary:

> The part of this study which follows cannot be given to the public without extensive explanations and apologies. For it is nothing other than a faithful (and often word-for-word) repetition of the first part [of the third Essay]. . .[8]

---

[8] The passage in question is short, about two pages. The discussion here refers to Strachey, K. Jones, and to the original German edition (*SE*, 1939/1991, pp. 103–4; Freud, 1967, pp. 131–3; Freud, 1939, pp. 183–5).

The additional words in square brackets are from Strachey; Katherine Jones does not presume to say that the "faithful repetition" concerns "the first part *of the third essay*" or "the first part *of the book in general*." In the parlance of deconstruction, the choice between them is undecidable. In any case, Freud apologizes for what is *oft wörtliche Wiederholung*, often a verbatim repetition. Continuing:

> For it is nothing other than a faithful (and often word-for-word) repetition of the first part, abbreviated in some of its critical enquiries . . .

The repetition "which follows" in part II is the same, sometimes exactly the same, as other parts of *Moses*, only now in "abbreviated" or shortened form, *verkürzt*. Freud is already playing, enjoying himself – as he sets up the punch line. Enough to say that, through his rhetoric, Freud is invoking Haeckel's theory of recapitulation, according to which the totality of evolutionary development is repeated again at the individual level – only in abbreviated fashion. As I've argued throughout, this theory is typically invoked alongside Lamarck's theory about the inheritance of acquired characteristics, and forms the metapsychological foundation of Freud's mature theory of repetition. Freud continues:

> . . .abbreviated in some of its critical enquiries and augmented by additions relating to the problem of how the special character of the Jewish people arose.

Jewish character is acquired, augmented by additions (*vermehrt um Zusätze*) that are experienced over the course of history. These "additions" are the accumulated experiences of trauma. Such is the origin of the Jewish specificity, or difference, including a heightened sense of guilt and, along with it, the development of intellectuality. Freud closes the paragraph:

> I am aware that a method of exposition [*Darstellung*] such as this is no less expedient than it is inartistic. I myself deplore it unreservedly.

Freud's disapproval of his own representation – *Ich mißbillige sie selbst uneingeschränkt* – is total; he gives it without reservation. Like the man Moses, he is not a very good communicator. After his conflicts with Jung, Adler, Rank, Ferenczi, and so on, he has no sons he can trust, certainly no brother Aaron to communicate difficult truths on his behalf.[9] And so he stutters and bumbles along by himself, just as he did in *Beyond* and in

---

[9] For this insight about Aaron, Moses's brother, I thank the panel on Freud at the PAMLA gathering in late 2016, Fuhito Endo, Keiko Ogata, and Takayuki Tatsumi, and also members of the audience.

Civilization. In Strachey and Jones the next three sentences are rolled into the first paragraph, the difference between first and second paragraphs silently erased. But in Freud's original German they warrant their own paragraphs. This second paragraph, incidentally, is possibly the most clever of the entire book, for it poses and then answers a very good question about Freud's "inartistic" representation:

> Why have I not avoided it [the method of exposition]? The answer to that is not hard for me to find, but it is not easy to confess. I found myself unable to wipe out the traces of the history of the work's origin, which was in any case unusual.

The punch line, not easy to admit or confess (*einzugestehen*), could not be more amusing – or appropriate. The unorthodox, eccentric, irregular *features* of *Moses and Monotheism*, its *Darstellung* or representation, are themselves repetitions of the *arguments* of *Moses and Monotheism*. Or again, the *style* of *Moses* analogously repeats and so performs the *metabiology* that makes it all possible: it repeats, abbreviates, encapsulates, augments, and thereby records its own genesis (essay one, essay two, preface one, preface two, essay three, part one, summary and recapitulation, part two), even as it reveals, through psychoanalysis, the repressed history of repetitions, abbreviations, encapsulations, augmentations, and ultimately the genesis of the man Moses and monotheistic religion.

Freud thought he would never live to see the publication of the third essay – the "dangerous" residue or "remainder" (*Rest*) of the first two essays. But the move to England made its publication too tempting. For the book he tried to rearrange and edit the two early essays, but failed. "And so it has come about," Freud writes, "that I have adopted the expedient of attaching a whole piece of the first presentation to the second unchanged – which has brought with it the disadvantage of involving extensive repetition" (p. 104). In other words, the final version of *Moses and Monotheism* retains aspects of its development that are vestigial. On the other hand, repetition has its uses. Some things, Freud says, "should be said more than once"; indeed some things "cannot be said often enough" (p. 104). Still, the "clumsiness" or awkwardness (*Ungeschicklichkeit*) remains for the author. As for the work itself, it "grows as it will" (*das Werk gerät, wie es kann*) and, assuming a life of its own, "sometimes confronts its author as something independent, even alien" (p. 104; Freud, 1967, p. 133, translation modified).

The independent, objective existence of the work – which appears, Freud says with a lyrical flourish, "like a dancer balancing on the tip of one toe" (*SE*, 1939/1991, p. 58) – has justified its means or, if you prefer, has validated all the stages in its development between at least 1934 and 1938. Like a grown child, it lives an independent life, one separate from its father. If so, it makes little sense to complain about what appears clumsy or "inartistic," no more than one should complain about the vestigial in the history of the development of the species or bemoan the extravagances of children once they are born and grown up. And so Freud reflects upon and apologizes for his own repetition. Or rather he "apologizes," since the theory of repetition he invokes undermines his sincerity: he could have edited out the repetitions, but did not; he just kept it all. The reasons, recall, are easy for him to know but hard to confess; he could not erase the development of his work on development. As in *Civilization*, in other words, the apology is just a piece of ironical civility directed at those readers who, as Nietzsche would have it, don't have ears big enough to hear Freud's meta-commentary aside, his confession and creation story, about *Moses and Monotheism* – readers, I'm afraid, like Grubrich-Simitis and Said.

* * *

In *Moses* Freud repeatedly invokes the analogy between individual psychology and the history of the group. But Freud treats the analogy like a strict correspondence. For example, in the third essay he says that the analogy between individual and group psychology is very nearly "an identity," if not "more like a postulate" (*SE*, 1939/1991, p. 72). Yerushalmi calls this assumption Freud's "most audacious step" (1991, p. 30), one that is "impossible to accept" (p. 87). But Yerushalmi, like Bernstein after him, neglects to connect the audacious analogy to the audacious theory of compulsive repetition that drives it. And then, because he neglects the *Wiederholungszwang*, Yerushalmi neglects to connect the repetition compulsion to the death drive theory of *Beyond the Pleasure Principle*.

In *Moses* Freud is not just describing that form of repetition called the "return of the repressed." He is also describing *the mechanism* by which that return is made possible. To this end Freud stresses two points about "neurotic phenomena": traumas are either "positive" or "negative," and all traumas are subject to compulsive repetition. The "positive trauma" is the re-presentation of an emotionally charged experience from the past but now "in an analogous relationship with someone else." Freud continues:

> We summarize these efforts under the name "fixations" to the trauma and as a "compulsion to repeat." They may be taken up into what passes as a normal ego and, as permanent trends in it, may lead to unalterable character-traits, although, or rather precisely because, their true basis

[*wirkliche Begründung*: their real justification] and historical origin are forgotten. (*SE*, 1939/1991, p. 75; Freud, 1939, p. 136)

It is here that Freud introduces two examples of "positive traumas": the case of the young boy who, so attached to Mommy, spends his adult life looking for a wife with whom he can recreate that dependency; and the woman who, sexually abused as a child, spends her adult life recreating the conditions of her abuse. In other words, by "positive" Freud just means that the formative emotional experience, often traumatic, is still "present" long after the event. Formula: it is a ghost that haunts the person.

"Negative trauma" is just the opposite: the traumatic experience is neither recalled nor repeated. Even so, Freud argues that it is still a form of fixation, albeit one with "a contrary purpose" (p. 76): namely, it functions as a "defensive reaction" that presents as avoidance, inhibitions, and phobias. So although "negative traumas" still matter for the development of character, Freud cannot point to the reproduction of the original trauma. By "negative," then, Freud just means that the emotional experience, often traumatic, is only present as a lack or "absence" or avoidance. Formula: it is a haunting that presumes a ghost.

In *Beyond the Pleasure Principle*, Freud has trouble producing convincing examples of repetition compulsion. Recall that they include the spawning of salmon, the migratory patterns of birds, child's play, the facts of embryology, the transference neurosis, and the man whose protégés constantly turn against him. Freud speculates that these kinds of "demonic" repetitions point to something beyond the pleasure principle – a "beyond" he associates with a death drive that is both older than and independent of psychoanalysis. Freud cannot be convinced of his examples, however, because in the end he insists that the death drive primarily does its work in silence; like the "negative trauma," it is virtually unknowable aside from affects owing to an admixture of life and love. Recall our earlier metaphor: it is like an invisible black hole known only by its indirect effect on planetary bodies.

Moses is a continuation of these lessons first drawn in *Beyond*. Knowledge of the repressed may be an abstract, theoretical knowledge, but it is still comprehensible because of the "characteristic of compulsion" (p. 72). One cannot underestimate the utility of such compulsiveness, without which the ghosts from the past could not speak to us in the present. Freud writes:

All these [neurotic] phenomena ... have a *compulsive* [*Zwangscharakter*] quality: that is to say that they have great psychical intensity and at the same time exhibit far-reaching independence of the organization of the other mental processes, which are adjusted to the demands of the real external world and obey the laws of logical thinking. They are insufficiently or not at all influenced by external reality, pay no attention to it or to its psychical representatives, so that they may easily come into active opposition to both of them. They are, we might say, a State within a State, an inaccessible party, with which cooperation is impossible, but which may succeed in overcoming what is known as the normal party and forcing it into its service. (*SE*, 1939/1991, p. 76)

Compulsive repetition is set apart from ordinary repetition and from the ordinary functioning of the pleasure principle. The relationship between inaccessible trauma on the one hand and its representation on the other, between the repressed past and its recovery in the present, is just like the relationship between metapsychology and psychoanalysis, the death drive and the life drive. Or, truly, it is more than an analogical relationship, for the two realms overlap and are practically identical. Like the compulsion to repeat, metapsychology is a "State within a State," a theoretical field that Freud relies upon but that is *set apart and yet is within* psychoanalysis proper.

At stake in *Moses*, as in the rest of the late works, is the question of contact between the two realms, one "normal" and one "inaccessible." At stake is not only the question of reality but of the potential loss of reality – of psychosis. If the intense and independent "State" or "party" overwhelms normal functioning, if "internal psychic reality" dominates "the reality of the external world," if one becomes fixated "to an early portion" of one's past, then we have a situation the "practical importance" of which "can scarcely be overestimated" (pp. 76–7). So all this abstract talk belies a serious, even practical matter. Compulsions matter.

The fact is that ghosts haunt us – or, at least, the belief in ghosts haunts us. Arguably this is the widest frame for understanding the Moses book. Like the repetition Freud describes and performs, Freud's *belief* in the project – compulsive, haunting; "it tormented me like an unlaid ghost" (p. 103) – is a part of the project, perhaps even the most decisive part. For as we are beginning to see, the compulsive belief attached even to delusion carries within it a "kernel of truth." The mark of its validity is measured precisely by the strength of a belief that goes beyond the pleasure principle; that is not just subject to recapitulation, *Wiederholung*, but to *compulsive* recapitulation, to *Wiederholungszwang* – the repetition compulsion. If so, and here is our own "kernel" of truth, we can finally say that *Moses and Monotheism* is Freud's first major work to venture "beyond the pleasure principle." As such it is also the first excuse he has to clarify a new concept that is equal to the enormity of the task: "historical truth."

This is of course a big claim. Let's turn to it now by way of "constructions in analysis," which is caught up, surprisingly, with the influence of Havelock Ellis and a long detour into the question of homosexuality.

3.3.2   Constructions, Havelock Ellis, and Homosexuality

Recall once more: Strachey characterizes the "construction" of *Moses* as unorthodox, eccentric, and irregular. By "construction" Strachey means the book's "organization" into three unequal chapters, in addition to its strange repetitive character. But construction has another more technical meaning in the context of *Moses*, one that determines, at least provisionally, the organization (or "construction" in Strachey's looser sense) of Freud's ideas. This is construction as artifice, model, just-so story – in a word, as interpretation – and Freud invokes the word numerous times in *Moses*. The invocations, often essential to the argument and tone of the book, include the following:[10] "According to this construction of ours, the Exodus from Egypt would have occurred during the period between 1358 and 1350 B.C." (*SE*, 1939/1991, p. 29); "At this point I expect to be met by an objection to my construction" (p. 31); "I am prepared to find myself blamed for having presented my reconstruction ... with too great and unjustified certainty" (p. 41); "I know myself that my construction has its weak spots, but it has its strong points too" (p. 41); "... we must admit that this discussion reveals a weak side of our construction" (p. 49); "My construction starts out from a statement of Darwin's and takes in a hypothesis of Atkinson's" (p. 81); "An essential part of the construction is the hypothesis that the events I am about to describe occurred to all primitive men" (p. 81); "But anyone who is inclined to pronounce our construction of primaeval history purely imaginary would be gravely under-estimating the wealth and evidential value of the material contained in it" (p. 84); "There is nothing wholly fabricated [*frei erfunden*] in our construction, nothing which could not be supported on solid foundations" (p. 84); "The killing of Moses by his Jewish people ... thus becomes an indispensable part of our construction" (p. 89); "The apparently rationalistic religions of the East are in their core ancestor-worship and so come to

---

[10]   Strachey is not always consistent in his translation of "*Konstruktion*," sometimes preferring "hypothesis" (as on page 31) or "structure" (as on page 41). Wherever necessary I make the change back to construction or reconstruction, but otherwise adopt Strachey's translation.

a halt, too, at an early stage of the reconstruction of the past" (p. 93); "Our construction of prehistory forces us to another explanation" (p. 121); "To this day I hold firmly to this construction [of the primal father from *Totem and Taboo*]" (p. 131).

Freud's invocation of *Konstruktion* and *Rekonstruktion* in *Moses and Monotheism* is unusual in the history of his thought. True, as Strachey says elsewhere, Freud's writings "contain many allusions" to constructions (*SE*, 23, p. 256). But nowhere else does Freud commit himself to applying the concept so doggedly. Consequently its appearance in *Moses* demands an explanation. That said, the best entrée into the question of construction is not *Moses and Monotheism* at all, but is rather the last complete essay that Freud ever wrote – his "Constructions in Analysis" of December 1937. This generally overlooked essay, written in September and October as Freud continued to revise his final essay on *Moses*, offers the historico-theoretical rationale for utilizing the concept of construction in *Moses*. It has another merit: it invokes an early group of essays wherein the idea of construction received its abortive test run, namely, Freud's "seduction" essays of 1896. At stake in 1896, as in 1937, is the problematic linkage, not just between the present and the repressed past but between objective and subjective reality, external and internal worlds – arguably the guiding question of the late Freud.

*   *   *

"Constructions in Analysis" opens with an anecdote. While "a certain well-known man of science" treated psychoanalysis fairly in the early days, he also once "gave expression to an opinion upon analytic technique which was at once derogatory and unjust" (*SE*, 23: 257). Freud continues:

> He said that in giving interpretations to a patient we treat him upon the famous principle of "Heads I win, tails you lose" [in English]. That is to say, if the patient agrees with us, then the interpretation is right; but if he contradicts us, that is only a sign of his resistance, which again shows that we are right. In this way we are always in the right against the poor helpless wretch whom we are analyzing, no matter how he may respond to what we put forward. (p. 257)

Like many readers, the French philosopher and lay analyst Jacques-Alain Miller (2010/2011) has wondered about the identity of this unnamed "man of science"; as Miller says, "we ought to find out who said that" (p. 14). Miller then links this man of science to the other "opponents" whom Freud invokes in works like *The Question of Lay Analysis* (see chapter 1).

The identity of the man in question is Havelock Ellis – a very real, as opposed to "imaginary," interlocutor (as utilized by Freud in *Lay Analysis* and *The Future of an Illusion).*[11] During a training session on November 6, 1934, Freud and a recent medical graduate of the University of Vienna, an American named Joseph Wortis, had been discussing the problem of suggestion when the "derogatory and unjust" remark about "heads I win" came up. Wortis records the following:

> Freud began to talk of Ellis's relation to psychoanalysis. Ellis had some years ago written of psychoanalysis and said it made use of a procedure which was the opposite of scientific. If a patient admitted something, said Ellis, the analyst accepted it. If, however, the patient denied something, the analyst decided it was an admission too, concealed by a conscious denial. This, said Ellis, was like "heads I win, tails you lose." (Freud used the English phrase.)
>
> "Now Ellis," said Freud, "was doing great harm to psychoanalysis by treating it so unjustly: it amounted to calling psychoanalysts a bunch of scoundrels [*Verbrecher*], and Ellis's opinions were likely to be influential."
> Ellis did not know what he was talking about, Freud went on to say. It was no great matter if a man did not know anything about psychoanalysis, only he ought not to talk about it. At any rate, Ernest Jones, the London psychoanalyst, attacked Ellis ... and Ellis thereupon wrote to Freud in protest.[12] Freud however felt it was his duty to say, as politely as he could, that Jones was in the right. (Wortis, 1954, p. 65)

As with Rolland, Freud was in 1934 concerned that an influential critic had done "great harm" to the reputation of psychoanalysis – harm that had, in fact, been realized in Adolf Wohlgemuth's *A Critical Examination of Psychoanalysis* (1923), where psychoanalysis was twice criticized for adopting the logic of "heads I win, tails you lose" (pp. 69, 238). Ellis was a critic, moreover, whom Freud basically admired, enjoyed as a correspondent, and whose framed and signed portrait ("With sincere regards and admiration") occupied a place on his waiting room wall (Guest, 1984, p. 213; Wortis,

[11] In *The Freud Files*, Borch-Jacobsen and Shamdasani propose (in a passing endnote) that "It seems that [Adolf] Wohlgemuth was the anonymous 'certain well-known man of science' whom Freud alluded to in 1937" (2012, p. 332, n. 152). Wohlgemuth was author of *A Critical Examination of Psycho-Analysis* of 1923, and remained an irritant to psychoanalysis by delivering, in the late 1920s, a harsh expert opinion to an ethics committee of the British Medical Association. Psychoanalysis, according to the psychology researcher, is fatally compromised by suggestion (Overy, 2009, pp. 138–39). Ernest Jones insisted on being made a member of this ethics committee, so it is likely that Freud knew about Wohlgemuth's views. Nonetheless, Wohlgemuth's "heads I win" quip actually originates in Ellis's work. (I thank Borch-Jacobsen for debating the issue with me and for pointing out unknown sources.)

[12] Concerning the letter of "protest" Ellis is supposed to have made to Freud about Jones's negative review (from 1928), it was actually made by Ellis's companion, François Lafitte-Cyon – whose pretense of being unconnected to Ellis, Grosskurth notes, did not fool Freud (Grosskurth, 1980, pp. 389–92). Ellis writes about this episode in a 1936 letter to Wortis (Wortis, 1954, pp. 172–3).

1954, p. 28). Ellis admired Freud as well, despite priority issues, disbelief in some tenets of psychoanalysis, distaste about discipleship, and the belief that Freud was an artist rather than a scientist (see Grosskurth, 1980, pp. 359–60, 387–93; Wortis, 1954, p. 176; *SE*, 1920b/1991, pp. 263–5). Referring to volume I of *Studies in the Psychology of Sex*, published in 1898, Ellis claimed to be "the first in English" to acknowledge Freud's unique contribution (Ellis, 1933/1948, pp. vii–viii).[13] Moreover, in an essay of 1898 Ellis was generally supportive of the sexual etiology that appeared in Freud and Breuer's *Studies on Hysteria* (1895b) – although he did caution, as Freud puts it, that they "put too much emphasis on early sexual trauma" (in Wortis, 1954, p. 92). One thus supposes that Ellis had earned the right to a position, as he says, of "always friendly but often critical" detachment from psychoanalysis (Ellis, 1933/1948, p. viii).

Ellis introduced the "heads I win" quip in a new supplementary section devoted to "eonism" – aka "sexoesthetic inversion" or, more simply yet, cross-dressing – in the third edition of volume two of *Studies in the Psychology of Sex*:[14]

> There are some psychoanalysts who when they see acknowledged signs of homosexuality, accept them, as most other people do, as the signs of homosexuality. But when they see the reverse, even a strong antipathy, they accept that also as a sign of homosexuality, the reaction of a suppressed wish. "Heads, I win," they seem to say; "tails, you lose." This is rather too youthful a method of conducting mental analysis. (1948, pp. 101–2)[15]

The context of Ellis's remark of 1915 is significant, and adds an important layer of complexity to Freud's invocation in "Constructions in Analysis." For it is clear from Ellis's remarks, and also from the context in which they are made (a volume devoted to "Sexual Inversion"), that he is not simply accusing psychoanalysis of turning every patient's "Yes" or "No" into

---

[13] Twice Grosskurth corrects Ellis about being the first to introduce the English to Freud (291n, 388n). The first English discussion of Freud was by J. Mitchell Clarke in 1896, and then J. W. H. Myers in 1897. But she ungenerously misreads Ellis. Ellis states that his was the first *book* in English to mention Freud.

[14] The publishing history of Ellis's volume on homosexuality is complex. Originally Ellis and a coauthor, John Addington Symonds, published *Contrary Sexual Feeling* in German in 1896. Symonds, however, died during its composition and his estate later asked for his contribution to be withdrawn. So Ellis rewrote the book and in time made the work volume 2 of the *Studies* (Grosskurth, 1980, pp. 179–83). The purged first edition in English appeared in 1897; a second edition appeared in the United States in 1901; and the third and revised edition, cited above, appeared in 1915. Ellis's discussion of psychoanalysis only begins in the 1915 edition.

[15] Brome (1979, p. 220) misattributes this passage to volume seven of *Studies in the Psychology of Sex* of 1928 – possibly because Ellis and Symonds' German edition appeared as the seventh volume of the *Bibliothek für Sozialwissenschaft*.

a confirmation. It is a rather more pointed criticism about the tendency of analysts to turn every patient's "Yes" or "No" into confirmation that they are actually "homosexual" (a pathological category of "inverted" sexuality). It is this specific tendency that reveals, for Ellis, that psychoanalysis is "rather too youthful a method." Always disinclined to offend, Ellis means by this elliptical phrase that the psychoanalytic method is immature, infantile – in a word, *homophobic*.

So Freud had three good reasons for agreeing with Jones's critical response to Ellis in 1928 (discussed with Wortis, above). One, Ellis had originated a dangerous criticism that psychoanalysis cannot be falsified – a criticism that had already doubled as a punch line for Wohlgemuth. Two, Ellis claimed that psychoanalysis overdetermines its constructions. And three, Ellis implied that such overdetermination was too often used as an excuse to diagnose repressed homosexuality.

Freud's discussion of Ellis during his analysis of Wortis in 1934–5 is part of his evolving response to the charge of finding homosexuality behind every "Yes" or "No," a charge that culminates in the more generalized arguments of "Constructions in Analysis." To this end Freud takes the time to disparage Ellis's understanding of psychoanalysis; so much so that this early and fair expositor of Freud's original views is now characterized as a know-nothing. It is no accident, furthermore, that Ellis's "heads I win" criticism occurs to Freud during the training of Wortis. For Wortis's analysis with Freud was supported by a fellowship, arranged by Ellis and Adolf Myer, "devoted to the scientific study of homosexuality" (Ellis in Wortis, 1954, p. 2). Here is how Wortis, decades later, describes the funding:

> I was a fortunate recipient of a fellowship, so I was very well situated. It was supposed to be a lifetime fellowship, but it terminated in seven years since I could not honestly go along with the hopes and wishes of the family of A. Kingsley Porter, a distinguished Harvard professor. Porter was a homosexual, in the closet, who in the 1930s could not afford to come out with his homosexuality. He fell in love with a young man, whom I knew, Alan Campbell, and the young man spurned him and [Porter] went into a deep depression. He had a summer home in Ireland and he threw himself off the cliffs; his body was never recovered. The bereaved widow, Mrs. Porter, went to Havelock Ellis, who was a friend of Kingsley Porter, saying she wanted to use her wealth to do something for the cause of homosexuality. (Wortis, 2007, pp. 14–15)

Wortis had little interest in sexology, let alone homosexuality, but took up the fellowship on the condition that he could use it to forward his postgraduate psychiatry training. And so it came about that, after some months of study in London, Wortis, against Ellis's advice (1954, pp. 10–11), approached Freud as part of his medical training – and to sound Freud out on homosexuality. Subsequently homosexuality became a topic prompted by the fellowship and, during the analysis, by Wortis's dreams about homosexuality.[16]

Imagine Freud's surprise, or skepticism, when he first heard that a protégé of Ellis – the very person who implied that the psychoanalytic method was homophobic – was now interested in a training analysis as part of a program to better understand homosexuality.

* * *

It is a notorious but well-known fact that Freud used analytic sessions to discover new information about colleagues, exchange gossip, and relay informal, sometimes highly personal, messages to absent third parties. Ellis had sent to Freud an inscribed copy of Isaac Goldberg's 1926 book, *Havelock, Ellis: A Biography and Critical Survey*, which Freud left in his waiting room (Wortis, 1954, p. 28). But Freud didn't know a lot about the man Ellis. That changed with his analysis of Hilda Doolittle. The American imagist poet and one-time lover of Ezra Pound, better known as H.D., had an analysis with Freud from March to May of 1933, and then again in the fall of 1934 (Guest, 1984, pp. 297, 217). Both Hanns Sachs and Havelock Ellis wrote to Freud recommending H.D. for analysis (p. 207). Freud agreed, and they had six sessions weekly at 5:00 in the afternoon (p. 210). H.D. writes to Ellis: "Freud says openly [that] he cannot take on people who have nothing to offer in return, any more . . . or words to that effect" (in Guest, 1984, p. 214). What H.D. could offer Freud was information about his friend and rival, Havelock Ellis – but also information about her first brief analysis with Freud's colleague Hanns Sachs and a third person named Annie Winnifred Ellerman.

Ellis had already treated H.D. in 1919 not long after she began her affair with Ellerman, heiress and author of boy's adventure stories better known as "Bryer" and "Bryher" (Grosskurth, 1980, p. 294; Guest, 1984, pp. 105–28).[17]

---

[16] While in Vienna for analysis Wortis discovered early work on the insulin shock treatment, which he brought back to the States as a treatment for schizophrenia. He remained open to psychoanalysis as a profession, but drifted toward biological psychiatry.

[17] H.D. was pregnant and separated from her husband, Richard Aldington, when Bryer, a fan of her poetry, eight years her junior, tracked her down in July 1918. H.D., desperate, sick with pneumonia, and opportunistic, was open to the adventure; beyond that Bryer was lonely, depressed, and potentially suicidal. So they needed each other. In time the women enjoyed an open arrangement that lasted through Bryer's two marriages until H.D.'s death in 1961 (Guest, 1984).

Through Sachs, her analyst, Bryer had become a benefactor to the psycho-analytic cause. In the 1930s she bailed out the *Psychoanalytic Review*, which Freud's son Martin was about to manage (having been pushed out of his banking job by the Nazis) (Guest, 1984, p. 212); paid very high fees to Freud for H.D.'s analytic treatment; and, at the end of H.D.'s treatment, estab-lished emergency funds to be used at Freud's discretion (pp. 211–12).[18] So Freud had three good reasons (Ellis, Sachs, Ellerman) for accepting H.D. into treatment.

To those reasons we can add a plausible fourth. In October 1918 Freud had begun analyzing his own daughter, Anna, six days a week at 10:00 in the evening; an open secret among Freud's close associates, but unknown to the general public until it was revealed in 1969 by the Freud scholar Paul Roazen (1969, p. 43; 1976, pp. 438–40).[19] This analysis, which lasted almost four years – and was repeated again in 1924 for another year – flew in the face of every technical recommendation that Freud or any analyst ever made. According to literary critic and lay analyst Patrick Mahony, it was "an impossible and incestuous treatment," and "a momentous and bizarre event by any standard" (1991, p. 307). That sounds about right. Mahony connects Freud's 1919 essay on moral and sexual masochism called "A Child Is Being Beaten," not only to *Beyond the Pleasure Principle* of 1920 but to Anna's essay "Beating Fantasies and Daydreams" of 1923 – a work that gained her entry to the Vienna Psychoanalytic Society as a recognized analyst (pp. 307–9; Roazen, 1976, p. 438). Mahony's inter-pretation: Freud's essay of 1919, along with Anna's acceptance of Freud's ideas, reflects the fact that Freud was "in the process of beating" his daughter – a daughter subject, therefore, to "an iatrogenic seduction and abuse" (p. 308). That too sounds about right.

Far less has been said about the possible relevance of another essay Freud published in 1920, "The Psychogenesis of a Case of Homosexuality in a Woman."[20] In it Freud narrates the case of a "clever girl" who belonged to

---

[18] H.D. paid about $25 per session, while Wortis paid $20; other Viennese analysts at this time charged American patients $10 (Roazen, 1976, p. xxiv). Freud preferred payment in pounds or US dollars. Guest writes: "Freud explained that he was forced to charge his wealthy and foreign clients more, so that he might charge the Viennese less" (1984, p. 211). To put this in perspective, "a secretary would [at that time] earn about twenty dollars a month." So Bryer's and Wortis's foundations were paying exorbitant fees.

[19] Anna's private view of Roazen, written in a letter: "he is a menace whatever he writes."

[20] The essay ends with a discussion of Eugen Steinach's experiments as a possible "cure" of homo-sexuality (1920c/1991, pp. 171–2). A pioneer in endocrinology, Steinach's use of the vasectomy ("vasoligation") to reinvigorate fading libido led Freud to get "Steinached" after the cancer diagnosis of 1923. In short, Eros was brought to bear against Thanatos. One can only speculate about the possible connection between Steinach's work on homosexuality and its connection to Freud's

"a family of good standing" and had fallen in love with an older "society lady" who, although married, was reputed to live with a female companion with whom they shared an open relationship. "After she had been punished for her over-affectionate attitude to a woman," Freud writes, "she realized how she could wound her father and take revenge on him. Henceforth she remained homosexual out of defiance against her father" (*SE*, 1920c/1991, p. 129). It cannot be the case that in 1920 Freud was talking about his daughter Anna's relationship with Dorothy Burlingham, the Tiffany heiress with whom she was to spend the rest of her life.[21] For Burlingham only arrived in Vienna in 1925. Yet it does make sense that Freud's newfound interest in female homosexuality, and with it the role of the mother in psychoanalysis, came up precisely when he began to analyze his own lesbian daughter in 1918. It is also possible that some aspects of the case study on homosexuality are derived from his analysis of Anna.

Certainly the analysis of H.D. in 1933, years after his first analysis of Anna, must have been uncanny for Freud. By that time he had discovered in the relationship of H.D. and Bryer a repetition of his daughter's relationship with Burlingham, and a repetition of the anonymous relationship discussed in "The Psychogenesis"; each relationship involved a younger woman and an older, more independent, financially stable woman.[22]

Back to Ellis and H.D. Not long into her treatment with Ellis in 1919, H.D. and Bryer had invited Ellis on a summer vacation to Greece paid for by Ellerman's father, the English shipping tycoon Sir John Ellerman.[23] Apparently the two lovers took to calling Ellis by the name "Chiron" – immortal god, centaur, son of Kronos (Guest, 1984, p. 122). So H.D. knew Ellis very well by the time she arrived in Vienna over a decade later. From H.D.'s book *Tribute to Freud* (1944), we also know that Freud and his

---

operation in November 1923 to fend off the cancer (itself sometimes cast in the light of narcissism and repetition compulsion). See Gay, 1988, p. 426; Dufresne, 2000, pp. 38, 190 n. 15; and, in a fascinating exploration, Gherovici, 2010, pp. 79–83.

[21] Burlingham lived at 19 Berggasse in 1929; they bought a summer house together; Anna analyzed all four children, which the two women raised together; like Anna, Burlingham became a child analyst; and they ultimately lived together in Freud's house in Hampstead after Martha Freud's death in November 1951. Readers always ask about Anna's sexual orientation, a question usually avoided altogether in the literature. Finally, though, in the French introduction to the letters of Freud and Anna, historian Elisabeth Roudinesco (2012) spells it out: Anna was gay, and the long avoidance of admitting it as such is simply homophobic. I agree.

[22] It is also significant that Freud analyzed Burlingham as well, thus closing the family circuit (Roazen, 1976, p. 448).

[23] Probably the richest man in England. At his death in 1935, his fortune was estimated at $30,000,000. Adjusted to today's dollars, that would make Ellerman a billionaire a few times over.

patient spent time discussing Ellis. One session on March 10, 1933, is especially relevant: Freud delivers a criticism of Ellis that doubles as a direct response to Ellis's charge that the psychoanalytic method is "too youthful." Having teased out her own negative reactions to Ellis – "I had spoken of my disappointment with Havelock Ellis" (1974/1944, p. 147) – Freud tells H.D.: "He [Ellis] records so many funny things that people do but never seems to want to know *why* they do them. You see I lose him a little, but I always thought there was something immature about his *Psychology of Sex*" (p. 148). Touché – Freud delivers the same charge of immaturity back at Ellis's work, and indeed at his life.

But Freud's diagnosis of Ellis's "immaturity" was neither guesswork nor an analytic "construction"; it was derived from his discussions with H.D. First of all, from biographers we know that Ellis had good reason to be sensitive about sexual "inversion": his first wife, the novelist Edith Lees, was gay and, as their marriage evolved, had serial affairs with women. H.D. let Freud know this fact (Guest, 1984, p. 213). Incidentally, Ellis's personal connection to homosexuality was indirectly the reason that he was on friendly terms with A. Kingsley Porter, the wealthy Harvard professor. As early as 1931 Porter had written to Ellis about his newfound homosexuality. In the summer of 1932 Porter and his wife visited Ellis about Porter's depression over the situation, which included worry about losing his job at Harvard (Grosskurth, 1980, pp. 418–20). It was Ellis himself, having confided in the couple about his own unconventional first marriage, who connected Porter with Alan Campbell, an aspiring novelist. Grosskurth writes, Campbell "moved into the Porters' beautiful home in Cambridge, Massachusetts, a few months later [after July 1932], and there apparently a *ménage a trois* was established" (p. 418). When Campbell subsequently left for California, Porter once again fell depressed and, in the summer of 1933, killed himself near his summer home in County Donegal, Ireland. One final detail about this incestuous family romance: having recommended Alan Campbell to the Porters in 1932, Ellis then recommended Wortis in 1934 for the Porter fellowship to study homosexuality. Recall, as well, that Wortis admitted to already knowing Campbell socially (Wortis, 2007, p. 15). So Ellis was intimately involved – therapeutically, humanely – with Porter's struggles, both before and after his suicide.

For all his admirable tolerance of flexible sexual relationships, Grosskurth characterizes Ellis as initially quite naive about homosexuality, plagued by stereotypes about gender, and "bewildered" and hurt when his own wife Edith began to act upon her desires (Grosskurth, 1980, pp. 154–7). We also know that Ellis was a virgin when he married Edith at age 31, was predominately asexual in his relations with women, and was impotent most of his life. In his 60s, however, Ellis finally discovered sexual pleasure through urolagnia, pleasure derived by the sight (or experience) of a woman urinating. His late romantic partner, Françoise Lafitte, was for this reason affectionately called his "Naiad" or water nymph (p. 287). There's more. We also know that H.D. had direct access to Ellis's proclivities: during 1919 she urinated on Ellis for his pleasure. Five years later Ellis would recount the sensuous episode in his autobiography, foolishly entitled *The Fountain of Life* (1924). At her insistence, Ellis disguised H.D.'s identity as "Person":

> Person's tall form languidly rose and stood erect, taut and massive it seemed now with the length of those straight adolescent legs still more ravishing in their unyielding pride, and the form before me seemed to be some adorable Olympian vase, and a large stream gushed afar in the glistering liquid arch, endlessly, it seemed to my wondering eyes, as I contemplated with enthralled gaze this prototypical statue of the Fountain of life. (in Guest, 1984, p. 121)

As far as gossip goes, it doesn't get any better. It is therefore no wonder that Freud, having learned of these intimate details about Ellis from H.D., would declare his rival "immature." In a letter to her lover, Bryer, H.D. repeats Freud's response, albeit differently than in the public version recounted in *Tribute*: "Ah," Freud said, "I always thought between OURSELVES that that man's work was inconclusive and in some way he may be immature. AND NOW I KNOW" (in Guest, 1984, p. 213; her emphasis). Now he knows; the man who dared to call Freud's method "too youthful" was himself sexually immature, technically a "pervert" once married to an "invert." One can practically hear the glee in Freud's discovery.

Naturally the shy twenty-eight-year-old Joseph Wortis could never compete with worldly Hilda Doolittle, twenty years older, who was not only beautiful, smart, interesting, and connected to massive wealth, but had been on intimate terms with Havelock Ellis. She was also a fairly well-known author. By the time Wortis arrived at 19 Berggasse, H.D.'s book of poems was inscribed and included with the others (e.g., Malinowski, Woodsworth, Einstein) in Freud's waiting room (Wortis, 1954, p. 28).[24] So the two patients were in different leagues. But Wortis managed to prove his usefulness, as well. Practically his first act as patient

---

[24] They did share Freud as an analyst for a few months in the fall of 1934, but never met. Wortis was too shy when Ellis suggested he ought to meet her (1954, p. 87). As for Freud, he told Wortis that he "should break himself of that" shyness.

was to share with Freud some of Ellis's derogatory remarks written in private letters (see Wortis, 1954, p. 17). "If you are psychoanalysed," Ellis had cautioned his young protégé in one such letter of September 1934, "you either become a Freudian or you don't. If you don't, you remain pretty much where you are now; if you do – you are done for! – unless you break away, like Jung or Adler or Rank (and he has done it too late)" (in Wortis, 1954, p. 11).

By 1920 Freud had already considered Ellis's reduction of Freud's work to artistry to be a "highly sublimated form of resistance" (Jones, 1957, p. 21). For example, in a short essay published anonymously (and in the third person) in 1920, Freud directly responded to Ellis's claim about artistry as it appeared in *The Philosophy of Conflict* (1919). "We are inclined," says Freud, "to meet it with a most decided contradiction" (*SE*, 1920b/1991, p. 263) – in short, with a "No."[25]

The upshot is that when Wortis revealed Ellis's private remarks about Freud in 1934, it only confirmed that Ellis had further distanced himself from psychoanalysis. As Freud therefore told Wortis, "Ellis, in a fundamental sense, has rejected analysis" (Wortis, 1954, p. 16). Always careful to play both sides, Wortis protested Freud's conclusion: actually, Wortis insists, Ellis is "sympathetic in many ways, especially toward Freud personally" (pp. 16–17). Freud responded by linking Ellis to another colleague, the Swiss lay analyst Pastor Oskar Pfister: "I know," Freud said. "Ellis is one of the friendliest persons I know. A man can only accept

---

[25] Actually Ellis's claim was even more mischievous, since he goes on to connect artistry to the origins of the free association technique. This he does by pointing to the work of J. J. Garth Wilkinson, a physician who, Ellis says, is "more noted as a Swedenborgian mystic and poet than as a physician" (cited by Freud, *SE*, 1920b/1991, p. 263). Apparently in 1857 Wilkinson adopted "a kind of exalted laissez-faire" or "Impression" method in writing a volume of "mystic doggerel verse." Freud cites Ellis as follows: "it is easy to see that essentially it is the method of psycho-analysis applied to oneself, and it is further proof how much Freud's method is an artist's method" (in *SE*, 1920b/1991, p. 264). Freud felt it necessary to disown this heritage, and to this end he points to an even earlier source of the free association technique, a volume by Ludwig Börne called "The Art of Becoming an Original Writer" (1823). In that book, known to Freud as a boy and still sitting on his shelf, Börne advises would-be writers to hone their originality by (essentially) free associating to ideas. Freud simply bows before the possibility of "cryptomnesia" in this case, thereby undercutting Ellis's connection of free association to mysticism – but at the price, ironically, of conceding that it is indeed tied to an artist's search for originality. Although Freud had forgotten all about Börne's technique, he confesses that he did in fact often recall other snippets from "The Art of Becoming an Original Writer." With this in mind Freud nearly closes his little essay by citing one such snippet, which, arguably, doubles as finger wagging at a troublesome Havelock Ellis. "It is not lack of intellect but lack of character," Börne tells us, "that prevents most writers from being better than they are . . . Sincerity is the source of all genius, and men would be cleverer if they were more moral" (in *SE*, 1920b/1991, p. 265). No doubt Freud felt that Ellis's provocation about Freud-as-an-artist, connected to the history of mysticism, was actually not so very clever.

so and so much of psychoanalysis. Pfister, author of *Love-life of Children*, could only go to a certain limit because after all he was a minister" (p. 17).

As with the saintly Pfister and the humanitarian Rolland, Ellis could not abide a metapsychology wedded to a "beyond" of life and love, namely to the death drive. In 1930 Freud had sent Ellis a copy of *Civilization and Its Discontents*. In a response of March 24, 1930, Ellis discusses the "oceanic feeling," the claim that introduces Freud's book. (Ellis couldn't know that the remark about the "oceanic feeling" came from Romain Rolland, a fact only revealed in the second edition of 1931.) Ellis admits that he sympathized with the anonymous author of the idea, since he shares "a very similar attitude towards the universe"; an attitude, he says, sounding very much like Rolland, "allied to mysticism, but not to any of the pseudo-intellectual religious creeds" (in Grosskurth, 1980, p. 392). Moreover Ellis adds that he cannot accept "the primary impulse of aggression," which, he says, the abundance of life contradicts (p. 393). A few years later Ellis formalized these complaints in a book called *My Confessional* (see Brome, 1979, pp. 22–3).

We already know Freud's diagnosis of the oceanic love that Pfister, Rolland, and now Ellis brought to bear against Freud's brooding late Romanticism: it was an illusion, better perhaps than organized religion but ultimately just a kind of infantile narcissism. But clearly Freud had another trick in his arsenal to use against their overinvestments in love, group feeling, and mystical oneness with the universe. Like each of their overzealous expressions of friendliness, it revealed a civility "inverted" to the point of homosexuality. Moreover, according to Freud, narcissism and homosexuality are related. "We have discovered," Freud declares in "On Narcissism" (1915), that in the cases of perverts and homosexuals "their later choice of love-objects" coincide with "their own selves. They are plainly seeking *themselves* as a love-object, and are exhibiting a type of object choice which must be termed 'narcissistic'" (*SE*, 1915/1991, p. 88). Or as he echoes in an essay of 1922, "In the light of psychoanalysis we are accustomed to regard social feeling as a sublimation of homosexual attitudes towards objects" (1922b/1991, p. 232). And sure enough, civility and homosexuality come up during the Wortis sessions. Wortis: "Do you mean that socially good people like Einstein and Romain Rolland are doing nothing but sublimating their sexuality?" Freud: "Exactly" (Wortis, 1954, p. 87). Freud again: "Our entire government, our bureaucracies, our official life, all operate on the basis of homosexual impulses, which are of course unconscious and not manifest; but there would be havoc if they were to become manifest" (p. 100). By the same token, we also know from

Civilization that Freud believed that the excessive "Yes" to life and love only betrayed its opposite, namely repressed feelings of hatred and the death drive ("No"). As a result, loving people are faced with a "heads I win" double bind – homosexual no matter what they say.

Of course these kinds of overdetermined observations reflect back on Freud himself, and not always to his benefit. Consider two of his overtly seductive remarks made to H.D. during her analysis. First remark: while "beating with . . . his fist, on the head-piece of the old-fashioned horse-hair sofa," Freud says to H.D.: "The trouble is – I am an old man – *you do not think it worth your while to love me*" (1974, pp. 15–16). We know that H.D. loved Ellis. Surely she had some love left over for Freud, as well? It is all the more amazing that Freud's dramatic remarks were uttered during the *very first* session of H.D.'s analysis (Guest, 1984, p. 208). Second remark: moments after hearing gossip about Ellis, Freud confides to H.D. the true quality of his own masculinity: "And – I must tell you (you were frank with me [about Ellis] and I will be frank with you), I do *not* like to be the mother in transference – it always surprises and shocks me a little. I feel so very masculine" (pp. 146–7). This confidence H.D. later characterizes to Bryer as "some scraps of flea morsel" (in Guest, 1984, p. 213). Surely to everyone's surprise it was Ellis who occupied the "father transference" – and not Freud (p. 214). What does it all mean? Between the urolagniac Ellis and the bisexual H.D., Freud in 1933 clearly felt obliged to call attention to his own rather different, *heterosexual* proclivities. Either that or Freud opened himself up to the very obvious charge that perhaps he doth protest too much; that sometimes a cigar is, indeed, a penis.

* * *

Through H.D. and Wortis, messages were given and messages were received: the young, bisexual American poet and the young American doctor and investigator of homosexuality were willing playthings circulated between the two famous sexologists and professional rivals. Both patients were emotionally attached to Ellis, and so endlessly talked and dreamed about him during their analyses with Freud. Their attachments were reinforced by the fact that they both maintained an active correspondence with Ellis during treatment. Wortis, however, took it one further step. In 1936 he sent Ellis a box full of 4×6 recipe cards, filled out in detail immediately after each session in the Café Astoria near Freud's home, about his training analysis with Freud (Wortis, 1954, pp. x, 166–81), notes that were eventually transcribed and published in 1954 as *Fragments of an*

Analysis with Freud. With this act Wortis proved his devotion to his mentor, Ellis – and became a boogie-man within Freud studies ever after.

Naturally Ellis was curious to read what transpired and to learn what Freud really thought about him. In an awkward moment, Ellis would even learn how Wortis's analysis accidentally crossed over into H.D.'s. At one point late in the analysis the topic returns to the psychology of Havelock Ellis. "I feel sure," Freud told Wortis, "that Ellis must have some sexual abnormality, else he would never have devoted himself to the field of sex research" (p. 154). Then Freud excludes himself from that same logic. Wortis records that he thought Freud was "being vulgar and unfair." At the end of the session Wortis complains: "I hope that people won't speak of me as you speak of Ellis." Freud just shrugs his shoulders.

The next day Wortis expresses his "discomfort" with Freud's remarks.

> I said that was the sort of lay opinion that made Ellis's life so difficult and cheapened his accomplishment. Freud then gave the reasons: *I had said his wife was homosexual*; besides, he had no children, and a man who makes so few judgments is suspect of being impotent. I insisted I never said his wife was homosexual; ... Shakespeare made few judgments too – he saw too many sides to an argument.
>
> Freud was angrier than I had ever seen him. He sputtered: "Do you know Shakespeare, then, as well as you know Ellis?" (1954, p. 156; my emphasis)

Until that moment Wortis had not, in fact, said anything about Ellis's wife being gay – and neither had Freud. And just like that Freud was caught out: he knew intimate details about Ellis's personal life that Wortis did not. Cue the back-pedaling, obsequiousness replacing angry defensiveness: during the next session Wortis found that Freud was "remarkably friendly" (p. 157), and praised Ellis "as a wonderful man, etc." His conjecture about Ellis was "based, as he now saw, on incorrect evidence, and he took it back" (p. 157). In other words, Freud lied to Wortis to cover over his unwise attempt to launder gossip from H.D. as analytic acumen before Wortis (and ultimately before Ellis).

In October 1936 Ellis finally had his say. To Wortis, Ellis claims that he is "not at all annoyed at the suggestion that my interest in sex was due to a perversion" (p. 177). But he invokes the same exemption as Freud: "not in my case." Then he denies that his wife, Edith, was gay – a lie – and then either guesses more than is in evidence in Wortis's notes, or shows by his discussion that Wortis has excised Freud's full remarks in the published version of his "fragments" (which is far more likely). For Ellis indirectly invokes the passage cited earlier about H.D. urinating on him from his book *The Fountain of Life*, although misdirects Wortis (or Wortis misdirects us) that the passage is from his book *Impressions and Comments*. "The 'Person' in question," Ellis writes, "is H.D. I had, in the first place, obtained her consent to print it, with some difficulty, though she said, when I read it to her, that it was so beautiful it almost brought tears to her eyes, and is generally considered by critics my finest piece of prose" (in Wortis, 1954, pp. 177–8). Next Ellis mentions H.D.'s claim that he had helped her during this time, but feigns to not know why – namely, her breakdown in 1919 after the birth of her daughter and lesbian turn to Bryer. Then Ellis denies the charge of personal impotence – after explaining impotence in terms that, Grosskurth shows, perfectly applied to Ellis: impotence caused by premature ejaculation ("hyperaesthetic over-rapidity of nervous reaction, reaching its climax before entrance is effected") and the anxiety generated therein (Grosskurth, 1980, p. 422). The very long letter to Wortis ends with a quip that "Freud is an extravagant genius" (Wortis, 1954, p. 179). None of these remarks, save perhaps for the last, are credible – and even the final quip about Freud is undone by the specter of sour grapes at having read Freud's unguarded remarks.

Years later, even after reading Grosskurth's biography, Wortis was still unable to see clear on Ellis, and almost certainly didn't understand the interpersonal quagmire he had opportunistically courted and fueled back in the 1930s. Grosskurth, Wortis says, had mistakenly filtered her interpretations through Ellis's sexuality, which was not in fact central; and in any case, Ellis wasn't necessarily impotent; and while Ellis was indeed "fascinated by urination," it was "a harmless interest" (Wortis, 2007, p. 23). It calls to mind the "kettle logic" that Freud discusses in the *Dream* and *Joke* books: when asked for the return of a kettle, the borrower claims that he already returned the kettle undamaged, that it was already damaged when he borrowed it, and that he had never borrowed it in the first place. The point: one does not need to be a Freudian to appreciate the relevance of sexual proclivities for someone, like Ellis, who devoted his life to the field of sexuality.

3.3.3   Constructions, Apologia, and the "Seduction of Analogies"

Back to Freud. It is clear that Ellis's criticisms of psychoanalysis, conveyed by Wortis during his analysis in late 1934 and early 1935, even as Freud dug into his "historical novel" on Moses, were fresh insults that called up all the other insults – including the "heads I win" criticism from 1915. Rarely one to ignore an insult, especially made in public, Freud took time out in 1937 – near the end of his life, suffering from the ravages of cancer as well as an exhausting and stressful relocation to London – to formally, albeit anonymously, rebut his old friend Ellis. We have seen this highly personal, mildly ugly strategy before, as when Freud made use of Romain Rolland's private remarks at the beginning of *Civilization and Its Discontents*.

Fortunately this detour into homosexuality, politics, and gossip among therapists pays a major dividend: now we know for sure that Freud's "Constructions in Analysis" (1937) is a pointed response to Havelock Ellis. It is a conclusion that helps unpack the significance of "Constructions" in ways hitherto unacknowledged. For example, in addition to the dramatic interpersonal subtext of the "heads I win" criticism, it helps explain why Freud in "Constructions" revisits the old sexology the two men held in common – a sexology that is surprisingly relevant to the thinking behind *Moses and Monotheism*. Let's get back to this essay now.

"Constructions in Analysis" is divided into three sections. The first section introduces the idea of construction in analysis, and once again invokes the analogy of archeology. Also featured is the theme of recovered memory. The second section discusses patient responses to the analyst's constructions and the kind of confirmations that give constructions their objectivity and therapeutic efficacy. The final and most conceptually challenging section opens up what Freud calls "a wider perspective" (*SE*, 23, p. 266). It begins with instances of "ultra-clear" ephemera that patients bring to the analyst's constructions, and ends with a discussion of the concept of historical truth. Framing it all is surprising levity: at key moments in the essay Freud invokes the role of Polonius in Shakespeare's *Hamlet*, and the role of the manservant ("Gluthammer," the locksmith) in Johann Nestroy's *Der Zerrissene* (1844) – *A Man Full of Nothing*.

Let's begin with the "apologia," as Freud calls his response to Ellis, that informs sections one and two of "Constructions." Freud states that psycho-analysis aims to induce the patient to abandon repressions of the past and "replace them by reactions of a sort that would correspond to a psychically mature condition" (p. 257). That "mature condition," we know from previous chapters, is informed by an understanding of the real (external) world – Freud's peculiar brand of positivism that arrives most insistently in the late works. Freud repeats himself on the next page: the patient "has to be induced to remember [*soll dazu gebracht werden*] something that has been experienced by him and repressed" (p. 258; *GW*, 1937/1991, p. 396). In turn the patient places "raw material" at the analyst's disposal, of which

Freud names dreams, free associations, repetitions, and the transference. These are the materials that "put him on the way to recovering [*wiederzu-gewinnen*] the lost memories" (p. 258).

However, the patient's recovery of lost memories is only one "portion" of the work. The other portion belongs to the analyst's constructions, which Freud says form a "link between the two portions of the work of analysis" (p. 259). Freud continues: the analyst's task

> is to make out what has been forgotten from the traces which it has left behind or, more correctly, to construct it . . . His work of construction, or, if it is preferred, of reconstruction, resembles to a great extent an archaeologist's excavation of some dwelling-place that has been destroyed and buried or of some ancient edifice. The two processes are in fact identical, except that the analyst works under better conditions and has more material at his command to assist him. . . (p. 259)

As in chapter one of *Civilization and Its Discontents*, Freud invokes his right to interpret the repressed on the back of archeology: both psycho-analysis and archeology "have an undisputed right to reconstruct by means of supplementing and combining the surviving remains" (p. 259; cf., Miller, 2010/2011, p. 8). Like the "identity" Freud posits between individual and mass psychology (*SE*, 1939/1991, p. 72), the "processes" of archeology and psychoanalysis "are in fact identical [*identisch*]" – an incredibly bullish (actually absurd) remark, but typical of the late Freud. There are differences, however. Freud concludes the section by pointing out that while analysis has many advantages over archeology, it is complicated by the fact that re/construction is for the former "only a preliminary labour" (p. 260).

In section two Freud keeps to the "preliminary labour," attempting to show that analysts do not ignore the patient's "Yes" or "No" to construc-tions, since neither response is conclusive. Actually this is old territory. Freud discussed the patients' denial (their "No") in an essay of 1925, "Negation," a fact that Wortis mentions during the same training session cited above. At the time Wortis also addresses an issue that often comes up in connection with constructions, namely suggestion:

> "It's true," said Freud, "that an analyst accepts an affirmation as such, because it means the patient consciously accepts the suggestion. If, however, the patient denies the suggestion it may either mean that it is true or untrue – that depends. The patient may simply not want to admit it. Generally, a patient simply neglects an inappropriate suggestion; if he reacts to it at all, it is generally a sign that there is something to it." (Wortis, 1954, p. 66)

In "Constructions" Freud is rather more circumspect; he insists that the patient's "Yes" is not immediately accepted by the analyst. Freud's essential point: the patient is not a helpless victim of a logic that finds confirmations no matter what is said. As he asserts at the end of section II in "Constructions," there "is no justification for the reproach" of the kind made by Ellis (*SE*, 1923, p. 265).

It must be said, though, that Freud's argument in defense of Ellis's reproach is incredibly weak. He begins, sensibly, by considering *false constructions* made in analysis. Miller describes it well:

> Freud tackles the problem of error. What happens if we say something false? If we, the analyst, say something false? What guarantee do we have? The word "guarantee" is in the text: "What guarantee [do] we have, during the work on construction, that we are not going wrong?" So, we have the problem of error, of guarantee, and in a certain sense, of the guarantee of truth. (2010/2011, p. 6)

Later Miller adds: "What does Freud's confidence rest on?" (p. 18). Freud's answer is that "analytic experience" should afford analysts some comfort – precisely the gesture that Lacan would make in the following decades. "For we learn by it," Freud says, "that no damage is done if we happen to make a mistake and offer the patient the wrong [*unrichtige*] construction as the probable historical truth" (*SE*, 1923, p. 261); translation adjusted slightly; 1937/1991, p. 399). True, the analyst wastes time and does not "create a very good impression." But the patient, Freud claims, will be utterly unspoiled or "untouched" (*unberührt*) by false constructions – to Wortis he says that the patient will "neglect" them – and at some point the analyst can simply correct the mistake without compromising his own "authority" (pp. 261–2). Although this claim is problematic, let's grant it and follow the rest of Freud's argument, which is even less convincing.

Enter Polonius, the inept fool in Shakespeare's *Hamlet*. Freud is still discussing false constructions: "In this way the false construction drops out, as if it were never made; and, indeed, we often get the impression as though, to borrow the words of Polonius, our bait of falsehood had taken a carp of truth" (p. 262). Naturally Miller finds in this reference a reassuring opening for Lacanianism: the truth is found precisely by means of an indirection equal to the unconscious, namely, "off to one side," "out of kilter," and beyond the patient's "Yes" or "No" (2010/2011, pp. 18–21).[26] And that's just fine, since Freud does indeed privilege what he calls the

---

[26] Lacan: "La méprise du sujet supposé savoir," "the unconscious does not remember what it knows" (in Miller, 2010/2011, p. 17).

"indirect forms of communication" in "Constructions" (*SE*, 1923, p. 263). But "the bait of falsehood" remark is significant beyond a thesis about indirection. Consider Freud's words more carefully: "our bait of falsehood had taken the carp of truth. The danger of our leading a patient astray by suggestion, by persuading him to accept things which we ourselves believe but which he ought not to, has certainly been enormously exaggerated" (p. 262).

It is appropriate that the Jewish clown Polonius, of all the fictional characters in Freud's vast and learned repertoire, takes the stage at the very moment Freud addresses false constructions and the problem of suggestion. For it was Freud, according to his own version of events, who had unwittingly played the fool during his early experiences with false constructions: patients had reported false memories about childhood sexual abuse and Freud had mistakenly believed them. Luckily for Freud, so the story goes, he had, like Polonius, caught a "carp of truth," *Wahrheitskarpfen*, in the "bait of falsehood" (*GW*, 1937/1991, p. 399). The false memories about "seduction" ultimately gave way to a genuine understanding of the true cause of hysteria: repressed infantile sexual fantasy. That is to say, instead of being sexually abused *in fact*, Freud "discovered" that even children wished to be sexually abused *in fantasy*. The birth of psychoanalysis was itself the carp of truth that redeemed the false constructions that anteceded it.

In this passage Freud openly links constructions in analysis to the problem of suggestion. And in truth it must be admitted: they point to the same thing, although the one word, suggestion, normally applies to the lives of patients, while the other word, construction, normally applies to the records of ancient history; or, if you prefer, a suggestion seeks the affirmative "Yes" of Freud's *patients*, while a construction seeks the affirmative "Yes" of Freud's *readers*. Arguably, then, the words "suggestion" and "construction" could be swapped out with little consequence – much as one might swap out the words "psychoanalysis" and "archeology." Both processes provide the connection between objective and subjective reality, present and past – including the present and past of psychoanalysis itself.

Freud himself discussed these issues in *Beyond the Pleasure Principle*. In chapter three, he admits that the goals of analytic technique had shifted since the early years. It began, he says, as an "interpretive art" that, through the analysis of resistance, tried "to compel the patient to confirm the analyst's constructions through his own memory" (Freud, 2012, p. 60; *SE*, 1920a/1991, p. 18). The art was then set on trying to get the patient to give up their resistance. "This was the locus of suggestion," Freud writes, "operating as 'transference'" (2012, p. 60; *SE*, 1920a/1991, p. 18). The problem with early psychoanalysis was that confirmation did not come from memories at all:

> But it became ever clearer that the established aim of making the unconscious conscious is not fully achievable in this way either [through suggestion in the guise of the transference]. The patient cannot remember everything repressed in him – maybe not even the most important thing – and thus gets no convincing evidence that the construction communicated to him is accurate. Indeed, he is compelled to *repeat* the repressed content as current experience instead of *remembering* it, as the physician would prefer, as part of the past.

In *Beyond* Freud duly adds a note to his own essay of 1914, "Remembering, Repeating and Working-Through," wherein the importance of repetition in this regard is first registered. Freud himself understood very well that constructions are linked to confirmations – either in the form of memories or, more likely, repetitions. Suggestion in the form of transference generates confirmation through repetition, or, better put, through a *behavior* and not through the declarations of the patient. This was Freud's clever way around the entire problem of assent to his constructions, the "Yes," that he claimed was at work in his earliest practice. Confirmation of a given construction through a patient's recollection (for example, of childhood sexual abuse) is neatly sidestepped with the theory of repetition.

Freud, of course, knew what his earliest critics said about his seduction etiology: it was the overeager therapist who inadvertently suggested his results about the repressed content. Sophisticated critics such Eugen Beuler and J. Mitchell Clarke claimed that the "memories" reported were determined by the analyst's theory, what we nowadays call a "contamination bias," a form of epistemic looping or feedback (Borch-Jacobsen, 1996a; Dufresne, 2003, p. 17).[27] This is no doubt why Richard von Krafft-Ebing,

---

[27] As Mikkel Borch-Jacobsen puts it, "Psychoanalysis is the product of this feedback, the magical fulfillment of its own prophesy" (1996a, p. 33). Informed discussion has demolished the claim, first advanced by Jeffrey Masson in *The Assault on Truth: Freud's Suppression of the Seduction Theory* (1984), that Freud abandoned the seduction theory because it generated controversy, and because Freud was afraid of the rampant sexual abuse that he had uncovered. Borch-Jacobsen's work just cited is a good place to start. Suffice to say that Freud never spoke about recovered memories *at all* in these original works, and was, in any case, hardly afraid of controversy. Freud only spoke about his patients' resistance to narratives of sexual abuse that *he himself had constructed*. When Freud dropped the seduction theory he dropped his own etiology – his own stories. He didn't run away from their "recovered memories" of sexual abuse because there *weren't* any reports of memories. He just stopped interpreting their "No" (to his constructions) as proof that he was in any case correct ("Yes") about repressed seductions. In turn he reinterpreted their "No" as proof that they only *wished* they had been sexually abused at the level of fantasy (his new "Yes"). Hence the birth of psychoanalysis

the sexologist famous for his work on *Psychopathia Sexualis* (1886), bluntly dismissed Freud's seduction etiology as "a scientific fairy-tale" (Freud & Fliess, 1985, p. 184). And this may be why Ellis, one of Freud's earliest English readers, ultimately charged Freud with mistaking his patients' denial of his constructions (that they were homosexual, in a narrow context), their "No," as proof they were therefore true.

We also know that Freud never indulged his early critics nor accepted responsibility for the blunder of his mistaken seduction etiology. Instead he retreated into his self-imposed isolation and, not incidentally, began to deliver his ideas to a more receptive audience of fraternal lodge members at the local B'nai B'rith. Consequently it was only years later that the reading public, including Freud's own critics, could have known that he had privately dropped the seduction etiology, thereby conceding, belatedly, that the etiology he published in 1896 was indeed based on "false constructions"; or again, that "psychoanalysis," a practice introduced in 1896, was no longer concerned with repressed sexual abuse but with sexual fantasy, the basis of a new practice introduced after the seduction debacle (in 1897). Worse, when Freud did publicly address the new foundations of "psychoanalysis" it was only to muddy the waters further. One of the least offensive strategies he employed was credulity at the role of suggestion in analysis. This strategy is much in evidence in "Constructions in Analysis," where Freud chalks up the "danger" of suggestion to an "enormous exaggeration" (*SE*, 23: 262) on the part of his *critics*. Then he adds:

> An analyst would have had to behave very incorrectly before such a misfortune [i.e., suggesting a false memory, instilling belief in a false construction] could overtake him; above all, he would have to blame himself with not allowing his patients to have their say. I can assert without boasting that such an abuse of "suggestion" has never occurred in my practice. (p. 262)

But Freud's assertion is indeed a boast, and not a little one, either. Wortis pressed Freud about the possibility that perhaps Ellis "was not altogether wrong" in his quip about psychoanalysis always finding what it wants – the very same criticism, incidentally, that Wohlgemuth mentions at the end of his chapter on homosexuality.[28] "An unskillful analyst," Wortis remarked, "could put together any kind of arbitrary theory on this basis" (1954, p. 65). Freud's reply: "Of course. It all depends on the analyst. But we are sure he

---

proper. The "assault on truth" is actually, and ironically, Masson's. For an overview, see Dufresne, 2003, pp. 35–47.

[28] Wohlgemuth, who examines suggestion at length, states that the "psycho-analytic method merely discovers in the patient what the psycho-analyst has been putting there himself" (1923, pp. 159–60).

will use his judgment and experience" (p. 65). Freud offers his personal assurance. But what of the analyst who fails to "use his judgment and experience"? Freud himself delivers the appropriate verdict to Wortis. Such unskillful analysts would rightly be called *Verbrecher*, criminals – a word that Wortis generously translates as "scoundrels" (p. 65).

Unfortunately for Freud, one does not avoid the criminal "misfortune" of suggestion by simply allowing "patients to have their say." Notwithstanding his empty boast about his own avoidance of suggestion, which he effectively reduces to a moral issue of right intentions, here and elsewhere Freud is remarkably naive about how suggestion actually works; something, again, that perceptive critics understood very well in the 1880s. Even so, there is no need to contradict Freud on this score either. The rather more complicated truth is that Freud neither suggested memories to his early patients nor did he accept their botched constructions. If we ignore Freud's later version of events and simply read the original essays on seduction, we know very well that his patients never reported *belief in memories* at all. Instead, Freud described how his patients reported a *disbelief in the constructions that Freud had offered to them*: despite analytic investigations of their repressed pasts, Freud plainly admits that the patients had "no feeling of remembering the scenes" (*SE*, 1896/1991, p. 204). And of course they didn't, because Freud had merely asked his patients to "visualize" his own "reconstructions." Memory was not a factor because the treatments never got that far. Consequently, the patients exhibited neither belief nor the effects of suggestion. This is no doubt what Freud means when he asserts – however simplistically – that patients always ignore or neglect false constructions/suggestions.

It was only Freud who failed to ignore or neglect his own constructions, only Freud who fell victim to an auto-suggestive belief in the reality of his own visualizations and reconstructions about the traumatic content of repression. How can we be so sure? Because Freud published his seduction etiology not once but three times in one year – once in French, twice in German. And in these essays Freud *did* in fact take his patients' explicit denial of his constructions as confirmations that they were true. The persistent "No" had indeed become a "Yes" – exactly the point that Ellis makes. In retrospect it is therefore hard to imagine that Freud, as he puts it in "Constructions," made "a very good impression" on these early patients.

In Miller's informal commentary on "Constructions in Analysis," constructions are only incidentally linked to suggestion, and so are never connected to the seduction debacle, that is, to the birth of psychoanalysis.

Miller simply notes that Freud does not accept the charge of suggestion (2010/2011, p. 10), and that in any case the focus is rightly on an unconscious that presents only through falsehoods (p. 18). This is indeed Freud's highly opportunistic strategy: turn a defeat (a serious debacle) into a win. Freud tried to sidestep suggestion. But it is actually very clear in Freud's "Construction" essay – ultra-clear even – that Freud in 1937 was still not done exorcising the ghost of a badly buried suggestion, the stink that followed him, thanks to sexologists like Ellis, to the end of his life. In other words, "constructions in analysis" were always driven by "seductions in analysis."

Freud ends section II by invoking Nestroy's farce, *Der Zerrissene – The Torn* – which deals with Herr von Lips, a "man full of nothing." The gist of Freud's invocation is this: in psychoanalysis we listen to our patients, weighing their words carefully, and make our constructions accordingly. "In short," Freud concludes, "we conduct ourselves on the model of a familiar figure in one of Nestroy's farces – the manservant [Gluthammer] who has a single answer on his lips to every question or objection: '*In the course of events everything will become clear*'" (*SE*, 1923, p. 265, translation adjusted; 1937/1991, p. 403). But what exactly is "made clear" in *Der Zerrissene*? That life (under capitalism) is absurd, that fate is capricious, that society is full of discontents. And, moreover, that the women from our pasts – in Gluthammer's case, Madame Schleyer – may one day return to cause us serious trouble, or, better, may return to reveal the truth of our absurd, capricious, and discontented existence. If Freud closes section II with Gluthammer's answer to every question ("in the course of events everything will become clear"), it is precisely because he is about to re-engage the women of his own past and clear up some niggling questions that torment psychoanalysis. In short, "Constructions in Analysis" is a final reckoning – the final scene in a farcical play that began in the 1880s.

* * *

We are not quite finished with the theme of recovered memory. In the third, final, and most important section of "Constructions in Analysis," Freud moves on to phenomena that, in less creative hands, would count as immediate disconfirmation of a given construction: ephemera that patients "recall" in response to the analyst's construction. This is where Freud opens the discussion onto what he calls "a wider perspective" (*SE*, 1923, p. 266):

> I have been struck by the manner in which, in certain analyses, the communication of an obviously apt construction has evoked in the patients a surprising and at first incomprehensible phenomenon. They have had

lively recollections [*lebhafte Erinnerungen*] called up in them – which they themselves have described as "ultra-clear" – but *what they have recollected has not been the event that was the subject of the construction* but details related to that subject. For instance, they have recollected with abnormal sharpness [*überscharf*] the faces of the people involved in the construction or the rooms in which something of the sort might have happened, or, a step further away, the furniture in such rooms – on *the subject of which the construction had naturally no possibility of any knowledge*. (p. 266, my emphasis; *GW*, 1937/1991, pp. 403–4)

If these "ultra-clear" (*überdeutlich*) recollections aren't obvious *dis*confirmations of an analyst's constructions, they are at least noteworthy. The "surprising" ultra-clear recollections are "at first incomprehensible"; they also exhibit inconsequential but ultrasharp details that can never be contradicted (or falsified). More significant is Freud's remark, in the next paragraph, that ultra-clear recollections are linked thematically, not just with dreams but with "waking fantasies" (*Wachen in phantasieartigen Zuständen*) such as hallucinations, delusions, madness, and psychoses (*GW*, 1937/1991, p. 404). As such they are a part of the turning away from the real external world that concerns the late Freud. Put otherwise, ultra-clear recollections are actually the patient's willing fantasies in response to an analyst's construction – the patient's "Yes" to his or her constructions.

On the one hand, Freud has thereby reduced ultra-clear recollections to the product of a classic folie à deux – a "waking fantasy" or delusion shared between the doctor and the patient. That is of course an apt description of the hypnotic trance, which is always made possible by willing role-playing. As Anna O. at one point admits to her doting physician, Josef Breuer, "the whole business [i.e., her hysteria] had been simulated" (1895b/1991, p. 46; cf. Borch-Jacobsen, 1996b; Dufresne, 2003, pp. 4–25). It was a response that Freud, when it came time to publish the first case of the talking cure, turned into a negative *confirmation* of the existence of hysteria. Her "No" became a "Yes."

On the other hand, the late Freud knows very well how to avoid the dead end into which he nearly drove his argumentation back in 1896. The trick is the shift away from "material truth" to "historical truth," a shift that begins in "Constructions" with a tortured sentence.

> Perhaps it may be a general characteristic of hallucinations to which sufficient attention has not hitherto been paid that in them something that has been experienced in infancy and then forgotten returns – something that the child has seen or heard at a time when he could still hardly speak and that

now forces its way into consciousness, probably distorted and displaced owing to the operation of forces that are opposed to this return. (p. 267)

Freud then wonders if, during the experience of such delusion, the "turning away from reality (*die Abwendung von der Realwelt*) is exploited by the upward drive of the repressed in order to force its content into consciousness" (*GW*, 1937/1991, p. 404). If true, then the resulting distortions are just like that madness we call dreams, and thus rightly subject to analytic interpretation.

According to Freud, this revised view of delusion (even the shared delusion of a folie à deux) brings clarity to the foreground (*SE*, 1923, p. 267). It is also close to the raison d'être of the essay, which was referred to in Freud's *Diary* in September 1937 by the heading "Idea about delusion and construction" (in Freud, 1992, p. 222). "The essence of it," Freud writes, "is that there is not only *method* in madness, as the poet has already perceived, but also a fragment of *historical truth*; and it is plausible to suppose that the compulsive belief [*zwanghafte Glaube*] attached to delusions derives its strength precisely from infantile sources of this kind" (*SE*, 1923, p. 267, his emphasis; *GW*, 1937/1991, p. 405). This is the second time Freud invokes an insight from Polonius, albeit this time unnamed and once-removed as a function of "the poet," namely Shakespeare. "Though this be madness," Polonius says in an aside about Hamlet's ranting, "yet there is method in't" (Act 2, Scene 2). The madness Hamlet spouts is meaningful, first of all as pointed mockery of Polonius. Fair enough. Freud's additional point is that there is *more* than method in the madness, because there is also historical truth. As with false constructions of seduction in analysis, waking fantasies reveal a carp of truth – an *historical truth*, a concept for understanding repressed ancient prehistory that functions exactly the same way that *fantasy* functions for an analyst's understanding of an individual's repressed past. While the one is utilized for recovering repressed *Kultur*, the other is utilized for recovering the repressed psyche. The bridge between them, built on the strength of analogy, is a key feature of *Moses and Monotheism*.

It is, therefore, perhaps not surprising that historical truth has the structure of an argument made by a prankster or, perhaps, a court jester. It begins in "Constructions" when Freud offers up reminiscences (his own?) as proof: "All that I can produce today in support of this theory are reminiscences, not fresh impressions" (*Mir stehen heute, um diese Theorie zu erweisen, nur Reminiszenzen zu Gebote, nicht frische Eindrücke*) (p. 267; *GW*, 1937/1991, p. 405). At this point it isn't clear how far back in time the reminiscences go. But the path back is broached as follows:

> The vain effort would be abandoned of convincing the patient of the error of his delusions or of its contradiction of reality; and, on the contrary, the recognition of its kernel of truth would afford common ground upon which the therapeutic work could develop. That work would consist in liberating the fragment of historical truth from its distortions and its attachments to the actual present day and in leading it back to the point in the past to which it belongs. (p. 268)

Hallucinations, waking phantasies, delusion, dreams, madness, psychoses – phenomena found individually and collectively, in the present and in the archaic past – contain within them a "kernel of truth," *Wahrheitskern* (*SE*, 1923, p. 268). And by truth Freud means that they contain a core of objective reality, to wit, a trace of real but repressed traumatic events. As Freud puts it, the neurotic's foreboding sense of doom is "under the influence of a repressed memory . . . that something which was at that time terrifying did really happen" (p. 268). We should probably underline Freud's claim: what is recovered by psychoanalysis "did really happen" (*etwas damals Schreckhaftes sich wirklich ereignet hat*); although distorted by delusion, the trauma itself was *real* (*GW*, 1937/1991, p. 405).

Let's pause for a moment to recall *Moses and Monotheism*. In the fourth subsection of the third essay, "Application," Freud repeats these remarks from "Constructions." Belief in the absurd – a facet of religious belief associated with Tertullian and discussed in *The Future of an Illusion* – also returns. Freud's aim here in *Moses* is to argue that "a forgotten truth lies hidden in delusional ideas" (*SE*, 1939/1991, p. 85), most especially in abiding, absurd, compulsive, obsessive, delusional ideas. "The compulsive conviction," Freud writes, "arises from this kernel of truth [*Wahrheitskern*] and spreads out on to the errors that wrap around it" (p. 85; translation modified). This kernel of truth "may be called *historical* truth," *historische Wahrheit*.

And so the late Freud abandons the "vain effort" of disabusing someone of their delusion, a recommendation he also makes in a 1935 "Postscript" to *An Autobiographical Study* (1925). This is the moment that Freud announces the existence of "historical truth" as an alternative to "material" or factual truth.[29] As Strachey tells us, "the first explicit reference [to historical truth] is in the (1935) 'Postscript' to the *Autobiographical Study* (1925), where, oddly enough, the idea is mentioned as being already in the world, though in fact it was not put into print before 'Constructions in

---

[29] "Historical truth" does appear a few times in passing (at the end of chapter eight) in *The Future of an Illusion* of 1927, but is only developed as a *concept* in 1935.

Analysis'" (*SE*, 1939/1991, p. 130, n. 1). Strachey is referring to Freud's passing qualification in the "Postscript" about the "negative valuation of religion" made in *The Future of an Illusion*. Having posited in the *Future* that individual psychology repeats "the very same processes repeated upon a wider stage," Freud in 1935 adds the following caveat: "Later, I found a formula which did better justice to it [religion]: while granting that its power [of persuasion, its affective power] lies in the truth it contains, I showed that that truth was not a material but a historical truth" (*SE*, 1925c/1991, p. 72). The more just formula from later on is actually found in *Moses*, still unfinished in 1935 and unavailable in 1927 – which as Strachey says, perplexed by Freud's use of the past-tense ("I showed . . ."), existed only as an unfinished draft on Freud's desk. It is only in 1935 that the concept of historical truth enters the public realm. (I argue in the Coda that it probably makes its first *indirect* debut, as a concept, in 1931.)[30]

As Freud admits elsewhere, what is true of the archeologist is also true of the psychoanalyst: it is sometimes a tricky or "ticklish" (*heikel*) problem determining the "relative age of his finds" (*SE*, 1923, p. 259; *GW*, 1937/1991, p. 397). For example, sometimes an archeological relic discovered at one layer of sediment really originates in another. The mistake is understandable. Of course the relative age of Freud's own concepts is also a major problem for the historians (or "archeologists") of psychoanalysis. For Freud always, even compulsively, revised the history of psychoanalysis – adding but not always acknowledging new notes, new sentences, new paragraphs, and new findings in serial editions of favored old works (e.g., *The Interpretation of Dreams* and *Three Essays on the Theory of Sexuality*). As a result, he frequently leaves readers with a very imperfect sense of the past, present, and future of psychoanalysis. Much of Strachey's considerable value as an editor lies precisely in untangling the development of Freud's thinking for bewildered readers (which is why his editorial apparatus has been translated and directly imported into Freud's later German editions as well). So it is perhaps not entirely surprising that, in the 1935 "Postscript," Freud himself confuses the genesis of the concept of historical truth, treating it as though it already existed when it was still waiting for Moses.

The ironic and performative self-entanglement of these efforts is not over; indeed, we have only now arrived at the most self-reflexively

---

[30] Although the idea has never been widely recognized, Reik could in 1958 write: "What we psychoanalysts search for is the matter in the myths, the fact in the fable. That means the kernel of historical truth" (1958a, p. 51).

humorous part of "Constructions in Analysis." Freud has established the vain futility of correcting a patient's delusion, since it is far more productive to attend to "its kernel of truth." This truth is historical, not material. He adds that psychotics and also neurotics often transpose "a forgotten past on to the present or on to an expectation of the future" (*SE*, 1923, p. 268). They are, recall, "under the influence of a repressed memory" that was at once both real and terrifying. Having recalled in 1937 his old, even heretical interest in the recovery of actual (material, real) memories, Freud now invokes what he calls *der Verlockung einer Analogie*, the "seduction of an analogy":

> I am aware that it is of small service to handle so important a subject in the cursory fashion that I have here employed. But nonetheless I have not been able to resist the seduction of an analogy. The delusions of patients appear to me to be the equivalents of the constructions which we build up in the course of an analytic treatment – attempts at explanations and cure, though it is true that these, under the conditions of a psychosis, can do no more than replace the fragment of reality that is being disavowed in the present by another fragment that had already been disavowed in the remote past. (*GW*, 1937/1991, p. 405)

Strachey has Freud say that he "is unable to resist." And of course it's true: Freud is very often "seduced" or tempted by analogies, including what philosophers call "arguments from analogy." But these passing fancies are rarely offered as a cute invocation of a theory that caused Freud so much trouble in the 1890s: the theory of childhood sexual seduction (*sexueller Verführung*), the seduction theory. Freud had been unable to offer any proof for his new theory of historical truth – at least not beyond (his own?) "reminiscences" (p. 267). It would seem that Freud means this literally. Continuing:

> It will be the task of each individual investigation to reveal the intimate connections between the material of the present disavowal and that of the original repression. Just as our construction is only effective because it recovers a fragment of lost experience, so the delusion owes its convincing power to the element of historical truth which it inserts in the place of the rejected reality. In this way a proposition which I originally asserted only of hysteria would apply also to delusions – namely, that those who are subject to them are suffering from their own reminiscences. (p. 268)

Freud's chutzpah in this passage is frankly stunning. Neurotics, psychotics, delusionary patients, religious fanatics are just like the hysterics described in *Studies on Hysteria* in 1895. "Hysterics," in Freud and Breuer's original formulation, "suffer mainly from reminiscences" (*SE*, 1895b/1991, p. 7). In other words, Freud in "Constructions in Analysis" cannot offer proof, so he offers reminiscences about his old theory of reminiscence. What he once said only of hysteria – *den ich früher einmal nur für die Hysterie ausgesprochen habe* – he can now say about these delusions (*GW*, 1937/1991, p. 406). These reminiscences of reminiscences of psychoanalysis, in psychoanalysis, and about psychoanalysis are his fundamental grounds for believing in historical truth.

* * *

What does it all mean? Minimally it means, as the analyst-philosopher Jonathan Lear rightly argues, that the late Freud of *Moses and Monotheism* was unable to shake off the seduction theory, that while the theory may have failed at the individual level it still worked at the archaic level, and that Freud, indeed, "was seduced by the seduction hypothesis" (2000, p. 148). So far so good – but there is more going on. In "Constructions in Analysis," his last complete essay, the late Freud revisits and reaffirms the past, including the false construction called the seduction theory (according to which hysteria is caused by repressed childhood sexual abuse), because he has rebranded and tweaked a very old formula: not material truth, but historical truth; not sexual abuse *in fact*, but sexual abuse *in fantasy*. Freud thus finds a way, not only of rationalizing and validating the pre-psychoanalytic past, but also of embracing his old commitment, never really abandoned, of recovering real but totally distorted traumas from the past. What is true is an historical event – a trauma – so inaccessible to confirmation or disconfirmation that Freud can't lose: despite false constructions of childhood sexual abuse and the hunt for fantasies of patricide, this history is absolutely real. This is "reality" structured like a dream or myth, the "external world" structured like a waking fantasy.

What haunts us in the present is always a phylogenetic past that lives on as *compulsively believed delusions*. The same holds for constructions in analysis, which are after all the "equivalents" to the delusions of patients, i.e., they are explanations compulsively believed in by someone (*SE*, 1923, p. 268). Each "portion" in the analytic encounter reflects the other side. As Miller cleverly formulates it, delusion is the patient's (pathological) construction; construction is the analyst's (methodical) delusion (2010/2011, p. 4). Both compulsive beliefs have the flavor of what Freud in 1907 calls "individual religiosity" (*SE*, 1908/1991, p. 126) – a kind of "private religion." Belief, therefore, is reason enough for believing – a circularity no less vicious than those reminiscences that reminisce, and those seductions that seduce. Which is to say – incredibly vicious.

Consequently, just as belief in the primal father of *Totem and Taboo* finds "confirmation" in Freud's obsessive belief in an Egyptian Moses, so too does Freud's old belief in childhood seduction find "confirmation" in enduring fantasies of sexual abuse that point to the traumatic reality of an ancient sexual abuse – rapes, one supposes, rendered inevitable by the primal father's dominance over all women, including his own daughters. In other words, while the "material truth" proves Freud *literally* wrong about the etiology of hysteria in 1896 and, indeed, about the origins of monotheism in 1939 – one is fantastical, the other is fictional – the "historical truth" totally validates Freud's obsessive belief. *Obsession is enough to make it true.* And so it is that the so-called pre-psychoanalytic period is brought within the orbit of psychoanalysis proper.

So, yes, strictly speaking, the patient's "Yes" or "No" is never decisive. What is decisive is a kernel or carp of truth, historical truth, that presents as an indirection perfectly suited for interpretation, construction, conjecture – three words Freud uses almost interchangeably in "Constructions in Analysis." It is a truth beyond life, love, and psychoanalysis, and thus beyond clinical substantiation. For it is a truth that is *meta*, for instance metaphysical, metabiological, and metapsychological. The takeaway message? The external world *necessarily* reflects the truths – deeply fantastical, historical, biological – "discovered" by psychoanalysis and its metapsychology. Psychoanalysis is the method that discovers the actual traumatic past because it is the science of obsession, compulsion, and repetition.

By the "seduction of an analogy" Freud can therefore conclude that humankind is just as likely as individuals to have developed delusions that "contradict reality" (*SE*, 1923, p. 269). That these delusions persist over millennia, returning to haunt *Kultur* and its individuals, proves that they are (let's just say) really real. "They owe their power," Freud concludes the essay, "to the element of *historical truth* which they have brought up from the repression of the forgotten and primaeval past" (p. 269).

In the course of events everything has become clear: psychoanalysis, with the help of metapsychology, has validated psychoanalysis. Circuit complete.

* * *

From his correspondence it is widely known that Freud originally called his *Moses* an "historical fiction," a fact that lends credence to the many interpretations that effectively reduce Freud's efforts to fiction, to self-analysis, to a forgettable outlier (see Grubrich-Simitis, 1997, p. 8). Yet two things must be noted. First, this wasn't the first time that Freud explicitly acknowledged the role of fiction in psychoanalysis. Already in *Studies on Hysteria* in 1895 Freud admitted that "It still strikes me, myself, as strange that the case histories I write should read like short stories and that, as one might say, they lack the serious stamp of science" (*SE*, 1895b/1991, pp. 160–1). He echoes this conclusion in his Dora case study and again in his psychoanalysis of Leonardo da Vinci; the works sound like fiction, like a novel. So Freud's thinking about *Moses* as an historical novel or fiction is by no means an aberration or quirk of his late style. Second, it must also be acknowledged that, in the case of his Moses book, Freud also *dropped* the term "historical novel" by 1937. We know this because he stopped using the term and abandoned altogether an early introduction that rationalized the Moses project in these terms (see Yerushalmi, 1989, p. 379). In fact Freud had already concluded in November 1934, in a letter to Max Eitingon, that "I am no good at historical romances. Let us leave them to Thomas Mann" (in Jones, 1957, p. 194). But even at the beginning of the project Freud was uncertain about his own reliance upon fiction. As he admits in the aborted introduction, "To me fiction and invention are easily associated with the blemish of error" (in Yerushalmi, 1991, p. 17).

The influential scholar of Jewish history and culture Yosef Yerushalmi provides the definitive account for why Freud finally abandoned the rubric of historical fiction, *historischen Roman*: (1) Freud's initial use of the term was essentially defensive, that is, it was a clever way of disarming criticism, but at the cost of drawing attention to the weakness of his reconstructions; (2) in time Freud came to believe in his reconstructions, largely on account of corroborating support from Ernst Sellin, a German theologian (see Yerushalmi, 1991, pp. 25–7); (3) Freud found solace in the concept of "historical truth"; and (4) ultimately Freud erred on the side of science and truth rather than art and fiction (1989, p. 390). While these four reasons are interconnected, the third is easily the most significant. It can be restated more emphatically yet: Freud dropped the category of historical fiction, a medium mastered by his novelist friends Thomas Mann and Arnold Zweig, because he had developed the more psychoanalytical defensible idea of historical truth. For historical truth subsumes historical fiction; or, better put, historical truth is *the truth of historical fiction*, the science behind the fiction. Freud's preference is therefore epistemologically motivated – and perfectly logical. In other words, Freud's argumentation is intellectually *coherent*; it is not simply the result of old age and a faltering command of detail.

According to Yerushalmi, Freud's shift from fiction to history is decisive and underlines "a fundamental difference" between the mythological and ahistorical *Totem and Taboo* and the historical *Moses and Monotheism* (1991, p. 21). Moses is not, for this reason, merely the "final telescoping of a series of analogies" (p. 21). Instead Freud set aside myth and for the first time engaged in the practice of history proper. To this end Yerushalmi cites Freud's letter to his son Ernst upon the publication of *Moses*: "It is my first appearance as a historian; late enough!" (in Yerushalmi, 1991, p. 18). "For the first time," Yerushalmi writes, "he must attempt to corroborate a psychoanalytically derived truth with historical facts quite beyond the purview of psychoanalysis" (p. 21).

Two remarks. First, Yerushalmi's claim is false. From about 1922 to 1932 Freud and William C. Bullitt attempted just such an historical work "beyond the purview of psychoanalysis" in *Thomas Woodrow Wilson: A Psychological Study*. According to Bullitt, Freud "was dissatisfied by his studies of Leonardo da Vinci and of the Moses statue by Michelangelo because he had been obliged to draw large conclusions from few facts, and he had long wished to make a psychological study of a contemporary with regard to whom thousands of facts could be ascertained" (Freud & Bullitt, 1966, p. vi). Freud was not only worried about the status of his historical novel in the 1930s, but had long been concerned that "applied" works of psychoanalysis might bring psychoanalysis into disrepute. Second, Yerushalmi's attempt to set *Moses and Monotheism* apart from everything that came before it confuses the new *theories* of Moses for its *subject*. True, unlike the Primal Father of prehistory the "man Moses" exists within historical time, and this fact is what gives Freud the discomfort of actually having to bother with the protocols of historical evidence. Yerushalmi is obviously right about this.[31] But his deduction is false, since the historical time of the man Moses is nonetheless largely inaccessible to us; it is broken by what Freud himself calls, in a letter to Arnold Zweig, an "unbridgeable gap" between the present and the past (Freud & Zweig, 1970, p. 77). As Yerushalmi (1989) himself expertly demonstrates, Freud actively dissuaded Zweig from writing his own historical novel about Nietzsche precisely because, Freud says, one should not invent details (for example about Nietzsche's sexuality) when the subject is "so near to us in time" (Freud & Zweig, 1970, p. 77). In the case of President Wilson, Freud was

---

[31] As is Ernest Jones when he rightly credits Abraham for providing the first application of psychoanalysis "to the elucidation of purely historical problems" (Jones, 1954, p. 33). The work in question was Abraham's essay on the monotheistic cult of Aton, "Amenotop IV," published in 1912. Freud doesn't even mention it in his *Moses and Monotheism*.

able to draw on Bullitt's extensive research, including original interviews with key personages, about the life of Wilson; research, Bullitt says, that "ran to more than fifteen hundred typewritten pages" (Freud & Bullitt, 1966, p. vii). Unlike Zweig's proposed Nietzsche project, that is, Freud and Bullitt had done their homework before attempting to flesh out a psychological portrait.

In Freud's *Moses* this "unbridgeable gap" is indeed surmounted with the help of all the old analogies that Freud brings to bear – "telescoping," in Yerushalmi's metaphor – on the man Moses. If so, Yerushalmi's attempt to set the historical project of *Moses and Monotheism* apart from the wild speculations of, say, *Totem and Taboo* is entirely wrongheaded – another strategy to save Freud from Freud. Let's put it categorically: Freud was never interested in history per se; he was always only interested in the truth. In this respect he was far more of a metaphysician than an historian. And this is why everything in *Moses and Monotheism* turns on the new concept of "historical truth," that "kernel of truth" built on the back of his renewed interest in "constructions in analysis." Historical truth is the truth of all the other narrative forms we utilize in our creative and scientific endeavors: fictions, delusions, religions, case studies, analogies, biographies, and histories.

Put otherwise, the concept of historical truth is the perfect alibi for the paleopsychologist. For with historical truth Freud need not, in the end, give a damn about the niceties of historical research, including the authority, accuracy, and validity of his sources. For example, Abraham Shalom Yahuda reports that in 1938 he told Freud that Ernst Sellin had, in fact, recanted his claims about the murder of Moses. Freud didn't argue. He just said (and this is quintessential Freud): "And yet it might be true, for it fits so well in the frame of my thesis" (in Ludwig, 1973, p. 246). The same point holds for Freud's Olympian disinterest in anthropological fieldwork that contradicted the fancies of *Totem and Taboo* (see Freud, 1967, pp. 167–8). True, Freud's research into history makes him a *kind of historian* – namely a bad one. But even that is saying too much. Freud was not so much a bad but indifferent historian. For, once again, the concept of historical truth did not make Freud a historian at all, good or bad; it merely reconfirmed him as a psychoanalyst who recovers memories of the past that others, including historians, cannot. That is the privilege of psychoanalysis, the reason why, in *Civilization* as in "Constructions," he insists that analysts and archeologist have "the right" to find what is repressed alongside what is preserved. Without such an alibi there could be no psychoanalysis at all – not of the individual's repressed history, and not of society's repressed history. The glue that holds the analogy of individual and culture together is historical truth. That the concept arrives on the analytic scene only at the end of Freud's life is not ironic, or only ironic. What the arrival of historical truth does is reveal how the entire edifice had been functioning, willy-nilly, all along. Less charitably: the concept of historical truth confirms what good readers of Freud should have known from simply reading Freud's arguments. In the end Freud finally spells it out for us, exclaiming it, in fact, for those with ears too small to hear.

* * *

Freud's own fantasy life very obviously revolved around the work of archeology, the wonder of nineteenth-century discovery that inspired Freud's tales about the unbridgeable, unknowable, and so necessarily *inventable* past. And this, given the exigencies of reality, always filtered through the strict but metaphorically rich language of science and positivism. The many players in Freud's life, including famous men like Rolland and Ellis, made the game worth playing – real, objective, valuable, and significant. *Moses and Monotheism* was Freud's last major attempt, and his most magnificent gambit, to close the gap between the known present and the repressed past and thus provide the epistemological grounds that always eluded him. It is perhaps best called a work of *applied metapsychology*, the fulfillment of his psychoanalytic dreams in the late period, if not the abbreviated culmination of every major feature of the "late Freud." If so, it is also the end game of psychoanalysis, the *non plus ultra* beyond which nothing more can be said.

If so, then what's left to say when we can no longer believe, and thereby validate, the many intricate fantasies of psychoanalytic constructions? The answer must be stories – stories about the men and women who inspired Freud's work, and who advanced the cause of psychoanalysis. Stories about the external world called the psychoanalytic movement, which is true even if the theories it embodies are not. What is left to think is not only the fantastical depths of psychoanalysis, its metapsychology, but its very surface. What's left is the sociopolitical or human dimension.

Let's skim it once more, and bring this discussion to a human end. Havelock Ellis was one of the first people Freud reached out to upon arriving in London – the first letter sent. Freud even asked their mutual friend H.D. to arrange a meeting (in Freud, 1992, p. 261). But by then Ellis was too weak to travel from Suffolk, where he was convalescing, to Freud's home in north London (Brome, 1979, p. 248). In late May of 1939, presumably after the appearance of the English translation on the nine-teenth, Freud sent Ellis a copy of his final masterwork, *Moses and Monotheism* (p. 249; cf., Freud, 1992, p. 260). Ellis replied that he was physically and mentally incapacitated, and so not able to read it (pp. 248–9). About seven weeks later Freud recorded a simple note in his *Diary*: "Havelock Ellis +" (Freud, 1992, p. 261). Ellis died of a heart attack on July 8, 1939, and his cremated remains were interned at Golders Green Cemetery. Freud followed him to Golders Green in September.

The two correspondents, very different in temperament yet brothers in a field they helped define, never did meet in life. However, fate arranged it so that they would remain neighbors in death. Somehow the irony, well beyond any reasonable expectation, seems appropriate and also poignant.

In the Conclusion that follows I finally turn to the role that ethics, and ultimately Jungian thinking, plays in the cultural works. This means a return to the period of time before the writing of *Beyond the Pleasure Principle*, in particular to the period of time that Jung and other followers were engaged with what is sometimes called "paleopsychology" – the psychological examination of prehistory. So far my basic argument has been that the cultural works are determined by Freud's metabiology, by his psycho-Lamarckianism; that one understands nothing of Freud's so-called sociology without an appreciation of this scientist framework. What I want to add in this concluding chapter is a not inconsiderable wrinkle: namely, that the turn toward prehistory, and by extension to cultural problems, was actually begun by followers like Jung and Abraham during early days of institutional psychoanalysis, long before the death drive theory made it all uniquely Freudian. Let's consider this prehistory now.

Conclusion
Ethics, Spirituality, and Psychoanalysis:
Prequel to the "Late Freud"

Freud's late interest in the wider purview of culture is evidenced by his discussions of group psychology, ego instincts, religion, telepathy, mysticism, guilt, sublimation, archaic history, and more. However, all of it is based on his early work on the unconscious dynamics of the individual psyche. So the "sociological" work is logically continuous with the psychology of individuals that came before. Indeed, what seems new or even revolutionary in the late Freud – in particular the death drive – actually works to entrench some of Freud's oldest prejudices. As always, late Romanticism dictated in advance the color of everything else, even when Freud was at his most positivistic.

It is well known that Freud's late interest in culture matches up with his early interests, forming neat bookends to his life's work. It is less well appreciated that Freud took his cues on many aspects of his late work from Carl Jung and the "Zurich School of psychoanalysis." For although Freud may have cracked the door open on the archaic meaning of dreams and myth, it was Jung who kicked it open. As for Freud's interest in religion and (indirectly) mysticism, it was Freud who followed Jung's lead. The real question, then as now, is just how far Freud followed Jung in these pursuits, and just how much, if at all, the encounter with Jung transformed the meaning of Freud's psychoanalysis.

It was in fact a relatively unknown Viennese analyst, Herbert Silberer, who named the shift in tone announced by Jung's work. A gentile like Jung, Silberer was attracted to what he called the "anagogic" potential of psychoanalysis, a word derived from the Greek *anagōgē*, meaning to "lift up." By this neologism Silberer attempted to provide an alternative to Freud's dark conclusions about the unconscious, where sexuality means something more than just pathology and disorder. In other words Silberer was pointing to the positive, ethical, moral, uplifting side of the study of the unconscious – precisely the side that critics, even friendly critics like Oskar Pfister, felt was missing in Freud's work.

Naturally Freud resisted any move to prettify the unconscious. Yet in the end he accepted, if not the content, then at least the direction demanded by analysts such as Adler, Jung, Stekel, Silberer, Pfister, Wittels, Rank, and others. For Fritz Wittels it came down to a characteristic "cryptomnesia" on Freud's part, where every good idea was not only resisted but "forgotten" until Freud could put his own stamp on it and declare his priority. "When others try to introduce their thoughts into his system," Wittels writes, "he denies them hospitality. He can only come back to such thoughts after a long detour, and by way of cryptomnesia" (Wittels, 1924/1971, p. 195). A less charitable view would call Freud's tendency a combination of papal arrogance and intellectual theft. Either way the effect was the same: Freud constantly rejected talented disciples who dared to outthink him, or who more quickly followed his arguments to their logical conclusions; and then, after some time had passed, he circled back and raided their original insights.

Silberer's work on the uplifting aspects of the unconscious, which is connected to his innovations in dream interpretation, is a case in point. It also provides a glimpse into how lesser figures in the psychoanalytic movement could exert a considerable impact on Freud's thinking, including the substance and direction of the "cultural" Freud. Moreover, while we have come to understand very well what the "cultural Freud" means in the wake of the death drive theory, we have still not quite addressed how it all came to be. In short, we turn now to the necessary although still not sufficient conditions that made the late Freud possible – in a word, to the prequel. To this end I start with Silberer's contributions to psychoanalysis, followed by the role of the two great Viennese dissidents of this period, Alfred Adler and, most especially, Wilhelm Stekel. Then I move on to Jung's critically important position in the evolution of psychoanalytic ideas, not just about myth and archaic inheritance, but about spirituality more generally.

1   Herbert Silberer and "Anagogic Psychoanalysis"

In June 1909, a sports journalist, balloonist, and wealthy gentile named Herbert Silberer sent Freud an essay called "Report on a Method of Eliciting and Observing Certain Symbolic Hallucination Phenomena." To Jung Freud writes, "An outsider has given me a short but very significant piece about dreams to submit to you for the *Jahrbuch*" (Freud & Jung, 1988, pp. 238–9). When asked who the outsider is, Freud replies: "Silberer is an unknown young man, probably a better-class degenerate; his father is a well-known figure in Vienna, a member of the city council and an 'operator'" (p. 242). Silberer's essay was duly published in the first issue of *Jahrbuch für psychoanalytische und psychopathologische Forschungen*, the "Yearbook" created in 1908 under Jung's editorship (see Freud & Ferenczi, 1993, p. 148, n. 2; Roazen, 1976, p. 338). Freud met Silberer for the first time in July of 1910, and in October the "outsider" formally joined the Vienna Psychoanalytic Society. On January 18, 1911, Silberer presented his first (and seemingly only) Society presentation on "Magic and Other Topics" (Nunberg & Federn, 1975, Vol. 3, pp. 126–32). Several essays by Silberer followed in the *Yearbook* and in *Zentralblatt für Psychoanalyse*, the *Central Journal of Psychoanalysis*; and, after 1920, in an English-language journal called *Psyche and Eros*. By 1911 Freud was able to commend everything Silberer wrote as "valuable" (Freud & Jung, 1988, p. 453).

In the early "Report on a Method" Silberer discusses the relationship between hypnagogic states (the threshold between waking and sleeping) and self-observation; ideas eagerly adopted by Freud, the lattermost feature anticipating Freud's mature view of conscience. But Silberer was also interested in myth, ethics, alchemy, "hermetic art" (magic, Rosicrucianism, Freemasonry, etc.), and mystic symbolism (Silberer, 1914/1917, pp. 36–7; cf., Shamdasani, 2003, pp. 139–40). In addition to essays on the occult published in the *Central Journal*, in 1914 Silberer published a lengthy book called *Problems of Mysticism and Its Symbolism*. In the broadest sense it's a contribution to the "prospective theory of dream interpretation," that is, to the ethical and spiritual interpretation of dreams (Kerr, 1993, pp. 448–9).

In *Problems* Silberer is remarkably liberal with his references – catholic, curious, generous. Take his claim that myth is expressed through Haeckel's theory of recapitulation. Silberer dutifully cites (without providing a full reference) Freud's own speculations about myth as "the displaced residues of wish phantasies of entire nations, the dreams of ages of young human-ity" (in Silberer, 1914/1917, p. 36). He also refers favorably to Karl Abraham's small book *Dreams and Myths: A Study in Race Psychology*, a 1910 study of the Prometheus legend. "For [Abraham]," writes Silberer, "the myth is the dream of a people and a dream is the myth of the individual" (Silberer, 1914/1917, pp. 36–7; Kerr, 1993, p. 350; see Abraham, 1913, p. 72). Silberer's *bona fides* were thus established, although he was venturing into the most speculative side of psychoanalysis. At the same time it was not Freud or Abraham but Jung who provided Silberer with the greatest inspiration. Silberer writes: "The dreamer thus approaches his own childhood, as he does likewise the childhood of the human race, by reaching back for the more primitive perceptual mode of thought. [On the second kind of regression the Zurich psychiatrist, C.G. Jung, has made extraordinary interesting revelations. His writings will occupy our attention later]" (1914/1917, p. 35). Immediately after this acknowledgment Silberer cites a lengthy passage from Nietzsche's *Human, All Too Human*: "In sleep," Nietzsche writes, "we pass through the entire curriculum of primitive mankind" (p. 35).

It would certainly appear that Silberer was among the most informed, most widely read of commentators, fluent in an intellectual context that included both psychoanalytic literature and philosophy. In fact Silberer's impressive erudition was lifted directly – plagiarized – from Jung's "Two Kinds of Thinking" of 1912. In a section called "The Psychology of the Unconscious," we find not only Jung's full reference to Freud – complete with the page and title, "The Poet and Daydreaming" – but the exact references to passages Silberer cites from Abraham's book of 1910 and to Nietzsche as well. Moreover, the context of Silberer's remarks is identical to Jung's. "The supposition," Jung writes, "that there may also be in psychology a correspondence between ontogenesis and phylogenesis therefore seems justified. If this is so, it would mean that infantile thinking and dream thinking are simply a recapitulation of earlier evolutionary stages" (p. 27). Back to Jung and phylogenesis in a moment.

A less derivative take-away message from Silberer's *Problems of Mysticism and Its Symbolism* is "the problem of multiple interpretation." Through the analysis of myth Silberer finds three competing interpretations: psycho-analytic, "anagogic" (ethical), and "chemical" (natural philosophical) (1914/1917, p. 216). "The multiple interpretation of works of fantasy," Silberer says, "has become our problem, and the diametrical opposition of the psychoanalytic and the anagogic interpretation has particularly struck us" (p. 233). Silberer then moves on to the issue of "introversion." Introversion, he says, "is no child's play," but "leads to abysses" (p. 269). The turning inward to the soul or inner life is a withdrawal from outer reality that "presents two possibilities, either to gain what the mystic work seeks, or to lose oneself" (p. 269). Recall how highly Rolland, in the late 1920s, thought of creative introversion, and also what Freud thought about it: mystic introversion is a return to infantile narcissism. It would seem that Freud's grappling with Silberer's ideas had prepared him for his disagreement with Rolland years later.

The terms "introversion" and "extroversion" were first introduced at the Psychoanalytic Congress in 1913, a time marking the end of Freud and Jung's friendship. In "A Contribution to Psychological Types," Jung had expounded upon the new terms and concluded in provocative fashion that introversion and extroversion applied to the characters of Freud and Adler-Stekel, respectively (Roazen, 1976, pp. 262–3). In *Problems* of 1914, Silberer essentially repeats this distinction – wittingly or not – contrasting psychoanalysis and anagogic interpretation, introversion and extroversion (1914/1917, p. 233). In this way Silberer allied himself with Jungian terminology and an Adlerian concern for the social or "extroverted" sphere of life.

Silberer's contributions are acknowledged in a scattering of references in Freud's work after 1913. In a footnote in a brief essay for *Scientia*, Freud in late 1913 includes Silberer in a list of followers able to "confirm and amplify" his work on dream interpretation; the list includes other stalwart followers like Rank, Jones, Abraham, and Ferenczi (*SE*, 1913c/1991, p. 170). In his polemical attack on Jung, "On the History of the Psychoanalytic Movement," Freud in 1914 mentions the Zurich school penchant for finding a "higher 'anagogic' meaning (as Silberer calls it) which made it possible for them to be employed in the abstract trains of thought of ethics and religious mysticism" (*SE*, 1914a/1991, p. 62). The curiosity is that it was a Viennese member, Silberer, who named this "Zurich School penchant." In his "Wolfman" case study of 1914 (published in 1918), Freud mentions Silberer's "anagogic" explanation in passing (*SE*, 1918/1991, p. 102). Then in his seminal essay of the same year, "On Narcissism," Freud speaks glowingly about Silberer's contribution to a "functional" understanding of dreams as first argued in "Report on a Method."[1] As Freud characterized it, Silberer shows us that "in states between sleeping and waking we can directly observe the translation of thoughts into visual images," and can also understand the "part played by observation . . . in the formation of dreams" (1914b/1991, p. 97). If Silberer's contribution to the interpretation of dreams had been "overlooked," Freud says, it is because hypnagogic imagery is usually reserved for those "gifted philosophically and accustomed to introspection." Subtext: people not like Freud. In these passages Freud is circling around what will in 1923 become his theory of conscience and the superego; a capacity for self-observation that he calls "endo-psychic perception" (Freud & Jung, 1988, p. 388), but which is more often associated with another human sense, that of hearing. This is the "voice" of conscience. In 1914 Freud readily admits that Silberer's work on

---

[1] The discussion of the hypnagogic state was developed in "Phantasy and Mythos" of 1910, "Magic and Other Topics," a full Society lecture of 1911, "Some Little Half-Sleep Experiences" of 1920, and elsewhere (in Freud & Jung, 1974, p. 388, n. 9; Nunberg & Federn, 1975, Vol. 3, pp. 126–32). Silberer defines his terms as follows: "Hallucinations of the sleep-waking state are classified as 'hypnogogic,' i.e., those leading to sleep, and 'hypnopomic,' i.e., those leading away from sleep. Thus hypnogogic hallucinations occur when we fall asleep, hypnopomic when we wake up" (1920, p. 63).

"this critical observing agency" is "one of the few indisputably valuable additions to the theory of dreams." To prove his point, Freud twice refers to and cites from Silberer's hypnagogic experiments ("finely perceptive observations") in a new 1914 edition of *The Interpretation of Dreams* – a signal to everyone that Silberer had arrived (*SE*, 1900/1991, pp. 344, 503). In 1919 Freud once again adds Silberer to another new edition of the *Dream Book* – but this time about anagogic and psychoanalytic interpretations. About this feature of his work Freud has become more openly critical: Silberer has "not given any evidence" that dreams have two possible interpretations (p. 524). "I must [therefore] object," Freud says, "that the alleged fact is non-existent." Then in "A Child Is Being Beaten," also from 1919, Freud once again refers favorably to Silberer's claims about a "functional phenomenon" of "being watched" during hypnagogic states (*SE*, 1918/1991, p. 194).

In retrospect, the critical remark added to the 1919 edition of *The Interpretation of Dreams* marks a turning point in Freud's relationship with Silberer. Obviously Freud valued Silberer's early contributions to dream interpretation. But the "anagogic" ideas from *Problems of Mysticism and Its Symbolism* of 1914 and other works were another matter. The book exhibits traits that Freud would not have appreciated: Silberer's open reliance on the major defectors from psychoanalysis, Adler, Stekel, and Jung; his subject matter, mysticism and hermetic interpretation; the invocation of and reliance upon the Jungian concept of "introversion"; and the contrast drawn between psychoanalysis and ethical or anagogic interpretation, usually to the detriment of the former.

Certainly the timing of *Problems of Mysticism*, published just as Jung exited psychoanalysis, could not have been worse. Beyond that, Silberer was either remarkably uninformed or remarkably reckless about the inner workings of psychoanalytic politics. Normally one would expect a Viennese analyst to tread more carefully into territory already branded as "Swiss." In a letter of April 12, 1912, Freud wrote the following to the Swiss psychiatrist Ludwig Binswanger:

> Silberer has a sensitive mind with a strong penchant for the occult, which he came upon his way to psychoanalysis and has only used psychoanalysis to further his favourite interest. On a personal level he is not part of the Vienna group at all. He is a convinced Christian and well-to-do, his father a conservative provincial civil servant, sportsman and aviator. (Freud & Binswanger, 2003, p. 82)

On a professional level Silberer certainly did continue to attend many meetings of the Vienna Psychoanalytic Society, his last recorded attendance being April 28, 1915. But he must have kept his distance from the other Viennese members. It is possible, therefore, that Silberer was simply not privy to the internecine politics of psychoanalysis or, just as likely, didn't care – a disregard that wouldn't have impressed Freud, either.

The situation with Jung was obviously confusing for many observers, but most especially to those outside Vienna. In 1913 Jung was still president of the International Psychoanalytic Association (IPA), was still the main editor of the *Yearbook* (until October, when he resigned), and was still being invited to lecture abroad as one of the best-known representatives of psychoanalysis. And in fact Jung was still a psychoanalyst. As such he was only too happy to go about refining and indeed redefining the meaning of psychoanalysis in public lectures and in new publications. Even after resigning as editor of the *Yearbook*, Jung planned on creating a new publishing vehicle for the Zurich analysts to be called "Psychological Studies: Works of the Zurich School of Psychoanalysis" (1973, p. 28). Clearly psychoanalysis was morphing into a beast with two heads, two competing centers of influence – and only Jung's carried the prestige of the Burghölzli, the psychiatric hospital associated with the University of Zurich in Switzerland.

Behind the scenes Freud did his best to undermine Jung's standing (see Shamdasani, 2005, p. 95). But by 1914 Freud felt obliged to escalate his campaign, and consequently went public with his complaints. The goal of a new polemic (intended for the *Yearbook*) was to declare what was and was not psychoanalysis once and for all – and to blacklist Jung and the "Zurich School." "Although it is a long time now since I was the only psychoanalyst," Freud sniffs, "I consider myself justified in maintaining that even today no one can know better than I do what psychoanalysis is, how it differs from other ways of investigating the life of the mind, and precisely what should be called psychoanalysis and what would be better described by some other name" (*SE*, 1914, p. 7). Perhaps Jung caught wind of the forthcoming essay, for on April 20, 1914, he finally stepped down as president of the IPA (Clark, 1980, pp. 335–6). Nonetheless Freud went ahead and published "On the History of the Psychoanalytic Movement" in July, which announced the new situation to the readers of a journal edited by Jung only months before. No one could fail to understand the message: Jung's innovations upon psychoanalysis were not psychoanalysis at all. And so, three weeks after the essay appeared, Jung finally withdrew as a member of the IPA, taking with him the rest of the "Zurich school of psychoanalysis" (see Roazen, 1976, p. 264; Shamdasani, 2009, p. 26). As per Freud's insistence, Jung stopped referring to himself as a psychoanalyst and stopped publishing works of psychoanalysis, Swiss or otherwise. Jungian psychoanalysis was thereafter rebranded "analytical psychology," the Swiss group now formally reorganized as the Association for Analytical Psychology.

In 1921, two years after his unfavorable remarks about Silberer's "anagogic" interpretation of dreams, Freud added an aggressive new critique in "Dreams and Telepathy." "Viewed superficially," Freud writes, we can sometimes find a "mental structure with a twofold aspect" (*SE*, 1922a/ 1991, p. 216). Continuing:

> In Silberer's nomenclature the structure has an *anagogic* [ethical] content. On deeper investigation it reveals itself as a chain of phenomena belonging to the region of the repressed life of the instinct – it displays *psychoanalytic* content. As you know, Silberer, who was among the first to issue a warning to us not to lose sight of the nobler side of the human soul, has put forward the view that all or nearly all dreams permit such a twofold interpretation, a purer, anagogic one beside the ignoble, psychoanalytic one. This is, however, unfortunately not so. On the contrary, an over-interpretation of this kind is rarely possible. To my knowledge no valid example of such a dream-analysis with a double meaning has been published up to the present time.

So much for Silberer's "superficial" opposition of psychoanalysis to ethico-spiritual matters. Moreover, in "Dreams and Telepathy" Freud shows Silberer how such work is actually done – and so makes his first public foray into paranormal psychology, a field not just popular with analysts like Jung, Silberer, and Ferenczi, but with a wider stable of scholars that included the famous American philosopher William James. Freud's essay appeared in *Imago* in January 1922 (Jones, 1957, p. 81). By April Silberer and Freud were not speaking, although not for want of Silberer trying. The literature is unclear about what happened. We do know that, on April 17, 1922, Freud sent Silberer a note consisting of two sentences: "I request that you do not make the intended visit with me. As the result of the observation and impressions of recent years I no longer desire personal contact with you" (in Roazen, 1976, p. 339).

Silberer's unconventional proximity to the Zurich school made him an easy target. For here was another gentile with ideas closely aligned to Carl Jung, a colleague perfectly welcome in 1910 but *verboten* after 1913. It is therefore tempting to characterize Freud's rejection of Silberer in 1922 as delayed collateral damage of his break with Jung years before, or, in more Freudian terms, as a deferred effect of the old trauma. Tempting – but not entirely true. In the end the problem was not just Silberer's intellectual affinity to Jungian ideas, but his relationship with another apostate – Wilhelm Stekel. Let's turn to this second forbidden relationship now.

2   "Science Friends" and the "Transition to a Higher Life"

The story of Freud's first dissidents is well known but worth recalling. Freud's two earliest and most prominent followers in Vienna were Wilhelm Stekel and Alfred Adler. When Freud in 1909 took steps to shift the center of power from Vienna to Jung's Zurich, the Viennese were understandably insulted; it was a betrayal. In an emotional plea to his Viennese colleagues at the Second Psychoanalytic Congress of 1910, complete with tears, Freud is reported to have said that "They begrudge me the coat I am wearing; I don't know whether in the future I will earn my daily bread" (in Stekel, 1950, p. 129). "An official psychiatrist," Freud continued, "and a Gentile must be the leader of the movement." Apparently Fritz Wittels remarked: "Freud does not think much of us, his Viennese pupils. If he knew the Swiss as well as he knows us, he would like them still less!" (Wittels, 1924/1971, p. 177). And to be sure, Freud really was "trading-up" with the better-trained, better-educated Zurich followers (Roazen, 1976, p. 227). That summer Wittels resigned from the Society (Wittels, 1924/1971, p. 142).

At the center of the outrage were Stekel and Adler, whose collaboration with Freud began in 1900 and 1902, respectively (Wittels, 1924/1971, p. 233; Stekel, 1950, p. 105). Freud did his best to placate his Viennese friends and colleagues. First, he resigned from the presidency of the Vienna Psychoanalytic Society in the fall of 1910, thereby clearing the way for Adler's and Stekel's election to president and vice president, respectively. Second, he made the two men editors of the new *Central Journal of Psychoanalysis*. Third, he shifted the Wednesday meetings from his own home to a larger, neutral, less personal space at the Viennese Medical Society (Jones, 1955, pp. 130–1; Wittels, 1924/1971, p. 142). But Freud's Viennese colleagues were still not satisfied. To his Hungarian friend, Ferenczi, Freud complained that "I am getting terribly angry with Adler and Stekel. I have been hoping it would come to some kind of clean separation, but things are getting reconciled again, so I have to go on slaving away with them despite my belief that nothing can be done with them" (Freud & Ferenczi, 1993, p. 236; Jones, 1955, p. 131). Of course Freud was right, nothing could be done – and he was the cause of the trouble.

Ultimately meetings of the Society were called, positions were debated, and in February 1911 Adler and Stekel stepped down as president and vice president of the Society. Adler was the first to resign from the *Central Journal* and, in June 1911, founded his own psychoanalytic organization called the "Society for Free Psychoanalytic Research" – the implication, clear enough, that psychoanalysis under Freud was not free (Wittels, 1924/ 1971, pp. 150–1; Bjerre, 1920, p. 88; Jones, 1955, p. 133). In October the Vienna Psychoanalytic Society declared that analysts could not be members of both organizations, a policy that obliged analysts to take sides (Adler, 2002, p. v). As Jung would do a few years later, Adler finally dropped the word "psychoanalysis" from his work, and his society of free analysts morphed into the "Society for Individual Psychology" – the first major offshoot of the "Freud School" of psychoanalysis. It would be years until commentators stopped referring to the "three schools of psychoanalysis" (Freudian, Adlerian, and Jungian), precisely the outcome Freud had sought to avoid (Strachey in *SE*, 1914a/1991, p. 4).

Stekel stayed around a bit longer, in part because his work was never that divergent from Freud's, and in part because Freud actively campaigned to keep him around. According to Wittels, Freud told Stekel that "I have made a pygmy [Adler] great, but I have overlooked a giant close at hand. A single one among the many dream symbols you have discovered is worth more than the whole 'Adlerei' put together" (1924, p. 225; cf., Stekel, 1950, p. 142). To add tribute to the praise, Freud in 1911 sent Stekel an "agate bowl" – Stekel calls it a "valuable ashtray" (1950, p. 142) – and a letter that reads: "I cannot conceive that anything could ever come between us" (Wittels, 1924/1971, p. 226).

But of course something did come between them. In May of 1912 Freud asked Stekel to appoint Victor Tausk, a follower who joined the group after the move to the Viennese Medical Society, as the new book review editor of the *Central Journal*. But Stekel hated Tausk. Apparently Tausk had impuned Stekel's honor in a public lecture, insinuating that Stekel invented his published case studies (Stekel, 1950, p. 142). Beyond that, Stekel believed that he had "the right of veto" over any paper in the *Central Journal* (p. 143); a right he wasn't willing to cede to Tausk. Consequently, Jones says, Stekel "declared that he would not allow a line from Tausk's pen to appear in *his Zentralblatt*" (Jones, 1955, p. 136). "His" journal. "Stekel behaved in a most impertinent and foolish way," Jung recalled, "so that Freud had to give up the editorship of the *Zentralblatt*. Unfortunately the publisher [Bergmann] remained on the side of Stekel, hence Stekel kept the *Zentralblatt* and Freud was dismissed" (1973, p. 27; cf., Stekel, 1950, p. 145). Freud responded by asking the various regional societies to withdraw their support for Stekel's journal. As a result the

Central Journal soon folded (Jones, 1955, p. 137) – although Stekel claimed only that "World War I put an end to it" (Stekel, 1950, p. 145). By November of 1912 Stekel was no longer a member of the Vienna Psychoanalytic Society, the only analyst actively pushed out of Freud's circle for "personal" reasons. As for the Society, it formed yet another house journal, the *International Journal of Medical Psychoanalysis*, under the editorship of Rank and Ferenczi (Bjerre, 1920, p. 89).[2] In time both Rank and Ferenczi would also go their own way from Freud.

How does this unedifying but typical intrigue within psychoanalysis relate to Herbert Silberer? In July 1920 a group of international editors launched yet another journal, this one out of New York, called *Psyche and Eros: An International Bi-Monthly Journal of Psychanalysis, Applied Psychology and Psychotherapeutics*.[3] Of the five European editors, two were Viennese psychoanalysts: Wilhelm Stekel and Herbert Silberer. The other three were from Geneva: Professors Charles Baudouin, Ferdinand Morel, and Édouard Claparède. Silberer's new affiliation with the journal was a public declaration of independence from Freud and from the Vienna Psychoanalytic Society. In other words he was once again an "outsider," but from Freud's perspective something worse – an apostate who had betrayed Freud's trust and support.

Arguably, then, when Freud in April 1922 speaks of "observations and impressions of recent years," he is referring to Silberer's public allegiance to Stekel and the founding of a new journal. Furthermore, *Psyche and Eros* was problematic for three related reasons. The first problem was the journal's name or, more pointedly, its long subtitle. The editors obviously knew that the word "psychoanalysis" was an ungrammatical and therefore ugly

---

[2] After 1920 they dropped the word "medical"; the journal still exists today.

[3] The title changed over the years, the ampersand coming and going in the second issue; the words "psychotherapeutics" and "Applied Psychology" reversing position after the first issue; and the subtitle finally settling on "An International Bi-Monthly Journal of Psychanalysis, Psychotherapeutics, Applied Psychology and Therapeutic Psychognosis" in the seventh issue (July–August 1921). The editors also underwent some change over the short life of the journal. By the third issue the Swiss editors, Professors Charles Baudouin, Ferdinand Morel, and Édouard Claparède, dropped off. Then Baudouin came back as the lead editor for the fourth issue, demoting Samuel A. Tannenbaum from New York. That arrangement lasted until the eleventh issue of March–April 1922, when Stekel, Silberer, and Baudouin all dropped off leaving only Tannenbaum as the sole editor of the last two issues. In the last issue of May–June 1922, Tannenbaum includes an "Important Announcement" on the inside back cover "temporarily" suspending the journal: "In its place we shall begin the publication... ... of a new journal, THE JOURNAL OF SEXOLOGY AND NEO-PSYCHOANALYSIS." It was slated to begin in September 1922. The first issue appeared in 1923 under the editorship of Tannenbaum and William J. Robinson, but they dropped the prefix "neo" and kept the "o": Journal of Sexology and Psychoanalysis.

neologism. For Latin does not permit the conjunction of two vowels, "oa."
Knowing commentators like Swedish psychiatrist Poul Bjerre (*The History
and Practice of Psychanalysis*, 1920) therefore began to telegraph their higher
learning by utilizing the correct Latinate word "psychanalysis" without the
"o" or, in a British compromise, by hyphenating it as "psycho-analysis."
In fact Jung was among the first to utilize the word "psychanalysis" in
essays written in 1906 and 1908 (see Jung, 1961, p. 3, n. 3). In his biography
of 1924, Fritz Wittels claims that "there is a fierce struggle between those
who write 'psychoanalysis' and those who write 'psychanalysis.'
Philosophical considerations would certainly lead us to prefer the shorter
form. The founder considers that the use of the 'o' makes the word more
euphonious, and its use is incumbent upon all of the faithful" (1924/1971,
p. 144, n. 2). However, Jones, Freud's faithful bulldog, contests this
interpretation. According to Jones, Freud stated that "It is impossible for
me to conceive a matter on which I could be more completely indifferent"
(Jones, 1924, p. 485, n. 1).

German historian Horst Gundlach has published the definitive commentary on the missing "o" in analysis: "Psychoanalysis and the Story of
'O': An Embarrassment" (2002, pp. 4–5). The impression one gets, Jones's
version notwithstanding, is that Freud surely did not appreciate these
unsubtle corrections of his neologism, and would have chalked them up
to symptomatic expressions of a knowing superiority. "Psychanalysis,"
a modification derived of embarrassment, was inevitably a form of public
shaming that drew attention to itself and to Freud's apparent poverty of
learning.

Freud's problem with the journal would have extended to its provenance
and editorship. On the title page of each issue of *Psyche and Eros* is
included, in brackets, the following claim, "Successor to *Zentralblatt für
Psychoanalyse*." With the new journal Stekel had boldly resurrected and
poached upon the symbolic capital of the old *Central Journal* – in short,
poached upon Freud's international reputation. The *Central Journal*
belonged to Stekel, after all, first as the spoils of the war between the
Vienna and Zurich schools of psychoanalysis; and then as the orphaned
journal of official psychoanalysis in Vienna. And so, while Adler and Jung
had stopped calling their version of Freud's ideas psychoanalysis, confusion
over what psych(o)-analysis really was continued unabated because of
dilettantes like Stekel. That the journal boasted Swiss editors was similarly
problematic. So too was the fact that the journal was published in English
and in New York, a highly significant battleground for the future of
psychoanalysis.

The second major problem was the journal's contributors. *Psyche and Eros* was utilized by some of Freud's close supporters, like Oskar Pfister (in a two-part essay of 1921). But it was also the new home for analysts that Freud had rejected, such as Max Kahane (Roazen, 1976, p. 339 n.; Wittels, 1924/1971, p. 216) – one of the early members of the Wednesday society (Stekel, 1950, p. 116). But, most of all, the journal was the unofficial mouthpiece of Stekel's unauthorized form of psychoanalysis. Stekel wrote the lead article in the first, second, and eleventh of twelve total issues; and contributed articles another eight times. Just as important, Stekel wrote a total of fifty reviews of various lengths about current essays and/or books related to psychoanalysis – including reviews of Freud's own works. For example, in the November–December issue of 1920 he reviewed Freud's essay "The Uncanny." Beyond Stekel's involvement, the journal also became the home of "anagogic psychoanalysis." For example, the Swedish psychotherapist Emanuel von Geijerstam published a three-part essay (1921–2) called "Anagogic Psychoanalysis," the appearance of which may have contributed to Freud's decision to formally delegitimize this trend in his "Dreams and Telepathy" of January 1922. That ethics was being institutionalized as a trend within psychoanalysis but beyond Freud's own control would not have been appreciated. It certainly helps flesh out Freud's hostility to ethics in the late period.

The third problem created by *Psyche and Eros* was the substance of Silberer's own contributions. Silberer was not as prolific as Stekel – his articles appear seven times (sometimes as continuations); and he contributed only eleven reviews of varying lengths. But the content of two review essays in particular would have angered Freud. One, called "Beyond Psychoanalysis," was published in May–June of 1921; the other, a biting review of *Group Psychology and the Analysis of the Ego*, was published in March–April of 1922. Both essays gave Freud plenty of reasons to cut off relations with Silberer once and for all in mid-April of 1922 – assuming that the other major problems with the journal didn't already guarantee that outcome. Let's turn now to these two forgotten contributions.

* * *

In "Beyond Psychoanalysis" Silberer does something that surprisingly few reviewers of *Beyond the Pleasure Principle* bother to do: he takes Freud's biological arguments seriously. The problem with this approach is that Freud admits, perhaps as a defensive tactic, that his arguments are highly speculative and therefore inconclusive. The "principle of charity" thus obliges reviewers to tiptoe around all the logical absurdities – and make up excuses for what they find. But Silberer was not feeling charitable. In a way, though, he simply amplifies Ellis's private response to *Civilization and Its Discontents*, noted earlier: the abundant evidence of life and evolution proves the death drive theory wrong. "To postulate instincts which are not instincts to live, but the contrary" writes Silberer, "would be a biological contradictio in adjecto" (1921, p. 143) – a contradiction in terms. Silberer's rhetoric in the review essay is indicative of his overall approach: "The author [Freud] has 'decided,' without having any particular proof" (p. 145); "Freud probably overlooks the fact that our instincts are after all a part of life" (p. 147); "to attribute death, the end of life, to the instincts would be pure arbitrariness" (p. 147); "the whole of Freud's suggestive theory is in danger of collapsing" (p. 148); "a tour de force consisting of an arbitrary application to biology of the well-known psychoanalytic conception of manifest and latent tendencies" (p. 148); "as might be expected, his thesis comes out of the wordy contest unharmed" (p. 148); "It is but a feeble argument . . ." (p. 148); "Freud's conclusion . . . seems to me to be wrong" (p. 148); "thus far Freud has failed . . ." (p. 150); "The author having lost himself in this impenetrable thicket finds no earthy [*sic*: earthly?] way out" (p. 150); "this thesis has already gone surprisingly far into the airy realm of fantasy" (p. 150); and so on.

Toward the end of the review essay Silberer finally cuts to the chase and names his major problems: in *Beyond the Pleasure Principle* Freud has abandoned empiricism (pp. 150–1); and death, including suicide, is not about instinct at all but about a consciousness that has abstracted itself and "become independent and foreign to the biological goals" of life (p. 151). About the latter point – the missing anagogic content concerning death – more in a moment. As for the former point, let's take off from Silberer's remarks about Freud's "airy realm of fantasy":

> I do not deny that even in this realm, which calls for a special quality of thinking and writing, much that is valuable may be produced. When I recall Fechner's charming capricios I could even wish to hear his masterhand improvising on this theme of Freud's. Not that I mean to imply that Freud is not himself a master; but it is on the firm ground of empirical knowledge that he rules, sometimes despotically. His admirable powers lie within the bounds of psychoanalysis, not beyond it. (pp. 150–1)

Freud rules "sometimes despotically." In the next paragraph Silberer remarks upon how completely Freud misunderstands Kant (the same complaint Pfister makes in 1928). The overall implication is that Freud is out of his depth in his speculations about the death drive, and should stick to what he is good at, namely an empirical psychoanalysis. These other depths, at times charmingly laughable as in Fechner, are better left to people like Silberer. "Is there any occasion for such a dizzy flight?" asks Silberer. "Certainly not" (p. 151). Silberer is clearly "schooling" his old master – and, he goes on, not as severely as Freud deserves. "I have not shown up all the author's inexactitudes, cabrioles and sinuosities; there is no need to do so; perhaps they even have a charm of their own" (p. 151). "Perhaps," he says – but implies that they do not. The schooling slips easily into condescension.[4] However, to be fair, there is nothing critical a slave *can* say that is not (as a *contradictio in adjecto*) bound to be received by the master as condescension.

If "Beyond Psychoanalysis" did not adequately convey Silberer's newfound freedom from, equality with, or even contempt toward the "despotic" ruler of psychoanalysis, then his review of Freud's next book certainly did. Appearing in March–April of 1922, the review could have been written (in part) as a salvo in response to Freud's criticism of anagogic psychoanalysis in "Dreams and Telepathy" published in January of that same year.[5] Most of Silberer's review of *Group Psychology and the Analysis of the Ego* is exegesis – although his discussion of Freud's view of the psychology of the group, of the leader, and of the infantile dependence therein obviously resonates with autobiographical significance. When Silberer switches to critique he mentions all the negative things he could or might have said about Freud and *Group Psychology*: "One could take exception ... to all the great certainty with which the theory of the primitive herd is accepted"; "One might attempt a defence of the primary herd instinct ..."; "One might object to his theory of suggestion ..." (1922a, p: 115). And then Silberer gets to his point: "Here we shall speak of only two of his extravagances, because they are of a less general nature" (pp. 115–16). The first: Freud in *Group Psychology* claims that the father of the mass is a kind of hypnotist, and that he gets his authority "by the power of his glance." Silberer is probably referring to chapter ten, "The Group

---

[4] Cabriole: "A jump in which one leg is extended into the air forward or backward, the other is brought up to meet it, and the dancer lands on the second foot." Sinuosity: "The ability to curve or bend easily and flexibly."

[5] It is also notable that Silberer's review appears in the same issue where Stekel provides an aggressive review of Ernest Jones's new work, "The Treatment of Neurosis." "Freud is a monarch," Stekel begins the review, who is surrounded by "representative[s] in every province" (1922, p. 118). One of these designates, Jones, "lets it be known far and wide that no psycho-therapeutist has the right to call himself a psychoanalyst unless he accepts all of Freud's teachings, bag and baggage" (1922, p. 118). Then the coup de grace: "But psychoanalysis is not merely a science, it has become a religion" (p. 119). This is the kind of criticism that made *The Future of an Illusion* increasingly necessary in the 1920s.

and the Primal Horde," where Freud mentions that "to be alone with him [the father], 'to look him in the face,' appears a hazardous exercise" (*SE*, 1921/1991, p. 127). At the same time, Silberer argues, Freud denigrates all other forms of hypnosis. "Need I remind the reader that no information has come down to us about the glance of the herd-father?" (p. 116). Presumably Silberer is calling on Freud to account for and perhaps analyze his own hypnotic power – similar to the charge that Jung makes in a letter of 1912 (Freud & Jung, 1988, pp. 534–5). Silberer's second point is even less clear, but is charged with an emotional intent that's hard to miss. It constitutes the concluding paragraph of the review, and is probably the last thing Silberer ever published about Freud:

> Recently Freud has enunciated a primary "oral" phase of the libido-organization in which the individual incorporated, by eating, the desired and treasured object and in so doing destroyed it. In a passage relating to this, he says: "The cannibal, as we know, has not progressed from this phase; he loves 'to devour' his enemies, and he eats only those whom he loves." [Comment unnecessary.] (1922a, p. 116)

Or as Strachey translates the passage from *Group Psychology*: "The cannibal, as we know, has remained at this standpoint: he has a devouring affection for his enemies and only devours people of whom he is fond" (*SE*, 1921/1991, p. 105). Silberer merely adds, in brackets, that any comment is "unnecessary" – except of course the very words that declare the comment unnecessary. It is not quite silent, therefore, and not quite unnecessary either; it is more like an aside or, better yet, like the wagging of a finger, an accusation. What Freud says speaks for itself, and speaks for Silberer and for all of Freud's debased followers. Arguably it cashes out as follows: Freud is a cannibal who destroys what he loves, a despotic father who breaks the followers that he makes. If so, then Freud is the one who has failed to progress beyond a brutal primal phase, who fails to achieve anything close to a personal ethics in his relations with the group – let alone the heights of an anagogic psychoanalysis. In short, Freud's "love" is a consuming hatred.

The finger wagging appears in the March–April 1922 issue *Psyche and Eros*. In April Silberer nonetheless seeks out a meeting with the primal despot – thereby admitting, indeed, that more remained to be said. But recall that the despot refuses the request and breaks off all further communication: "As the result of the observation and impressions of recent years," Freud declares, "I no longer desire personal contact with you." Freud will not lay his eyes upon Silberer, will not risk entrancing his follower again. Silberer is not eaten up by the father-cannibal, but is unceremoniously spit out. No more cabriolets and sinuosities. No more identification. Skip ahead nine months: on January 12, 1923, the forty-year-old Silberer hangs himself from the window bars in his house, "leaving a flashlight," Roazen says, "shining on his face as he strangled so his wife could see him when she came home" (1976, p. 339).

Viennese analysts were in fact rocked by two consecutive suicides, Silberer on the 12th and Max Kahane on the 11th. According to Felix Deutsch, Silberer's suicide was "allegedly on account of 'mental overstimulation,'" while Kahane had "slit his Radialis" – his wrist – "supposedly because of neediness" (in Roazen, 1985, p. 209). "Among the psychoanalytic members," Deutsch reports of the suicides, "there is a rather subdued mood." Then he adds: "I'm curious as to how Prof. takes these things."

Freud greeted Silberer's death with silence. Or very nearly. In his first letter of the new year to Ferenczi, about a week after Silberer's suicide, Freud writes: "There are all kinds of new things with us, some that one should be happy about, but everything is so mixed with cares and qualms, and one has gotten out of practice with joy" (Freud & Ferenczi, 1993, p. 93). Presumably Silberer's death was one of the "new things" Freud could be happy about, a sentiment he also felt about Tausk after his suicide in 1919 ("I confess I do not really miss him; I had long take him to be useless, indeed a threat to the future" [in Roazen, 1969, p. 140]). And given the Freudian interpretation of suicide, Freud's refusal to acknowledge Silberer's death was entirely justified: unable to kill Freud, Silberer had taken his own life instead. Wittels summarizes this view perfectly: "No one thinks of suicide unless he has wished for another's death. His suicide is punishment for the death wish" (1924/1971, p. 241).

* * *

In his review essay of *Beyond the Pleasure Principle*, Silberer insists that death, including suicide, cannot be reduced to a biologically innate drive or instinct. "Even if we disregard the fact of suicide," Silberer writes, "a yearning for death is often enough manifested in life and in art. But these impulses cannot be called instincts, nor can they be considered as something of a primary nature" (1921, p. 151). On the contrary, for Silberer they are features of a consciousness perverted in its aim – which is tied up with the assessment of pleasure and displeasure. About consciousness he writes:

> the light thus kindled grew beyond its biological purpose, became independently dominant and succeeded in setting itself up over the biological purpose. Here, at the extreme summit of development, we find the basis for the super-biological, including the death impulses, which sometimes

appear deceptively like instincts in their behavior. They are late blossoms on an old system – reversal phenomena running counter to the natural impulse. They are manifestations of consciousness which have become independent and foreign to the biological goals. (p. 151)

It is probably too much to interpret these words as a direct rationalization and foretelling of Silberer's own suicide. But they dramatize, tragically so, the differences between the two men. Silberer conceived of suicide and the impulse to die as perversions of a consciousness turned against itself – a "reversal phenomena." The impulse to die is therefore not an instinct, and is therefore unknowable by Freud's botched biology, his absurd speculations, and his psychoanalysis. Simply put, it is not *unconscious*. The impulse to die is rather a product of social and ethical forces ("the extreme summit of development") and so better understood by Silberer's own anagogic psychoanalysis. It is *conscious*, in other words, a product of social relations punctuated by experiences of pleasure and displeasure. Or as his title would have it, the so-called death drive is "beyond psychoanalysis" – not biological and *metapsychological*, as Freud fashioned it, but *anagogical*.

An anonymous one-paragraph obituary was published in the *Bulletin of the International Psycho-Analytical Association* in 1923. The year of Silberer's death is incorrectly recorded as 1923, and emphasis is placed on the fact that "Silberer's interest obviously lay outside the domain of psycho-analysis proper" (p. 399). The author mentions the two major psychoanalytic journals where he published work, but fails to mention *Psyche and Eros*.

The following year Stekel wrote a much longer, far more personal obituary for yet another new journal, *Fortschritte der Sexualwissenschaft und Psychoanalyse* (Progress in Sexology and Psychoanalysis). It fills in some details missing in the secondary literature. According to Stekel, Silberer "was very careful and skeptical" when he came to psychoanalysis (1924, p. 410; my translation). Then he recounts their relationship in some detail. "When I separated from Freud," Stekel writes, Silberer "was the only one of all the Freudians who remained true to me. (He would pay a high price for this friendship [*Freundschaft teuer bezahlen*]). He saw clearly that it was only scientific differences that pushed Freud to get me to voluntarily resign from the Society" (p. 411). Stekel then goes on to name the founding of *Psyche and Eros* as the precipitating cause of the rupture between Freud and Silberer:

Silberer was a permanent participant of evening gatherings where my adherents and I shared experiences. When Dr. Tannenbaum asked me to establish with him an English analytical journal, *Psyche and Eros*, I immediately thought of Silberer as [editorial] assistant. I pointed out that his participation in the journal would damage his standing with Freud. He saw the truth of my warnings, but after thinking about it for 24 hours he accepted the position of editor. After that Freud was finished with Silberer. This also explains the otherwise incomprehensible fact that the Psychoanalytic Press has not published a collection of Silberer's lesser and greater writings. (This debt of honor could still be made up later.) (Stekel, 1924, pp. 411–12; my translation)

Stekel also mentions how Freud's followers mistreated Silberer during Society meetings. When Stekel asked Freud to account for "the deeper reason for this bitchiness" (*Gehässigkeit*) toward Silberer, Freud apparently told him: "'The man is a Jesuit!'" (1924, p. 415). Thereafter, Stekel writes, Silberer knew there was "a deep, unbridgeable chasm between himself and his beloved and revered teacher."

Stekel makes a point of demonstrating that Silberer was nonetheless sympathetic to Freud and to the scientific issues he raised. To drive the point home he tells the story of the demise of their journal, *Psyche and Eros*. Their coeditor Samuel Tannenbaum had visited Vienna with a "mission" to mediate the hostilities between Freud, Adler, and Stekel. When it failed, Tannenbaum "transformed from a fanatical Freudian into an even more fanatical anti-Freudian" (p. 416; cf., Stekel, 1950, p. 189). One consequence was that Tannenbaum began to publish comic and absurd essays "against his master." Silberer and Stekel immediately agreed to suspend their support for *Psyche and Eros*, which for Silberer came with "a large financial loss."[6] As a consequence the two Viennese men fell out with their "American counterparts" – a price they paid willingly, although with no apparent credit from Freud. Given the timing of his requested meeting with Freud, it is likely that Silberer wanted to inform Freud about the turn of events with the journal and, perhaps, undo some of the damage done on its account. When Freud refused to meet with him, Silberer became a man with few allies – an unrecognized, unheralded martyr to psychoanalysis.

Stekel does not lay the blame for Silberer's suicide on Freud's rejection, although the pain it caused him is a dominant theme of the obituary. With touching pathos Stekel confronts the problem that suicide raises for psychoanalysis:

[6] Their names drop off the masthead beginning with issue eleven of March–April 1922, the issue wherein Silberer attacks Freud's *Group Psychology and the Analysis of the Ego*. The following issue of May–June contains nothing from Stekel or Silberer, and includes the "important announcement" about the journal's temporary suspension.

I have no idea what demonic forces hid beneath his serene exterior. Had he confided in me, perhaps I could have saved him!

An analyst who commits suicide is incomprehensible, since analysis is the best way to prevent suicide.

Silberer shared the fate of many gifted people who concerned themselves with analysis without being thoroughly analyzed. (I refer only to the brilliant Viennese researchers Schroetter and Tausk, who also committed suicide.) (p. 417)

There are in fact many suicides in the history of psychoanalysis – including, in 1940, Wilhelm Stekel.[7] As for Silberer, he apparently maintained a facade that belied his inner turmoil. And so his friendship with Stekel was "very peculiar," *eine sehr merkwürdige* (1924, p. 417). Silberer would discuss his patients' dreams with Stekel, who was reputed to be a master of interpretation, but never his own (p. 417). So they were, Stekel says, "*Duzfreunde,*" science friends; but Silberer "never shared a word with me about his spiritual life" (p. 417).

Toward the end of his tribute, Stekel notes that Silberer had discussed death as a "transition to a higher life" in a conversation with "a well-known Viennese philosopher" not long before he committed suicide. No doubt Silberer was retracing some of the views he raised in his criticism of Freud's *Beyond the Pleasure Principle*, against which he posited the higher anagogic, strictly cultural and interpersonal, reasons for suicide. It is no doubt with this contribution in mind that Stekel closes out the obituary with words that Silberer adopted as his own in *Problems of Mysticism and Its Symbolism*: "*Versinke denn! Ich könnt auch sagen: steige!*" "Sink then! But I could also say: ascend!" Stekel may not have realized that these are originally words uttered by Mephistopheles in Goethe's *Faust* (see Spielrein, 1994, p. 158).

If Silberer was a martyr to psychoanalysis, then he was also a martyr to anagogic considerations or, more accurately, to that marriage of concepts that failed him in the end, an *anagogic psychoanalysis*. His death, after all, did not confirm Freud's pessimism about human biology; it confirmed merely that social death could precipitate death by suicide. His suicide proved the value of anagogics.

As for Carl Jung, who had originally influenced the direction of Silberer's interests, he was at once grateful and contemptuous. Years after the suicide, Jung acknowledged Silberer's priority in the field of psychology and alchemy – admitting that, at the time, he only paid attention to

---

[7] On June 25, 1940, after years of suffering the effects of diabetes, including gangrene of the foot, Stekel committed suicide by aspirin poisoning (Stekel, 1950, pp. 18, 22–3).

Silberer's work on ethics (Jung, 1961/1989, p. 204). "As his tragic death shows," Jung said in 1961, "Silberer's discovery of the problem [of the psychology of alchemy] was not followed by insight into it" (p. 204). Or as Jung put it, rather less generously, in a letter of December 22, 1935: "Analytical psychology . . . has its roots deep in Europe, in the Christian Middle Ages, and ultimately in Greek philosophy. The connecting-link I was missing for so long has now been found, and it is alchemy as Silberer correctly surmised. Unfortunately, rationalistic psychologism broke his neck for him" (Jung, 1973, p. 206).

For Jung, Silberer wasn't a martyr to ethics. He was just a sad proponent – and victim – of the very kind of rationalism that Freud championed in his later years. Let's turn, finally, to Jung's interpretation of Freud's supposed rationalism; a rationalism best associated with *The Future of an Illusion* of 1927.

3 "The Black Tide" and "Hair-Shirted John of the Locusts": On Jung and Freud

It is noteworthy that, before the First World War, the Vienna Psychoanalytic Society hosted a meeting with a "telepathist" (Roazen, 1976, p. 233) and that Freud himself "participated in at least one telepathic séance" (p. 237). Freud's essays on telepathy (1921 and 1922) were, technically speaking, his first forays into research of the occult and paranormal.[8] But the truth is that his speculations about death, repetition, and the death drive are also significant contributions to the field. *Beyond the Pleasure Principle* is a ghost story, after all, an account of compulsive repetitions that are purportedly "demoniacal." As for the theme of death, it is the pinnacle of occult research. For what is "beyond" everyday pleasure is, almost by definition, outside the bounds of normal scientific research.

Investigations into the occult were de rigueur by the 1920s, when it became easier for Freud to go public with his speculations. Other major scientific figures, like Albert von Schrenck-Notzing and Albert Moll, were investigating the field of parapsychology – and would examine mediums, the occult, telepathy, séances, and more. Jones tells us that in 1921 Freud was asked to be coeditor of "three different periodicals devoted to the study of occultism" (Jones, 1957, p. 392). Freud refused. But in one letter of reply Freud nonetheless claimed that, "If I had my life to live over again I should devote myself to psychical research rather than to psychoanalysis."

---

[8] The first essay, "Psychoanalysis and Telepathy," was published posthumously in 1941.

In lecture thirty of the *New Introductory Lectures* of 1932, "Dreams and Occultism," Freud states that when occult concerns "first came into my range of vision more than ten years ago, I too felt a dread of a threat against our scientific *Weltanschauung*, which, I feared, was bound to give place to spiritualism or mysticism if portions of occultism were proved true. Today I think otherwise" (*SE*, 1933a/1991, p. 54).

Freud's "dread" of the occult can be traced back to the writing of *The Interpretation of Dreams* – at least in the negative. For as he says straight off in the first preface, "I have not, I believe, trespassed beyond the sphere of interest covered by neuropathology" (*SE*, 1900/1991, p. xxii). In Jung's obituary for Freud, he writes that while the book was "a source of illumination" for younger psychiatrists, "for our older colleagues it was an object of mockery" (in Jung, 1989, p. 147, n. 2). Like the use of hypnosis, dream interpretation was just more hocus pocus, coin of the realm for hucksters, charlatans, and mystics. Clearly Freud had many good reasons to tread carefully.

Jung became interested in psychoanalysis as a young assistant at the Burghölzli after his boss, famed psychiatrist Eugen Bleuler, asked him to review the *Dream Book* in 1900 (in Evans, 1964, p. 27). When Jung and Freud first met in March 1907, they supposedly spoke for thirteen hours straight (in Jung, 1989, p. 149). Freud, immediately concerned about Jung's interest in mysticism, urged him to stay true to the theory of sexuality. "We must make a dogma of it," Freud insisted, "an unshakeable bulwark." Jung: "A bulwark against what?" Freud: "Against the black tide of mud . . . of occultism" (p. 150). Such was, for Jung, Freud's "flight from himself, or from that other side of him which might perhaps be called mystical" (p. 152). *Fin de siècle* Vienna was in fact a hotbed of interest in what Ellenberger calls "the cult of *Anti-Physis*, that is, of everything that is the opposite of nature" (1970, p. 282). This included interest in hypnosis, unusual mental states, eroticism, and also mysticism. In this sense Freud was wary of a trend that had garnered a lot of attention. But from Jung's perspective, Freud's recourse to a crude positivism in the face of changing mores was just a form of overcompensation in the face of "virtually every-thing that philosophy and religion, including the rising contemporary debate of parapsychology, had learned about the psyche" (in Jung, 1989, pp. 150–1).

Jung was never convinced by the "dogma" of sexuality. The problem was that the field of sexuality, so dear to Freud, was itself barely established as a science. "To me," Jung rightly contends, "the sexual theory was just as occult" (p. 151). But because of researchers like Krafft-Ebing and Ellis, sexuality had at least established a modest pedigree. The same held for hypnotism, used by Freud in his early practice, which had already been laundered by medical hypnotists like James Braid in Scotland and Hippolyte Bernheim in France (the Nancy school). In these respects Freud was not really an innovator but an early adopter. So long as psychoanalysis could trace its unusual interests in dream interpretation and sexuality to medicine, then the dangers of being associated with paranormal research were minimized. Psychoanalysis was science – not a worldview or, worse, a form of palmistry.

Despite Jung's very apparent interest in mysticism, Freud felt that he needed him. In a letter of 1909, Freud told Jung that, "If I am Moses, then you are Joshua, and will take possession of the promised land of psychiatry, which I shall only be able to glimpse from afar" (Freud & Jung, 1988, pp. 196–7). "If I am Moses" – with good humor and fantasy, Freud did his best to match Jung's own robust enthusiasm. Still, the grandiosity of the remark, so typical of their correspondence, bodes ill for the future; it also puts Freud's late interest in the murder of Moses in an interesting light. Obviously Jung could never live up to Freud's enormous expectations or endure his constant manipulations. Who could? The answer, we know, was nearly no one, least of all the best and brightest among Freud's followers. The best always went their own way. "The best always leave," Freud is reported to have complained, "and the goody-goodies are no good" (Roazen, 1969, p. 303). That is exactly right.

From the outset Freud's Viennese colleagues were suspicious of Jung: Swiss, Christian, a psychiatrist. Robust. Charismatic. But Freud always insisted that these were the qualities needed to take psychoanalysis out of its Jewish ghetto in Vienna and make it real, objective, and universal – and now centered at an influential powerhouse of medical training, the Burghölzli Psychiatric Clinic in Zurich. The means was unapologetically political, but the end was always truth; or, at least, the belief in such truth.

As it happened the Freud–Jung relationship did not survive even six good years, roughly 1907 to 1913. During this time they debated the future of psychoanalysis, schemed, swapped ideas as well as gossip, exchanged thoughts about Jung's lover, the Russian Sabina Spielrein, and even shared her as a patient and colleague. In time Jung would be reviled by Freudians as a mystic and, even before his collaboration with the Nazis, an anti-Semite. Yet it must be said: Freud knew about Jung's "racial" background of Swiss Protestantism and knew about his peccadillos well before their break in 1913. Consider the period just prior to the founding of the IPA in March 1910, when Jung was elected the first president (Freud & Jung,

1988, p. 304). One of the first issues facing the IPA was an offer made to Freud a few months earlier by Alfred Knapp, a Bern pharmacist: perhaps the IPA would like to join the new International Order for Ethics and Culture? Freud mentions the offer in a letter to Jung in January 1910, and asks: "Mightn't it be a good idea for us to join as a group?" (p. 288). The Swiss psychiatrist Auguste Forel had already joined; beyond that, Germans during this period were keen to establish and join new associations (Kerr, 1993, p. 283).

Jung's response in February contains in miniature many of the features that would eventually destroy his relationship with Freud. It begins with his discomfort about ethics and follows with what he would later call his "rampages of fantasy" (Freud & Jung, 1988, p. 296). The letter is worth citing at length:

> I am so thoroughly convinced that I would have to read myself the longest ethical lectures that I cannot muster a grain of courage to promote ethics in public, let alone from the psychoanalytic standpoint! At present I am sitting so precariously on the fence between the Dionysian and the Apollonian that I wonder whether it might not be worthwhile to reintroduce a few of the older cultural stupidities such as the monasteries. That is, I really don't know which is the lesser evil ... If a coalition is to have any ethical significance it should never be an artificial one, but must be nourished by the deep instincts of the race. Somewhat like Christian Science, Islam, Buddhism. Religion can be replaced only by religion... 2000 years of Christianity can only be replaced by something equivalent. An ethical fraternity, with its mystical Nothing, not infused by any archaic-infantile driving force, is a pure vacuum and can never evoke in man the slightest trace of that age old animal power which drives the migrating birds across the sea and without which no irresistible mass movement can come into being. I imagine a far finer and more comprehensive task for [psycho-analysis] than alliance with an ethical fraternity. I think we must give it time to infiltrate into people from many centres, to revivify among intellectuals a feeling for symbol and myth, ever so gently to transform Christ back into the soothsaying god of the vine, which he was, and in this way absorb those ecstatic instinctual forces of Christianity for the *one* purpose of making the cult and the sacred myth what they once were – a drunken feast of joy where man regained the ethos and holiness of an animal. That was the beauty and purpose of classical religion ... What infinite rapture and wantonness lie dormant in our religion, waiting to be led back to their true destination! A genuine and proper ethical development cannot abandon Christianity but must grow up within it ... (p. 294)

Jung, heir apparent and future president of the IPA, imagines a psycho-analysis that transcends Christianity but from within Christianity – a religion to replace all previous religions. To top it all off, he also invokes a return of the "god of the vine," to wit, the pagan god Dionysius. All of which makes sense, since Jung, so obviously functioning beyond ethical norms in his own clinical practice, was not just "on the fence" between Dionysus and Apollo but had already embraced the "drunken feast of joy" and "infinite rapture and wantonness" of his Dionysian exploits with Spielrein (and then with others). In this respect psychoanalysis was Jung's intellectual *rationale* for his lapse in professional ethics, not an opportunity for ethical self-reflection. As Jung adds near the end of his letter, invoking Goethe's *Faust*, psychoanalysis "makes me 'proud and discontent,' I don't want to attach it to Forel, that hair-shirted John of the Locusts, but would like to affiliate it with everything that was ever dynamic and alive" (p. 294).

Freud was flattered by Jung's eager devotion; a devotion echoed by all of Freud's successful colleagues. Already in 1907 Jung had confessed that his "veneration" for Freud had "something of the character of a 'religious' crush" (1988, p. 95). One would expect the theorist of the transference to immediately quash such infantile devotion, but he did not. Instead he used it. Yet obviously Freud had to set Jung straight when he equated psychoanalysis and religion (in the passage cited earlier). "You mustn't regard me," Freud cautions, "as the founder of a religion" (p. 295). And later in the same paragraph: "I am not thinking of a substitute for religion; this need must be sublimated." In the same letter Freud also feels obliged to justify his own interest in the International Order for Ethics and Culture, which was, he claims, "purely practical" and "diplomatic." "I suspect," Freud says, "Knapp is a good man, that [psychoanalysis] would bring him liberation, and I thought: if we join this Fraternity while it is in *statu nascendi* [in a nascent state], we shall be able to draw the moralists to [analysis] rather than let the analysts be turned into moralists" (p. 295). Freud was not really interested in becoming a moralist. But that was his point. Freud's discussion of joining forces with an ethical Order was really just an unsubtle way to bludgeon the philanderer Jung, reminding Jung that he had been dragged into his moral quagmire with Sabina Spielrein. But Jung wouldn't heed the advice.

It's highly unlikely that Freud was sincerely interested in joining the ethical Order at all; he just wanted to remind Jung about his moral obligations, both to his wife, Emma, and to psychoanalysis. And Jung surely understood this. If that's true, then Jung's frenzied rejection of the request to join the Order was also a pointed rejection of Freud's advice-cum-blackmail. Jung would not change, would never become a "hair-shirted John of the

Locusts." He was too "dynamic and alive" for anything so pedestrian. In his letter of response Jung also makes it clear that his situation in Zurich continued apace. His pregnant wife, Emma, had "staged a number of jealous scenes" – probably because in 1910 Jung was gearing up for his next affair (with Toni Wolff). "The prerequisite for a good marriage," Jung quips, "is the license to be unfaithful" (1988, p. 289).

In general, though, Freud was inclined to ignore, indulge, and downplay Jung's proclivities – or, better, use them to his own strategic advantage. Referring to Jung's affair with Spielrein, Freud wrote to Jung on June 7, 1909, that "I myself have never been taken in quite so badly, but I have come very close to it a number of times and had *a narrow escape*. I believe that only grim necessities weighing on my work, and the fact that I was ten years older than yourself when I came to [psychoanalysis], have saved me from similar experiences" (pp. 230–1). Freud even adds, bizarrely but characteristically, that "no lasting harm is done" in such affairs and, in any case, such experiences "are a '*blessing in disguise*.'" Freud always had a talent for turning a debacle into a blessing. Clearly Freud was not only willing to look the other way with Jung, but was remarkably nonplussed about it. It was neither the first nor the last time that he would rationalize the gross manipulation of patients and followers, or excuse ethically dubious decisions or behaviors, when it was a question of forwarding "the cause" of psychoanalysis.

But that was Freud's excuse. How could Jung, in his letter, have so badly misunderstood Freud's own scientistic, antireligious view of things? How could he say that psychoanalysis was a kind of religion, and that it must grow out from within Christianity? The answer is very simple: because this exchange between Freud and Jung occurred in 1910. The "late Freud" that we have been exploring had yet to write *The Future of an Illusion* or *Civilization and Its Discontents*, let alone *Totem and Taboo*. Freud's tremendous disdain for religion, mystical feeling, and even introspection was still a matter for the future. That said, Freud had written an early attack on religion in 1907, "Obsessive Actions and Religious Practices," in which the kernel of *Totem and Taboo* is indeed presented, and Jung most assuredly read it. So there still remained in Jung a level of willful disregard for the master's viewpoint.

Like Rolland years later, Jung refused to accept that religion and mystical experience were anything *verboten*; nor were they illusions, as Freud would eventually argue. But Jung also never really understood what motivated Freud's critique. In a new foreword (1950) to his venerable "Psychology of the Unconscious" of 1912, Jung strikes a familiar note:

"Although Freud's book *The Future of an Illusion* dates from his later years, it gives the best possible account of his earlier views, which move within the confines of the outmoded rationalism and scientific materialism of the late nineteenth century" (Jung, 1956, p. xxiii). Jung simply repeats the common but entirely superficial interpretation of *The Future of an Illusion*; the interpretation first put forth by Pfister in 1928. Let's just repeat once again that this view, correct so far as it goes, neglects to consider the dominant strain of late Romanticism that made *Beyond the Pleasure Principle* not just the founding text of the late "cultural" Freud, including *The Future of an Illusion*, but the belated realization of Freud's penchant for the darkest, most troubling, and also most fascinating speculations began many years before. What's more, unlike the positivism that peppers his work, the speculative impulse in Freud's late work brings him far closer to Jung and "Jungianism" than even Jung seems to have understood. Let's consider this mildly heretical claim now.

4 Phylogenetic Inheritance and Jung

During the 1920s Freud was busy correcting all the "misinformation" about social, cultural, intellectual, and technical issues circulated by former students like Adler, Stekel, Jung, and Silberer; by current students like Pfister, Rank, and Ferenczi; and by prominent thinkers outside of psychoanalysis like Rolland and Ellis. But the late Freud was not only concerned with laying down the law, like Moses, on religion, ethics, spirituality, and mystical phenomena. The work of criticism, and with it the voice of conscience (the superego), was also the excuse he needed to embrace interests that he had carefully avoided for most of his personal and professional life. This includes both the archaic origins of society and the occult. Arguably this excuse would come to have a proper name – Carl Gustav Jung – the ghost that propels much of what would become known as the cultural Freud.

Without denying the enormous impact that other analysts had on Freud's work, it was Jung's impact that is impossible to overestimate. It runs across nearly everything Freud wrote after 1913 – sometimes operating in the background of debates with other people. Here is a short list: *Totem and Taboo* was motivated by and explains Jung's attempted patricide within the psychoanalytic movement, even as it "proves" that the Oedipus complex, denied by Jung, actually exists, and precisely in the "archaic" terms Jung had already championed (Wittels, 1924/1971, p. 191); "Moses of the Michelangelo" was, as Puner says, a "disguised analogue" for the Zurich defection and very obviously a "record of his own emotions of betrayal" (1947, p. 246); "On the History of the Psychoanalytic Movement," Freud's word on what is and is not psychoanalysis, was explicitly a polemic against Jung and the Zurich school of psychoanalysis; the Wolfman case study brought empirical data about the importance of sexuality to bear against Adler and most especially Jung (Strachey in *SE*, 1918/1991, p. 5); "On Narcissism" was in large part written, as Strachey puts it, to "offer an alternative to Jung's non-sexual 'libido' and to Adler's 'masculine protest'" (in *SE*, 1914b/1991, p. 70); *Beyond the Pleasure Principle* established the late dualism (the life/death drives) against Jung's monistic thinking about sexuality, even as it drew a line in the sand between the Jung and post-Jung eras of psychoanalysis; *The Future of an Illusion* demonstrates that psychoanalysis is most emphatically not a religion meant to replace other religions, as Jung imagined, but a science; *Civilization and Its Discontents* proves once and for all that mysticism, love, and religion, characteristics valued by Jung, cannot save humankind from an essential unhappiness and guilt; and *Moses and Monotheism* reconfirms that Freudianism can draw a comprehensive picture of the repressed archaic past that effectively out-speculates Jungian interpretations. In short, the cultural Freud is driven by the concerns raised by Jung during his correspondence with Freud but only solved by psychoanalysis.

Consider again the *Moses* book, the culmination of all the trends of the late period. The tricky thing about this final attempt to out-speculate Jung is that Freud utilizes ideas that sound very close to Jung's theories of "archetypes" and the "collective unconscious." It is true that Freud explicitly, albeit quickly, rejects this connection in *Moses*; an assertion that Freud and Jung scholars have mostly repeated or at best tweaked (for example, see Clark, 1980, p. 331; Frey-Rohn, 1990, p. 132). "It is not easy," Freud claims, "for us to carry over the concepts of individual psychology into group psychology; and I do not think we gain anything by introducing the concept of a 'collective' unconscious. The content of the unconscious is in any case collective, the common property of the people [*der Menschen*]" (*SE*, 1939/1991, p. 132; translation adjusted).[9] For Freud the idea of a "collective unconscious" is not wrong so much as

[9] Although Jung coined the term, the idea of a "collective unconscious" was handed down for decades by thinkers like Carl Gustav Carus and Eduard von Hartmann. As Sonu Shamdasani says, it is an irony that Jung is the person most often associated with the collective unconscious when "it could almost have been regarded as a commonplace" in the late nineteenth century (2003, p. 235; Shamdasani, 2005, pp. 89–90).

redundant; the unconscious already presupposes its collective nature. But that means that Freud is not actually disavowing the "collective unconscious" at all; he is simply disavowing a contemporary most often associated with the term. Roazen spells things out in his *Freud and His Followers* of 1975:

> In *Moses and Monotheism*, as it *Totem and Taboo*, Freud argued that acquired guilt feelings could be passed on genetically, and the Oedipus complex did in the end assume for Freud archetypal status. Although Freud wrote that [in *Moses*] "I do not think we gain anything by introducing the concept of a 'collective unconscious,'" Jung's theory of archetypes could find support in Freud's theory of symbolism; Freud's thought symbols were a phylogenetic inheritance. To Jung, Freud's notion of "super-ego" denoted Jung's collective unconscious . . . (1976, pp. 295–6)

The truth is that Freud and Jung were heavily influenced by each other – and by other significant authors like Karl Abraham and Sándor Ferenczi. It is just that, after decades of denigrating Jung's ideas and disowning the connections to paleopsychology, few can see it very clearly in the works of Freud and his close followers. Abraham, for example, speaks very plainly about the connection between individual dreams and collective myths – what he calls the "collective spirit of a people" (1910/1913, p. 5; cf., Abraham, 1920/1955, pp. 131–5). It is an idea that Theodor Reik, among others, would continue to echo for years. As Reik claims in "Myths and Memories," myths are for analysts what flint axes are for archeologists (1958a, p. 50).

One obvious hurdle in our understanding has been Jung's collaboration with the Nazis. In June 1933, the Nazis reorganized German psychotherapy around the International General Medical Society for Psychotherapy – of which Jung became its first president (see Roazen, 1976, pp. 292–3). He only stepped down in 1940. Jung claimed that he took the job to protect individual psychotherapists, and this may be true. But no matter. It was a calamitous and foolish decision. Jung himself, in a letter of 1946, blamed Freud for his poor reputation: "The story of my anti-semitism and Nazi-sympathies originally started with the holy father Freud himself. When I disagreed with him he had to find a reason for my most incomprehensible disagreement and found that I must be an anti-semite" (in Shamdasani, 2003, p. 93, n. 103). There is little doubt that Freud, after their break, opportunistically used the charge of anti-Semitism against Jung. But Jung's words ring hollow given his collaboration in the 1930s. Beyond that there is the not inconsiderable issue of Jung's belief in the Jewish and Christian unconscious. "The mere fact that I speak of a difference between Jewish and Christian psychology," Jung once wrote, "suffices to allow anyone to voice the prejudice that I am an anti-Semite" (in Roazen, 1976, p. 292).

On the one hand, the problematic implications of Jung's argument about the racialized unconscious are clear enough: it confirms that National Socialists were not exactly wrong to think of Jews as fundamentally unsuited to Western Christian culture. It also helps explain why Jung, already in his "rampages of fantasies" letter, spoke of a psychoanalysis that must be derived from *within the Christian tradition*. On the other hand, *Moses and Monotheism* makes it very clear that Freud fully agreed with and even amplified Jung's idea that Jewish psychology is different than Christian psychology – for it represents the inheritance of a different prehistory, and a different set of myths and symbols. And by "inheritance," just to spell it out again, Freud means the Lamarckian inheritance of acquired characteristics and their transmission according to Haeckel's theory of recapitulation (ontogeneny repeats phylogeny). This psychobiological inheritance means that the different histories of Christians and Jews accumulate and evolve, for example, as a reverence for muscles and intellect, respectively. If true, nothing could be more significant for our understanding of individual and mass psychology today, and *Moses* is the work that crowns this lifelong tendency in Freud's thinking.

In short, Jung was in significant ways no more of an anti-Semite than Freud.

In these respects it is hardly incidental that both Freud and Jung enjoyed archeology, symbolism, and archaic history, and that their speculations were made possible by a shared belief in phylogenetic inheritance. On December 25, 1909, Jung writes to Freud that "we shall not solve the ultimate secrets of [current] neurosis and psychosis without mythology and the history of civilization, for *embryology* goes hand in hand with *comparative anatomy*, and without the latter the former is but a freak of nature whose depths remain uncomprehended" (Freud & Jung, 1988, p. 279). A thoroughgoing comprehension of everyday psychopathology requires a thoroughgoing comprehension of ancient history. In *Moses* Freud effectively closes the circle and proves Jung's point. But Freud was already willing to meet Jung halfway during their intense correspondence, as he would a few years later with Ferenczi, with whom he worked out the details of his metabiology – and, once again, on the basis of their shared enthusiasm for phylogenetic explanations. Concerning symbolism, Freud writes to Jung the following remarks on February 2, 1910: "what you write now about [symbolism] is only a hint, but in a direction where I too am searching, namely, *archaic regression*, which I hope to master through mythology and the *development of language*" (p. 291). What Jung suggests is for Freud "only a hint," just a beginning, but one that Freud will eventually "master": the jostling for priority is abundantly clear and entirely characteristic of Freud. In the 1911 preface to *The Interpretation of Dreams*, Freud would add that "My own experience, as well as the works of Wilhelm Stekel and others, have since taught me to form a truer estimate of the extent and importance of symbolism in dreams (or rather in unconscious thinking)" (*SE*, 1900/1991, p. xxvii).

Years later Jung would say, arguably with pride, that "I alone logically pursued the two problems which most interested Freud: the problem of 'archaic inheritance,'[10] and that of sexuality" (1961/1989) – clarifying, however, that his investigation of sexuality focused on its "spiritual aspect and its numinous meaning," the territory that Silberer designated by the words anagogic psychoanalysis. The "cult of the archaic," as Wittels put in in 1924, was indeed evident in Freud's work at least since the time of *The Interpretation of Dreams* (Wittels, 1924/1971, p. 182). The upshot: if Jung went his own way in 1913, it is not too fanciful to say that it was still the way of Freud – the Freud, from Jung's perspective, unafraid to plumb these far greater depths; and the Freud, from my perspective, unafraid to apply individual psychology to the group and to its ancient history, to wit, the "cultural Freud" of the late period.

Sonu Shamdasani provides a masterful overview of the history of the "phylogenetic unconscious" in Jung. To this end he reveals the rich antecedents of Jung's collective unconscious in the work of "organic memory theorists and psychologists" that both Jung and Freud read and admired: these include Ewald Hering, Théodule Ribot, Auguste Forel, and Stanley Hall (2003, p. 232). According to Shamdasani, Jung's collective unconscious was in this respect actually the culmination of trends that were "widespread in philosophy, physiology and psychology in the latter half of the nineteenth century" (p. 235), the very Romantic period that was to prove so influential to Freud. Jung, however, came to reject strict Lamarckianism. For the later Jung, phylogenesis was not about the repetition of inherited *ideas* per se, but about the *conditions* from which such ideas might arise again and again (p. 233). In other words, while Freud and the early Jung believed that biology captured prehistorical (and historical)

---

[10] Strachey provides a useful discussion of Freud's use of the two terms, *archaisches Erbteil* and *archaisches Erbschaft*, in a long note in the *Moses* book (see *SE*, 1939/1991, p. 102, n. 1). Both translate as "archaic inheritance," but Freud only introduced the second term in 1919 and, as Strachey says, "thereafter the concept and the term appear frequently" – but is most fully discussed in *Moses and Monotheism*.

experiences (Jung, 1961, p. 173), after 1913 Jung shifted away from the inheritance of actual experiences and toward the inheritance of archetypes. This means that Jung, after his break with Freud, began to favor Kant's "categories of the mind": the very categories that Jung's Swiss colleague, Oskar Pfister, would throw at the epistemologically "naive" Freud in "The Illusion of a Future." At the same time Shamdasani is careful to point out that Jung's use of Kant's categories, which Jung married to organic memory theory, functioned more like intellectual cover than as a convincing application of Kantian philosophy to psychology (p. 237). And arguably this admission is essential, because the foundation for Jung's ideas is really not, I think, so very different from the various forms of neo-Lamarckianism and psycho-Lamarckianism popular in the late nineteenth century.

In fact, Jung sounds remarkable similar to Freud and the other organic theorists of memory on the question of phylogenetic inheritance. In a paper of 1927, "The Structure of the Soul," Jung explicitly makes a connection between the past experiences of the world and the eventual creation of archetypes (or "primordial images") in the psyche. In this respect Jung sounds very much like Freud in *Beyond the Pleasure Principle*, when Freud claims that human evolution essentially repeats our ancient experiences of the earth and sun. And like Freud, Jung in his lectures on Nietzsche in 1934 would couch this compulsive repetition in Nietzschean terms as the "eternal return of the same." "Consequently," as Shamdasani puts it, "the archetypes were originally real situations"; and again, "it would appear that the archetypes, as timeless structures, were themselves built up through history" (p. 238). Ferenczi would say the same thing in his work on the "Development of a Sense or Reality" (1913) and in *Thalassa*, where he argued that real environmental "catastrophes," such as the Ice Age, left their literal marks on human evolution. And we know that Freud wholeheartedly agreed with Ferenczi, both in private and in the late works – beginning with *Beyond the Pleasure Principle*. Such phylogenetic inheritance is the key to understanding not just Freud's mature theory of repetition compulsion and the death drive, but also his late understanding of how human beings acquire knowledge about reality, the object world, science itself. Therefore, although Freud and Jung may differ as to the *content* of our repressed, archaic past, the *method* is essentially the same – so much so that the major theoretical difference between them is Freud's inconsequential refusal, in *Moses* and elsewhere, to adopt Jung's language of the *collective* unconscious.

The American psychiatrist and psychoanalysis, Ely Smith Jelliffe, was among the first to notice the significant overlap between Jung and

Freud – and precisely in terms of what he too calls "paleopsychology" (in Burnham, 1983, p. 204). Jelliffe flitted between Jung and Freud between roughly 1910 and the early 1920s; in 1917 he also translated into English Silberer's *The Problems of Mysticism and Its Symbolism*.[11] By the mid-1920s Jelliffe finally sided with Freud over Jung (Burnham, 1983, p. 80). But even after that time he remained loyal to the Jungian belief in so-called "thought fossils" (p. 242), an allegiance that cashed out as Jelliffe's belief in heredity and his position within the psychobiological tradition in American medicine. For John C. Burnham, Jelliffe's thought is, therefore, theoretically neo-Lamarckian – and precisely in Jung's own terms (1983, pp. 124–34). "Jelliffe," writes Burnham, "always remained partially a Jungian. He never surrendered the use of ancestral psychological accretions, recapitulation, and neo-Lamarckianism in general" (p. 125). And indeed, in a letter of December 18, 1920, Jung explicitly confirms Jelliffe's approach to the theory of archaic memory: "With regard to the Paleopsychological formulation," Jung writes, "I think it is indisputable that a principle analogous to geological stratification exists" (1983, p. 204). Recall, again, that this is also how Brill characterized *Freud's* thinking, namely, as the work of a "paleopsychologist of the mind" (1944/1962, p. 225). And of course let's also not forget that it was Freud himself who repeatedly invoked archeology and geology as analogous to psychoanalysis. It's also interesting to note that an unwavering Freudian like Theodor Reik had no trouble invoking phylogentic inheritance, Palaeolithic men, and an unconscious that was collective; one that reflects, for instance, "the common adventures of mankind of the Old Stone Age." In these respects Reik also went ahead and cited Joseph Campbell, a famous popularizer of *Jungian* ideas (1958a, p. 55).

Scholars have nonetheless preferred to ignore the overlap between Jung and Freud, and have been slow to explore Freud's lifelong commitment to psychobiology. Perhaps it's fear of a still forbidden Jungianism. Or perhaps, just as likely, it's fear that a biological Freud fails to conform to popular belief that psychoanalysis represents an uncomplicated leap forward from biology to psychology. But let's be honest: the facts, made so abundantly clear by the "cultural Freud," are far less fickle than the wishes of partisan Freud scholars. Commentators like Jelliffe, Brill, Jones, and Sulloway are telling us something fundamental about Freudianism that is not only troubling, but is essential to our understanding of why it is that Freud offers the sometimes head-scratching conclusions he draws in

---

[11] It is interesting to note that Jeliffe was a rare supporter of the death drive theory, although his contributions are mostly superficial (see Jelliffe, 1933).

works of the late period. Without Freud's embarrassing metabiology, in other words, and along with it a strong whiff of Jungian mysticism, there is no way of comprehending the meaning of works like *Civilization and Its Discontents* and *Moses and Monotheism*. For in the end the Freudian science was very obviously anything but science. True, Freud aggressively contrasted the rhetoric of objectivity, science, and reality against delusion, mysticism, and religion. But, as we have seen again and again, this is the rhetoric of disguise and dissimulation. What is actually revealed by the late Freud is the incredibly speculative, undeniably nonempirical, and quasi-Jungian grounds of psychoanalysis after 1920 – if not immediately upon Jung's departure in 1913.

Of course, it is incredibly easy to go wrong in Freud studies. Consider a letter Freud wrote to Jung on January 10, 1912. "Your demonstration of unconscious heredity in symbolism," Freud writes, "which amount to a demonstration of the existence of innate ideas, and Ferenczi's proofs of thought-transference [telepathy], lead us far beyond the original limits of [psychoanalysis], and that we should not follow" (Freud & Jung, 1988, p. 293). It would be easy to cite this passage as proof that Freud was nothing but a cautious, sensible scientist – a positivist even – and would never follow such disreputable paths. That was the view held by Pfister, Rolland, Jung, and countless commentators on psychoanalysis. But we know very well that Freud did indeed follow Jung and Ferenczi in both instances: in time he was just as committed as Jung to "unconscious heredity," and was, like Ferenczi, similarly convinced of the reality of telepathy. If one takes the long view of Freud's life and work the proper inference is undeniable: positivism was important to Freud, not because he simply and naively believed in it, but because the *fundamentally occult nature of psychoanalysis demanded nothing less*. For the tincture of positivism helped launder psychoanalysis as a new kind of *science*. Yet it is actually very obvious that Freud's ultimate interests lay elsewhere.

What was "new" in psychoanalysis was precisely its courageous wrangling with the occult aspects of the unconscious, sexuality, dreams, death, and everything else that was beyond traditional science and its philosophy. Precisely the themes, in short, that attracted a group of young thinkers around Freud, including Jung, in the early years of the twentieth century.

5   Final Act: Moses from 1912 to 1939

In 1912 Karl Abraham published a long essay called "Amenhotep IV: A Psychoanalytical Contribution towards the Understanding of His

Personality and of the Monotheistic Cult of Aton." Relying heavily on American historian and archeologist James Henry Breasted's *A History of Egypt*, published in 1906, Abraham speculates about the "parent-complex" of the Egyptian king and discusses the origins of monotheism. As a Freudian he dutifully applies the Oedipus complex to Amenhotep IV, who rebelled against his father and his father's religion, Amon, and then changed his own name to Akhetaton. Of this son Abraham writes:

> He declared war above all upon Amon. He sought to obliterate all traces of the god after whom his father and himself had been named. Never again was that hated name to be uttered. He therefore caused the name of Amon, well as that of his father, Amenhotep [III], to be removed from all inscriptions and memorials. In this strange act of purification the ancient, long-suppressed or sublimated hostility of the son breaks through in an aggressive manner. This action of the king seems like the realisation of an ancient oriental curse directed against a malignant foe, expressing the wish that his memory be extinguished. [Akhetaton] strove to erase the memory of Amon, and with it that of his own father. (1955a, pp. 273–4)

Akhetaton replaced the old Amon religion with the "monotheistic cult of Aton," a new religion based on love, infinite goodness, and peace (p. 275). For love to prosper, the father had to be erased from memory. Abraham also connects it all to the Mosaic tradition. As he says, Akhetaton was "a forerunner of Moses the lawgiver" (p. 275) – "the precursor of Moses and his monotheism, in which the one and only god unmistakably bears the features of the patriarch, the sole ruler of the family" (p. 287).

Two things are immediately fascinating about this essay. First, Abraham wrote it in advance of Freud's *Totem and Taboo*, his tale about the origin of civilization in a prehistorical murder of the primal father. Second, Freud failed to even acknowledge this essay in *Moses and Monotheism*, a work that relies on Breasted's book, is heavily invested in Egyptian lore, and has a lot to say about Moses and the origin of monotheism. Yet if Freud ignored Abraham's essay in 1939, it was not because it failed to leave an impression. Here's why. On November 24, 1912, a handful of analytic colleagues met in Munich to discuss the fallout from Stekel's usurping of the *Central Journal*. At one point the analysts, thinking about Abraham's essay, discussed Akhetaton's erasure of his father's name and memory from the public record. According to a note found in Jones's papers,[12] Jung interjected the

---

[12] Jones's official version has none of this. Instead he hangs the faint on a discussion about the Swiss (Jung and Riklin) penchant for "expounding psychoanalysis" without citing Freud's name (Jones, 1953, p. 317). In this version, this erasure precipitates Freud's fainting. The alternative version, from his own notes, seems more likely.

following: "Yes, he did [erase his father's name], but you cannot dismiss him with that. He was the first monotheist among the Egyptians. He was a great genius, very human, very individual. That is his main merit. That he scratched out his father's name is not the main thing at all" (in Clark, 1980, pp. 327–8). Jung's own version of the discussion is similar, but includes his reflections as well. Jung says that he was annoyed by Abraham's claim that Akhetaton's erasures reflected a "father-complex," that is, "a negative attitude towards his father." "This sort of thing irritated me," Jung admits, "and I attempted to argue that Amenophis [another name for Akhetaton] had been a creative and profoundly religious person whose acts could not be explained by personal resistances toward his father" (1989, p. 157). Jung added that it wasn't uncommon for pharaohs to erase the names of their predecessors and, more to the point, that they had "a right to do so since they were incarnations of the same god."

In response to Jung's remarks Freud fainted. Jones has Freud collapsing to the floor, while in Jung's version Freud slides off his chair. "As I was carrying him [to the sofa]," Jung says, Freud "half came to, and . . . looked at me as if I were his father." Freud's first words: "How sweet it must be to die" (Jones, 1953, p. 317; cf., Roazen, 1976, p. 247; Clark, 1980, pp. 326–7).

This was in fact the second time that Freud, rather famously, fainted in Jung's presence. The first time occurred in a restaurant in Bremen, Germany, the day before Freud, Jung, and Ferenczi took their transatlantic trip to America in August 1909. Jung had been speaking about the discovery of "peat bog corpses" in Northern Germany – the naturally preserved remains of ancient people. The discussion annoyed Freud. "He was inordinately vexed by the whole thing," Jung says, "and during one such conversation, while we were having dinner together, he suddenly fainted. Afterwards he was convinced that all this chatter about corpses meant that I had death-wishes toward him" (Jung, 1989, p. 156). Jung very reasonably concludes that Freud's "fantasy of father-murder" was connected to both fainting episodes (p. 157). In a letter to Jung in December 1912, Freud himself connects the two episodes – conceding that there is a "psychic factor which unfortunately I haven't had time to track down" (Freud & Jung, 1988, p. 524) – and mentions two more episodes. "Six years ago," he confesses, "I had a first attack of the same kind there, and four years ago a second. A bit of neurosis that I ought to really look into." The other two episodes happened in Wilhelm Fliess's presence, Freud's close friend whom he broke off with in 1906. Moreover, the Fliess faints also happened in the same restaurant in the Park Hotel, Munich (Jones, 1953, p. 317; cf., Roazen, 1976, pp. 246–50).

In the days and weeks immediately following the fourth fainting episode, Freud proffered various excuses, only rarely diagnosing the cause. But on December 8, 1912, Freud admitted to Jones that "There is some piece of unruly homosexual feeling at the root of the matter" (p. 317). Jung had become a substitute for Fliess, just as Fliess had become a substitute for Freud's mentor Josef Breuer. Freud was well aware of how those relationships had ended – badly. According to Jones, therefore, Freud was in the thrall of "a repetition," something Freud would later call a repetition compulsion. Another plausible psychoanalytic interpretation: as a kind of suicidal gesture, fainting was the introjection of Freud's own murderous hatred of his young rivals.

At the Munich meeting in late 1912, Freud and Jung's relationship was winding down. The prodigal son would soon conduct his own campaign to remove Freud's name from psychoanalysis. At a gathering of almost one hundred psychiatrists and neurologists at Fordham University in New York (Clark, 1980, p. 321), Jung delivered nine lectures on "The Theory of Psychoanalysis." The effect of his lectures was to water down the very feature that Freud had originally warned him to protect dogmatically, the theory of sexuality. Freud was displeased. As for Jung's annoyance about the "father-complex" discussion, it may suggest that his defense of the patricidal son, Akhetaton, was not entirely innocent. In any case, it was clearly more than Freud could bear.

Although Jung hung on to psychoanalysis well into 1914, Freud and Jung's relationship took a fatal turn just a few weeks after the Congress. In a blunt letter of December 18, 1912, Jung finally told Freud what he thought of him.

> I admit the ambivalence of my feelings toward you ... I would, however, point out that your technique of treating your pupils like patients is a *blunder*. In that way you produce either slavish sons or impudent puppies (Adler-Stekel and the whole insolent gang now throwing their weight about in Vienna). I am objective enough to see through your little trick. You go sniffing out all the symptomatic action in your vicinity, thus reducing everyone to the level of sons and daughters who blushingly admit their faults. Meanwhile you remain on top as the father, sitting pretty. For sheer obsequiousness nobody dares to pluck the prophet by the beard and inquire for once ...: "*Who's* got the neurosis?" (Freud & Jung, 1988, pp. 534–5)

Freud's response was restrained – and a little superior. Analysts, he says, are accustomed to admitting their own neuroses. But anyone who behaves "abnormally" even as he shouts out his normality "lacks insight into his illness" (p. 539). And so, Freud says, "I propose that we abandon our personal relations entirely." As we know, it took 1913 and much of 1914 for Freud to disentangle their professional relations as well.

In the meantime Freud licked his wounds and embraced those analysts who still supported him. To his loyal friend, Sándor Ferenczi, Freud writes (July 9, 1913): "We will carry on our cause quietly and with superior assurance. I had intended to thank Jung for the feeling that the children are being taken care of, which a Jewish father needs as a matter of life and death; I am now happy that you and our friends are giving it to me" (Freud & Ferenczi, 1993, p. 500). The children would be "taken care of," but never again by a father other than Freud.

For all of his retrospective contempt for Silberer who, recall, committed suicide after Freud refused to see him in 1922, Jung didn't fare particularly well after his angry letter to Freud at the end of 1912. Jung suffered what is routinely referred to in the literature as a "nervous breakdown," what he calls "a state of disorientation" that lasted about seven years (1961/1989, pp. 170, 195). "When I parted from Freud," Jung says, "I knew that I was plunging into the unknown. Beyond Freud, after all, I knew nothing; but I had taken the step into darkness" (p. 199). Certainly Jung's own description of his "descent into empty space" (p. 181) is not only highly mystical and grandiose; as he acknowledged, it is very nearly psychotic (see Shamdasani, 2009, pp. 27–9). Having become his own patient, Jung began to *live the myths* he had, until that time, examined only as a thinker. What followed was eighteen years of a "scientific experiment" with the unconscious, punctuated by Jung's cosmic interpretations of dreams, waking fantasies, and visions as recorded in his "Black Books" (Jung, 1961/1989, pp. 178, 188). As a result Jung slowly fashioned the technique of "active imagination," basically a kind of introspective dia-loguing with the self that formed the revised foundation for all of his interpretations and clinical practice after the break with Freud (Shamdasani, 2009, p. 39). This self-experiment, later transcribed and elaborated in beautifully rendered (full color) paintings in the famous "Red Book," holds the same importance for Jung that *The Interpretation of Dreams* holds for Freud. As Jung puts it, the "primal stuff" of his unconscious formed the autobiographical backbone of what became Analytical Psychology (1989, pp. 175, 192, 199). But unlike Freud's highly filtered experiment, Jung's private, experimental, and sometimes troubled "confrontation with the unconscious" kept *The Red Book* out of the public domain until 2009. Jung himself, however, created *The Red Book* – seemingly modeled on Nietzsche's *Thus Spoke Zarathustra* and *Dante's Inferno* – for the reading public (Shamdansani, 2009, pp. 30–1). Whether it will ever become the "bible" of Jungian thinking, as Freud's *Dream Book* once was for Freudians, is yet to be seen. But one suspects that Jungians missed out on a golden opportunity.

How much of Jung's experiment in introversion Freud knew about is hard to say. But at the Psychoanalytical Congress in Munich in 1913, Jung was already advancing his newfound interest in the categories of introversion and extroversion. Note that Jung clearly allied himself, not with the extroverted Adler and Stekel but with the introverted Freud. By the time Romain Rolland was making his own mystical claims for introversion in the mid-1920s, Freud was totally unwilling to concede that introversion could help us understand anything about the external world; at best it had value as an "embryology of the soul when correctly interpreted" (in Parsons, 1999, p. 177). Of course everything turns on those three words: *when correctly interpreted*. Recall what Freud said about Jung in a letter to Rolland:

> Concerning the criticism of psychoanalysis, you will permit me a few remarks: the distinction between *extrovert* and *introvert* derives from C. G. Jung, who is a bit of a mystic himself and hasn't belonged to us for years. We don't attach any great importance to the distinction and are well aware that people can be both at the same time, and usually are. (in Parsons, 1999, p. 176)

In the margin of the letter Rolland scribbled his own parenthetical remark: "that smells of excommunication" (in Fisher, 1976/1991, p. 57). For Freud, Rolland's "oceanic feeling" was a form of narcissism; introversion led him to the wrong conclusions, to illusions, to mysticism. As Jung himself complained in 1939, Freud felt that introversion was "abnormal, morbid, and otherwise objectionable" (in Roazen, 1976, p. 292). Yet Jung and Rolland were only utilizing the introspection that Freud himself had used to create psychoanalysis – precisely to reveal the "embryology of the soul."

In the late phase of Freud's work the final measure of all things became the external world – a measure that undid much of what made *The Interpretation of Dreams* so attractive to people like Jung and Rolland. A significant cause of this reframing was the rising popularity of introversion as a legitimate, seemingly "Freudian," way of doing science; and the rise of mysticism and occultism more generally. I have argued that the late Freud took this new route, positivistic on its face, for purely defensive or, if you prefer, reactive reasons: to defend psychoanalysis from its enemies; enemies who thereby became, ironically, the cause of the development (shifts, changes, innovations) of psychoanalysis. And so Freud fought off

those who would reduce psychoanalysis to religion, mysticism, occultism –
or even to the "Russian introspection" of the kind associated with
Dostoevsky and the rise of a new philosophy, existentialism (see *SE*,
1927b/1991, p. 37). That is how psychoanalysis in the final period became
increasingly associated with the rhetoric of science – even as Freud took
steps to vitiate that very rhetoric with his remarkably wild and unscientific
speculations about archaic history.

Freud knew that the pastor's son, Carl Jung, embodied all of the
dangerous traits of magical thinking. But he was a gentile and a well-
connected psychiatrist, and so useful to the cause. Had Freud succeeded in
converting him to the *science* of psychoanalysis, the father could (perhaps)
have vested his authority in the son. But Jung refused to play along, and
was therefore "excommunicated." According to Jung, his *Psychology of the
Unconscious* (1911–12) was "declared to be rubbish; I was a mystic, and that
settled the matter" (1961/1989, p. 162). By the time of *Beyond the Pleasure
Principle* (1920), Jung could honestly report that "there is a large group of
Freudians fighting against me as if I were the devil himself" (in Burnham,
1983, p. 200; translation adjusted). These Freudians, of course, took their
cues from Freud. As for Freud, his major turn to the subject of religion in
1912–13, like his turn to the problems of mysticism, the occult, and *Kultur*
in the 1920s and 1930s, was nothing less than an elaborate defense of
psychoanalysis from the darkness, the "black tide of mud," that threatened
it on all sides. In still other words, these were Freud's sustained attempts to
preserve and enhance the science he had created – but always by
a procedure of creative destruction of his enemies, none more so than Jung.

And so Freud out-speculated Jung, just as he out-speculated Rolland,
and in the process showed everyone, once more, how it's done. *Moses and
Monotheism* is in this respect a return to Karl and Carl. To a debate, begun
in 1912, about Akhetaton and the Egyptian origins of monotheism. And to
a debate about the "father complex," on the one hand, and the supposed
rights of the son to patricide, on the other. In the *Moses* book Freud simply
erases the one son, Karl Abraham, from the record. He outthinks and
outlasts Abraham (who died in 1925) – and annihilates his contribution.[13]

---

[13] Note, however, that Freud also does this to the loyal Theodor Reik, who delivered lectures at the
Vienna and Berlin Psychoanalytic Societies in 1914 and 1915 and then published the results as lengthy
essays on archaic inheritance. Some of these essays include substantial discussions about the archaic
origins of Judaism and the role of Moses therein. The works were later collected as a book of 1919,
Probleme der Religionspsychologie – for which Freud wrote an introduction – then published in
English as *Ritual* (1931). Archaic inheritance was then taken up again in a new book of 1958, *Myth and
Guilt*, only judiciously updated with consideration of Freud's *Moses* book.

Then Freud demonstrates to the other son, Carl Jung, how Christian and Jewish character came to exist – and does so with a phylogenetic tale every bit as collective, fantastical, and grandiose as anything Jung imagined. Jung could have his waking fantasies about the present, his illusions, and his archetypes of the mind. He could have his *Red Book*. Freud had the historical truth, which trumped everything and everyone.

Sometimes in history all the accumulated experiences of truth and justice add up to someone or something important. Sometimes, for example, it adds up to a single genius and his science. The upshot? This time in history the *Jewish father* wins because psychoanalysis wins – and because the father is wise enough to destroy all the sons before they can destroy him. *Moses and Monotheism* is not only Freud's first successful venture beyond the pleasure principle; it is the first successful *applied metapsychology*. It is the dying Freud's first attempt to openly declare his satisfaction, his hard-won happiness, in the face of everyone who dared oppose him in life. No more fainting. No more repressed and "unruly homosexual feeling." And no more love – just undisguised resentment and contempt. In terms appropriate to the act, the Moses book was Freud's final *fuck you* to everyone, but first and foremost to his would-be son and successor, Carl Jung.

Coda
"Undisguised Resentment," War, and the Challenge of Being Cultured

> This is the problem: Is there any way of delivering mankind from the menace of war?
>
> (Einstein to Freud, July 30, 1932 [*SE*, 1933b/1991, p. 199])

In the early 1930s Freud produced two short works, not linked by theme but linked in spirit. The first, written at the end of 1931, revisits at greater length a claim about the acquisition of fire originally made in a short but unforgettable footnote in *Civilization and Its Discontents*. The second, written in August 1932, was Freud's reply to Einstein's open letter about the avoidance of war.[1] By way of conclusion, I want to explore the connections between these two works: between, essentially, Freud's impulse to embrace a paleopsychology of the deep past, on the one hand, and his late theory of the evolutionary future of culture, on the other. For as we will see the whole story of the late Freud is almost perfectly encapsulated in miniature in the thinking behind these two brief contributions.

The first work, what Ernest Jones calls a "brilliant little paper" (1957, p. 326), is a minor classic of the late Freud. In this essay, called "The Acquisition and Control of Fire," Freud provides an interpretation of the Prometheus myth, reveals the analytical symbolism associated with subduing fire, insists on a homosexual prequel to sociality, relates it all to the late theory of the life and death drives, and makes what is probably his

---

[1] Freud's open letter to Einstein was intended as part of a little pamphlet dedicated to issues of importance to the International Institute of Intellectual Cooperation, an organization created by the League of Nations and precursor to what became the United Nations. The institute was tasked with stimulating useful dialogue between scholars and, where appropriate, publishing the results as pamphlets for popular consumption. To this end Albert Einstein was asked to select a suitable interlocutor for a discussion about war. Einstein agreed and suggested Freud, whom he and his wife had met personally once in late December 1926 at Freud's son's (Ernst Freud) apartment in Berlin. The result is "Why War?," published almost too late to have any impact – especially in Germany, where it was immediately banned.

first indirect reference to the concept of "historical truth" (only explicitly developed in 1935). The six-page essay really has it all.

The occasion for the essay was some contemporary discussion about Freud's footnote concerning the acquisition of fire in *Civilization and Its Discontents*. But that footnote itself harkens back to the final remarks of Freud's "Character and Anal Eroticism" of 1908, to some discussion about bedwetting made in the Dora case study of 1905, and before that to *The Interpretation of Dreams* of 1900. In short, the discussion of fire in 1932 goes back to the meat and potatoes of psychoanalytic interpretation of personality, and back to the origins of psychoanalysis as the interpretation of sexual fantasy.

In "The Acquisition" Freud argues that the control of fire, and with it the rise of civilization, is connected to the renunciation of an ancient infantile desire to extinguish fire altogether. As always, with Freud, cultural evolution is possible only at the expense of already present drives, drives that are essentially antisocial. So in the case of fire, man's "great cultural conquest" begins with his decision to not urinate on the flames (*SE*, 1930/ 1991, p. 90). In chapter three of *Civilization*, Freud writes as follows (part of the footnote appearing here in parentheses):

> If we go back far enough, the first acts of civilization were the use of tools, the gaining of control over fire [*die Zähmung des Feuers*], and the construction of dwellings. Among these, the control over fire stands out as a quite extraordinary and unexampled achievement ... (Psychoanalytic material, incomplete as it is and not susceptible to clear interpretation, nevertheless admits of a conjecture – a fantastic-sounding one – about the origin of this human feat. It is as though primal man had the habit, when he came in contact with fire, of satisfying an infantile desire connected with it, by putting it out with a stream of his urine.) (p. 90)

Thus begins Freud's fantastical argument, buried in a footnote, about the historical importance of taming fire – and its connection to male anatomy.

It is not entirely clear why Freud came to believe that fire is connected to urine, or why enuresis (for example, in cases of bedwetting) is connected to ambition. Let's begin with enuresis, the involuntary discharge of urine. The connection between bedwetting and ambition is first raised in the essay on character of 1908, but is very far from developed. Freud merely mentions the possibility that zones other than the anus may lend themselves to analyses of character. "At present," Freud says, "I only know of the intense 'burning' ambition of people who earlier suffered from enuresis" (*SE*, 1932/1991, p. 175). The word "burning," *brennenden*, is placed in quotation marks, indicating a figure of speech about urination that lends itself to thinking about fire. The ever-careful Strachey remarks that this is Freud's first mention of the connection between bedwetting and ambition, adding that in 1914 Freud went on to insert one new sentence about it in a new edition of *The Interpretation of Dreams*. The sentence: "We have also learned from the psychoanalysis of neurotic subjects the intimate connection between bed-wetting and the character trait of ambition" (*SE*, 1900/1991, p. 216).

By 1914 Freud simply asserts the connection between enuresis and ambition, the result, one might assume, of clinical observation – "the psychoanalysis of neurotic subjects." And it is certainly true that Freud cites bedwetting in a few case studies. In the *Dream Book* he discusses his own bedwetting problem, and his mortification before his father (*SE*, 1900/1991, p. 216). Then in the Dora case of 1901, bedwetting is linked to masturbation (*SE*, 1905a/1991, pp. 74–5); Freud repeats the claim again in his *Three Essays on the Theory of Sexuality* of 1905 (*SE*, 1905b/1991, p. 190). And in the Wolfman case of 1914 (published in 1918), Freud mentions the connection between enuresis and fire in another footnote. "The regular relation," Freud says in the note, "that is found to exist between incontinence of the bladder and fire also provides matter for reflection. It is possible that these reactions and relations represent precipitates from the history of human civilization derived from a lower stratum than anything that is preserved for us in the traces surviving in myths and folklore" (*SE*, 1918/1991, p. 92, n. 1). Note that, in this passage, it is not clinical *observation* that proves the connection between fire and urination, but clinical *technique*: the principle that dream symbols are sometimes better turned on their heads, better reversed. And in fact Freud mentions the natural antithesis of "water" and "fire" in the Dora case (*SE*, 1905a/1991, p. 72, 89) and in "The Acquisition and Control of Fire" (*SE*, 1932/1991, p. 192). So when Freud says that the connection between involuntary urination and ambition is gleaned from "the psychoanalysis of neurotic subjects," he simply means that it's a feature of the psychoanalytic worldview. Presumably the *failure* called enuresis is connected to the *success* of ambition because of overcompensation – and because psychoanalysis says so. Of course such reversals (fire/water, success/failure) are present in most psychoanalyses, and are largely responsible for the surprising and ironical tone of psychoanalysis in general. Reversing symbols is, quite simply, a technical part of what Freud calls the *analyst's construction*. As such it is a matter of *interpretation*, not *observation*. This of course is the very practice that earned a pointed reproach from Havelock Ellis – the complaint that every "Yes" is turned into a "No" by psychoanalysis – and that provoked

Freud's late response in his essay "Constructions in Analysis," including his unexpected allusion to the territory of homosexuality.

Ambition is certainly characteristic of any man's attempt, or any group of men's attempt, to put out fire with urine. For Freud the act is highly significant. Here is the remainder of the footnote from *Civilization and Its Discontents*:

> It is as though primal man had the habit, when he came in contact with fire, of satisfying an infantile desire connected with it, by putting it out with a stream of his urine. The legends that we possess leave no doubt about the originally phallic view taken of tongues of flame as they shoot upwards. Putting out fire by micturating ... was therefore a kind of sexual act with a male, an enjoyment of sexual potency in a homosexual competition. The first person to renounce this desire and spare the fire was able to carry it off with him and subdue it to his own use. By damping down the fire of his own sexual excitation, he had tamed the natural force of fire. This great cultural conquest was thus the reward for his renunciation of instinct.

At this point Freud mentions the missing female in this story about boys-being-boys, and trots out, implicitly, a formula that has always aggrieved sensitive readers: the claim, adapted from Napoleon's remark about history, that "anatomy is destiny" (see *SE*, 1912/1991, p. 189; *SE*, 1924b/1991, p. 178). Freud continues:

> Further, it is as though the woman had been appointed the keeper [*Hüterin*] of the fire which was held captive on the domestic hearth, because her anatomy made it impossible for her to yield to the temptation of this desire. It is remarkable, too, how regularly analytic experience testifies to the connection between ambition, fire, and urinary eroticism [*Harnerotik*]. (*SE*, 1930/1991, p. 90; translation adjusted)

So on the one hand we have the primal men, *der Urmensch*, engaged in a homosexual competition to extinguish the fire. As Freud says: *[Es] war also wie ein sexueller Akt mit einem Mann, ein Genuß der männlichen Potenz im homosexuellen Wettkampf*, rendered literally, "it was like a sex act with a man, a pleasure of male potency through homosexual competition." On the other hand we have the woman who protects home and hearth. On the surface it seems as though we have stumbled upon the natural origin, based on anatomical difference, of public and private, masculine and feminine realms. But in fact the primal men don't belong to the public realm at all, but to a realm beyond the private/public distinction. Primal men belong to what is *meta*, a realm more ancient than and independent of sociality. Analogically, in other words, Freud is in this passage still discussing his metapsychology – albeit in strikingly anthropocentric terms. As for public and private realms, they actually denote the positions taken, respectively, by the man who steals the fire and the woman who protects it. But to this end everything depends on the man first able to overcome his anatomy, specifically his penis – first, as it fuels his desire (*Lust*) to extinguish the fire, and second, as it fuels his joy in competing with other men. Culture is his "reward."

It is only in "The Acquisition and Control of Fire" that Freud considers more carefully this unusual man of culture from prehistory, the one able to renounce his instinct – *Triebverzicht*, his drive – for the greater good of culture. But, already in the context of this footnote from *Civilization*, it is not too much to say that, for Freud, the founding of culture is dependent on a shift toward the feminine; a shift toward heterosexuality, hetero-normativity, or, more simply, to life. Instead of enjoying with men the "tongues of flame" – a game that has nonexistence as its raison d'être; a game Freud associates with the death drive – the man sets up house with a woman who thereafter becomes the keeper of the flame, of human culture. In this respect, it is the woman who helps man maintain the renunciation of drive, helps him achieve what it is best for the group, for culture. *Kultur* may begin with man but it is maintained or regulated by woman.

Freud doesn't quite say that this man of culture is a bit like the Greek god Prometheus, the one responsible for creating humankind out of clay and then stealing fire for them. But it is implied, at least in "The Acquisition and Control of Fire," where Freud's discussion of fire hinges on an elaborate interpretation of the Prometheus legend. There Freud repeats his earlier claim from the footnote in *Civilization* and updates it with his nascent interest in "historical truth." He writes:

> I think that my assumption[2] – that, in order to gain control over fire, men had to renounce the homosexual pleasure of extinguishing it with a stream of urine – can be confirmed by an interpretation of the Greek myth of Prometheus, provided that we bear in mind the distortions which must be expected to occur in the transition from facts to the contents of a myth. (*SE*, 1932/1991, p. 187; translation amended)

"The transition from fact": by 1931 Freud understands that a psychoanalysis of the Prometheus legend must dig down to "the essential content of humankind's distorted recollection" (p. 188; translation amended); and

---

[2] Strachey has Freud say "hypothesis" when he actually says "assumption," *daß meine Annahme*.

again, in the same language later used in "Constructions in Analysis," that it must aim to reach "the historical core of the myth" (p. 191), *der historische Kern des Mythus*. And why wouldn't he think this? Karl Abraham already admitted in 1910 that he was inspired to analyze the Prometheus myth on the strength of Freud's own analysis of the Oedipus myth (see 1910/1913, p. 69); and had to this end very explicitly formalized the relationship between dreams and myths.[3]

In the "Wolfman" case study of 1914 Freud wonders if the "precipitates from the history of human civilization" can be gleaned from myth and folklore. By the time of "The Acquisition" he realizes that there may, indeed, be just such a myth as it concerns urination, fire, and culture. And so the game begins: what is now mythical and distorted must once again become factual. Psychoanalysis thus becomes not only archeology but also paleopsychology, an analysis of Prometheus bent on confirming the claims made about fire and urination first ventured in *Civilization*. Not expand upon but *confirm them by interpretation* – a very bullish claim about the powers of depth psychology.

* * *

Man's turn toward culture comes at a cost, first, to his natural appetite for destruction, and second, to his social relations with other "primal men." For among men "driven by their instincts," the "culture-hero" arouses only their "undisguised resentment" (*SE*, 1932/1991, 22: 189; translation adjusted). "We know," Freud says, "that a demand for a renunciation of instinct, and the enforcement of that demand, call out hostility and aggressiveness, which is only transformed into a sense of guilt in a later phase of psychical development" (pp. 189–90). Culture, society, or civilization is founded upon the theft of fire made possible by the renunciation of a homoerotic bond

---

[3] "The myth," writes Abraham, "is a fragment of the repressed life of the infantile psyche of the race. It contains (in disguised form) the wishes of the childhood of the race" (1910/1913, p. 36). Moreover Abraham makes the linchpin of his argument the same thing as Freud: the theory of phylogenesis, according to which *prehistorical* myths of the collective are preserved in *historical* dreams of individuals (p. 72). As the ever compliant Abraham said already in a letter of April 1908, "My expositions are, naturally, based entirely on yours, and I very much hope that you will agree with the conclusions I drew for the myth from the interpretation of dreams, etc." (Freud & Abraham, 2002, p. 34). Other Freudians, like Otto Rank, Hanns Sachs, and Theodor Reik, would pursue the same course. As Reik would say about *Totem and Taboo*, "We were enthusiastic and we immediately understood that here was an intellectual challenge for generations of psychologists and historians of civilization" (1958a, p. 9). Two decades later Freud could perhaps be forgiven for believing that he was merely building on a way of thinking implicit in his own thought, and only developed in the work of people like Abraham, Jung, and the other followers including Herbert Silberer. Perhaps that is why Abraham's name, let alone the title of his Prometheus study, doesn't even appear in Freud's own analysis of the Prometheus myth.

with other primal men, men whose aggressivity toward fire has now shifted to an aggressivity toward the fire-stealing culture-hero. Apparently primal men resent having their control over fire transferred to women; women who do not share their aggressiveness toward fire, but on the contrary are inclined by anatomical difference to care for it. Freud was amazingly blunt about the role destined for women in *Civilization and Its Discontents*, where he writes:

> [W]omen soon come into opposition to civilization and display their retarding and restraining influence – those very women who, in the begin-ning, laid the foundations of civilization by the claims of their love. Women represent the interests of the family and of sexual life. The work of civiliza-tion has become increasingly the business of men, it confronts them with ever more difficult tasks and compels them to carry instinctual sublimations [*Triebsublimierungen*] of which women are little capable [*wenig gewachsen sind*]. (*SE*, 1930/1991, p. 103; *GW*, 1948b/1991, p. 463)

Freud goes on to say that the "business of men," *Sache der Männer*, requires the "constant association with men," their *Zusammensein*, which in turn alienates men from women and family and then alienates women from men and culture (*SE*, 1930/1991, p. 104). What begins with homosexual competition ends, it would seem, with homoerotic cooperation at the expense of women. But in "The Acquisition and Control of Fire" very little is said about women beyond their caretaker function concerning fire/culture. In this regard one is reminded of Freud's quip from an essay of 1925: "We must not allow ourselves to be deflected from such conclusions by the demands of the feminists, who are anxious to force us to regard the two sexes as completely equal in position and worth" (*SE*, 1925b/1991, p. 258). In "Acquisition," all we can assume is that Freud's women are able to rekindle a different kind of erotic fire for the male culture-hero; that women are a force that tempts the men back to home and hearth, and thus to nature.

Which brings us to "Why War?," the work that follows "The Acquisition and Control of Fire." In this open letter Freud attempts to answer the "why" of war and the "how" of perpetual peace. But as it concerns the former, Einstein steals Freud's thunder. The reason human beings go to war, Einstein suggests, is "because man has within him a lust for hatred and destruction" (*SE*, 1933b/1991, p. 201). We know very well that this was Freud's own view as well, hence his droll remark: "though you have taken the wind out of my sails I shall be glad to follow in your wake and content myself with confirming all that you have said by amplifying it to the best of my knowledge – or conjecture" (p. 203). Freud promises an amplification that is *either* knowledge or conjecture. Surprisingly, Freud concedes, right at the outset, that his "knowledge" is equivalent to "suspicion" or "speculation," *oder Vermuten*. More about this in a moment.

Freud's first step is to summarize everything that he has learned between 1920 and 1932, roughly everything between *Beyond the Pleasure Principle* and *Civilization and Its Discontents*. It is familiar territory. Life in a state of nature is a life of violence, a state dominated by muscles and brute force. The development of weapons, however, is a step forward in intellectuality. Group cohesion and therefore society depend upon emotional bonds between people. In time social feeling and justice civilize humankind. But hostility still exists and will always exist until everyone bonds under a "supreme agency," for example, under the authority of a League of Nations or, in our time, the United Nations. But that may be just a dream. Until this imaginary future, the answer to all the riddles of life boils down to an eternal battle between Eros and the death drive.

Freud's characterization of this final shibboleth is no less surprising than his opening admission – a kind of world-weary shrugging of the shoulders – that his knowledge is conjecture. "It may perhaps seem to you," Freud tells Einstein, "as though our theories are a kind of mythology and, in the present case, not even an agreeable one. But does not every science come in the end to a kind of mythology like this? Cannot the same thing be said today of your own physics?" (*SE*, 1933b/1991, p. 211). Freud makes a similar claim in *Beyond the Pleasure Principle*. Toward the end of chapter six, Freud admits that his speculations are strange and difficult to follow. He isn't quite ready to say that this difficulty is due to the *mythological* nature of psychoanalysis (and its metapsychology), but because of its *metaphorical* nature; the language of psychoanalysis, he says, is unavoidably "figurative" (Freud, 1920/2011, p. 96; *SE*, 1920a/1991, p. 60). But Freud then calls out the terminologies of physiology and chemistry as in no way less figurative than those of psychoanalysis. As such Freud's remarks in *Beyond* function as a kind of torched earth defense of psychoanalysis. In the open letter to Einstein, Freud does the same thing, only now with physics: psychoanalysis is mythology, but then so too is physics.

Two paragraphs later in his open letter, Freud again refers to the late dualism as "our mythological theory of instincts [drives]" (*SE*, 1933b/1991, p. 212). Of course this is a stunning admission: the metapsychology really is a mythology. Freud does seem to have become "Jungian." But the truth is, Freud was already so convinced by the emergent concept of historical truth, generated by his growing interest in the psychoanalysis of Moses, that he could afford to appear cavalier about his characterization of psychoanalysis as conjecture and metapsychology as mythology. For the truth of psychoanalytic conjecture, like that of mythological metapsychology, was already assured. Myth only obscures its kernel of truth; it doesn't destroy it. So what appears to many readers as incredible and even laudable self-deprecation is anything but. On the contrary, it represents the late Freud at his most ironically self-confident – and on the verge of his final breakthrough concept, historical truth. Moreover, the fact that truth has the structure of myth just shows the depths that psychoanalysis has penetrated – even though, to lay readers, it is bound to seem, as he says in *Beyond*, like "false profundity or even mysticism."

Freud is not done. In the last few pages of "Why War?" he risks his most interesting and also most self-aggrandizing thoughts about war; thoughts that resonate perfectly with everything we now know about the cultural works. Freud stops "amplifying" on Einstein's insight about innate human aggressivity, the "why" of war, and finally addresses the "how" of perpetual peace – the how of a future without war. His shift to this question follows immediately upon his retread of the territory covered in *The Future of an Illusion*. Ideally, Freud says, humankind would subordinate their drives "to the dictatorship of reason" (*SE*, 1933b/1991, p. 213). But he is no more convinced by this ideal than he was at the end of the *Future*. "Nothing else could unite people so completely and so tenaciously, even if there were no emotional ties between them. But in all probability that is a Utopian expectation" (translation amended).

Freud admits that the results of an "unworldly theorist" don't add up to much, *es kommt nicht viel dabei heraus*. As Strachey freely translates, the results are "not very fruitful." So Freud duly moves on to more fruitful territory and slowly returns us to the "culture-hero" discussed in "The Acquisition and Control of Fire." He begins with a question to Einstein, and to all the other good men he has known in his life – men of peace like Oskar Pfister, Romain Rolland, and Havelock Ellis. "Why," Freud asks, "do we resist war so strongly – you and I and so many others? Why do we not accept it as another of the many unpleasant difficulties of life?" Freud's pithy answer: "we can't help it" (p. 214; translation modified). "We are pacifists," he clarifies, "because we are obliged to be for organic reasons." The cause of this obligation is a "process of culture-evolution" (*Prozeß der Kulturentwicklung*), a process that results in "psychical modifications" to some people.

This is precisely the territory that will later inform the conclusions of *Moses and Monotheism*, where Freud is very clear about an evolutionary shift from muscles to intellect over the time of deep history. In his letter to

Einstein, Freud is already laying down the basic outline of this view. "Of the psychological characteristics of civilization," Freud writes, "two appear to be the most important: a strengthening of the intellect, which is beginning to govern instinctual life, and an internalization of the aggressive impulse, with all its consequent advantages and perils" (pp. 214–15). War is the basest rejection of this shift toward culture. In the terms discussed in "The Acquisition and Control of Fire," war is what happens when the oldest and most hateful instincts, represented by the anger of primal men, revenge themselves on the culture-heroes.

Freud's point is that pacifism is not just an *attitude* or *feeling*, but an organic *development* – and so a concrete leap forward in the evolution of culture. "We pacifists," Freud says, "have a constitutional intolerance of war, an idiosyncrasy magnified, as it were, to the highest degree" (p. 215). The language of constitutionality and obligation is, of course, the now-familiar language of Freud's troublesome metabiology. Pacifists like Freud are constitutionally different from other people. As such they have no choice but to be pacifists; they are driven to it by nature, that is, by the natural accumulation of culture over a millennia. To put it plainly, Freud and Einstein are culture-heroes – a bit like the first man who turned away from the nihilism of a homosexual community devoted to destroying any trace of fire.

Strachey rightly adds, in a footnote, that Freud's discussion of the evolution of culture is developed further in *Moses and Monotheism*, especially in the third essay where Freud discusses such things as historical truth and intellectuality. "It figures prominently," says Strachey, albeit "in rather different terms" (in *SE*, 1933b/1991, p. 215). But actually the terms are the same. The only thing missing in the open letter of 1932 is the candor or, if you prefer, the chutzpah of 1939 – where the "progress of spirituality or intellectuality," of *Geistigkeit*, is quite explicitly understood to be a special characteristic of Jews. We pacifists, we intellectuals, we culture-heroes, we Prometheans, we Jews – Freud and Einstein – we are the future of culture evolution and the hope of humanity. The self-congratulatory flattery is breathtaking.

As for the rest of humankind, Freud, as always, is less impressed. That said, he is also less pessimistic than he was in the closing pages of *The Future of an Illusion*. Here are Freud's closing remarks to "Why War?":

> And how long shall we have to wait before the rest of humankind become pacifists too? There is no telling. But it may not be Utopian to hope that these two factors, the cultural attitude and the justified dread of the consequences

of a future war, may result within a measurable time in putting an end to the waging of war. By what paths or by what side-tracks this will come about we cannot guess. But one thing we *can* say: whatever fosters the growth of civilization works at the same time against war. (p. 215; translation adjusted)

Recall that, in the *Future*, Freud says that "the primacy of the intellect certainly lies far, far ahead, but probably not infinitely far" (Freud, 1927/2012, p. 111; *SE*, 1927b/1991, p. 53). In his letter to Einstein he is able to moderate his pessimism to conclude that such a hope "may not be Utopian." May not be: *vielleicht ist es keine utopische Hoffnung*. No mention, this time, of unmeasurable "geological time," only of "measurable time." And that, simply put, is the extent of Freud's optimism in the late cultural works. In an open letter designed to explore the causes and limits of war, a letter designed for mass consumption as a pamphlet, Freud offers us highly qualified hope. Maybe humankind will live to see an improvement to our natural predisposition to hostility and war. Maybe guilt will finally accumulate in the mental lives of humankind. And maybe – there is no telling when – maybe one day culture-heroes like Freud and Einstein will outnumber primal men. That's as good as it gets with Freud.

Freud of course knows he has not delivered on the promise of the exchange – to "deliver mankind from the menace of war" and so he closes out the letter with "I trust you will forgive me if what I have said has disappointed you"; *Ich grüße Sie herzlich und bitte Sie um Verzeihung, wenn meine Ausführungen Sie enttäuscht haben*. Full stop. And then his closing remark: "Yours, Sigmund Freud." But the English gentleman in Strachey can't leave it at that, and so in his translation he invents for readers a modest closing flourish: "and I remain, with kindest regards, Sincerely yours, Sigmund Freud." That, in a nutshell, is how the English Freud became, word by word, a more courteous culture-hero than he is in the original German.

On December 3, 1932, Einstein replies to Freud that "You have made a most gratifying gift to the League of Nations and myself with your truly classic reply."[4] Freud was less impressed. In a letter to Max Eitingon, Freud referred to the exchange as "tedious and sterile" (in Jones, 1957, p. 175). The truth is somewhere in between. In his essay Freud crystallized his thinking about culture after *Beyond the Pleasure Principle*, and pointed the way to arguments he would develop in *Moses and Monotheism*. In the process he found the privileged place for himself and for people like him – cultured

---

[4] See www.public.asu.edu/~jmlynch/273/documents/FreudEinstein.pdf.

people. The cultural elite exists as a glimpse into the utopian future of humankind.

* * *

In 1818 a young Mary Shelley published *Frankenstein: Or, the Modern Prometheus*, a novel that translates the Prometheus legend for the Romantic era. Where traditionally Prometheus represents human striving and culture, after Shelley he becomes more commonly associated with singular genius – for instance, the creative genius of Dr. Victor Frankenstein. Like Prometheus, Frankenstein creates life and steals fire from the gods, in his case the fire of electrical current.

With psychoanalysis Freud, too, steals fire from the gods – the hellfire he associates with the unconscious, and the energy he associates with the drives – and thereafter plays the part of embattled culture-hero repeatedly punished for his transgression. Our modern Moses-cum-Prometheus[5] even earns the Hercules, the savior and culture-hero, he so richly deserves: not the vigorous Jung, the creative Rank, or the sympathetic Ferenczi, but the vicious Ernest Jones. In these respects and more, psychoanalysis is not just a theory about consciousness. It is always a description of the way Freud views the inner and outer worlds, the reality, of his fellow human beings. Beyond that it is an elaborate rationale for how a genius, culture-hero, and Jew can expect to be treated in a world haunted by primal hostility and dominated by hordes of unthinking automatons. It is tempting to say that psychoanalysis is, therefore, a project rich in overcompensation and, moreover, is true only of itself, that is, of Sigmund Freud. And, actually, one would be right on both counts.

But perhaps it is more just, more realistic even, to end by simply agreeing with everything that motivated Freud's project. It is true that human beings rarely think about the conditions that form and indeed haunt their everyday lives. It is true that human beings are the end products of a history that includes evolution and geological time. It is true that culture is precious and constantly imperiled by base instincts and that human beings are, after all, still animals. It is true that culture is precious and fragile, a thin veneer that only imperfectly covers over our basic incivility. And it is true that death is an unavoidable part of life, and at times the dominant part. Furthermore, let's concede that Freud was a prodigious synthesizer and genius; a gifted thinker and genuine culture-hero; a secular

---

[5] According to Abraham, comparative mythology allows us to link Moses and Prometheus: "The biblical Moses ascends, like Prometheus, to heaven and brings the laws down – as he did the fire" (1910/1913, p. 50).

Jew who dared appropriate, willy-nilly, the troubling ideologies of race and anti-Semitism and turn them to his own advantage and to the advantage of *Kultur* more generally.

Fine. But at the same time, let's also admit that Freud's incredibly complex answers to all the riddles of life are wrong. Indeed, very few thinkers in the history of Western thought have been so wrong about so many important things.

And yet – the fire still burns. So while it is incontestable that psychoanalysis is literally unbelievable, can no longer be accepted as even passably correct or scientific, is fatally unreliable as a means for uncovering individual or collective histories, and is peppered with results that are fantastical Frankenstein monsters, nonetheless, despite it all, Freud's lifework remains a stunningly ambitious, startlingly imaginative, and in many respects worthwhile way to think about the project of being human. For all of his foibles and faults, Freud demonstrates over and over again how it's done – albeit in the most singular and eccentric way possible. So while the results are not repeatable, not universal, and finally not applicable to anyone but Sigmund Freud, the colossal effort of it all is still exemplary, still amazing, and somehow still encouraging. Arguably it represents the grandeur of a life spent not just *doing*, but *thinking*. A life of the mind. Of what Freud, at one point in "The Acquisition and Control of Fire," calls the "sheer pleasure of representation" (*SE*, 1932/1991, p. 191). That sounds just about right: Freud's lifework recalls for us the nearly lost pleasure of representation, *Darstellungslust*, of joyful creation and cultural engagement with self and other.

We could do worse.

Or, if you prefer, we could be so lucky.

One thing is certain: Sigmund Freud was among the last of his kind, a Prometheus both brave and foolish enough to risk big answers to all the big questions of life and death. Who among us is Herculean enough to meet him even half way in this quest? Who among us is as brave – or foolish? Silence in the face of the challenge tells us nothing about the mysterious death drive. But it does tell us that our current reality, objectively speaking, has been diminished by timidity, cowardice, and indifference toward the glory of thought; and that our naive recourse to and reliance upon science, realism, and objectivity does little to preserve and enhance human existence in the world. Freud, in short, still teaches us to speculate and dream big – however wrong he was about all the riddles of life.

* * *

So what have we learned? Let's summarize one last time. Freud reached out and was attracted to significant advocates of peace, love, and pacifism – Pfister, Rolland, Ellis, and Einstein – who were constitutionally similar to him, but unable to bear witness to the uncomfortable realities of our everyday existence. And so Freud painted their psychologies of love and compassion as narcissistic, illusory, and hopelessly unrealistic, but also tainted with "homosexuality" and, indeed, with the death drive. In the end, the clamor of life and love only proved to Freud, as noisily as possible, the truth of the silent death drive: frightened by an older and more powerful drive for destruction, these idealistic advocates of Eros recoiled, and so overcompensated. The same logic informs the psychoanalysis of *Kultur*. Society wraps itself in love and community, as though by reaction formation, because it is actually the end product of deep evolutionary developments that begin with death and destruction. Individual and group life begin with nonexistence and forever seek its return, even as society demands from us life and love. And that is how, simply put, the life and death drives provide an answer to "all the riddles of life" – all of them, everything. The progress called life, love, and culture is just a thin veneer, really an illusion, that is unequal to the more original regress called death, hate, and nature. Their interplay is the stage upon which we enact the drama of human existence.

The late Freud theorized the internal world of the psyche, measured it against the external world of material reality, grounded it in the truth of archaic prehistory and myth – one reconstructed on the basis of our shared psycho-biology – and presented the totality, a psychoanalysis wedded to the "Witch Metapsychology," as the bridge between our animal past and our human future. Psychoanalysis was thereupon revealed as the most important science among all sciences. These are the essential premises and conclusions – difficult, provocative, coherent, but also dogmatic, unbelievable, embarrassing – upon which Freud psychoanalyzed modern Western society. He was not only mistaken, but brilliantly mistaken – and that's not nothing.

The upshot? Freud's legacy lies not with his botched science at all but rather with the philosophy and culture that motivated and finally embodied his most grandiose beliefs. True, Freud would have hated this conclusion. But the alternative is that Freud was, indeed, just a "bad scientist" destined for the dustbin of history. This is, no doubt, an ironic conclusion. For what saves Freud from irrelevance are the very works on culture that are often deemed, by friends and foes alike, as superfluous, merely imaginative, probably symptomatic, and definitely incoherent.

What saves Freud is his radical yet consistent application of the theories of psychoanalysis to human *Kultur*. What is most true of psychoanalysis lies, therefore, with Freud's phylogenetic fantasies, with the metapsychology, and with the late Romantics, and not with empiricism, positivism, science, realism, objectivity, and falsifiability.

In his best moments Freud only wanted the truth. We should give it to him. That has to be enough – even for a creative genius. Of course, it also has to be enough for us, too.

References

Abraham, K. (1913). *Dreams and myths: A study in race psychology* (W. A. White, Trans.). New York, NY: The Journal of Nervous and Mental Disease Publishing Co. (Original work published 1910).

(1955a). IV: A psychoanalytical contribution towards the understanding of his personality and of the monotheistic cult of Aton. In H. C. Abraham (Ed.), *Clinical papers and essays on psycho-analysis* (pp. 262–90). London, England: Hogarth Press (Original work published 1912).

(1955b). The cultural significance of psychoanalysis. In H. C. Abraham (Ed.), *Clinical papers and essays on psycho-analysis* (pp. 116–36). London, England: Hogarth Press (Original work published 1920).

(1979). A short study of the development of the libido, viewed in the light of mental disorders. In *Selected papers of Karl Abraham* (D. Bryan & A. Strachey, Trans., pp. 418–501). New York, NY: Brunner/Mazel (Original work published 1924).

Adler, A. (2002). Preface: To the reader (1911). In H. T. Stein (Ed.), *The neurotic character: Fundamentals of individual psychology and psychotherapy.* Bellingham, WA: Alfred Adler Institute of Northwestern Washington.

Bakan, D. (July 19 1996). [Interview with author].

Berlin, B. & Levy, E. (1978). On the letters of Theodor Reik to Arthur Schnitzler. *Psychoanalytic Review*, 65, 109–30.

Bernstein, R. (1998). *Freud and the legacy of Moses.* Cambridge: Cambridge University Press.

Bersani, L. (2002). Introduction. In S. Freud (Ed.), *Civilization and its discontents* (D. McLintock, Trans.) (pp. vii–xxii). London, England: Penguin Books.

Bjerre, P. (1920). *The history of psychoanalysis* (Rev. ed., E. N. Barrow, Trans.). Boston, MA: Richard G. Badger.

Borch-Jacobsen, M. (1996a). Neurotica: Freud and the seduction theory. *October*, 76, 15–43.

(1996b). *Remembering Anna O.: A century of mystification.* New York, NY: Routledge.

Borch-Jacobsen, M. & Shamdasani, S. (2012). *The Freud files: An inquiry into the history of psychoanalysis.* Cambridge: Cambridge University Press.

Brill, A. A. (1962). *Freud's contribution to psychiatry.* New York, NY: Norton (Original work published 1944).

Brome, V. (1979). *Havelock Ellis: Philosopher of sex, a biography*. London, England: Routledge & Kegan Paul.

Brown, N. O. (1959). *Life against death: The psychoanalytical meaning of history*. London, England: Routledge.

Burke, J. (2006). *The sphinx on the table: Sigmund Freud's art collection and the development of psychoanalysis*. New York, NY: Walker & Company.

Burnham, J. C. (1983). *Jelliffe: American psychoanalyst and physician and his correspondence with Sigmund Freud and C. G. Jung*. Chicago, IL: University of Chicago Press.

Burston, D. (1991). *The legacy of Erich Fromm*. Cambridge, MA: Harvard University Press.

Choisy, M. (1963). *Sigmund Freud: A new appraisal*. New York, NY: Philosophical Library.

Clark, R. (1980). *Freud: The man and the cause*. New York, NY: Random House.

Cocks, G. (1997). *Psychotherapy in the Third Reich: The Goering Institute* (2nd ed.). New Brunswick, NJ: Transaction Books (Original work published 1985).

Crabtree, A. (1993). *From Freud to Mesmer: Magnetic healing and the roots of psychological health*. New Haven, CT: Yale University Press.

Deleuze, G. (1991). Coldness and cruelty. In G. Deleuze & L. von Sacher-Masoch (Eds.), *Masochism: Coldness and cruelty; Venus in furs* (J. McNeil, Trans.) (pp. 7–138). New York, NY: Zone Books.

Derrida, J. (1987). *The post card: From Socrates to Freud and beyond*. Chicago, IL: University of Chicago Press (Original work published 1980).

   (1996). *Archive fever: A Freudian impression* (E. Prenowitz, Trans.). Chicago, IL: University of Chicago Press.

Doolittle, H. D. (1974). *Tribute to Freud*. New York, NY: New Directions.

Dostoevsky, F. (1918). *Notes from underground*. New York, NY: Vintage (Original work published 1864).

Dufresne, T. (2000). *Tales from the Freudian crypt: The death drive in text and context*. Stanford, CA: Stanford University Press.

   (2003). *Killing Freud: 20th century culture and the death of psychoanalysis*. London, England: Continuum.

Ehrenwald, J. (1971). On the so-called Jewish spirit. In *The Jews of Czechoslovakia: Historical studies and surveys, volume II*. Philadelphia, PA: The Jewish Publication Society of America (Original work published 1938).

Eliot, T. S. (1928). Review of *The future of an illusion*, by S. Freud. *The Criterion, 8*, 350–3.

Ellenberger, H. (1970). *The discovery of the unconscious: The history and evolution of dynamic psychiatry*. New York, NY: Basic Books.

Ellis, H. (1948). *Psychology of sex*. London, England: William Heinemann (Original work published 1933).

Evans, R. I. (1964). *Conversations with Carl Jung and reactions from Ernest Jones*. New York, NY: D. Van Nostrand.

Ferenczi, S. (1952). The problem of acceptance of unpleasant ideas – Advances in knowledge of the sense of reality. In *Further contributions to the theory and technique in psycho-analysis* (J. I. Sutie, C. M. Baines, O. Edmonds, E. G. Glover, & J. Rickman, Trans., pp. 366–79). New York, NY: Basic (Original work published 1926).

(1956). Stages in the development of the sense of reality. In *Sex in psycho-analysis* (E. Jones & C. Newton, Trans.). New York, NY: Dover Books (Original work published 1913).

(1968). *Thalassa: A theory of genitality* (H. Bunker, Trans.). New York, NY: Norton (Original published 1924).

(1995). *The clinical diary of Sándor Ferenczi* (J. Dupont, Ed., M. Balint & N. Z. Jackson, Trans.). Cambridge, MA: Harvard University Press (Original work published 1932).

Fisher, D. J. (1982). Reading Freud's *Civilization and its discontents*. In D. LaCapra & S. L. Kaplan (Eds.), *Modern European intellectual history: Reappraisals and new perspectives* (pp. 251–79). Ithaca, NY: Cornell University Press.

(1988). *Romain Rolland and the politics of intellectual engagement.* Berkeley: University of California Press.

(1991). *Cultural theory and psychoanalytic tradition.* New Brunswick, NJ: Transaction Press (Original work published in 1976).

Freud, S. (1895a). Project for a scientific psychology. In J. Strachey (Ed. & Trans.), *The standard edition of the complete psychological works of Sigmund Freud* [*SE*] (Vol. 1, pp. 281–397). London, England: Hogarth, 1953–1974 (Reprint published 1991).

(1895b). Studies on hysteria. In *SE* (Vol. 2).

(1896). The aetiology of hysteria. In *SE* (Vol. 3, pp. 187–221).

(1900). The interpretation of dreams. In *SE* (Vols. 4–5).

(1905a). Fragment of an analysis of a case of hysteria. In *SE* (Vol. 7, pp. 1–122).

(1905b). Three essays on the theory of sexuality. In *SE* (Vol. 7, pp. 123–243).

(1908). Obsessive actions and religious practices. In *SE* (Vol. 9, pp. 115–27).

(1909). Analysis of a phobia in a five-year-old boy [Little Hans]. In *SE* (Vol. 10, pp. 1–149).

(1912). On the universal tendency to debasement in the sphere of love. In *SE* (Vol. 11, pp. 179–90).

(1913a). Introduction to Pfister's The psychoanalytic method. In *SE* (Vol. 12, pp. 329–31).

(1913b). Totem and taboo. In *SE* (Vol. 13, pp. 1–161).

(1913c). The claims of psychoanalysis to scientific interest. In *SE* (Vol. 13, pp. 163–90).

(1914a). On the history of the psychoanalytic movement. In *SE* (Vol. 14, pp. 3–66).

(1914b). On narcissism. In *SE* (Vol. 14, pp. 67–102).

(1915). Thoughts for the times on war and death. In *SE* (Vol. 14, pp. 271–300).

(1916). On transience. In *SE* (Vol. 14, pp. 303–7).

(1918). From the history of an infantile neurosis. In *SE* (Vol. 17, pp. 1–133).

(1919). Preface to Reik's Ritual. In *SE* (Vol. 17, pp. 259–63).

(1920a). Beyond the pleasure principle. In *SE* (Vol. 18, pp. 1–64).

(1920b). A note on the prehistory of the technique of analysis. In *SE* (Vol. 18, pp. 263–5).

(1920c). The psychogenesis of a case of homosexuality in a woman.

(1921). Group psychology and the analysis of the ego. In *SE* (Vol. 18, pp. 65–143).

(1922a). Dreams and telepathy. In *SE* (Vol. 18, pp. 195–220).

(1922b). Some neurotic mechanisms in jealousy, paranoia, and homosexuality. In *SE* (Vol. 18, pp. 221–32).

(1923). The ego and the id. In *SE* (Vol. 19, pp. 1–66).

(1924a). The economic problem of masochism. In *SE* (Vol. 19, pp. 155–70).

(1924b). Dissolution of the Oedipus complex. In *SE* (Vol. 19, pp. 173–9).

(1925a). A note upon the "mystic writing-pad." In *SE* (Vol. 19, pp. 225–32).

(1925b). Some psychical consequences of the anatomical distinction between the sexes. In *SE* (Vol. 19, pp. 248–58).

(1925c). An autobiographical study. In *SE* (Vol. 20, pp. 3–74).

(1926) The question of lay analysis. In *SE* (Vol. 20, pp. 179–250).

(1927a). Postscript. In *SE* (Vol. 20, pp. 251–8).

(1927b). The future of an illusion. In *SE* (Vol. 21, pp. 1–56).

(1930). Civilization and its discontents. In *SE* (Vol. 21, pp. 57–145).

(1932). The acquisition and control of fire. In *SE* (Vol. 22, pp. 183–93).

(1933a). New introductory lectures on psychoanalysis. In *SE* (Vol. 22, pp. 1–182).

(1933b). Why war? In *SE* (Vol. 22, pp. 195–215).

(1933c). Sandor Ferenczi. In *SE* (Vol. 22, pp. 225–9).

(1935). Postscript [to "An autobiographical study"]. In *SE* (Vol. 20, pp. 71–4).

(1936). A disturbance of memory on the Acropolis. In *SE* (Vol. 22, pp. 238–48).

(1937). Analysis terminable and interminable. In *SE* (Vol. 23, pp. 209–53).

(1939). Moses and monotheism. In *SE* (Vol. 23, pp. 3–137).

(1937). Constructions in analysis. In *SE* (Vol. 23, pp. 255–69).

(1940). An Outline of Psychoanalysis. In *SE* (Vol. 23, pp. 140–207).

(1925). *Studien über Hysterie*. In A. Freud & M. Bonaparte (Eds.), *Gesammelte werke: chronologisch geordnet [GW]* (Vol. 1, pp. 3–238). London: Imago, 1940–1952, Vols. 1–17. Frankfurt am Main: Fischer Verlag, 1968, Vol. 18. (Reprint published 1991).

(1932). Zur Gewinnung des Feuers. In *GW* (Vol. 16, pp. 3–9).

(1936). Brief an Romain Rolland (Eine Erinnerungsstörung auf der Akropolis). In *GW* (Vol. 16, pp. 250–7).

(1937). Konstruktionen in der Analyse. In *GW* (Vol. 16, pp. 41–56).

(1948a). Die Zukunft einer Illusion. In *GW* (Vol. 14, pp. 323–80).

(1948b). Das Unbehagen in der Kultur. In *GW* (Vol. 14, pp. 421–506).

(1939). *Der Mann Moses und die monotheistische Religion: Drei Abhandlungen*. Amsterdam: Allert de Lange.

(1960a). *Briefe 1873–1939* (E. Freud & L. Freud, Eds.). Frankfurt: S. Fischer Verlag.

(1960b). *Letters of Sigmund Freud, 1873–1939* (E. L. Freud, Ed., T. Stern & J. Stern, Trans.). London, England: Hogarth Press.

(1967). *Moses and monotheism* (K. Jones, Trans.) New York, NY: Vintage (Original work published 1939).

(1987). *A phylogenetic fantasy: Overview of the transference neuroses* (I. Grubrich-Simitis, Ed., A. Hoffer & P. T. Hoffer, Trans.). Cambridge, MA: Belknap Press (Original work published 1915).

(1992). *The diary of Sigmund Freud, 1929–1939: A record of the final decade* (M. Molnar, Trans.). New York, NY: Scribner.

(2011). *Beyond the pleasure principle* (T. Dufresne, Ed., G. C, Richter, Trans., pp. 49–99). Peterborough, ON: Broadview (Original work published 1920).

(2012). *The future of an illusion* (T. Dufresne, Ed., & G. C, Richter, Trans.). Peterborough, ON: Broadview (Original work published 1927).

Freud, S. & Abraham, K. (2002). *The complete correspondence of Sigmund Freud and Karl Abraham, 1907–1925* (Completed ed., E. Falzeder, Ed., C. Schwarzacher, C. Trollope, & K. M. King, Trans.). London, England: Karnac.

Freud, S. & Andreas-Salomé, L. (1966). *Sigmund Freud and Lou Andreas-Salomé: Letters* (E. Pfeiffer, Ed., W. Robson-Scott & E. Robson-Scott, Trans.). London, England: Hogarth Press.

Freud, S. & Binswanger, L. (2003). *The Sigmund Freud–Ludwig Binswanger correspondence, 1908–1938* (G. Fichtner, Ed., A. J. Pomerans. Trans.). New York, NY: Other Press.

Freud, S. & Bullitt, W. C. (1966). *Thomas Woodrow Wilson: A psychological study.* Boston, MA: Houghton Mifflin.

Freud, S. & Ferenczi, S. (1993). *The correspondence of Sigmund Freud and Sándor Ferenczi, 1908–1914* (Vol. 1, E. Falzeder & E. Brabant. Eds., P. Hoffer, Trans.). Cambridge, MA: Belknap Press.

(2000). *The correspondence of Sigmund Freud and Sándor Ferenczi, 1920–1933* (Vol. 3, E. Falzeder & E. Brabant. Eds., P. Hoffer, Trans.). Cambridge, MA: Belknap Press.

Freud, S. & Fliess, W. (1985). *The complete letters of Sigmund Freud to Wilhelm Fliess, 1887–1904* (J. M. Masson, Ed. & Trans.). Cambridge, MA: Belknap.

Freud, S. & Jones, E. (1993). *The complete correspondence of Sigmund Freud and Ernest Jones, 1908–1939* (R. A. Paskauskas, Ed., R. Steiner, Trans.). Cambridge, MA: Belknap Press.

Freud, S. & Jung, C. (1988). *The Freud/Jung letters: The correspondence between Sigmund Freud and C. G. Jung* (W. McGuire, Ed., R. Manheim & R. F. C. Hull, Trans.). Cambridge, MA: Harvard University Press.

Freud, S. & Pfister, O. (1963). *Psychoanalysis and faith: The letters of Sigmund Freud and Oskar Pfister* (H. Meng, Ed., E. Mosbacher, Trans.). London, England: Hogarth Press.

Freud, S., & Zweig, A. (1970). *The letters of Sigmund Freud and Arnold Zweig* (E. Freud, Ed., W. Robson-Scott & E. Robson-Scott, Trans.). London, England: Hogarth Press.

Frey-Rohn, L. (1990). *From Freud to Jung: A comparative study of the psychology of the unconscious.* Boston, MA: Shambhala (Original work published in 1974).

Fromm, E. (1950). *Psychoanalysis and religion*. New Haven, CT: Yale University Press.

(1970). Freud's model of man and its social determinants. In *The crisis of psychoanalysis* (pp. 30–45). New York, NY: Holt, Rinehart, Winston.

(2011). A humanist response to the death instinct theory [1973]. In T. Dufresne (Ed.), *Beyond the pleasure principle* (G. C. Richter, Trans., pp. 275–83). Peterborough: Broadview.

Gay, P. (1988). *Freud: A life for our times*. New York, NY: Norton.

Gherovici, P. (2010). *Please select your gender: From the invention of hysteria to the democratizing of transgenderism*. New York, NY: Routledge.

Guest, B. (1984). *Herself defined: The poet H. D. and her world*. New York, NY: Quill.

Gundlach, H. (2002). Psychoanalysis and the story of "O": An embarrassment. *Semiotic Review of Books, 13*(1), 4–5.

Grosskurth, P. (1980). *Havelock Ellis: A biography*. Toronto, ON: McClelland & Stewart.

Grubrich-Simitis, I. (1997). *Early Freud and late Freud* (P. Slotkin, Trans.). London, England: Routledge.

Harrison, I. B. (1966). A reconsideration of Freud's "Disturbance of memory on the Acropolis" in relation to identity disturbance. *Journal of the American Psychoanalytic Association, 15*(3), 518–27.

Irwin, J. E. G. (1973a). Oskar Pfister and the Taggert report: The "first pastoral counselor" and today's role problems. *Journal of Pastoral Care, 27,* 189–95.

(1973b). Pfister and Freud: The rediscovery of a dialogue. *Journal of Religion and Health, 12*(4), 315–27.

Jelliffe, S. E. (1933). The death instinct in somatic and psychopathology. *Psychoanalytic Review, 20,* 121–32.

Jones, E. (1924). [Review of Sigmund Freud: His personality, his teaching and his school, by F. Wittels]. *International Journal of Psycho-Analysis, 5,* 481–6.

(1953). *The life and works of Sigmund Freud* (Vol. 1). New York, NY: Basic Books.

(1954). Introductory memoir. In *Selected papers of Karl Abraham* (D. Bryan & A. Strachey, Trans., pp. 9–41). London, England: Hogarth Press (Original work published 1926).

(1955). *The life and works of Sigmund Freud* (Vol. 2). New York, NY: Basic Books.

(1957). *The life and works of Sigmund Freud* (Vol. 3). New York, NY: Basic Books.

Jung, C. G. (1956). Symbols of transformation. In *The collected works of C. G. Jung* (Vol. 3, R. F. C. Hull, Trans.). New York, NY: Pantheon Books.

(1961). Freud and psychoanalysis. In *The collected works of C. G. Jung* (Vol. 4, R. F. C. Hull, Trans.). New York, NY: Pantheon Books.

(1973). *C. G. Jung letters, I: 1906–1950* (G. Adler, Ed., R. F. C. Hull, Trans.). London, England: Routledge & Kegan Paul.

(1989). *Memories, dreams, reflections* (A. Jaffe, Ed., R. Winston & C. Winston, Trans.). New York, NY: Vintage (Original work published 1961).

Kant, I. (1970). An answer to the question: "What is enlightenment?" In H. Reiss (Ed.) *Kant's political writings* (H. B. Nisbet, Trans., pp. 54–60). Cambridge, England: Cambridge University Press (Original work published 1784).

(1993). *Critique of pure reason* (N. K. Smith, Trans.). London, England: Macmillan Press (Original work published 1781).

Kanzer Mark. (Winter 1969). Sigmund and Alexander Freud on the Acropolis. *American Imago, 26*(4).

Kerr, J. (1993). *A most dangerous method: The story of Jung, Freud, and Sabina Spielrein.* New York, NY: Vintage.

Kiell, N. (1988). *Freud without hindsight: Reviews of his work (1893–1939).* Madison, CT: International Universities Press.

Klein, D. B. (1985). *Jewish origins of the psychoanalytic movement.* Chicago, IL: University of Chicago Press.

Klein, M. (1981). *"Love, guilt, and reparation" and other works, 1921–1945.* London, England: Hogarth Press.

(2011). "On the development of mental functioning [1958]." In T. Dufresne (Ed.), *Beyond the pleasure principle* (G. C. Richter, Trans., pp. 175–85). Peterborough: Broadview.

Kupper, H. & Rollman-Branch, H. (1973). Freud and Schnitzler: (Doppelgänger). In H. M. Ruitenbeek (Ed.), *Freud as we knew him* (pp. 412–27). Detroit, MI: Wayne University Press.

Laforgue, R. (1973). Personal memories of Freud. In H. M. Ruitenbeek (Ed.), *Freud as we knew him* (pp. 341–52). Detroit, MI: Wayne University Press (Original work published 1956).

Last, H. (1928). Chapter XI: The founding of Rome. In S. A. Cook, F. E. Adcock, & M. P. Charlesworth (Eds.), *The Cambridge ancient history* (Vol. 7, pp. 333–69). Cambridge, England: Cambridge University Press.

Lear, J. (2000). *Happiness, death, and the remainder of life.* Cambridge, England: Harvard University Press.

Lehrer, R. (1995). *Nietzsche's presence in Freud's life and thought.* New York, NY: SUNY Press.

Lieberman, E. J. (1985). *Acts of will: The life and work of Otto Rank.* New York, NY: Free Press.

Ludwig, E. (1973). *Doctor Freud.* New York, NY: Manor Books.

Mahony, P. (1992). Freud as family therapist: Reflections. In T. Gelfand & J. Kerr (Eds.), *Freud and the history of psychoanalysis* (pp. 307–17). Hillsdale, NJ: The Analytic Press.

Marcuse, H. (1966). *Eros and civilization: A philosophical inquiry into Freud* (2nd ed.). Boston, MA: Beacon Books (Original work published 1955).

(2011). "A decisive correction": Non-repressive progress and Freud's instinct theory. In T. Dufresne (Ed.), *Beyond the pleasure principle* (pp. 250–60). Peterborough: Broadview (Original work published 1970).

Marcuse, L. (1973). Freud's aesthetics. In H. M. Ruitenbeek (Ed.), *Freud as we knew him*. Detroit, MI: Wayne State University Press.

Marx, K. (1982). *A contribution to the critique of Hegel's philosophy of right* (Vol. 3., J. O'Malley. Ed., A. Jolin & J. O'Malley, Trans.). Cambridge, England: Cambridge University Press (Original work published 1843).

Meissner, W.W. (1984). *Psychoanalysis and religious experience*. New Haven, CT: Yale University Press.

Miller, J. (2010/2011). Marginalia to "Constructions in analysis." *NLS Messager*, 31, 1–22. Retrieved from www.amp-nls.org/page/fr/62/22-lacanian-practice-2011.

Molnar, M. (1994). The bizarre chair: A slant on Freud's light reading in the 1930s. In S. Gilman, J. Birmele, & J. Geller (Eds.), *Reading Freud's reading* (pp. 252–65). New York, NY: New York University Press.

Nemiah, J. C. (2000). A psychodynamic view of psychosomatic medicine. In *Psychosomatic Medicine, 62*, 299–303.

Nestroy, J. (1967). A man full of nothing. In *Three comedies* (T. Wilder, Trans.). New York, NY: Frederick Ungar.

Nietzsche, F. (1974a). On truth and lie in an extra-moral sense. In W. Kaufmann (Ed. & Trans.), *The portable Nietzsche* (pp. 42–7). New York, NY: Viking (Original work published 1873).

   (1974b). Twilight of the idols. In W. Kaufmann (Ed. & Trans.), *The portable Nietzsche* (pp. 464–563). New York, NY: Viking (Original work published 1888).

Nunberg, H. & Federn, P. (Eds.). (1975). *Minutes of the Vienna Psychoanalytic Society* (M. Nunberg, Trans.). 4 vols. New York, NY: International Universities Press.

Obituary [of Silberer]. (1923). Bulletin of the International Psycho-Analytical Association, *4*, 399.

Overy, R. (2009). *The morbid age: Britain between the wars*. London: Penguin.

Parsons, W. B. (1999). *The enigma of the oceanic feeling: Revisioning the psycho-analytic theory of mysticism*. London, England: Oxford University Press.

Pfister, O. (2012). The illusion of a future. In T. Dufresne (Ed.), *The future of an illusion* (G. C. Richter, Trans., pp. 115–52). Peterborough, ON: Broadview (Original work published 1928).

Puner, H. W. (1947). *Freud: His life and his mind*. New York, NY: Howell, Soskin Publishers.

Reich, I. O. (1969). *Wilhelm Reich: A personal biography*. New York, NY: St. Martin's Press.

Reich, W. (1952). *Reich speaks of Freud*. New York, NY: Farrar, Straus, & Giroux.

Reik, T. (1942). *From thirty years with Freud*. London, England: Hogarth Press.

   (1958a). Myths and memories. In *Myth and guilt: The crime and punishment of mankind* (pp. 48–57). London, England: Hutchinson.

   (1958b). *Ritual: Psycho-analytic studies* (D. Bryan, Trans.). New York, NY: International Universities Press (Original work published 1931).

   (1958c). The story of this book. In *Myth and guilt: The crime and punishment of mankind* (pp. 9–12). London, England: Hutchinson.

Rieff, P. (1961). *Freud: The mind of the moralist* (with S. Sontag). New York, NY: Doubleday.

Roazen, P. (1969). *Brother animal: The story of Freud and Tausk*. New York, NY: Knopf.

(1976). *Freud and his followers*. New York, NY: Meridian.

(1985). *Helene Deutsch: A psychoanalyst's life*. New York, NY: Anchor.

(1993a). Introduction to "The illusion of a future: A friendly disagreement with Prof. Sigmund Freud." *International Journal of Psychoanalysis, 74*, 557–8.

(1993b). *Meeting Freud's family*. Amherst: University of Massachusetts Press.

(1997). Nietzsche, Freud, and the history of psychoanalysis. In T. Dufresne (Ed.), *Returns of the "French Freud:" Freud, Lacan, and beyond* (pp. 11–23). New York, NY: Routledge.

Roazen, P. & Swerdloff, B. (1995). *Heresy: Sandor Rado and the psychoanalytic movement*. Northvale, NJ: Jason Aronson.

Robert, M. (1976). *From Oedipus to Moses: Freud's Jewish identity* (R. Manheim, Trans.). New York, NY: Anchor Books.

Rolland, R. (1916). *Above the battle* (C. K. Ogden, Trans.). Chicago, IL: Open Court (Original work published 1915).

(1920). *Liluli*. New York, NY: Boni and Liveright (Original work published 1919).

(1930) *The life of Ramakrishna* (E. F. Malcolm-Smith, Trans.). Calcutta, India: Adivaita Ashram.

(1931). *The life of Vivekananda and the universal gospel* (E. F. Malcolm-Smith, Trans.). Calcutta, India: Adivaita Ashram.

(1947). *Journey within* (E. Pell, Trans.). New York, NY: Philosophical Library.

(1948). *Essai sur la mystique et l'action de l'Inde vivante: La vie de Vivekananda et l'evangile universel*. Paris, France: Librairie Stock (Original work published 1930).

(1952). *Essai sur la mystique et l'action de l'Inde vivante: La vie de Ramakrishna*. Paris, France: Librairie Stock (Original work published 1929).

(1959). *Le Voyage intérieur, Song d'une vie*. Paris, France: Éditions Albin Michel.

Roudinesco, E. (1990). *Jacques Lacan & co.: A history of psychoanalysis in France, 1925–1985* (J. Mehlman, Trans.). Chicago, IL: University of Chicago Press.

(2012). Préface. In Ingeborg Meyer-Palmedo (Ed.), *Sigmund Freud et Anna Freud Correspondance, 1904–1938* (Olivier Mannoni, Trans.). Paris: Fayard.

Sachs, H. (1945). *Freud: Master and friend*. London: Imago.

Said, E. (2003). *Freud and the non-European*. New York, NY: Verso.

Shamdasani, S. (2003). *Jung and the making of a modern psychology: The dream of a science*. Cambridge, England: Cambridge University Press.

(2005). *Jung stripped bare by his biographers, even*. London, England: Karnac.

(2009). Introduction. In S. Shamdasani (Ed.), *The red book, Liber Novus: A reader's edition*. New York, NY: Norton.

Schopenhauer, A. (1893). *Studies in pessimism*. London: Swan Sonnenschein & Co. (Original work published 1851).

Schur, M. (1969). The background of Freud's disturbance on the Acropolis. *American Imago, 26*(4), 303–23.

(1972). *Freud: Living and dying.* New York, NY: International Universities Press.

Silberer, H. (1909). Bericht über eine Methode, gewisse symbolische Hallucinations-Erscheinungen hervorzurufen und zu beobachten. *Jahrbuch für psychoanalytische und psychopathologische Forschungen, 1,* 513–25.

(1917). *Problems of mysticism and its symbolism* (S. E. Jelliffe, Trans.). New York, NY: Moffat, Yard, & Co. (Original work published 1914).

(1920). Some little half-sleep experiences. *Psyche and Eros,* I (July) (1), 63–4.

(1921). Beyond psychoanalysis. *Psyche and Eros,* II (May–June) (3), 142–51.

(1922a). Review of Freud's group psychology and the analysis of the ego. *Psyche and Eros, III* (March–April) (2), 112–16.

(1922b). Review of Morel's essay on mystic introversion. *Psyche and Eros, III* (March–April) (2), 121–3.

Slochower, H. (1970). Freud's "déjà vu" on the Acropolis: A symbolic residue of mater nudam. *The Psychoanalytic Quarterly, 39,* 90–102.

Solomon, M. (1973). Freud's father on the Acropolis. *American Imago, 30*(2), 142–56.

Spielrein, S. (1994). Destruction as the cause of coming into being. *Journal of Analytical Psychology, 39*(2), 155–86.

Starr, W. T. (1971). *Romain Rolland: One against all.* The Hague, Netherlands: Mouton.

Stekel, W. (1922). Review of Ernest Jones' Treatment of the neuroses. *Psyche and Eros, III* (March–April) (2), 118–19.

(1924). In memorium Herbert Silberer. *Fortschritte der Sexualwissenschaft und Psychoanalyse, 1,* 408–20.

(1950). *The autobiography of Wilhelm Stekel: The life story of a pioneer psychoanalyst.* New York, NY: Liveright.

(1975). *Sadism and masochism: The psychology of hatred and cruelty.* New York, NY: Liveright (Original work published 1925).

Sterba, R. F. (1982). *Reminiscences of a Viennese psychoanalyst.* Detroit, MI: Wayne State University Press.

Stevenson, R. L. (1945). *The strange case of Dr. Jekyll and Mr. Hyde.* New York, NY: Random House (Original work published 1886).

Sulloway, F. (1979). *Freud, biologist of the mind: Beyond the psychoanalytic legend.* New York, NY: Basic Books.

Tolstoy, L. (1934). The death of Ivan Ilych. In *Ivan Ilych and Hadji Murad* (L. Maude & A. Maude, Trans.). London, England: Oxford University Press.

Tsai, S. Y. (1968). Eponym and identity: Benedict Augustin Morel (1809–1873) and Ferdinand Morel (1888–1957). *Archives of General Psychiatry, 19,* 104–9.

Vermorel, H. (2009). The presence of Spinoza in the exchanges between Sigmund Freud and Romain Rolland. *The International Journal of Psychoanalysis, 90,* 1235–54.

Vermorel, H. & Vermorel, M. (1993). *Sigmund Freud et Romain Rolland correspondance 1923–1936*. Paris: Presses Universitaires de France.

Viereck, G. (1930). *Glimpses of the great*. London, England: Duckworth.

Vitz, P.C. (1988). *Sigmund Freud's Christian unconscious*. Grand Rapids: William B. Eerdmans Publishing.

Wisely, A. C. (2004). *Arthur Schnitzler and 20th century criticism*. New York, NY: Camden House.

Wittels, F. (1971). *Sigmund Freud: His personality, his teaching, & his school* (E. Paul & C. Paul, Trans.). New York, NY: Books for Libraries Press (Original work published 1924).

Wohlgemuth, A. (1923). *A critical examination of psycho-analysis*. London: George Allen & Unwin.

Wortis, J. (1954). *Fragments of an analysis with Freud*. New York, NY: Simon & Schuster.

    (2007). "The man who was analyzed by Freud:" Joseph Wortis on Freud, Freudians, and social justice. In T. Dufresne (Ed.), *Against Freud: Critics talk back* (pp. 9–25). Stanford, CA: Stanford University Press.

Yerushalmi, Y. H. (1989). Freud on the "historical novel:" From the manuscript draft (1934) of Moses and monotheism. *The International Journal of Psychoanalysis*, 70, 375–95.

    (1991). *Freud's Moses: Judaism terminable and interminable*. New Haven, CT: Yale University Press.

Zilboorg, G. (1958). *Freud and religion*. Westminster, MD: Newman Press.

Zweig, S. (1921). *Romain Rolland: The man and his work* (E. Paul & C. Paul, Trans.). London, England: George Allen & Unwin.

Index